LIBRARY OF NEW TESTAMENT STUDIES

636

formerly the Journal for the Study of the New Testament Supplement Series

Editor
Chris Keith

Editorial Board
Dale C. Allison, John M. G. Barclay, Lynn H. Cohick, R. Alan Culpepper, Craig A. Evans, Robert Fowler, Simon J. Gathercole, Juan Hernández Jr., John S. Kloppenborg, Michael Labahn, Matthew V. Novenson, Love L. Sechrest, Robert Wall, Catrin H. Williams, Brittany Wilson

Common Property, the Golden Age, and Empire in Acts 2:42–47 and 4:32–35

Joshua Noble

LONDON • NEW YORK • OXFORD • NEW DELHI • SYDNEY

T&T CLARK
Bloomsbury Publishing Plc
50 Bedford Square, London, WC1B 3DP, UK
1385 Broadway, New York, NY 10018, USA
29 Earlsfort Terrace, Dublin 2, Ireland

BLOOMSBURY, T&T CLARK and the T&T Clark logo are trademarks of Bloomsbury Publishing Plc

First published in Great Britain 2021
This paperback edition published in 2022

Copyright © Joshua Noble, 2021

Joshua Noble has asserted his right under the Copyright, Designs and Patents Act, 1988, to be identified as Author of this work.

For legal purposes the Acknowledgments on p. viii constitute an extension of this copyright page.

All rights reserved. No part of this publication may be reproduced or transmitted in any form or by any means, electronic or mechanical, including photocopying, recording, or any information storage or retrieval system, without prior permission in writing from the publishers.

Bloomsbury Publishing Plc does not have any control over, or responsibility for, any third-party websites referred to or in this book. All internet addresses given in this book were correct at the time of going to press. The author and publisher regret any inconvenience caused if addresses have changed or sites have ceased to exist, but can accept no responsibility for any such changes.

A catalogue record for this book is available from the British Library.

Library of Congress Cataloging-in-Publication Data
Names: Noble, Joshua, author.
Title: Common property, the Golden Age, and Empire in Acts 2:42-47 and 4:32-35 / by Joshua Noble.
Description: London ; New York : T&T Clark, 2020. | Series: The library of New Testament studies, 2513-8790 ; 636 | Includes bibliographical references and index. | Summary: "Joshua Noble focuses on the rapid appearance and disappearance in Acts 2 and 4 of the motif that early believers hold all their property in common, and argues that these descriptions function as allusions to the Golden Age myth. Noble suggests Luke's claims that the believers "had all things in common" and that "no one claimed private ownership of any possessions" - a motif that does not appear in any biblical source - rather calls to mind Greek and Roman traditions that the earliest humans lived in utopian conditions, when "no one ... possessed any private property, but all things were common." "– Provided by publisher.
Identifiers: LCCN 2020022554 (print) | LCCN 2020022555 (ebook) | ISBN 9780567695819 (hb) | ISBN 9780567695826 (epdf) | ISBN 9780567695840 (epub)
Subjects: LCSH: Bible. Acts, II, 42-47–Criticism, interpretation, etc. | Bible. Acts, IV, 32-35–Criticism, interpretation, etc. | Right of property–Biblical teaching. | Personal belongings. | Commons.
Classification: LCC BS2625.6.P696 N63 2020 (print) | LCC BS2625.6.P696 (ebook) | DDC 226.6/067–dc23
LC record available at https://lccn.loc.gov/2020022554
LC ebook record available at https://lccn.loc.gov/2020022555

ISBN:	HB:	978-0-5676-9581-9
	PB:	978-0-5676-9643-4
	ePDF:	978-0-5676-9582-6
	ePUB:	978-0-5676-9584-0

Series: Library of New Testament Studies, ISSN 2513-8790, volume 636

Typeset by Integra Software Services Pvt. Ltd.

To find out more about our authors and books visit www.bloomsbury.com and sign up for our newsletters.

Contents

Acknowledgments		viii
List of Tables		ix
List of Abbreviations		x
1	Introduction	1
	Previous Research on the Literary Background of Acts 2:42–47 and 4:32–35	2
	Friendship Traditions	3
	Ideal State Descriptions	5
	Accounts of Distant Lands or Primitive Peoples	6
	Golden Age Accounts	7
	Reasons for Pursuing a Golden Age Interpretation of the Acts Summaries	9
	The Detection of Allusions	10
	The Structure of This Study	12
2	The Golden Age Myth in Greek and Latin Sources	15
	The Golden Age Myth before Hesiod	15
	The Golden Age Myth in Greek Sources	17
	The Golden Age Myth in Hesiod	17
	The Golden Age Myth in Plato	20
	The Golden Age Myth in Aratus	24
	Summary: The Golden Age Myth in Greek Sources	26
	The Golden Age Myth in Latin Sources	27
	The Golden Age Myth in Lucretius	27
	The Golden Age Myth in Virgil	30
	The Golden Age Myth in Ovid	35
	Common Property and the Golden Age in Other Sources	38
	Political Applications of the Golden Age Myth in Other Sources	46
	Summary: The Golden Age Myth in Greek and Latin Sources	52
3	The Golden Age Myth in Jewish and Christian Sources	55
	The Golden Age Myth in Philo of Alexandria	55
	The Golden Age Myth in Josephus	59
	Excursus: The Essenes in Philo and Josephus	64
	The Golden Age Myth in the Sibylline Oracles	67
	The Golden Age in Books 1–2 of the Sibylline Oracles	68
	The First Race: Sib. Or. 1.65–86	70

	The Sixth Race: Sib. Or. 1.283–306	71
	The Tenth Race: Sib. Or. 2.6–33	72
	The Blessings of the Righteous: Sib. Or. 2.313–338	73
	Summary: The Golden Age in Books 1–2 of the Sibylline Oracles	74
	The Golden Age in Book 8 of the Sibylline Oracles	74
	A Condemnation of Greed: Sib. Or. 8.17–36	75
	Equality in Hades: Sib. Or. 8.107–121	77
	The Blessings of the Righteous: Sib. Or. 8.205–212	77
	Summary: The Golden Age in Book 8 of the Sibylline Oracles	78
	The Golden Age in Book 14 of the Sibylline Oracles	79
	Summary: The Golden Age Myth in the Sibylline Oracles	80
	Summary: The Golden Age Myth in Jewish and Christian Sources	80
4	Preliminaries to a Golden Age Reading of the Acts Summaries	85
	Acts 2:42–47 and 4:32–35 as Eschatological Descriptions	85
	Eschatology in Luke-Acts: Conzelmann and His Responders	85
	Realized Eschatology in Acts 2:17–21	87
	The Text-Critical Debate Regarding ἐν ταῖς ἐσχάταις ἡμέραις in Acts 2:17	87
	Eschatology and the New Age in Acts 2:17–21	88
	The Pneumatological Context of Acts 2:42–47 and 4:32–35	89
	Conclusion: The Eschatological Character of Acts 2:42–47 and 4:32–35	90
	Luke-Acts and Rome	91
	Luke-Acts and Rome: Major Approaches	92
	Establishing Luke's Use of Imperial Language	94
	Interpreting Luke's Use of Imperial Language	100
	Previous Claims of Lukan Allusions to the Golden Age Myth	101
	Allen Brent on Luke-Acts and the Golden Age	101
	Michael Wolter on Luke-Acts and the Golden Age	102
	Stefan Schreiber on Luke-Acts and the Golden Age	104
	Summary: Preliminaries to a Golden Age Reading of the Acts Summaries	107
5	Reading Acts 2:42–47 and 4:32–35 as Golden Age Allusions	109
	Five Exegetical Issues	109
	The Meaning of κοινωνία in Acts 2:42	109
	The Meaning of ἐπὶ τὸ αὐτό in Acts 2:44, 47	110
	The Meaning of ἀφελότης in Acts 2:46	111
	The Meanings of ἔχειν χάριν πρός in Acts 2:47 and of χάρις in Acts 4:33	112

The Nature of the Property Arrangements in Acts 2:44–45 and 4:32,
    34–35   114
    "And [they] had all things in common" (2:44b); "and no one
        claimed private ownership of any possessions, but all
        things were common to them" (4:32c)   115
    "They would sell their possessions and goods" (2:45a); "for as
        many as owned lands or houses sold them" (4:34b)   116
    "And [they] brought the proceeds of what was sold. They laid
        it at the apostles' feet" (4:34c–35a)   117
    "And [they would] distribute the proceeds to all, as any had
        need" (2:45b); "and it was distributed to each as any
        had need" (4:35b)   117
    Summary: The Nature of the Property Arrangement   118
Identifying Acts 2:42–47 and 4:32–35 as Golden Age Allusions   118
    The Distinctiveness of Acts 2:42–47 and 4:32–35   119
        The Use of Distinctive Vocabulary in Acts 2:42–47 and 4:32–35 119
        Tensions between the Summaries and Their Immediate Contexts   120
        The Uniqueness of the Summaries in Their Broader Context   121
    Golden Age Features in Acts 2:42–47 and 4:32–35   122
        The Summaries in Acts: A Lost Age and a New Age   123
        The Summaries in Acts: Blessed with Divine Favor   124
        The Summaries in Acts: Marked by Unity and Harmony   124
        The Summaries in Acts: A Time when Property Was Common   125
        The Summaries in Acts: Associated with Imperial Ideology   128
        The Summaries in Acts: An Eschatological Image   131
        Summary: Identifying Acts 2:42–47 and 4:32–35 as Golden
            Age Allusions   134
    Interpreting Acts 2:42–47 and 4:32–35 as Golden Age Allusions   135
        Suggested Reasons for Luke's Utopian Language in Acts 2:42–47 and
            4:32–35   136
        The Golden Age Allusion as a Sign of the Universal,
            Eschatological Spirit   138
        The Golden Age Allusion as a Supra-Imperial Claim   141
    Summary: Reading Acts 2:42–47 and 4:32–35 as Golden Age Allusions 145

Conclusion   147

Bibliography   150
Ancient Sources Index   167
Subject Index   178

Acknowledgments

This book is the fruit of dissertation research that I conducted at the University of Notre Dame. I wish to first thank my advisor, John Fitzgerald, whose erudition, honesty, and eye for detail were key factors in bringing this project from a vague idea into a finished product. Next, I want to thank the other members of my dissertation committee, each of whom played a vital role not only in improving this study but also in my overall growth as a scholar. Blake Leyerle was the first member of the Theology department to reach out to me upon my arrival, and her kindness and encouragement continued to motivate me during the entirety of my graduate studies. Elizabeth Mazurek ensured that the Classics department was not a foreign territory, but a second home to me. Mary Rose D'Angelo constantly pushed me to think in new ways, and the germ of the idea for this book was the result of her prompting.

My greatest thanks belong to my wife, Amy. For seven long years she put up with the odd hours, recurrent stress, and innumerable other inconveniences that go along with being the spouse of a graduate student. She encouraged me in my failures, celebrated with me in my successes, and tirelessly supported me in the long, tedious stretches in between. Her love and friendship made the process a joy, and I simply could not have done it without her.

Finally, I want to dedicate this book to my children: Jack, Levi, Jude, and Emma. You are my absolute delight, and I love each of you more than I can ever say.

Tables

2.1	Common Property in Greek and Latin Golden Age Texts	45
3.1	Philo's Descriptions of the Messianic Age and the Essenes	66
3.2	Common Property in Jewish and Christian Golden Age Texts	81
3.3	Property Language in Golden Age Accounts	82
4.1	Examples of "Peace" (εἰρήνη) in Imperial Texts and in Luke-Acts	96
4.2	Examples of "Lord" (κύριος) in Imperial Texts and in Luke-Acts	96
4.3	Examples of "Savior" (σωτήρ) in Imperial Texts and in Luke-Acts	98
4.4	Examples of "Son of God" (υἱὸς θεοῦ) in Imperial Texts and in Luke-Acts	98

Abbreviations

Ancient Sources

Aelius Aristides
- Or. — Orationes

Aetn. — Aetna

Aratus
- Phaen. — Phaenomena

Aristotle
- Eth. eud. — Ethica eudemia
- Eth. nic. — Ethica nicomachea
- Pol. — Politica

Arrian
- Ind. — Indica

Bahm. Yasht — Bahman Yasht

2 Bar. — 2 Baruch

Calpurnius Siculus
- Ecl. — Eclogues

Cicero
- Amic. — De amicitia
- Flac. — Pro Flacco

Cons. Liv. — Consolatio ad Liviam

Corripus
- Laud. Just. — In laudem Justini minoris

Cyr. — Cyranides

Demosthenes
- Fals. leg. — De falsa legatione

Dio Cassius
    Hist. rom.   *Historia romana*

Diodorus Siculus
    Bib. hist.   *Bibliotheca historica*

Diogenes Laertius
    Vit. phil.   *Vitae philosophorum*

Dionysius of Halicarnassus
    Ant. rom.   *Antiquitates romanae*

1 En.   1 Enoch

Epictetus
    Diatr.   *Diatribai*

Euripides
    Alc.   *Alcestes*
    Andr.   *Andromache*
    Hipp.   *Hippolytus*
    Med.   *Medea*
    Orest.   *Orestes*

Germanicus
    Arat.   *Aratea*

Hesiod
    Op.   *Opera et dies*

Homer
    Il.   *Iliad*
    Od.   *Odyssey*

Horace
    Saec.   *Carmen saeculare*

Iamblichus
    Vit. pyth.   *De vita pythagorica*

Josephus
    A.J.   *Antiquitates judaicae*

	B.J.	Bellum judaicum
Jub.		Jubilees
Juvenal		
	Sat.	Satirae
LAB		Liber antiquitatum biblicarum
Lucian		
	Dial. meretr.	Dialogi meretricii
	Merc. cond.	De mercede conductis
	Sat.	Saturnalia
Lucretius		
	Rer.	De rerum natura
Lycurgus		
	Leocr.	Against Leocrates
Mah.		Mahabharata
Melito of Sardis		
	Pasch.	Peri pascha
Midr. Ps.		Midrash on the Psalms
Num. Rab.		Numbers Rabbah
Oct.		Octavia
Ovid		
	Am.	Amores
	Ars	Ars amatoria
	Fast.	Fasti
	Metam.	Metamorphoses
	Trist.	Tristia
Philo		
	Cher.	De cherubim
	Conf.	De confusione linguarum
	Decal.	De decalogo
	Flacc.	In Flaccum

Hypoth.   *Hypothetica*
Legat.   *Legatio ad Gaium*
Migr.   *De migratione Abrahami*
Mos.   *De vita Mosis*
Opif.   *De opificio mundi*
Praem.   *De praemiis et poenis*
Prob.   *Quod omnis probus liber sit*
Sacr.   *De sacrificiis Abelis et Caini*
Spec.   *De specialibus legibus*

Philostratus

Vit. Apoll.   *Vita Apollonii*

Plato

Crat.   *Cratylus*
Crit.   *Critias*
Gorg.   *Gorgias*
Leg.   *Leges*
Pol.   *Politicus*
Resp.   *Respublica*
Tim.   *Timaeus*

Pliny the Elder

Nat.   *Naturalis historia*

Plutarch

Cat. Min.   *Cato Minor*
Cim.   *Cimon*
Conj. praec.   *Conjugalia Praecepta*
Dem.   *Demosthenes*
Frat. amor.   *De fraterno amore*
Pyth. orac.   *De Pythiae oraculis*

Polybius

Hist.   *Histories*

Pompeius Trogus

    Ep.   *Epitome*

Porphyry

    Abst.   *De abstentia*

Pseudo-Hippocrates

    Ep.   *Epistulae*

Res gest. divi Aug.   *Res gestae divi Augusti*

Seneca the Elder

    Contr.   *Controversiae*

Seneca the Younger

    Apoc.   *Apolocyntosis*

    Clem.   *De clementia*

    Ep.   *Epistulae morales*

    Phaed.   *Phaedra*

    Polyb.   *Ad Polybium de consolatione*

Sib. Or.   Sibylline Oracles

Sophocles

    Oed. col.   *Oedipus coloneus*

Statius

    Silv.   *Silvae*

Strabo

    Geogr.   *Geographica*

Suetonius

    Tib.   *Tiberius*

T. Ab.   Testament of Abraham

T. Iss.   Testament of Issachar

T. Reu.   Testament of Reuben

Tibullus

    El.   *Elegiae*

Vettius Valens

    Anth.   *Anthologia*

Virgil

    Aen.   *Aeneid*

    Ecl.   *Eclogae*

    Georg.   *Georgica*

Xenophon

    Cyr.   *Cyranides*

Abbreviations of Periodicals and Series

AB	Anchor Bible
ABRL	Anchor Bible Reference Library
AGJU	Arbeiten zur Geschichte des antiken Judentums und des Urchristentums
AJP	*American Journal of Philology*
AnBib	Analecta Biblica
ANRW	*Aufstieg und Niedergang der römischen Welt: Geschichte und Kultur Roms im Spiegel der neueren Forschung. Part 2, Principat.* Edited by Hildegard Temporini and Wolfgang Haase. Berlin: de Gruyter, 1972–
ANTC	Abingdon New Testament Commentaries
BAFCS	The Book of Acts in Its First Century Setting
BECNT	Baker Exegetical Commentary on the New Testament
Bib	*Biblica*
BibInt	Biblical Interpretation Series
BibOr	Biblica et Orientalia
BKAT	Biblischer Kommentar, Altes Testament
BSOAS	*Bulletin of the School of Oriental and African Studies*
BTS	Biblical Tools and Studies
BZ	*Biblische Zeitschrift*
BZNW	Beihefte zur Zeitschrift für die neutestamentliche Wissenschaft
CBQ	*Catholic Biblical Quarterly*
CNT	Commentaire du Nouveau Testament

ClQ	Classical Quarterly
EKKNT	Evangelisch-katholischer Kommentar zum Neuen Testament
Enc	Encounter
ETL	Ephemerides Theologicae Lovanienses
EvQ	Evangelical Quarterly
EvT	Evangelische Theologie
ExpTim	Expository Times
FBBS	Facet Books, Biblical Series
FRLANT	Forschungen zur Religion und Literatur des Alten und Neuen Testaments
GR	Greece and Rome
HCS	Hellenistic Culture and Society
HDR	Harvard Dissertations in Religion
Herm	Hermanthena
HSCP	Harvard Studies in Classical Philology
HThKNT	Herders Theologischer Kommentar zum Neuen Testament
HUT	Hermeneutische Untersuchungen zur Theologie
ICC	International Critical Commentary
Int	Interpretation
JAAR	Journal of the American Academy of Religion
JAOS	Journal of the American Oriental Society
JBL	Journal of Biblical Literature
JRA	Journal of Roman Archaeology
JRS	Journal of Roman Studies
JSJ	Journal for the Study of Judaism in the Persian, Hellenistic, and Roman Periods
JSNT	Journal for the Study of the New Testament
JSNTSup	Journal for the Study of the New Testament Supplement Series
JSPSup	Journal for the Study of the Pseudepigrapha Supplement Series
JTS	Journal of Theological Studies
LCL	Loeb Classical Library

LNTS	The Library of New Testament Studies
NICNT	New International Commentary on the New Testament
NovT	*Novum Testamentum*
NovTSup	Supplements to Novum Testamentum
NTL	New Testament Library
NTOA	Novum Testamentum et Orbis Antiquus
NTS	*New Testament Studies*
QD	Quaestiones Disputatae
RB	*Revue biblique*
RBS	Resources for Biblical Study
ResQ	*Restoration Quarterly*
RevQ	*Revue de Qumran*
RHR	*Revue de l'histoire des religions*
SBB	Stuttgarter biblische Beiträge
SBLDS	Society of Biblical Literature Dissertation Series
SBLMS	Society of Biblical Literature Monograph Series
SBLSP	Society of Biblical Literature Seminar Papers
SBT	Studies in Biblical Theology
SHR	Studies in the History of Religions
SNTSMS	Society for New Testament Studies Monograph Series
SNTSU	Studien zum Neuen Testament und seiner Umwelt
SO	Symbolae Osloenses
SP	Sacra Pagina
StBibLit	Studies in Biblical Literature
STDJ	Studies on the Texts of the Desert of Judah
SUNT	Studien zur Umwelt des Neuen Testaments
SVTP	Studia in Veteris Testamenti Pseudepigraphica
SymS	Symposium Series
TAPA	*Transactions of the American Philological Association*
TAPS	Transactions of the American Philosophical Society

TGl   *Theologie und Glaube*

THKNT   Theologischer Handkommentar zum Neuen Testament

TZ   *Theologische Zeitschrift*

WGRWSup   Writings from the Greco-Roman World Supplement Series

WUNT   Wissenschaftliche Untersuchungen zum Neuen Testament

ZNW   *Zeitschrift für die neutestamentliche Wissenschaft und die Kunde der älteren Kirche*

Other Abbreviations

BCE   before the Common Era

BDAG   Danker, Frederick W., Walter Bauer, William F. Arndt, and F. Wilbur Gingrich. *Greek-English Lexicon of the New Testament and Other Early Christian Literature*. 3rd ed. Chicago: University of Chicago Press, 2000

BDF   Blass, Friedrich, Albert Debrunner, and Robert W. Funk. *A Greek Grammar of the New Testament and Other Early Christian Literature*. Chicago: University of Chicago Press, 1961

CE   Common Era

CIG   *Corpus Inscriptionum Graecarum*. Edited by August Boeckh. 4 vols. Berlin, 1828–1877

CIL   *Corpus Inscriptionum Latinarum*. Berlin, 1862–

FD III   *Fouilles de Delphes, III. Épigraphie*. Paris 1929– Fasc. 1, *Inscriptions de l'entrée du sanctuaire au trésor des Athéniens*. Edited by Émile Bourguet. Paris 1929

FGH   *Die Fragmente der griechischen Historiker*. Edited by Felix Jacoby. Leiden: Brill, 1954–1964

GELS   *A Greek-English Lexicon of the Septuagint*. Takamitsu Muraoka. Leuven: Peeters, 2009

HB   Hebrew Bible

IG   *Inscriptiones Graecae. Editio Minor.* Berlin: de Gruyter, 1924–

IMT   *Inschriften Mysia & Troas*. Edited by Matthias Barth and Josef Stauber. Leopold Wenger Institut. Universität München. Version of 25.8.1993 (Ibycus). Packard Humanities Institute CD #7, 1996

LSJ	Liddell, Henry George, Robert Scott, Henry Stuart Jones. *A Greek-English Lexicon*. 9th ed. with revised supplement. Oxford: Clarendon, 1996
LXX	Septuagint
NA[28]	*Novum Testamentum Graece*, Nestle-Aland, 28th ed.
NRSV	New Revised Standard Version
NT	New Testament
OCD	*Oxford Classical Dictionary*. Edited by Simon Hornblower and Antony Spawforth. 4th ed. Oxford: Oxford University Press, 2012
OGIS	*Orientis Graeci Inscriptiones Selectae*. Edited by Wilhelm Dittenberger. 2 vols. Leipzig: Hirzel, 1903–1905
OT	Old Testament
RE	*Realencyklopädie für protestantische Theologie und Kirche*
RIC	*The Roman Imperial Coinage*. Edited by C. H. V. Sutherland and R. A. G. Carson. London: Spink, 1984
RPC III	*Roman Provincial Coinage, Vol. 3: Nerva, Trajan and Hadrian (AD 96–138)*. Edited by Michel Amandry and Andrew Burnett. London: British Museum Press, 2015
SEG	Supplementum epigraphicum graecum
SIG	*Sylloge Inscriptionum Graecarum*. Edited by Wilhelm Dittenberger. 4 vols. 3rd ed. Leipzig: Hirzel, 1915–1924
TDNT	*Theological Dictionary of the New Testament*. Edited by Gerhard Kittel and Gerhard Friedrich. Translated by Geoffrey W. Bromiley. 10 vols. Grand Rapids: Eerdmans, 1964–1976

1

Introduction

In the first five chapters of Acts, Luke punctuates his narrative with three passages that summarize the lifestyle of the early Jerusalem community. The first two, Acts 2:42–47 and 4:32–35, describe the believers holding their property in common: they "had all things in common" (2:44), and again, "all things were common to them" (4:32).[1] These statements are quite conspicuous, as they are the only places in not only Luke-Acts but also the entire biblical canon where the idea of a community of property emerges. Luke describes individual acts of generosity elsewhere, but the general practice of common property appears abruptly in these summaries and disappears without comment.

Though Luke's portrayal of a community of property lacks biblical parallels, scholars have long observed that his language closely resembles that found in various Greek and Roman descriptions of common ownership. While some have assumed that Luke's only aim was to add luster to his sketch of the early church by depicting the fulfillment of a general cultural ideal, others have argued that the summaries contain a more precise allusion. Scholars have most often seen a reference to Hellenistic friendship ideals present in Luke's common property language, but some have also posited allusions to Plato or to contemporary ethnographic traditions. In each case, the specific referent is claimed to be interpretively significant: Luke's aim would not be merely to describe the economic arrangement of the believers but also to characterize them more particularly as a community of friends, an ideal state, or the virtuous exemplars of an *ethnos*.

One other context for common property has been suggested often as a model for the Acts summaries but rarely explored: the myth of the Golden Age. This myth, which appears as early as Hesiod, describes the decline of humanity from an initial ideal state through a series of races or ages, each corresponding to a metal. Toward the end of the first century BCE, the Golden Age myth exploded in popularity among Roman authors and began to be employed in imperial propaganda. Virgil's *Aeneid* announced that "Augustus Caesar ... will establish the golden ages again" (*Aen.* 6.792–793), and later emperors were often extolled for using Golden Age vocabulary.[2] Around the same time, Golden Age depictions began to include a new motif: the practice of common property.

In this book, I examine Luke's use of the common property motif in Acts 2:42–47 and 4:32–35 in light of the early imperial Golden Age myth. My central claim is that

---

[1] The third summary, Acts 5:12–16, mentions nothing about the community's economic practices. All biblical translations are from the NRSV; some have been modified to better reflect the Greek.
[2] Augustus Caesar ... aurea condet saecula qui rursus. All translations of classical texts are my own unless otherwise noted.

Luke's assertions regarding common property, along with other features of the summary descriptions, would have evoked the idea of the Golden Age for many in Luke's audience. An allusion to the Golden Age would have served two purposes: characterizing the coming of the Spirit as the beginning of a universal, eschatological restoration and making a supra-imperial claim for Christianity vis-à-vis the Roman Empire.

To prepare for building this case, in this first chapter I do four things. First, I review suggestions for the literary background of the common property motif in the Acts summaries, looking at the types of evidence mustered for each. Second, I show that a Golden Age reading of the summaries is relatively unexplored, potentially fruitful, and initially plausible, and thus well worth pursuing. Third, I lay out six criteria that will help establish whether or not a Golden Age allusion is present in the summaries. Fourth, I briefly summarize the structure of this book.

Previous Research on the Literary Background of Acts 2:42–47 and 4:32–35

Recognition of a Hellenistic background to Luke's descriptions in Acts 2:42–47 and 4:32–35 is often traced back to Johann Jakob Wettstein, whose 1751-2 Greek NT cites more than a dozen Greek and Roman authors who discussed common property.[3] As Luke Timothy Johnson observes, this recognition has been widely accepted subsequently: "Since the time of Wettstein the Hellenistic provenance of the language in this passage has been repeatedly affirmed and can be said to have the nearly unanimous approval of scholars."[4] Even those who minimize the importance of extra-biblical parallels for understanding the summaries often acknowledge that Luke's descriptions likely would have brought certain cultural ideals to the minds of many readers.[5]

Precisely which ideal these readers might primarily recall, however, has been more disputed. While many commentators speak of Luke as referring only to a general Greek ideal or to multiple traditions indiscriminately, others see an allusion to a more specific common property tradition.[6] Brian Capper helpfully divides the relevant literary traditions into four main strands:

[3] Johann Jakob Wettstein, *Novum Testamentum graecum* (Amsterdam: Officina Dommeriana, 1751-2), 2:470-71.
[4] Luke Timothy Johnson, *The Literary Function of Possessions in Luke-Acts*, SBLDS 39 (Missoula, MT: Scholars Press, 1977), 3. Recent studies have reiterated this judgment: in his 2005 dissertation, Rubén R. Dupertuis ("The Summaries in Acts 2, 4 and 5 and Greek Utopian Literary Traditions" [PhD diss., The Claremont Graduate University, 2005], 43–4) claims a "consensus among scholars" regarding Greek literary influence on Luke's summaries, and Douglas A. Hume's 2011 monograph (*The Early Christian Community: A Narrative Analysis of Acts 2:41–47 and 4:32–35*, WUNT 2/298 [Tübingen: Mohr Siebeck, 2011], 16) asserts that "historical studies generally agree" about the presence of this influence.
[5] So Eckhard Schnabel, *Acts*, Zondervan Exegetical Commentary on the New Testament 5 (Grand Rapids: Zondervan, 2012), 181, 269; Luise Schottroff and Wolfgang Stegemann, *Jesus and the Hope of the Poor*, trans. Matthew J. O'Connell (Maryknoll, NY: Orbis Books, 1986), 118.
[6] Hans Conzelmann (*Acts of the Apostles*, trans. James Limburg, A. Thomas Krabel, and Donald H. Juel, Hermeneia [Philadelphia: Fortress, 1987], 23–4) thinks that Luke derived the idea of common property from a broad range of sources, including friendship proverbs, portrayals of the Pythagorean

The theme of community of goods appears in a variety of contexts in the Graeco-Roman period. The most important are the Golden Age (an account of human beginnings), political theories of the proper organization for the state (beginning with Plato's *Republic*), the association of community of goods with the ideal of friendship, and its attribution to primitive peoples or location in fabled distant lands.[7]

Following Capper's division, I will briefly summarize the previous research into the literary background of Luke's common property descriptions using these four categories: (1) friendship traditions, especially the maxim "friends have all things in common" found in Aristotle and Plato, among others; (2) ideal state representations, particularly Plato's *Republic*; (3) descriptions of far-off fictional lands (such as the Islands of the Sun) or primitive peoples (such as the Scythians); and (4) versions of the Golden Age myth.

Friendship Traditions

The enduring popularity of the idea that Acts 2:42–47 and 4:32–35 draw upon friendship traditions is mostly due to the purported presence of two friendship proverbs in these summaries, proverbs that also appear together in Aristotle's discussion of friendship in the *Nicomachean Ethics*. Acts 4:32 contains the first possible proverb:

Eth. nic. 1168b	Acts 4:32
μία ψυχή	τοῦ δὲ πλήθους τῶν πιστευσάντων ἦν καρδία καὶ ψυχὴ μία.
One soul	Now the whole group of those who believed were of one heart and soul.[8]

The second possible friendship proverb occurs in this same verse, as well as in the first summary:

community, and Plato's depictions of ideal states. Martin Hengel (*Property and Riches in the Early Church: Aspects of a Social History of Early Christianity*, trans. J. Bowden [Philadelphia: Fortress, 1974], 8–9, 31) casts his net even wider, speaking of a "universal ideal of antiquity" and positing a background of accounts of the Scythians' lifestyle along with friendship proverbs, Golden Age myths, Pythagorean texts, and Platonic writings. Many recent commentators also propose a range of possible referents without adopting any one primary context of interpretation; examples include Rudolf Pesch (*Die Apostelgeschichte*, EKKNT 5 [Zurich: Benzinger, 1986], 184–5), Ben Witherington III (*The Acts of the Apostles: A Socio-Rhetorical Commentary* [Grand Rapids: Eerdmans; Carlisle: Paternoster, 1998], 162), Joseph A. Fitzmyer (*The Acts of the Apostles*, AB 31 [New York: Doubleday, 1998], 271), Craig S. Keener (*Acts: An Exegetical Commentary. Introduction and 1:1–2:47* [Grand Rapids: Baker Academic, 2012], 1013–19), and Carl R. Holladay (*Acts: A Commentary*, NTL [Louisville: Westminster John Knox, 2016], 109).

[7] Brian Capper, "Reciprocity and the Ethic of Acts," in *Witness to the Gospel: The Theology of Acts*, ed. I. Howard Marshall and David Peterson (Grand Rapids: Eerdmans, 1998), 504.

[8] Among friendship interpreters, a common analysis of Luke's statement is as a combination of the Greek friendship proverb μία ψυχή and the typical Septuagintal linking of καρδία and ψυχή (cf. the Shema, "with all your heart and with all your soul" [Deut 6:5 LXX, ἐξ ὅλης τῆς καρδίας σου καὶ ἐξ ὅλης τῆς ψυχῆς σου]). Whatever the precise origin of the expression καρδία καὶ ψυχὴ μία, Acts 4:32 contains its first extant appearance.

Eth. nic. 1168b κοινὰ τὰ φίλων Friends have all things in common.	Acts 2:44; 4:32 εἶχον ἅπαντα κοινά They had all things in common. ἦν αὐτοῖς ἅπαντα κοινά All things were common to them.

For Jacques Dupont, the joint appearance of two expressions similar to Aristotle's friendship proverbs is "not absolutely compelling, yet … strong enough to justify the hypothesis" that Luke is alluding to friendship traditions rather than the Golden Age myth or historical communes.[9] Johnson is still more confident, asserting that Luke's language "explicitly identified the community as a community of friends."[10] This remains the most popular interpretation among scholars who see a reference to a specific common property tradition in Acts 2 and 4.[11]

The first of these purported proverbs, the phrase μία ψυχή ("one soul"), undeniably does occur in discussions of friendship.[12] Prior to Plutarch, however, firsthand evidence of μία ψυχή as a friendship proverb is surprisingly sparse. By far the most common use of μία ψυχή (or ψυχὴ μία) is simply to designate an individual person, soul, or life.[13] A second function is to characterize the unity of multiple persons without any explicit

---

[9] Jacques Dupont, "The Community of Goods in the Early Church," in *The Salvation of the Gentiles: Essays on the Acts of the Apostles*, trans. John R. Keating, Paulist Press Exploration Books (New York: Paulist, 1979), 102.

[10] Johnson, *Literary Function*, 199.

[11] Others who identify an allusion to friendship traditions here include C. K. Barrett (*A Critical and Exegetical Commentary on the Acts of the Apostles*, ICC [Edinburgh: T&T Clark, 1994], 168, 254), S. Scott Bartchy ("Community of Goods in Acts: Idealization or Social Reality?" in *The Dead Sea Scrolls as Background to Postbiblical Judaism and Early Christianity: Papers from an International Conference at St Andrews in 2001*, ed. James Davila, STDJ 46 [Leiden: Brill, 2003], 311), Beverly Roberts Gaventa (*The Acts of the Apostles*, ANTC [Nashville: Abingdon, 2003], 81), Ernst Haenchen (*The Acts of the Apostles*, trans. Bernard Noble and Gerald Shinn [Philadelphia: Westminster, 1971], 233), Christopher M. Hays (*Luke's Wealth Ethics: A Study in Their Coherence and Character*, WUNT 2/275 [Tübingen: Mohr Siebeck, 2010], 200), Friedrich W. Horn ("Die Gütergemeinschaft der Urgemeinde," *EvT* 58 [1998]: 378), Hume (*Early Christian Community*, 36), Alan C. Mitchell ("The Social Function of Friendship in Acts 2:44–47 and 4:32–37," *JBL* 111 [1992]: 255), Gerhard Schneider (*Die Apostelgeschichte*, HThKNT 5 [Freiburg im Breisgau: Herder, 1980], 1:293, 1:365 n. 18), Schottroff and Stegemann (*Jesus and the Hope of the Poor*, 118), David P. Seccombe (*Possessions and the Poor in Luke-Acts*, SNTSU B/6 [Linz, AT: Fuchs, 1982], 202), Justin Taylor ("The Community of Goods among the First Christians and among the Essenes," in *Historical Perspectives: From the Hasmoneans to Bar Kokhba in Light of the Dead Sea Scrolls*, ed. David M. Goodblatt, Avital Pinnick, and Daniel R. Schwartz, STDJ 37 [Boston: Brill, 2001], 151–2), and Gerd Theissen ("Urchristlicher Liebeskommunismus: Zum 'Sitz im Leben' des Topos ἅπαντα κοινά in Apg 2,44 und 4,32," in *Texts and Contexts: Biblical Texts in Their Textual and Situational Contexts*, ed. Tord Fornberg and David Hellholm [Oslo: Scandinavian University Press, 1995], 699).

[12] See, for example, Plutarch, *Cat. Min.* 73.4; *Frat. amor.* 96f.

[13] See, for example, Num 15:27 LXX: "But if an individual [ψυχὴ μία] should sin unintentionally, he will present a one-year old female goat for a sin offering." This usage also appears in Euripides (*Alc.* 54; *Hipp.* 721; *Med.* 247), Sophocles (*Oed. col.* 499), Plato (*Gorg.* 501d, 513d; *Leg.* 10.898c), Lycurgus (*Leocr.* 100.61), Demosthenes (*Fals. leg.* 227), Polybius (*Hist.* 6.48.4; 8.3.3; 8.7.7; 9.22.1), Philo (*Legat.* 27; *Migr.* 60; *Sacr.* 3); T. Ab. 9:8 (rec. A), 11:12 (rec. B), 12:4 (rec. B), Lev 4:27 LXX, and Num 31:28 LXX.

invocation of friendship.[14] In contrast, the employment of μία ψυχή as a friendship proverb in Greek literature of this period is almost limited to Aristotle's oft-cited citations of it as such, along with a possible instance in Euripides' *Orestes*.[15]

As for the second friendship proverb, the expressions εἶχον ἅπαντα κοινά ("they had all things in common") and ἦν αὐτοῖς ἅπαντα κοινά ("all things were common to them") share only one word with the Aristotelian maxim they are supposed to reflect: κοινά.[16] Johnson's assertion that this is "an unmistakable allusion" to Aristotle's proverb reduces to the claim that the appearance of this word in the context of common property almost always invokes the friendship tradition.[17] Yet this is simply not the case. The term κοινά occurs in a wide variety of discussions of common property that make no appeal to friendship ideals, ranging from Plato's descriptions of primitive Athens (*Crit.* 110d) to Nicolaus of Damascus' depiction of the galactophages (*FGH* 90f.104).[18] The word κοινά can appear anywhere common property is discussed, often apart from ideas of friendship. As such, its mere presence in a description of a community of property is not evidence for a reference to friendship ideals specifically.

These observations do not disprove a Lukan friendship allusion, much less exclude the possibility that some of Luke's readers might have recalled friendship proverbs upon reading the summaries. Nevertheless, the lexical case for a clear reference to friendship ideals is far shakier than often supposed.

Ideal State Descriptions

While many have compared Luke's language to the friendship proverbs cited by Aristotle, others have drawn a connection to Plato, particularly to his description of the ideal state in the *Republic*. David Mealand is the most influential proponent of the idea that the accounts of common property in the Acts summaries use specifically Platonic vocabulary.[19] Mealand focuses on two phrases in Acts 4:32; the first is οὐδὲ εἷς ... ἴδιον:[20]

---

[14] For example, Philo highlights the agreement of Moses and Aaron "when they came to Egypt with one mind and soul" (*Mos.* 1.86, γνώμῃ καὶ ψυχῇ μιᾷ), and 1 Chr 12:39 LXX describes Israel as being "of one mind [μία ψυχή] to make David king." See also the pseudo-Hippocratic *Ep.* 13.5 (on the unity of a city) and Dionysius of Halicarnassus, *Ant. rom.* 6.10.1 (on the unity of an army).

[15] *Eth. eud.* 1240b; *Eth. nic.* 1168b. Electra remarks to Orestes about his "having one soul with your sister" (*Orest.* 1046, ἔχων τῆς σῆς ἀδελφῆς ... ψυχὴν μίαν). There is indirect evidence for the use of this Greek phrase as a friendship proverb prior to 100 CE from later Greek reports and from Latin versions of the phrase (Cicero, *Amic.* 25.92: "as if one soul comes to be from many" [unus quasi animus fiat ex pluribus], e.g.).

[16] For other appearances of this proverb, see Brian Capper, "The Palestinian Cultural Context of Earliest Christian Community of Goods," in *The Book of Acts in its Palestinian Setting*, ed. Richard Bauckham, BAFCS 4 (Grand Rapids: Eerdmans, 1995), 325 n. 5.

[17] Luke Timothy Johnson, *The Acts of the Apostles*, SP 5 (Collegeville, MN: Liturgical Press, 1992), 58; "Making Connections: The Material Expression of Friendship in the New Testament," *Int* 58 (2004): 159.

[18] Other instances include Plato's description of the guardians' lifestyle (*Resp.* 5.464d), Aristotle's report of the Tarentines' economic practices (*Pol.* 1320b), Strabo's accounts of the Scythians (*Geogr.* 7.3.9) and the scholars of the Alexandrian museum (*Geogr.* 17.1.8), Philo's notion of the proper attitude of the wealthy (*Spec.* 4.72), Josephus' portrait of the Essenes (*A.J.* 18.20), Lucian's satirical petition to Cronus (*Sat.* 31), and Iamblichus' presentation of the Pythagoreans (*Vit. pyth.* 168).

[19] David L. Mealand, "Community of Goods and Utopian Allusions in Acts II–IV," *JTS* 28 (1977): 96-9.

[20] This is one of four places in Plato that Mealand cites where οὐδέν or μηδέν is combined with ἴδιον; the others are *Crit.* 110d, *Resp.* 8.543b, and *Tim.* 18b.

Resp. 5.464d	Acts 4:32
διὰ τὸ μηδὲν ἴδιον ἐκτῆσθαι πλὴν τὸ σῶμα Because they possess nothing of their own except their body.	οὐδὲ εἷς τι τῶν ὑπαρχόντων αὐτῷ ἔλεγεν ἴδιον εἶναι No one claimed private ownership of any possessions.

Mealand also points to Platonic uses of the expression ἅπαντα κοινά:[21]

Crit. 110d	Acts 2:44; 4:32
ἅπαντα δὲ πάντων κοινὰ νομίζοντες αὐτῶν Considering all of their things common to all.	εἶχον ἅπαντα κοινά [They] had all things in common. ἦν αὐτοῖς ἅπαντα κοινά All things were common to them.

Other scholars make even stronger claims for a direct use of Plato by Luke. Lucien Cerfaux argues that certain expressions in the summaries have "been mechanically transposed from Plato or from a source derived from the *Republic*," and Rubén Dupertuis suggests that Luke "had a copy of Plato before him" when composing these passages.[22]

These arguments run into the same problem as those of friendship interpreters: similar language appears as or more often outside of the proposed referent. Both οὐδέν/μηδέν ... ἴδιον and ἅπαντα/πάντα ... κοινά occur not only in Plato but also in descriptions of friendship, marriage, and the lifestyles of certain primitive, philosophical, or religious communities.[23] Again, the case for a specific reference, this time to Plato, based on vocabulary alone is unconvincing.[24]

Accounts of Distant Lands or Primitive Peoples

Gregory Sterling argues that Luke's summaries primarily belong to the genre of "description of religious or philosophical groups" rather than to friendship or

---

[21] Mealand notes only this passage, but the phrase appears as well in *Leg.* 7.802a; *Resp.* 4.424a.

[22] Lucien Cerfaux, "La première communauté chrétienne a Jérusalem (Act., II, 41–V, 42)," *ETL* 16 (1939): 27; "été transpose méchaniquement de Platon ou d'une source dérivée de la République"; Dupertuis, "Summaries in Acts," 171. Alan J. Thompson (*One Lord, One People: The Unity of the Church in Acts in Its Literary Setting*, LNTS 359 [London: T&T Clark, 2008]) also sees an intentional allusion to Plato's *Republic*.

[23] οὐδέν/μηδέν ... ἴδιον: Euripides, *Andr.* 376; Musonius Rufus, frag. 13a, 4; Plutarch, *Conj. praec.* 140f; Epictetus, *Diatr.* 4.4.39; Philo, *Hypoth.* 11.4; Diogenes Laertius, *Vit. phil.* 8.23.4. ἅπαντα/πάντα ... κοινά: Aristotle, *Eth. nic.* 1159b; Musonius Rufus, frag. 13a.4; Plutarch, *Conj. praec.* 143a; Strabo, *Geogr.* 7.3.7, 9; Iamblichus, *Vit. pyth.* 168; Lucian, *Merc. cond.* 20.6.

[24] Dupertuis ("Summaries in Acts," 131–2) also proposes three "striking thematic similarities" between the *Republic* and Acts to bolster his claim of a literary relationship: (1) both present the founding of a city, (2) both use the term κοινωνία in the context of common property, and (3) both link the organization of the community with the authority of its leaders. The first and last similarities are only dubiously present in Acts, however, and κοινωνία, like the other highlighted vocabulary, is by no means peculiar to Plato.

ideal state discourses.²⁵ He supports this claim by selecting ten exemplars of this ethnographic tradition and identifying twenty-five standard topoi present in them.²⁶ Sterling finds thirteen of the topoi in Acts 2:41–47, allowing him to locate this passage in the aforementioned tradition.²⁷

Several of the shared topoi are of questionable value.²⁸ In particular, almost all of the instances of the most significant topoi, gathered under the heading "common life," occur in descriptions of the Essenes. With the remaining exemplars providing negligible attestation, it is debatable whether common property is a standard feature of an ethnographic literary tradition in general or, instead, of Essene accounts specifically.²⁹ Sterling's study does have two strengths that should be highlighted. First, he argues mostly on the basis of shared themes rather than shared vocabulary. Given the wide use of the common property language found in Acts, Sterling's approach has a greater likelihood of success. Second, Sterling points out that any interpretation of the summaries must deal with their uniqueness: Luke describes no other Christian group as he does the Jerusalem believers of Acts 2 and 4.³⁰ This is a fact often emphasized by those who read the summaries against a Golden Age background.

Golden Age Accounts

While exploring the literary background of common property descriptions in Acts 2:42–47 and 4:32–35, many interpreters note that this motif also occurs in accounts of the Golden Age, when "no one ... possessed any private property, but all things were common and undivided to all persons" (Pompeius Trogus, *Ep.* 43.1.3).³¹ Eckhard Plümacher, for instance, claims that the summaries depict "the church's Age of Saturn," an alternative title for the Golden Age.³² Plümacher does not explore this

---

²⁵ Gregory Sterling, "'Athletes of Virtue': An Analysis of the Summaries in Acts," *JBL* 113 (1994): 688.
²⁶ Sterling's ten exemplars consist of five descriptions of the Essenes (Philo, *Prob.* 75–91; *Hypoth.* 8.11.1–18; Josephus, *B.J.* 2.120–61; *A.J.* 18.18–22; Pliny, *Nat.* 5.73), three depictions of contemporary foreign sages (Arrian, *Ind.* 11.1–8; Philostratus, *Vit. Apoll.* 3.10–51; 6.6), and two accounts of groups at hundreds of years remove from the authors (Porphyry, *Abst.* 4.6–8; Iamblichus, *Vit. pyth.* 96–100).
²⁷ Sterling, "Athletes of Virtue," 688. The number of topoi found in individual exemplars ranges from five in Pliny's account of the Essenes to eighteen in those of Philo and Josephus.
²⁸ Luke's only mention of "domiciles" is his remark that the believers "broke bread at home" (2:46). "Time in temple" occurs in only two of the ten exemplars. "Community structure" is not explicitly discussed in Acts 2:41–47. "Initiation" occurs in v. 41 (baptism), but the summary is more commonly thought to begin with v. 42 (see Maria Anicia Co, "The Major Summaries in Acts: Acts 2,42–47; 4,32–35; 5,12–16: Linguistics and Literary Relationship," *ETL* 68 [1992]: 58–61).
²⁹ The two exceptions are Philostratus on the Indian sages, who "have the things of all" (*Vit. Apoll.* 3.15.3, τὰ πάντων ἔχειν), referring to their practice of living outside, and Iamblichus on the Pythagorean community; only the latter seems comparable to the Acts summaries.
³⁰ Sterling "Athletes of Virtue," 695–6.
³¹ neque quicquam privatae rei habuerit, sed omnia communia et indivisa omnibus fuerint.
³² Eckhard Plümacher, *Lukas als hellenistischer Schriftsteller: Studien zur Apostelgeschichte*, SUNT 9 (Göttingen: Vandenhoeck & Ruprecht, 1972), 16–17, 18 n. 61; "das Saturnische Zeitalter der Kirche."

idea at any length, but in line with this interpretation he considers Acts 2 and 4 to be describing "heroic, unrepeatable beginnings."[33]

Capper has written the most extensive consideration of the Golden Age myth as a possible literary context for the Acts summaries, devoting eight pages to the topic in an essay on the idea of reciprocity in Acts.[34] Capper argues that Luke's theme early in Acts is "new beginnings," and he connects this with the nature of the Golden Age myth as "an account of human beginnings."[35] Like Plümacher, Capper also thinks that Luke's use of Golden Age imagery implies that the practice of common property is not a general standard for Christian communities: "Readers familiar with the contemporary relegation of community of goods to the past Golden Age ... would have been cued to employ a reading strategy which would not demand that earliest Christian community of property would persist into the present experience of the Church."[36] Instead, Capper believes that Luke uses the Golden Age idea primarily to show that "foundation-events of unique import for world history were taking place."[37]

The most promising Golden Age reading of the summaries to date is found not in any study of Acts but rather in Stefan Schreiber's monograph on Luke 1–2.[38] Schreiber argues that Luke's infancy narrative alludes to the Golden Age myth, and he sees a reference to this same myth in the motif of a community of goods in the Acts summaries.[39] Schreiber notes this only in passing and offers no arguments for a Golden Age interpretation of the summaries. His advance consists in recognizing the political aspects of the Golden Age myth in the early Roman Empire and that a

---

[33] Ibid., 18 n. 61; "heroischen, unwiderholbaren Anfangen." Hans-Josef Klauck ("Gütergemeinschaft in der klassischen antike, in Qumran und im Neuen Testament," *RevQ* 11 [1982]: 47–79) gives a very similar interpretation of the summaries, placing them "in the Golden Age of the beginning" (ibid., 73, in der goldenen Zeit des Anfangs) and stating that this era's "heroic greatness is unrepeatable for the present" (ibid., 73-4, heroische Größe für die Gegenwart uneinholbar ist). So too Daniel Marguerat (*Les Actes des apôtres (1–12)*, CNT 5A [Geneva: Labor et Fides, 2007]), who sees the summaries as an "idealized portrait of a Golden Age" (ibid., 100, portrait idéalisé d'un âge d'or). Marguerat also denies that the summaries are intended as a model: "This portrait belongs to a Golden Age. The author of Acts does not invite imitation" (ibid., 109, ce portrait ... appartient à un âge d'or. L'auteur des Actes n'invite pas à l'imitation).

[34] Capper, "Reciprocity," 504–12. Despite his detailed consideration of the Golden Age myth here, Capper does not use this interpretation exclusively or even predominately in his writings. In the second half of this same study, Capper reads the summaries through the lens of friendship traditions, concluding that "the earliest community in Jerusalem realised the vaunted Greek ideal of friendship" (ibid., 516). Elsewhere, Capper's ideas about the most applicable literary context are similarly varied: in one essay ("Community of Goods in the Early Jerusalem Church," *ANRW* 26.2:1751) he suggests that Luke's description indicates that he was "passingly familiar with the Hellenistic accounts on Pythagorean communism," while in another ("Palestinian Cultural Context," 325) he states that Luke presents "the early Christians in Jerusalem in the dress of Greek thinking about ideal political organization."

[35] Capper, "Reciprocity," 504, 509.

[36] Ibid., 509.

[37] Ibid.

[38] Stefan Schreiber, *Weihnachtspolitik: Lukas 1–2 und das Goldene Zeitalter*, NTOA, SUNT 82 (Göttingen: Vandenhoeck & Ruprecht, 2009). See Chapter 4 for an evaluation of Schreiber's claims with respect to Luke 1–2.

[39] Ibid., 76.

Golden Age allusion would therefore indicate that "being a follower of Jesus must have political consequences."[40]

Reasons for Pursuing a Golden Age Interpretation of the Acts Summaries

Compared to other Greek and Roman literary traditions that involve common property, the Golden Age myth is relatively unexplored as a context for understanding the Acts summaries. The friendship, ideal state, and ethnographic traditions each have advocates who have put forward comprehensive cases for reading the summaries through these lenses. Not so the Golden Age myth, which is typically mentioned only in passing and without any systematic study of the myth. Still, relative inattention is not a sufficient justification for pursuing a Golden Age reading of the summaries. Why think that Luke might be alluding to an ancient Greek utopian myth?

What makes such a reading far more initially plausible and enticing are two facts noted by Schreiber but typically ignored by commentators on Acts. First, the Golden Age myth is not just one among many old Greek myths in the early Empire. Beginning with the Augustan poets, the Golden Age becomes a ubiquitous literary motif, leading the classicist Denis Feeney to label it *"the* great Roman myth."[41] Second, the Golden Age myth acquires unmistakable political connotations during this period. Beginning with Augustus, Roman emperors are regularly credited with bringing about a return of the Golden Age. The political import of the Golden Age myth constitutes potential evidence for an allusion to this tradition by Luke, the Gospel author most interested in the relationship between the nascent Christian movement and the Roman Empire. Furthermore, should such an allusion be accepted, the use of this myth in both imperial propaganda and criticisms of Rome opens up a new and exciting range of interpretive possibilities for the Acts summaries.

Inattention to these aspects of the Golden Age myth is likely responsible for how little scholars have explored its implications for reading the early chapters of Acts. While a few objections have been raised to a Golden Age interpretation of the summaries, none hold up under examination. Alan Mitchell, for instance, argues that "in these summaries, it is evident that having all things in common did not require the absence of private property for all, usually associated with non-Platonic versions of the golden age myth."[42] The accuracy of this statement could be questioned on both ends: Capper and others do posit an absence of private property in the Acts summaries, while many Golden Age accounts only deny that fields were marked as private possessions without making any explicit claim to a complete absence of private property.[43] More to the

---

[40] Ibid., 92; "Anhänger Jesu zu sein, muss ... politische Folgen haben."
[41] Denis C. Feeney, *Caesar's Calendar: Ancient Time and the Beginnings of History* (Berkeley: University of California Press, 2007), 112.
[42] Mitchell, "Social Function of Friendship," 260–1.
[43] Germanicus, *Arat.* 118–119; Ovid, *Am.* 3.8.41–42; *Metam.* 1.135–136; Seneca, *Phaed.* 528–529; Tibullus, *El.* 1.3.43–44; Virgil, *Georg.* 1.126–127.

point, even if the context in Acts did indicate that private property was widely retained, this would not preclude a literary allusion by Luke to a tradition characterized by a full community of property.

David Seccombe and Christopher Hays have a more general objection that a Golden Age allusion would amount to Lukan endorsement of mythology: "It is doubtful that a Christian writer, as immersed in the OT as Luke, would consciously have imitated pagan mythological conceptions."[44] This claim may be refuted by considering Josephus' use of the Golden Age myth in the *Jewish Antiquities*. As Chapter 3 will show, Josephus consciously incorporated elements of this myth in his retelling of Genesis, interweaving Golden Age details into the biblical narrative. Josephus was certainly no less "immersed in the OT" than Luke and even prefaced his work with a claim to "have added nothing" to Scripture, which is "pure of unseemly mythology" (*A.J.* 1.15–16, 17).[45] If this did not prevent Josephus from making use of the Golden Age myth, Luke's OT commitments cannot be used as grounds for ruling out an allusion to this same myth.

The Detection of Allusions

A Golden Age interpretation of the Acts summaries may be appealing and possible, but how can we be confident that an allusion to this myth is actually present? Studies of biblical allusion typically set forth criteria for verifying proposed allusions. The most influential proposal has been that of Richard Hays, but Christopher Beetham and Dennis MacDonald have employed their own, somewhat different, lists.[46] The three sets can be combined to produce six basic criteria:

(1) *Availability*:[47] The source of the proposed allusion must have been available to the author; that is, the source must both predate the writing of the alluding text and plausibly have been familiar to its author.
(2) *Markedness*:[48] The proposed allusion must be marked in some way to direct the audience back to the source. Most commonly, this occurs by the use of words or phrases borrowed from the source, with both the amount and the distinctiveness of the shared language contributing to the satisfaction of this criterion. Allusions

---

[44] Seccombe, *Possessions and the Poor*, 201; so also Hays, *Luke's Wealth Ethics*, 207 n. 42.
[45] οὐδὲν προσθείς; καθαρόν ... τῆς ... ἀσχήμονος μυθολογίας.
[46] Richard B. Hays, *Echoes of Scripture in the Letters of Paul* (New Haven: Yale University Press, 1989), 29–32; Christopher A. Beetham, *Echoes of Scripture in the Letter of Paul to the Colossians*, BibInt 96 (Leiden: Brill, 2008), 28–34; Dennis R. MacDonald, *The Homeric Epics and the Gospel of Mark* (New Haven: Yale University Press, 2000), 8–9, repeated with one significant addition in *The Gospels and Homer: Imitations of Greek Epic in Mark and Luke-Acts*, The New Testament and Greek Literature 1 (Lanham, MD: Rowman & Littlefield, 2015), 6–7.
[47] This includes the criteria labelled "availability" by Beetham (*Echoes of Scripture*, 28) and Hays (*Echoes of Scripture*, 29) and "accessibility" by MacDonald (*Homeric Epics*, 8).
[48] This includes the criteria labelled "word agreement or rare concept similarity" by Beetham (*Echoes of Scripture*, 29), "volume" by Hays (*Echoes of Scripture*, 30), and the three criteria called "density" (partially) "order," and "distinctiveness" by MacDonald (*Homeric Epics*, 8).

may also be marked by shared concepts or similarities in order, if these are sufficiently distinctive to be detectable in principle.
(3) *Sense*:[49] The proposed allusion must make sense in its context. Recognizing the allusion must aid in the interpretation of the alluding text, and this meaning must be plausible within the context of the alluding text.
(4) *Recurrence in the Same Author*:[50] If the same author refers to the same source more than once, this makes it more likely that otherwise uncertain allusions to this source are genuine.
(5) *Occurrence in Other Authors*:[51] If other authors also allude to the same source, this makes it more likely that otherwise uncertain allusions to this source are genuine.
(6) *Later Recognition*:[52] If later authors, ancient or modern, recognize a proposed allusion, this makes it more likely that the allusion is genuine.

These six criteria do not all carry equal weight. Beetham considers satisfaction of only the first three, availability, markedness, and sense, to be necessary for a genuine allusion.[53] The remaining three criteria, while they may "offer some aid in confirming an allusion," are not necessary for an allusion to be present and identifiable.[54] There is no reason to suppose that a given writer must allude to the same source multiple times, or that other authors must allude to this source as well, or that later readers must recognize and record the presence of an allusion. Fulfillment of these criteria may improve the case for an allusion, but a lack of fulfillment does not disqualify a potential allusion.

Of the six criteria collated here, one stands out as a potential stumbling block: markedness. Most allusions are identified by shared language, and distinctive verbal

---

[49] This includes the criteria labelled "essential interpretive link" and "thematic coherence" by Beetham (*Echoes of Scripture*, 30, 34), "thematic coherence," "historical plausibility," and "satisfaction" by Hays (*Echoes of Scripture*, 30–1), and "interpretability" by MacDonald (*Homeric Epics*, 9).
[50] This includes the criteria labelled "other verified references from the same OT context in Colossians" and "occurrence elsewhere in the Pauline corpus" by Beetham (*Echoes of Scripture*, 33), "recurrence" by Hays (*Echoes of Scripture*, 30), and "density" (partially) by MacDonald (*Homeric Epics*, 8).
[51] This includes the criteria labelled "Old Testament and Jewish interpretive tradition" by Beetham (*Echoes of Scripture*, 32) and "analogy" by MacDonald (*Homeric Epics*, 8).
[52] This includes the criteria labelled "scholarly assessment" by Beetham (*Echoes of Scripture*, 32) and "history of interpretation" by Hays (*Echoes of Scripture*, 31). In *Gospels and Homer* (6–7), MacDonald added a seventh criterion that belongs in this category, "ancient and Byzantine recognitions."
[53] Beetham, *Echoes of Scripture*, 28. These same criteria are recognized as necessary by others as well. Once markedness has been established in the form of a recognizable parallel, Richard F. Thomas ("Virgil's *Georgics* and the Art of Reference," *HSCP* 90 [1986]: 174) identifies "two absolute criteria … the model must be one with whom the poet is demonstrably familiar, and there must be a reason of some sort for the reference—that is, it must be susceptible of interpretation, or meaningful." Don P. Fowler ("On the Shoulders of Giants: Intertextuality and Classical Studies," *Materiali e discussioni per l'analisi dei testi classici* 39 [1997]: 20) assumes availability as a precondition and states the other two basic criteria: "We require a correspondence to stand out and to make sense …. We ask: show me that this is not common, and tell me something interesting."
[54] Beetham, *Echoes of Scripture*, 28.

agreement is correctly considered the best foundation for establishing an allusion.[55] In the Acts summaries as well, the main arguments for allusions to specific traditions have been based on shared language. As has already been shown, however, the words and expressions used in the summaries are not distinctive of any one tradition but appear in a wide variety of literary contexts. This presents a significant obstacle to claims for an allusion to any individual tradition, be it friendship, ideal state, ethnographic, or Golden Age.

With that said, it is also often acknowledged that allusions may be justifiably posited apart from any distinctive shared vocabulary: Beetham allows that the sharing of a "rare concept" may sufficiently mark an allusion without any verbal ties, and Ellen Finkelpearl points to an allusion in one of her own poems that has only the indefinite article in common with its source.[56] Nevertheless, the significance of the problem should be acknowledged. Criticizing two prominent attempts to establish Acts' dependence on a particular literary model, Craig Evans notes that most critics' "principle objection is that there are no actual quotations or sequences of words."[57]

I argue in this book that such an objection is not insurmountable with respect to the Acts summaries: a probable case for a Lukan allusion to the Golden Age myth can be made, and this allusion is ripe with interpretive possibilities. The absence of identifiable quotation in the Acts summaries requires that the argument for an allusion to a specific tradition be more in-depth than a simple noting of verbal similarities, however. The remainder of this book presents such an argument.

The Structure of This Study

The criterion of "later recognition" has already been met to some extent. Many scholars have recognized parallels or even an intentional allusion to the Golden Age myth in Acts 2:42–47 and 4:32–35. Such an allusion is far from universally accepted, but it is not a novel or even a rare suggestion, although its implications have been insufficiently investigated.

---

[55] Ellen D. Finkelpearl (*Metamorphosis of Language in Apuleius: A Study of Allusion in the Novel* [Ann Arbor: University of Michigan Press, 1998], 3) describes "similar phrasing" as the "sort of 'concrete' evidence one looks for above all" in detecting allusions, and Russell L. Meek ("Intertextuality, Inner-Biblical Exegesis, and Inner-Biblical Allusion: The Ethics of a Methodology," *Bib* 95 [2014]: 289) declares "shared language" to be "of utmost importance for determining the presence of an allusion."

[56] Beetham, *Echoes of Scripture*, 29; Finkelpearl, *Metamorphosis of Language*, 1–4; Finkelpearl states that, in context, her line "still on a dresser-top on Bartlett Street" alludes to the phrase "silent, upon a peak in Darien" at the end of Keats' poem "On First Looking into Chapman's Homer."

[57] Craig A. Evans, "The Pseudepigrapha and the Problem of Background 'Parallels' in the Study of the Acts of the Apostles," in *The Pseudepigrapha and Christian Origins*, ed. Gerbern S. Oegema and James H. Charlesworth, Jewish and Christian Texts in Contexts and Related Studies 4 (New York: T&T Clark, 2008), 140. Evans specifically criticizes Marianne Palmer Bonz, *The Past as Legacy: Luke-Acts and Ancient Epic* (Minneapolis: Fortress, 2000) and Dennis R. MacDonald, *Does the New Testament Imitate Homer? Four Cases from the Acts of the Apostles* (New Haven: Yale University Press, 2003).

Chapter 2 introduces the myth of the Golden Age, beginning with the most important Greek accounts of the myth. Latin Golden Age texts constitute the primary subject matter of the chapter. By presenting almost thirty references to this myth in the early Empire, this chapter clearly establishes its "availability" to Luke as a possible referent. Chapter 3 shifts attention to Jewish and Christian authors' utilization of the Golden Age myth, examining allusions by Philo, Josephus, and the Sibylline Oracles. An important general conclusion from this chapter is that some Jewish and Christian texts in the first couple of centuries CE do refer to the Golden Age idea. This fact increases the plausibility of a Lukan allusion to the same myth by fulfilling the criterion of "occurrence in other authors."

Chapter 4 narrows the focus to Luke-Acts, treating three broader issues that are preliminaries to the more specific analysis of Acts 2:42–47 and 4:32–35 in Chapter 5. First, I argue that the Acts summaries depict an eschatological lifestyle, which accords with the discovery in Chapter 3 that Jewish and Christian authors often use the Golden Age myth in eschatological passages. Second, I show that Luke not only has a particular interest in Rome but also uses imperial language on occasion; the chapter proposes that Luke's overall stance toward Rome is best described as "supra-imperial." Third, I evaluate the arguments of three authors who claim that Luke alludes to Roman Golden Age ideology elsewhere in Luke-Acts. I conclude they do not demonstrate that Luke alludes to the Golden Age motif specifically. As such, the optional criterion of "recurrence in the same author" cannot be considered to be conclusively satisfied in support of a Golden Age allusion in the Acts summaries.

Finally, Chapter 5 turns to the summaries in Acts 2:42–47 and 4:32–35. After treating the major individual exegetical issues, I present the evidence for reading these passages as Golden Age allusions. I identify four specific correspondences between the myth and the summaries: (1) both depict a lifestyle associated with a "new age," (2) both recount communities that are recipients of divine favor, (3) both emphasize the conditions of unity and harmony, and (4) both describe a time when property was held in common. In addition, other Jewish and Christian uses of the myth to portray the eschaton and to criticize Rome fit with the proposed allusion to the Golden Age in Acts. The convergence of this evidence constitutes sufficient "markedness" to confidently posit a Golden Age allusion in the Acts summaries. I then offer two complementary interpretations for this proposed allusion, showing how it satisfies the criterion of "sense" by significantly deepening the audience's understanding of the summaries. First, by characterizing the Jerusalem community by means of the Golden Age myth, Luke depicts the coming of the Spirit as marking the dawn of an eschatological "universal restoration" (Acts 2:17). Second, by presenting the community in terms that recall stock motifs of imperial propaganda, Luke's allusion to the Golden Age has a political meaning as well, implying that it is Jesus, and not Caesar, who has the power to restore unity among people and harmony between humanity and God. This interpretation fits with and offers a new contribution to the growing body of empire-critical studies of Luke-Acts.

2

The Golden Age Myth in Greek and Latin Sources

This chapter surveys the Golden Age myth as it occurs in Greek and Latin sources from its earliest appearance until the early second century CE. After a brief consideration of the myth's prehistory, I examine the three most important Greek accounts of the Golden Age, those of Hesiod, Plato, and Aratus. Each author describes the Golden Age as a period in the past when humans lived in harmony with each other and were blessed by the gods. Beginning with Lucretius, I then shift attention to the treatment of the myth by Latin authors, particularly Virgil and Ovid. Ovid emphasizes the Golden Age's attitudes toward wealth, while Virgil introduces three important innovations to the myth: the idea of the Golden Age's return, the attribution of the practice of common property to the Golden Age, and the explicit political application of the myth. I next survey further instances of these latter two additions to show their prevalence in Latin Golden Age accounts during the early Empire. More generally, this chapter demonstrates the ubiquity of the Golden Age myth during this period, satisfying the criterion of "availability" for a possible Lukan allusion to this myth.

The Golden Age Myth before Hesiod

Hesiod's *Works and Days* (ca. 700 BCE) contains the first extant account of the Golden Age myth, but the majority opinion is that Hesiod received rather than created this myth. The main internal evidence for this is the fact that four of his five races are associated with a particular metal, while the Heroic Race is not. As a result, this race is often considered to be an interpolation into a preexisting four-stage myth.[1] Externally, similar myths elsewhere suggest the existence of a source common to these and Hesiod's version. Almost a century ago, Richard Reitzenstein identified three parallels that continue to serve as the primary comparative material: Zoroaster's vision of a four-branched tree in the *Bahman Yasht*, Nebuchadnezzar's dream of a statue

---

[1] Ludwig Koenen, "Greece, the Near East, and Egypt: Cyclic Destruction in Hesiod and the Catalogue of Women," *TAPA* 124 (1994): 10–11; Richard Reitzenstein, "Altgriechische Theologie und ihre Quellen," in *Hesiod*, ed. Ernst Heitsch, Wege der Forschung 44 (Darmstadt: Wissenschaftliche Buchgesellschaft, 1966), 531; Pierre Sauzeau and André Sauzeau, "Le symbolisme des métaux et le mythe des races métalliques," *RHR* 219 (2002): 272; Martin L. West, ed., *Hesiod: Works and Days* (Oxford: Clarendon, 1978), 174. Roger D. Woodward ("Hesiod and Greek Myth," in *The Cambridge Companion to Greek Mythology*, ed. Roger D. Woodward [Cambridge: Cambridge University Press, 2007], 114) states that this position is held by "practically all classical scholars."

composed of different materials in Dan 2, and the description of four world-ages in the *Mahabharata*.² Since the extant versions of each of these postdate Hesiod, however, a pre-Hesiodic common source cannot be demonstrated, much less reconstructed in detail.

The *Bahman Yasht* is an apocalyptic Zoroastrian text whose final version likely dates to the ninth or tenth century CE.³ In this work, Ahura Mazda gives Zoroaster a vision of "a tree on which were four branches, one of gold, one of silver, one of steel, and one on [which] iron had been mixed" (*Bahm. Yasht* 1.3).⁴ Ahura Mazda then explains that the four branches represent four ages. A similar metallic series appears in Nebuchadnezzar's dream of a statue in Dan 2: "The head of that statue was of fine gold, its chest and arms of silver, its middle and thighs of bronze, its legs of iron, its feet partly of iron and partly of clay" (Dan 2:32–33).⁵ As in Hesiod and the *Bahman Yasht*, these metals symbolize a chronological succession, in this case, four successive kingdoms.⁶ The *Mahabharata*, an Indian epic that took form between the fourth century BCE and the fourth century CE, depicts a cycle of four ages, each associated with a specific color.⁷ The first age (white) was a time of ease, with "no human labor," when "fruits were obtained by wishing for them" (*Mah.* 3.148.12–13).⁸ After two inferior ages, marked by the colors red and yellow, the low point occurs with the appearance of the black age: "There are natural disasters, diseases, laziness, bad qualities such as anger and the like, calamities, and mental as well as physical suffering" (*Mah.* 3.148.34). The entire cycle then repeats itself.

Reitzenstein concluded that these various stories all stemmed from an original Near Eastern myth of the ages that was Hesiod's source.⁹ This has continued to be a popular position, but the case for Hesiod's account being an adaptation is not conclusive.¹⁰ The incongruity of the Heroic Race is disputable.¹¹ More importantly, the external parallels

---

2 Reitzenstein, "Altgriechische Theologie," 526–8; Reitzenstein first published his study in 1925.
3 Mary Boyce, "On the Antiquity of Zoroastrian Apocalyptic," *BSOAS* 47 (1984): 57–75; Carlo G. Cereti, *The Zand i Wahman Yasn: A Zoroastrian Apocalypse*, Serie Orientale Roma 75 (Rome: Istituto per il Medio ed Estremo Oriente, 1995), 13.
4 Translation is from Cereti, *Zand i Wahman Yasn*. A similar story is told in *Denkard* 9.8.
5 John J. Collins (*Daniel: A Commentary on the Book of Daniel*, Hermeneia [Minneapolis: Fortress, 1993], 38) dates the final chapters of Daniel between 167 and 164 BCE, but he suggests that the stories in chapters 2–6 circulated separately before this time.
6 The "mixed" iron stage in both Dan 2 and the *Bahman Yasht* suggests a close connection between the two accounts. John J. Collins (*The Sibylline Oracles of Egyptian Judaism*, SBLDS 13 [Missoula, MT: Scholars Press, 1974], 12) originally suggested that the *Bahman Yasht* borrowed from Daniel, but in his later commentary (*Daniel*, 164) he proposed a common Persian source for both. Klaus Koch (*Daniel: Kapitel 1,1–4,34*, BKAT 22.1 [Neukirchen-Vluyn: Neukirchener Verlag, 2005], 138) argues that the similarities between the two accounts indicate Daniel's dependence on Iranian texts.
7 Bodo Gatz (*Weltalter, goldene Zeit und sinnverwandte Vorstellungen* [Hildesheim: Olms, 1967], 12–13) links this color scheme to Hesiod's metals by tracing both back to Babylon. Koenen ("Greece, the Near East, and Egypt," 24 n. 58) correctly observes that Gatz's argument "builds on many assumptions."
8 Translations are from Luis González-Reimann, *The Mahabharata and the Yugas: India's Great Epic Poem and the Hindu System of World Ages*, Asian Thought and Culture 51 (New York: Lang, 2002).
9 Reitzenstein, "Altgriechische Theologie," 531.
10 Gatz (*Weltalter*, 3–4), Koch (*Daniel*, 130), and West (*Hesiod*, 174–6) propose a Near Eastern Ur-myth.
11 Glenn W. Most ("Hesiod's Myth of the Five [or Three or Four] Races," *Proceedings of the Cambridge Philological Society* 43 [1997]: 104–27) argues that the heroes fit integrally into the series.

all date from several centuries after Hesiod. While these may share a common source with Hesiod, Hesiod may actually be the source for these later versions.[12]

Given the uncertainty about the provenance and even the existence of a pre-Hesiodic version of the Golden Age myth, reconstruction attempts have been abandoned to some extent.[13] If the myths presented here derive from a single predecessor, this Ur-myth likely featured four successive periods of time, each associated with a metal, in a pattern of decline. Attempts to specify further details would devolve into pure speculation.

The Golden Age Myth in Greek Sources

The main focus of this chapter is on Latin accounts of the Golden Age myth, but Latin authors drew their material from Greek antecedents, joining ongoing debates about the nature of the Golden Age. The three most influential Greek versions were those of Hesiod, Plato, and Aratus.

The Golden Age Myth in Hesiod

The earliest attestation of the Golden Age myth occurs in Hesiod's *Works and Days*, written ca. 700 BCE.[14] Hesiod introduces the Golden Age myth with the stated purpose of showing "how gods and mortal humans came from the same source" (*Op.* 108), and he begins by describing the Golden Race:[15]

> Golden was the race of articulate humans that the immortals who live on Olympus made first. They lived at the time of Cronus, when he was king in heaven. They lived like gods, having a carefree heart, without toil and misery. Nor was miserable old age present, but they were always the same in their feet and their hands, and they delighted in festivities, free from all evils. They died as though overcome by sleep. All good things were theirs: the wheat-giving earth bore fruit spontaneously,

---

[12] This position is held by H. C. Baldry ("Who Invented the Golden Age?" *ClQ* 2 [1952]: 91), Koenen ("Greece, the Near East, and Egypt," 13), and Most ("Hesiod's Myth," 120–1).

[13] Helen van Noorden (*Playing Hesiod: The "Myth of the Races" in Classical Antiquity*, Cambridge Classical Studies [Cambridge: Cambridge University Press, 2014], 30) observes that "given the impossibility of certainty as to 'influences' on Hesiod, however, the debate in its original form is now almost extinct." Noncommittal positions are common; Jenny Strauss Clay (*Hesiod's Cosmos* [Cambridge: Cambridge University Press, 2002], 81), for example, allows that "Hesiod's account … may ultimately derive from Near Eastern or Indo-European traditions" but does not commit to any specific prehistory.

[14] Ralph M. Rosen ("Homer and Hesiod," in *A New Companion to Homer*, ed. Barry Powell and Ian Morris, Mnemosyne 163 [Leiden: Brill, 1997], 465) gives a "general consensus" date of 750–650 BCE.

[15] Hesiod and other Greek authors tend to speak of a "Golden Race" (χρύσεον γένος), while Latin authors often speak of a "Golden Age" (*aurea saecula* or *aurea aetas*). In this study, "Golden Age" will often be used as a generic term to cover both Greek and Latin expressions. For the shift in terminology, see Baldry, "Who Invented the Golden Age?" 87–90.

in abundance and without envy. Contented and at peace, they lived off their lands with many good things, rich in sheep, dear to the blessed gods. (*Op.* 109–120)[16]

The general picture is one of an easy, pleasant existence. Three specific details that reappear in later Golden Age accounts deserve mention. First, the idea of the earth producing food "spontaneously" (*Op.* 118, αὐτομάτη) becomes, with a few exceptions, "the essential feature of the Hesiodic Golden Age" for subsequent authors.[17] Second, the members of this race live "at peace" (*Op.* 119) with each other, another consistent characteristic of the Golden Age. Finally, the Golden Race enjoys a close relationship with the divine sphere, being "dear to the blessed gods" (*Op.* 120).

Next, the gods make the Silver Race, "much worse" (*Op.* 127) than its predecessor. Both interhuman and human-divine harmony are absent for this race:

> For they were not able to refrain from reckless outrage toward each other, nor were they willing to do service to the immortals or to offer sacrifice on the holy altars, as is right for humans according to their customs. (*Op.* 134–137)[18]

Due to this strife and impiety, Zeus puts an end to the race and creates another. Hesiod labels this new race "bronze" for obvious reasons:

> They were terrible and mighty, and they took interest in the woeful works of Ares and in wanton acts .... Bronze was their armor, bronze were their houses, and they worked with bronze. (*Op.* 145–151)[19]

The problem of human violence comes to a head in the Bronze Race, and eventually this race destroys itself, being "laid low by their own hands" (*Op.* 152).

The fourth race, "a divine race of heroic men" (*Op.* 159–160), momentarily halts the decline: they are the only race to be explicitly labeled "better" (*Op.* 158) than the preceding race. Nevertheless, this race too comes to an end, and Hesiod bemoans the arrival of its successor: "Would that I had never been among the fifth men, but had either died before or been born afterward!" (*Op.* 174–175). The poet predicts nothing but evil for this "Iron Race":

---

[16] χρύσεον μὲν πρώτιστα γένος μερόπων ἀνθρώπων/ἀθάνατοι ποίησαν Ὀλύμπια δώματ' ἔχοντες./οἱ μὲν ἐπὶ Κρόνου ἦσαν, ὅτ' οὐρανῷ ἐμβασίλευεν·/ὥστε θεοὶ δ' ἔζωον ἀκηδέα θυμὸν ἔχοντες,/νόσφιν ἄτερ τε πόνου καὶ ὀιζύος· οὐδέ τι δειλὸν/γῆρας ἐπῆν, αἰεὶ δὲ πόδας καὶ χεῖρας ὁμοῖοι/τέρποντ' ἐν θαλίῃσι κακῶν ἔκτοσθεν ἁπάντων·/θνῇσκον δ' ὥσθ' ὕπνῳ δεδμημένοι· ἐσθλὰ δὲ πάντα/τοῖσιν ἔην· καρπὸν δ' ἔφερε ζείδωρος ἄρουρα/αὐτομάτη πολλόν τε καὶ ἄφθονον· οἱ δ' ἐθελημοὶ/ἥσυχοι ἔργ' ἐνέμοντο σὺν ἐσθλοῖσιν πολέεσσιν./ἀφνειοὶ μήλοισι, φίλοι μακάρεσσι θεοῖσιν.

[17] Dimitri El Murr, "Hesiod, Plato, and the Golden Age: Hesiodic Motifs in the Myth of the *Politicus* 1," in *Plato and Hesiod*, ed. G. R. Boys-Stones and Johannes Haubold (Oxford: Oxford University Press, 2010), 290.

[18] ὕβριν γὰρ ἀτάσθαλον οὐκ ἐδύναντο/ἀλλήλων ἀπέχειν, οὐδ' ἀθανάτους θεραπεύειν/ἤθελον οὐδ' ἔρδειν μακάρων ἱεροῖς ἐπὶ βωμοῖς,/ἣ θέμις ἀνθρώποισι κατ' ἤθεα.

[19] δεινόν τε καὶ ὄβριμον, οἷσιν Ἄρηος/ἔργ' ἔμελε στονόεντα καὶ ὕβριες ... τῶν δ' ἦν χάλκεα μὲν τεύχεα, χάλκεοι δέ τε οἶκοι,/χαλκῷ δ' εἰργάζοντο.

They will not cease from toil and misery by day nor from being oppressed at night,
and the gods will give them grievous cares .... Father will not be united to children,
nor children to father, nor guest to host, and a sibling will not be dear as before ....
They will take justice into their own hands, and there will be no reverence. The evil
man will harm the better, speaking with crooked words and swearing with an oath.
And shrieking, evil-loving, horrible Envy will accompany all miserable humans.
(*Op.* 176–196)[20]

The Iron Race marks the nadir of the descent from the Golden Race. Ceaseless toil has replaced carefree reception of the earth's spontaneous bounty. Strife has penetrated into even the most intimate human relationships. Humans are no longer "dear to the blessed gods" (*Op.* 120); instead, the gods afflict humanity with oppressive burdens.

Certain fundamental features of Hesiod's myth remain obscure, and some critics reject even the basic idea of a decline from the past to the present.[21] The "better and more just" (*Op.* 158) Heroic Race precludes an unbroken descent through all five races, but some deny any deterioration at all.[22] Furthermore, Hesiod's wish that he had "been born afterward" (*Op.* 175) has led certain readers to posit that Hesiod envisions a cyclical process rather than a linear decline.[23] Finally, the role of the myth of the ages in the overall structure of the *Works and Days* is unclear, although in its immediate context the myth is most easily read as an explanation for the necessity of work.[24]

---

[20] οὐδέ ποτ' ἦμαρ/παύσονται καμάτου καὶ ὀιζύος οὐδέ τι νύκτωρ/τειρόμενοι· χαλεπὰς δὲ θεοὶ δώσουσι μερίμνας/ ... οὐδὲ πατὴρ παίδεσσιν ὁμοίιος οὐδέ τι παῖδες,/οὐδὲ ξεῖνος ξεινοδόκῳ καὶ ἑταῖρος ἑταίρῳ,/οὐδὲ κασίγνητος φίλος ἔσσεται, ὡς τὸ πάρος περ/ ... δίκη δ' ἐν χερσί καὶ αἰδὼς/οὐκ ἔσται· βλάψει δ' ὁ κακὸς τὸν ἀρείονα φῶτα/μύθοισι σκολιοῖς ἐνέπων, ἐπὶ δ' ὅρκον ὀμεῖται./Ζῆλος δ' ἀνθρώποισιν ὀιζυροῖσιν ἅπασιν/δυσκέλαδος κακόχαρτος ὁμαρτήσει, στυγερώπης.

[21] The traditional interpretation sees a continuous decline interrupted only by the Race of Heroes; so Gatz (*Weltalter*, 32), Willem J. Verdenius (*A Commentary on Hesiod*: Works and Days, vv. 1–382, Mnemosyne 86 [Leiden: Brill, 1985], 88), and West (*Hesiod*, 173).

[22] Seth Benardete ("Hesiod's *Works and Days*: A First Reading," *Agon* 1 [1967]: 156–9) and Jenny Strauss Clay ("*Works and Days*: Tracing the Path to *Arete*," in *Brill's Companion to Hesiod*, ed. Franco Montanari, Antonios Rengakos, and Christos Tsagalis [Leiden: Brill, 2009], 79–81) see the various races as successive attempts to create a functional human race. Jean-Pierre Vernant ("Le mythe hésiodique des races: Essai d'analyse structurale," *RHR* 157 [1960]: 21–54) makes the issue of decline irrelevant by a structuralist interpretation that views the various races as a representation of synchronic human statuses and functions; Juha Sihvola (*Decay, Progress, the Good Life? Hesiod and Protagoras on the Development of Culture*, Commentationes humanarum litterarum 89 [Helsinki: Societas Scientiarum Fennica, 1989], 48) rejects parts of Vernant's interpretation but also sees the myth as a synchronic presentation of the "social order according to the justice of Zeus." The traditional decline interpretation remains the most likely, but admittedly the deterioration is not always clear.

[23] R. H. Martin, "The Golden Age and the ΚΥΚΛΟΣ ΓΕΝΕΣΕΩΝ (Cyclical Theory) in Greek and Latin Literature," *GR* 12 (1943): 68; Woodward, "Hesiod and Greek Myth," 148. Hesiod's outburst is most likely a rhetorical expression of disgust that implies nothing about the possibility of a new Golden Age; so Lilah Grace Canevaro (*Hesiod's "Works and Days": How to Teach Self-Sufficiency* [Oxford: Oxford University Press, 2015], 144–5), Clay ("*Works and Days*," 81), Verdenius (*Hesiod*, 105), and West (*Hesiod*, 197).

[24] Hesiod sets the myth of the ages as a parallel account (*Op.* 106, ἕτερον ... λόγον) to the preceding Prometheus-Pandora myth, which clearly has the function of explaining humanity's need to work. Malcolm Heath ("Hesiod's Didactic Poetry," *ClQ* 35 [1985]: 248) sees the Golden Age myth as an etiology of the need to work, Benardete ("Hesiod's *Works and Days*," 153–4) and Verdenius (*Hesiod*, 75) as an etiology of evil, and Canevaro (*Hesiod's "Works and Days*," 149) as an exhortation against idleness.

Despite these uncertainties, some basic features of the myth can be ascertained. The Golden Race lives without toil, eating food spontaneously produced by the earth, and enjoying concord with each other and with the gods. Passing through a series of races identified with different metals (with one exception), the sequence culminates in the Iron Age, a time of toil and hostility. Hesiod's version of the Golden Age myth does not give much attention to the particular focuses of this survey, politics and property; not only is common ownership unmentioned, but even the general themes of wealth and greed are almost completely absent from Hesiod's account.[25]

The Golden Age Myth in Plato

After Hesiod, Plato is the Greek author most associated with the Golden Age myth.[26] The three main appearances of this myth in Plato occur in his political dialogues: the *Republic*, the *Statesman*, and the *Laws*.[27] Plato thus provides an early example of political application of the Golden Age idea, a significant aspect of the myth for this study.

In the third book of the *Republic*, Socrates describes the structure of an ideal city, dividing its citizenry into three classes: producers, auxiliaries, and guardians. To create a sense of unity, Socrates proposes telling a "noble lie" that makes use of Hesiod's races:[28]

> When the god was forming you, as many as were competent to rule, he mixed gold in with them in their formation; therefore they are held in the highest honor. He mixed silver in with as many as are auxiliaries, but iron and bronze in with farmers and other artisans. (*Resp.* 3.415a)[29]

In addition to encouraging unity, Socrates also finds this story useful for convincing the guardians and auxiliaries to accept strict limits on their possession of private property:

---

[25] Glenn W. Most's translation of the myth (LCL) seems to contradict this claim, as it translates *Op.* 118–119 in the following way: "And they themselves, willing, mild-mannered, shared out the fruits of their labors [ἔργ' ἐνέμοντο] together with many good things." This presents the Golden Age as a time of sharing, which, if not a claim of a community of property, tends in that direction. This is not a typical translation of ἔργ' ἐνέμοντο, however; van Noorden (*Playing Hesiod*, 67) and West (*Hesiod*, 181) render it as "lived off their fields," Clay (*Hesiod's Cosmos*, 86) as "looked after their works," and Verdenius (*Hesiod*, 84) as "had enjoyment of," none of which involves any notion of sharing. Verdenius and West point out similar wording in Homer, including *Il.* 2.751 and *Od.* 20.336–337.

[26] Gatz (*Weltalter*, 72) notes that Plato describes the Golden Age the most of any ancient author.

[27] Plato quotes parts of Hesiod's description of the Golden Race twice (*Crat.* 398a; *Resp.* 5.469a), and he arguably alludes to the myth in several other dialogues.

[28] Plato explicitly links his golden class with Hesiod's races in *Resp.* 5.468e–469a and 8.547a.

[29] ἀλλ' ὁ θεὸς πλάττων, ὅσοι μὲν ὑμῶν ἱκανοὶ ἄρχειν, χρυσὸν ἐν τῇ γενέσει συνέμειξεν αὐτοῖς, διὸ τιμιώτατοί εἰσιν· ὅσοι δ' ἐπίκουροι, ἄργυρον· σίδηρον δὲ καὶ χαλκὸν τοῖς τε γεωργοῖς καὶ τοῖς ἄλλοις δημιουργοῖς.

They will be told that they always have divine gold and silver from the gods in their soul and stand in need of no human thing, and that they should not defile holy things by mixing the possession of that gold with the possession of mortal gold. (*Resp.* 3.416e–417a)[30]

Though the *Republic* invokes the Golden Age myth multiple times, no specific details appear. Even the notion of a diachronic sequence is lacking; all that Plato takes over from Hesiod are the metals themselves and the idea of a gradation in value among them. It is tempting to locate the entrance of the common property motif into the Golden Age myth here, since aspects of a community of property do exist among the guardians and auxiliaries, who are represented by gold and silver in Plato's "noble lie."[31] Yet since the *Republic* never describes a temporal "Golden Age," it is impossible to ascertain from this work whether Plato regarded common property as characteristic of it.

Plato's later dialogue the *Statesman* contains a version of Hesiod's Golden Age myth that does present the period as part of a diachronic sequence. One interlocutor, the Elean Stranger, sets forth a two-stage cosmological myth.[32] In the first stage,

> Absolutely no war and no discord were present .... God himself tended and took care of them .... There were neither constitutions nor possession of wives and children .... But while all such things were absent, they had plentiful fruit from trees and much other growth, which sprang up without farming; the earth was yielding spontaneously. (*Pol.* 271e–272a)[33]

This is clearly Hesiod's Golden Age; like Hesiod, the Stranger locates it in the "time of Cronus" (*Pol.* 272b), and the motifs of spontaneous fertility, harmony, and divine-

---

[30] χρυσίον δὲ καὶ ἀργύριον εἰπεῖν αὐτοῖς ὅτι θεῖον παρὰ θεῶν ἀεὶ ἐν τῇ ψυχῇ ἔχουσι καὶ οὐδὲν προσδέονται τοῦ ἀνθρωπείου, οὐδὲ ὅσια τὴν ἐκείνου κτῆσιν τῇ τοῦ θνητοῦ χρυσοῦ κτήσει συμμειγνύντας μιαίνειν.

[31] Peter Garnsey (*Thinking about Property: From Antiquity to the Age of Revolution*, Ideas in Context 90 [Cambridge: Cambridge University Press, 2007], 6, 12) rejects the common characterization of the *Republic*'s city as a "communistic society": "There is no collective or communal ownership of property in the ideal polity of the *Republic*. Rather, Plato has Socrates prescribe for the political leadership and military ... an *absence* of property." The houses of the guardians and auxiliaries do seem to be common in some way, though, leading Garnsey to allow that "at best there is limited common use."

[32] The two stages are defined by the alternating direction of the universe's revolution. For one period of time, the god turns it in one direction; when he lets it go, the universe automatically turns the other way. Luc Brisson ("Interprétation du mythe du *Politique*," in *Reading the* Statesman: *Proceedings of the III Symposium Platonicum*, ed. Christopher J. Rowe, International Plato Studies 4 [Sankt Augustin, DE: Academia, 1995], 349–63) and Christopher J. Rowe ("On Grey-Haired Babies: Plato, Hesiod, and Visions of the Past (and Future)," in Boys-Stones and Haubold, *Plato and Hesiod*, 298–316) argue for a three-stage myth, but this is far from clear in the text and is rejected by the majority of interpreters.

[33] πόλεμός τε οὐκ ἐνῆν οὐδὲ στάσις τὸ παράπαν ... θεὸς ἔνεμεν αὐτοὺς αὐτὸς ἐπιστατῶν ... νέμοντος δὲ ἐκείνου πολιτεῖαί τε οὐκ ἦσαν οὐδὲ κτήσεις γυναικῶν καὶ παίδων ... ἀλλὰ τὰ μὲν τοιαῦτα ἀπῆν πάντα, καρποὺς δὲ ἀφθόνους εἶχον ἀπό τε δένδρων καὶ πολλῆς ὕλης ἄλλης, οὐχ ὑπὸ γεωργίας φυομένους, ἀλλ᾽ αὐτομάτης ἀναδιδούσης τῆς γῆς.

human concord are present. The *Republic*'s infamous proposal of common wives and children also reappears, but the idea of common property in general is not mentioned.

In the present, second stage, humanity has been "left destitute of the care of the god" (*Pol.* 274b, τῆς … δαίμονος ἀπερημωθέντες ἐπιμελείας). Suddenly lacking divine provision, humans had a difficult time adjusting to their new circumstances:

> They lacked resources and arts during the early times, since the spontaneous nourishment had ceased, and they did not know how to provide for themselves, because formerly no need had compelled them. Because of all these things, they were in terrible straits. (*Pol.* 274c)[34]

Yet despite the apparently preferable conditions found in the Age of Cronus, the Stranger unexpectedly raises the question whether it was truly a happier age than the present, concluding that the answer is unknowable.[35] There is little agreement as to the function of the myth here.[36] A few interpreters understand the Golden Age to be a positive paradigm, but most see a more complex relationship between the Age of Cronus and the present.[37]

Plato's final presentation of the Golden Age is more clearly favorable. In the *Laws*, another interlocutor, the Athenian Stranger, again brings up the example of the Age of Cronus while discussing a model city:

> It is said that there was a certain realm and settlement in the time of Cronus that was exceedingly happy, and the best of the current cities is governed in imitation of it. (*Leg.* 4.713b)[38]

---

[34] ἀμήχανοι καὶ ἄτεχνοι κατὰ τοὺς πρώτους ἦσαν χρόνους, ἅτε τῆς μὲν αὐτομάτης τροφῆς ἐπιλελοιπυίας, πορίζεσθαι δὲ οὐκ ἐπιστάμενοί πω διὰ τὸ μηδεμίαν αὐτοὺς χρείαν πρότερον ἀναγκάζειν. ἐκ τούτων πάντων ἐν μεγάλαις ἀπορίαις ἦσαν.

[35] Many find Plato's presentation of the Golden Age here to be highly ambiguous. Brisson ("Interprétation," 358) and El Murr ("Hesiod, Plato," 294) argue that Golden Age humans are insufficiently distinguished from animals; Klaus Kubusch (*Aurea saecula, Mythos und Geschichte: Untersuchung eines Motivs in der antiken Literatur bis Ovid*, Studien zur klassischen Philologie 28 [Frankfurt am Main: Lang, 1986], 33) and Friedrich Solmsen ("Hesiodic Motifs in Plato," in *Hésiode et son influence: six exposés et discussions*, ed. Olivier Reverdin, Entretiens sur l'Antiquité classique 7 [Geneva: Fondation Hardt, 1962], 186) think that Plato clearly implies that the Age of Cronus lacked philosophy and thus true happiness.

[36] "There is as yet no consensus about the main target of the story … every account of the myth involves an awkward reading of the text at some point" (Van Noorden, *Playing Hesiod*, 146).

[37] Presenting even a simplified taxonomy of interpretations is challenging; the following are some of the major suggestions: (a) the Golden Age is a model for the present (Sue Blundell, *The Origins of Civilization in Greek and Roman Thought* [London: Croom Helm, 1986], 152); (b) the Golden Age illustrates the difference between divine and human rule (John Ferguson, *Utopias of the Classical World*, Aspects of Greek and Roman Life [Ithaca, NY: Cornell University Press, 1975], 72–3; Rowe, "On Grey-Haired Babies," 300); (c) the Golden Age shows a rejection of the *Republic*'s philosopher-king model (Charles H. Kahn, "The Myth of the *Statesman*," in *Plato's Myths*, ed. Catalin Partenie [Cambridge: Cambridge University Press, 2009], 148–66); (d) the two ages represent two principles of order in the universe (Brisson, "Interprétation," 361; Kubusch, *Aurea saecula*, 35).

[38] λέγεταί τις ἀρχή τε καὶ οἴκησις γεγονέναι ἐπὶ Κρόνου μάλ᾽ εὐδαίμων, ἧς μίμημα ἔχουσά ἐστιν ἥτις τῶν νῦν ἄριστα οἰκεῖται.

Shortly afterward, the Stranger relates the traditional picture of this age:

> We have received a tradition of the blessed life of those at that time, how all things were plentiful and spontaneous …. God, loving humanity, set over us then a better race, that of the divine spirits, who … provided peace, reverence, good order, and an abundance of justice, and they made the human races free from discord and happy. (*Leg.* 4.713c–e)[39]

Again, the typical themes of spontaneous production and the concord of humans with both the gods and each other appear here, as they did in Hesiod's account. This description makes no mention of common possession of wives and children, nor is there any hint of common property. This absence is significant, as the *Laws* elsewhere upholds common property as an ideal.[40]

Across his dialogues, Plato shows some of the ways in which the Golden Age myth could be applied in political discourse. The *Republic* mobilizes the myth as a useful fiction for justifying and maintaining class structure. Both the *Statesman* and the *Laws* provide a more detailed picture of the Age of Cronus as a contrast to current political structures, and the *Laws* proposes this age as a model for the present. These latter two dialogues agree in describing the Golden Age as a period of concord, but neither makes common property a feature of it. *Pace* Capper and Dupertuis, Plato's Golden Age myth does not include a community of property.[41] Given the importance of the

---

[39] φήμην τοίνυν παραδεδέγμεθα τῆς τῶν τότε μακαρίας ζωῆς, ὡς ἄφθονά τε καὶ αὐτόματα πάντα εἶχεν … ὁ θεὸς ἄρα ὡς φιλάνθρωπος ὢν τότε γένος ἄμεινον ἡμῶν ἐφίστη τὸ τῶν δαιμόνων, ὃ … εἰρήνην τε καὶ αἰδῶ καὶ εὐνομίαν καὶ ἀφθονίαν δίκης παρεχόμενον, ἀστασίαστα καὶ εὐδαίμονα τὰ τῶν ἀνθρώπων ἀπειργάζετο γένη.

[40] The Stranger later states, "first is that city and constitution and best are those laws where the old saying comes to pass most of all throughout the entire city: 'friends truly have all things in common'" (*Leg.* 5.739b–c, πρώτη μὲν τοίνυν πόλις τέ ἐστι καὶ πολιτεία καὶ νόμοι ἄριστοι, ὅπου τὸ πάλαι λεγόμενον ἂν γίγνηται κατὰ πᾶσαν τὴν πόλιν ὅτι μάλιστα· λέγεται δὲ ὡς ὄντως ἐστὶ κοινὰ τὰ φίλων). Nevertheless, for the colony in question he proposes that they "distribute both the land and the houses and not farm in common, since such a thing would be too great given what has been said concerning their birth, rearing, and education" (*Leg.* 5.740a, νειμάσθων … γῆν τε καὶ οἰκίας, καὶ μὴ κοινῇ γεωργοῦντων, ἐπειδὴ τὸ τοιοῦτον μεῖζον ἢ κατὰ τὴν νῦν γένεσιν καὶ τροφὴν καὶ παίδευσιν εἴρηται). The Stranger still proposes that property be *thought* of as common, but André Laks ("Private Matters in Plato's Laws," in *Platon: Gesetze/Nomoi*, ed. Christoph Horn, Klassiker auslegen 55 [Berlin: Akademie, 2013], 172) points out that "Plato explicitly presents the allotment of land and the institution of households as a retreat from a *communitarian* principle."

[41] Capper argues from the fact that the guardians have something of a community of property and are represented by gold in Plato's "noble lie." Since the *Republic* never describes a temporal Golden Age, however, it is incorrect to assert that "community of goods seems to have first found its way into the myth of the Golden Age with Plato's *Republic*" ("Reciprocity," 506), especially since this feature is absent from all of Plato's more explicit versions of the myth. Dupertuis claims that "in both the *Timaeus* and the *Critias* the *kallipolis* of the *Republic* is placed in a recognizable historico-mytholigical setting of a primeval paradise or Golden Age" ("Summaries in Acts," 96), but neither the *Timaeus* nor the *Critias* either explicitly invokes the Golden Age motif or contains enough specific features of the myth to posit an allusion to the Golden Age myth.

subject for Plato, particularly the claim in the *Critias* that the primitive Athenians practiced common property, its absence from Plato's descriptions of the Age of Cronus is noteworthy.[42]

Even if Plato does not include common property in his descriptions of the Golden Age, his discussions of the benefits of this practice are still worth noting. Plato presents unity as the main advantage of a community of property: the absence of private ownership "keeps people from tearing the city apart" (*Resp.* 5.464c) by eliminating the sorts of objects that people quarrel about:

> Won't lawsuits and accusations against each other be almost absent among them, since they possess nothing privately except their body, but everything else is common? Won't it be possible for them to be free from discord, all the things that people quarrel about on account of possessing money or children and relatives? (*Resp.* 5.464d–e)[43]

Plato here associates common property with the possibility of life "free from discord" (ἀστασιάστοις), the same condition that prevailed during the Golden Age (*Pol.* 271e: οὐδὲ στάσις; *Leg.* 4.713e: ἀστασίαστα).[44] Nevertheless, the first appearance of the common property motif in the myth of the ages must be sought somewhere else than in Plato.

The Golden Age Myth in Aratus

The final Greek author examined here, the third-century BCE poet Aratus, transmitted a version of Hesiod's myth in his *Phaenomena* that had an even greater impact on Roman

---

[42] The *Critias* says about the warrior class of early Athens: "No one of them possessed anything as his own, considering all of their things common to all" (110c–d, ἴδιον μὲν αὐτῶν οὐδεὶς οὐδὲν κεκτημένος, ἅπαντα δὲ πάντων κοινὰ νομίζοντες αὐτῶν). Though Garnsey (*Thinking about Property*, 14) sees a "Golden-Age tinge" in this passage, the myth is not mentioned and none of its distinctive features (spontaneous fertility, Cronus, e.g.) appears. Blundell (*Origins of Civilization*, 164 n. 15) also points out that "proto-Athens" features "arts, crafts, agriculture, armies, and governments," all of which are typically excluded from the Golden Age.

[43] δίκαι τε καὶ ἐγκλήματα πρὸς ἀλλήλους οὐκ οἰχήσεται ἐξ αὐτῶν ὡς ἔπος εἰπεῖν διὰ τὸ μηδὲν ἴδιον κτῆσθαι πλὴν τὸ σῶμα, τὰ δ᾽ ἄλλα κοινά; ὅθεν δὴ ὑπάρχει τούτοις ἀστασιάστοις εἶναι, ὅσα γε διὰ χρημάτων ἢ παίδων καὶ συγγενῶν κτῆσιν ἄνθρωποι στασιάζουσιν;

[44] Aristotle reports that some "denounce the evils currently present in polities as happening because property is not common," giving as examples "lawsuits against each other concerning contracts, trials for perjury, and flattery of the rich" (*Pol.* 1263b18–23, κατηγορῇ ... τῶν νῦν ὑπαρχόντων ἐν ταῖς πολιτείαις κακῶν ὡς γινομένων διὰ τὸ μὴ κοινὴν εἶναι τὴν οὐσίαν ... δίκας τε πρὸς ἀλλήλους περὶ συμβολαίων καὶ ψευδομαρτυριῶν κρίσεις καὶ πλουσίων κολακείας). Aristotle, however, rejects this idea, declaring that "those who possess or share things in common quarrel much more than those who keep their possessions separate" (*Pol.* 1263b24–26, τοὺς κοινὰ κεκτημένους καὶ κοινωνοῦντας πολλῷ διαφερομένους μᾶλλον ... ἢ τοὺς χωρὶς τὰς οὐσίας ἔχοντας). Instead, Aristotle suggests that the preferable situation is for "possessions to be private, but to make them common in use" (*Pol.* 1263a39–40, εἶναι μὲν ἰδίας τὰς κτήσεις τῇ δὲ χρήσει ποιεῖν κοινάς).

reception of the Golden Age idea than Plato's.⁴⁵ The poem interprets constellations and weather signs, but Aratus seems to have written it more as a philosophical reflection than as a textbook.⁴⁶ Aratus relates his version of the Golden Age myth in a discussion of the constellation the Maiden (Virgo). In Aratus' telling, the Golden Race lived when the Maiden, "Justice," lived on earth among humans:

> At that time, they did not yet know wretched strife, nor harmful dispute, nor the din of battle, but they lived as they were. The harsh sea was left alone, and ships did not yet bring goods from far off, but oxen and plows and Justice herself, queen of the people, giver of what is right, provided all things without ceasing. During that time the earth still fed the Golden Race. (*Phaen.* 108–114)⁴⁷

Like both Hesiod and Plato, Aratus portrays the Golden Race as living in harmony with each other and with divine beings, in this case the goddess Justice. Unlike Hesiod, Aratus does not describe the fate of the Golden Race but instead moves on immediately to the Silver Race, which Justice criticizes and ultimately deserts:

> But she associated little and by no means readily with the Silver Race … and said she would no longer visibly come to them when they called: "What an inferior race the golden fathers left behind! But you will beget worse. And I suppose there will be wars and hostile bloodshed among humans, and the pain of their evils will weigh on them." When she had said this, she made for the mountains, and she left all the people as they were still looking at her. (*Phaen.* 115–128)⁴⁸

The decline from the Golden Race brings the end of human concord and the advent of war, as well as the loss of the goddess' presence, as she literally distances herself from humanity. These ill effects persist in the Bronze Race, the final stage in Aratus' scheme:

---

⁴⁵ Aratus' *Phaenomena* "became the most widely read poem, after the *Iliad* and *Odyssey*, in the ancient world, and was one of the very few Greek poems translated into Arabic" (G. J. Toomer, "Aratus [1]," *OCD* 132); at least six Latin translations of and twenty-seven commentaries on the work are attested (Emma Gee, *Aratus and the Astronomical Tradition*, Classical Culture and Society [New York: Oxford University Press, 2013], 5; van Noorden, *Playing Hesiod*, 170 n. 16). Paul himself quotes Aratus in Acts 17:28, in his speech at Athens: "for we too are his offspring" (*Phaen.* 5, τοῦ γὰρ καὶ γένος ἐσμέν). The most likely date and location of the *Phaenomena*'s composition are in the years after 276 BCE at Pella in Macedonia; so Marco Fantuzzi and Richard L. Hunter, *Tradition and Innovation in Hellenistic Poetry* (Cambridge: Cambridge University Press, 2004), 224; Gee, *Aratus*, 4.
⁴⁶ Aratus' poem was used as an astronomy textbook in antiquity, but it is most commonly treated as a philosophical work by modern scholars; see Katharina Volk, "Aratus," in *A Companion to Hellenistic Literature*, ed. James J. Clauss and Martine Cuypers (Chichester: Wiley-Blackwell, 2010), 198, 209.
⁴⁷ οὔπω λευγαλέου τότε νείκεος ἠπίσταντο/οὐδὲ διακρίσιος πολυμεμφέος οὐδὲ κυδοιμοῦ,/αὔτως δ' ἔζωον· χαλεπὴ δ' ἀπέκειτο θάλασσα,/καὶ βίον οὔπω νῆες ἀπόπροθεν ἠγίνεσκον,/ἀλλὰ βόες καὶ ἄροτρα καὶ αὐτή, πότνια λαῶν,/μυρία πάντα παρεῖχε Δίκη, δώτειρα δικαίων./τόφρ' ἦν, ὄφρ' ἔτι γαῖα γένος χρύσειον ἔφερβεν.
⁴⁸ ἀργυρέῳ δ' ὀλίγη τε καὶ οὐκέτι πάμπαν ἑτοίμη/ὡμίλει … οὐδ' ἔτ' ἔφη εἰσωπὸς ἐλεύσεσθαι καλέουσιν·/"οἵην χρύσειοι πατέρες γενεὴν ἐλίποντο/χειροτέρην· ὑμεῖς δὲ κακώτερα τεξείεσθε./καὶ δή που πόλεμοι, καὶ δὴ καὶ ἀνάρσιον αἷμα/ἔσσεται ἀνθρώποισι, κακὸν δ' ἐπικείσεται ἄλγος."/ὣς εἰποῦσ' ὀρέων ἐπεμαίετο, τοὺς δ' ἄρα λαοὺς/εἰς αὐτὴν ἔτι πάντας ἐλίμπανε παπταίνοντας.

They were the first to forge the harmful sword of the highwayman, the first to eat oxen used for plowing. And at that time Justice hated the race of those men and flew to the sky. Then she settled in that place, where she still appears to humans at night as the Maiden, being near far-seen Bootes. (*Phaen.* 131–136)[49]

Hesiod's poem provides the model, but Aratus makes substantial alterations. Most obvious is the reduction from five races to three, which has the myth conclude in the past rather than the present.[50] The most surprising change is the introduction of agricultural labor, "oxen and plows," into the Golden Age. Hesiod's Golden Race lived "without toil" (*Op.* 113), and the earth's spontaneous fertility is one of the most characteristic Golden Age motifs. Aratus' motivation for this change is unclear, but it likely indicates that the myth has a different function for Aratus than for Hesiod.[51] Like Hesiod, Aratus makes no political application of the myth and does not mention the idea of common property: the Golden Race is not marked by its presence, nor the Bronze Race by its absence.[52]

Summary: The Golden Age Myth in Greek Sources

This survey has highlighted certain differences among the major Greek accounts of the Golden Age myth, but the basic outline and features of the story have also become clear. The myth begins with an idyllic period in the past. Hesiod designates it as "the time of Cronus" (*Op.* 111) and its inhabitants as a "Golden … Race" (*Op.* 109); Plato mostly uses the former identifier, while Aratus adopts the latter. This race enjoys concord both with each other, being free from war and all forms of strife, and also with the divine realm, benefitting from the care and company of the gods. Hesiod and Plato portray this time as one when the earth produced food spontaneously, although Aratus rejects the idea.

The Golden Age is contrasted with one or several following ages, the last of which corresponds to the present.[53] In the current age, the divine presence has withdrawn: we have been "left destitute of the care of the god who used to possess and tend us" (Plato,

---

[49] οἳ πρῶτοι κακόεργον ἐχαλκεύσαντο μάχαιραν/εἰνοδίην, πρῶτοι δὲ βοῶν ἐπάσαντ' ἀροτήρων,/καὶ τότε μισήσασα Δίκη κείνων γένος ἀνδρῶν/ἔπταθ' ὑπουρανίη· ταύτην δ' ἄρα νάσσατο χώρην,/ἧχί περ ἐννυχίη ἔτι φαίνεται ἀνθρώποισιν/Παρθένος, ἐγγὺς ἐοῦσα πολυσκέπτοιο Βοώτεω.

[50] Fantuzzi and Hunter (*Tradition and Innovation*, 240) and Gatz (*Weltalter*, 63) think that ending the myth in the past is the point of the contraction, while Kubusch (*Aurea saecula*, 89) argues that the motive is structural, intended to make Justice's speech in the Silver Age the center of the account.

[51] Blundell (*Origins of Civilization*, 145) attributes the introduction of agriculture to an idealization of pastoral life resulting from urbanization, while Alessandro Schiesaro ("Aratus' Myth of Dike," *Materiali e discussioni per l'analisi dei testi classici* 37 [1996]: 14) sees labor as a realistic addition to give "didactic utility" to the myth, conceived of as a "moral paradigm." Stoic influence has also often been seen here, beginning with Eduard Norden (*Beiträge zur Geschichte der griechischen Philosophie* [Leipzig: Teubner, 1893], 426), who traces the origin of this change to Zeno.

[52] Schiesaro ("Aratus' Myth," 17–24) argues for a political interpretation of Aratus' version of the myth, based on its possible use of elements from Hesiod's fable of the Hawk and the Nightingale, which is addressed to kings. To conclude from this to a political function for Aratus' Golden Age myth is far-fetched.

[53] Aratus might seem an exception, but the final state of the Bronze Race persists into the present.

Pol. 274b). As a correlate of this withdrawal, strife and warfare now predominate. In the *Works and Days* and the *Laws*, ceaseless toil has replaced a life of leisure.

Finally, a few features that will figure prominently in later versions of the Golden Age myth are notably absent from these earlier Greek accounts. Although Plato invokes the myth primarily in political dialogues, none of these texts applies the Golden Age idea to any current political figure or situation. Nor do any foresee a return of Golden Age conditions. Finally, although Plato elsewhere describes a limited community of property in the ancient past, none of these authors hints at common property being a characteristic of the Golden Age, as the myth deals little with economic issues in general.

The Golden Age Myth in Latin Sources

In contrast to Greek accounts, Latin authors such as Ovid often discuss issues relating to wealth in their treatments of the Golden Age myth. Furthermore, many Latin versions add three specific features that are highly relevant to this study: the notion of a return of the Golden Age, the claim that common property was a characteristic of this age, and the application of the myth to contemporary politics. Virgil introduces all three aspects into the Golden Age myth, but Lucretius' use of the myth will be reviewed first, as Lucretius may have been Virgil's source for the idea of primeval common property.

The Golden Age Myth in Lucretius

Many familiar Golden Age motifs appear in the didactic poem *De rerum natura*, written by the Epicurean author Lucretius in the 50s or early 40s BCE.[54] Although Lucretius departs from the myth at many points, its influence is clear in his presentation of human history that concludes the fifth book of the poem. Lucretius' association of greed and private property with later stages of humanity is of particular interest, since these ideas are prevalent in subsequent Latin versions of the Golden Age myth.

Lucretius introduces the first "race of humans" as being "much hardier" (*Rer.* 5.925–926) than people are today:

> There was no firm guide of a curved plow, no one knew how to work the fields with iron .... What the sun and rain had given them, what the earth had created spontaneously, this gift was sufficient to satisfy their hearts .... At that time, the blooming newness of the world produced many things, rough fodder, abundant for wretched mortals. (*Rer.* 5.933–944)[55]

---

[54] The traditional date for the poem is ca. 55; so, for example, Don P. Fowler, "Lucretius and Politics," in *Philosopha Togata: Essays on Philosophy and Roman Society*, ed. Miriam T. Griffin and Jonathan Barnes (Oxford: Clarendon; New York: Oxford University Press, 1989), 121. G. O. Hutchison ("The Date of *De Rerum Natura*," *ClQ* 51 [2001]: 150) argues instead for a date "in or after 49."

[55] nec robustus erat curvi moderator aratri/quisquam, nec sciebat ferro molirier arva/ ... quod sol atque imbres dederant, quod terra crearat/sponte sua, satis id placabat pectora donum/ ... multaque praeterea novitas tum florida mundi/pabula dura tulit, miseris mortalibus ampla.

The absence of agriculture and the automatic provision of food recall the Golden Age accounts of Hesiod and Plato, but the descriptions of the food as "rough fodder" and the people as "wretched" add an unexpectedly negative note.[56] Lucretius also gives a mixed picture of early human interactions. On the one hand, cooperation was lacking:

> They were not able to look to the common good, and they did not know how to make use of customs or laws among themselves. Whatever gain fortune presented to each, that person would carry it off, having learned instinctively to be strong and to live for oneself. (*Rer.* 5.958–961)[57]

On the other hand, early humans did not kill each other en masse in warfare; the perils of sea travel were also unknown:

> But one day did not give over to destruction many thousands of men led under military standards, nor were violent seas dashing ships and men on the rocks …. The wicked art of navigation then lay hidden. (*Rer.* 5.999–1001, 1006)[58]

The absences of both war and seafaring are already features of the Golden Age in Aratus (*Phaen.* 108–111) and are ubiquitous in later Latin versions of the myth.

The humans of Lucretius' second stage acquire "huts, pelts, and fire" (*Rer.* 5.1011) and begin to cooperate: "Neighbors began to enter into friendship with each other, longing to neither injure nor be injured" (*Rer.* 5.1019–1020).[59] Although "harmony [*concordia*] still could not arise fully," nevertheless "a good many kept their agreements perfectly" (*Rer.* 5.1024–1025). The third stage brings more familiar traits of civilization:

> Kings began to found cities and to place fortresses as a protection and refuge for themselves, and they began to divide cattle and fields and to consign them to each in proportion to their beauty, strength, and natural ability. (*Rer.* 5.1108–1111)[60]

---

[56] Monica Gale (ed., *De rerum natura V*, Classical Texts [Oxford: Oxbow, 2009], 180) identifies the use of "negative phraseology … to undercut the apparently idyllic picture sketched in the preceding lines" as "a technique used repeatedly by [Lucretius] throughout this section."

[57] nec commune bonum poterant spectare, neque ullis/moribus inter se scibant nec legibus uti./quod cuique obtulerat praedae fortuna, ferebat/sponte sua sibi quisque valere et vivere doctus.

[58] at non multa virum sub signis milia ducta/una dies dabat exitio, nec turbida ponti/aequora lidebant navis ad saxa virosque/ … improba navigii ratio tum caeca iacebat.

[59] tunc et amicitiem coeperunt iungere aventes/finitimi inter se nec laedere nec violari. There is no consensus as to the number of stages in Lucretius' account. Benjamin Farrington ("*Vita Prior* in Lucretius," *Herm* 81 [1953]: 61) sees "two ways of life," while Gorden Lindsay Campbell (*Lucretius on Creation and Evolution: A Commentary on* De rerum natura, *Book Five, Lines 772–1104*, Oxford Classical Monographs [Oxford: Oxford University Press, 2003], 14), along with Daniel R. Blickman ("Lucretius, Epicurus, and Prehistory," *HSCP* 92 [1989]: 157), identifies "three stages." Alessandro Schiesaro ("Lucretius and Roman Politics and History," in *The Cambridge Companion to Lucretius*, ed. Stuart Gillespie and Philip R. Hardie, Cambridge Companions to Literature [Cambridge: Cambridge University Press, 2007], 44 n. 16) finds a separate fourth stage beginning at line 1112, and Fowler ("Lucretius and Politics," 142) traces "a five-stage analysis of social development."

[60] condere coeperunt urbis arcemque locare/praesidium reges ipsi sibi perfugiumque,/et pecua atque agros divisere atque dedere/pro facie cuiusque et viribus ingenioque.

Cities, fortifications, and private ownership of land will be standard features of the Iron Age in Latin accounts. Wealth also now enters the picture with its attendant problems:

> Property was invented and gold was discovered .... People wanted to be famous and powerful, so that their fortune might remain on a firm foundation and that they, being rich, might be able to live a peaceful life—in vain. (*Rer.* 5.1113–1123)[61]

> The human race always labors in vain and to no effect and wastes its life in useless concerns, surely because it does not understand the limit of possession. (*Rer.* 5.1430–1433)[62]

In contrast, Lucretius recommends a quieter life: "Now it is much better to submit quietly than to rule affairs with dominion and to possess kingdoms" (*Rer.* 5.1129–1130).[63]

Lucretius is certainly making use of the Golden Age myth.[64] The most distinctive motif is that of the earth producing food "spontaneously" (*Rer.* 5.938, *sponte sua*), and the absence of war, sailing, plows, cities, fortifications, and privately owned fields are all common features in Greek and/or Latin portraits of the Golden Age. On the other hand, Lucretius' account is itself not a version of this myth.[65] The first stage is not presented as clearly superior to subsequent stages.[66] While certain evils, such as war and sea travel, are missing, conditions are far short of ideal. In addition to subsisting on "rough fodder," early humans "were forced to hide their filthy limbs between shrubs to avoid the blows of winds and rain" (*Rer.* 5.956-957), often became "living fodder for wild beasts" (*Rer.* 5.991), and, being ignorant of medicine, "would call upon Death with horrible cries, until cruel aches stripped them of life" (*Rer.* 5.996-997). Thus, while adopting some of its elements, Lucretius "repeatedly exploits opportunities to invert, rationalize or ridicule elements of the traditional Golden Age myth."[67]

---

[61] res inventast aurumque repertum/ ... at claros homines voluerunt se atque potentes,/ut fundamento stabili fortuna maneret/et placidam possent opulenti degere vitam/—nequiquam.

[62] hominum genus incassum frustraque laborat/semper et in curis consumit inanibus aevom,/nimirum quia non cognovit quae sit habendi/finis.

[63] satius multo iam sit parere quietum/quam regere imperio res velle et regna tenere. If this statement represents "an astonishingly bold reversal of conventional Roman values" (Gale, *De rerum natura V*, 194), it is also a standard Epicurean position; see Fowler, "Lucretius and Politics," 122–6.

[64] Campbell, *Lucretius on Creation*, 14; Monica Gale, *Myth and Poetry in Lucretius*, Cambridge Classical Studies (Cambridge: Cambridge University Press, 1994), 159.

[65] Campbell, *Lucretius on Creation*, 12; Rhiannon Evans, *Utopia Antiqua: Readings of the Golden Age and Decline at Rome* (London: Routledge, 2008), 164; Gale, *Myth and Poetry*, 161.

[66] Blickman ("Lucretius, Epicurus, and Prehistory," 178) and Farrington ("*Vita Prior* in Lucretius," 61) do think that the first stage is preferable, although Farrington's first stage encompasses the first and second stages of other analyses. Campbell (*Lucretius on Creation*, 14) thinks the second stage "is the nearest to an Epicurean ideal state," while David J. Furley ("Lucretius the Epicurean: On the History of Man," in *Lucrèce: Huit exposés*, ed. David J. Furley and Olof Gigon, Entretiens sur l'Antiquité classique 24 [Geneva: Fondation Hardt, 1978], 10) and Gale (*Myth and Poetry*, 175) think Lucretius' point to be that *none* of the stages is ideal.

[67] Gale, *De rerum natura V*, 177.

Whatever his reasons for incorporating so many Golden Age elements while undercutting the myth itself, Lucretius' primary importance for this study lies in his use of several themes that Virgil will incorporate or respond to in his own Golden Age descriptions.[68] Lucretius' association of the later stages of humanity with greed and the failure to recognize a "limit of possession" (*Rer.* 5.1432–1433, *habendi finis*) reappears in Virgil and Ovid, who each connect the end of the Golden Age with "lust for possession" (*Aen.* 8.327; *Metam.* 1.131, *amor habendi*). Of particular significance is Lucretius' repeated characterization of the present age as the time when the earth was divided into private fields (*Rer.* 5.1110: *agros divisere*; 5.1441: *divisa … tellus*). His immediate source for this idea is unclear; Lucretius may have taken over much of his account from writings of Epicurus that are no longer extant, such as the twelfth book of the treatise *On Nature*.[69] Whatever Lucretius' source may have been, Latin authors from Virgil onward will make similar claims repeatedly about the Golden Age.

The Golden Age Myth in Virgil

Virgil's poetry represents a sea change in the Golden Age myth. He is the first to describe the Golden Age as a time without private property. Virgil also predicts for the first time an imminent return of this age and attributes the return to Augustus, reflecting the momentous political changes that occurred in the late first century BCE. Virgil was born ca. 70 BCE, in the last decades of the Roman Republic, and his lifetime spanned several civil wars and Octavian's creation of the Principate.

Virgil's first and most famous reference to the Golden Age occurs in his fourth *Eclogue*, written ca. 40 BCE, near the time of the treaty of Brundisium.[70] The poem's hopeful tone may reflect optimism regarding this truce between Octavian and Antony:

> Now the last age of the Cumaean song has come; the great series of ages is born anew. Now the Virgin also returns, the reign of Saturn returns; now a new race descends from the height of heaven. But you, chaste Lucina, show favor to the boy

---

[68] Campbell (*Lucretius on Creation*, 182) thinks that Lucretius uses "positive Golden Age associations" to temper the harshness of his Epicurean message: "he presents the reader as if with a brightly coloured sugared pill, the outer coating of the myth intact and attractive, but with Epicurean medicine inside." Gale (*Myth and Poetry*, 161) sees it as a useful tool for challenging "the progressivist assumption that all change is necessarily for the better."

[69] Furley ("Lucretius the Epicurean," 12) believes that "Lucretius found in his collection of works of Epicurus a fully worked out theory of the history of civilization," and Richard Sorabji (*Gandhi and the Stoics: Modern Experiments on Ancient Values* [Oxford: Oxford University Press, 2012], 172) suggests that Epicurus may have been Lucretius' source for the specific "idea that private property and gold were absent from primitive society."

[70] The date preferred depends on how much confidence one supposes Virgil had in his predictions. Alessandro Perutelli ("Bucolics," in *A Companion to the Study of Virgil*, ed. Nicholas Horsfall, Mnemosyne 151 [Leiden: Brill, 1995], 28) thinks that "everything points to … late 41," but Ian M. le M. Du Quesnay ("Virgil's Fourth *Eclogue*," *Papers of the Liverpool Latin Seminar* 1 [1976]: 31) claims that September, 40 BCE "alone suits our poem," arguing that Virgil's confidence would have been "inconceivable" prior to Brundisium. The *Eclogues* as a whole were likely published by 38 BCE (Perutelli, ibid., 30).

when he is born; because of him the Iron Race will now at last cease and a Golden Race will arise in the whole world. Now your Apollo reigns! (*Ecl.* 4.4–10)[71]

Details from prior versions of the myth are apparent here: the return of the Virgin from Aratus, the Golden and Iron Races from Hesiod, and the "reign of Saturn" that corresponds to the "time of Cronus" in both Hesiod and Plato.[72] But the unnamed speaker also introduces something completely new: for the first time in the extant literary history of the myth, a *return* of the Golden Age is announced.[73] The child who brings about this return remains perhaps the most perplexing aspect of the poem; the boy is never named, and a consensus as to his identity has yet to be reached.[74]

Whoever this child may be, this *Eclogue* predicts that he will enjoy the restoration of Golden Age conditions: peace among humans and community with the gods:

> He will receive the life of the gods and will see heroes intermingled with deities, and he himself will be seen by them. He will rule a world pacified by his father's valor. (*Ecl.* 4.15–17)[75]

The Golden Age motif that is most emphasized is spontaneous fertility: the earth will produce "without cultivation" (*Ecl.* 4.18), goats will come home "of their own accord" (*Ecl.* 4.21), and grapes will hang from "uncultivated brambles" (*Ecl.* 4.29). Sailing and plowing, Iron Age activities, are also banished:

> Even the traveler will depart the sea, nor will pine ships barter goods; every land will produce all things. The soil will not be afflicted with mattocks, nor the vine with a pruning-hook; now the hardy plowman will also take the yokes off his bulls. (*Ecl.* 4.38–41)[76]

---

[71] ultima Cumaei venit iam carminis aetas;/magnus ab integro saeclorum nascitur ordo./iam redit et Virgo, redeunt Saturnia regna;/iam nova progenies caelo demittitur alto./tu modo nascenti puero, quo ferrea primum/desinet ac toto surget gens aurea mundo,/casta fave Lucina: tuus iam regnat Apollo.

[72] For Virgil's identification of Saturn and Cronus, see Patricia A. Johnston, "Vergil's Conception of Saturn," *California Studies in Classical Antiquity* 10 (1977): 57–70.

[73] Virgil's originality in positing the Golden Age's return is unanimously acknowledged; see Gatz, *Weltalter*, 90; Gee, *Aratus*, 39; Karl Galinsky, *Augustan Culture: An Interpretive Introduction* (Princeton: Princeton University Press, 1996), 92; Kubusch, *Aurea saecula*, 93. Whether this age *already* has returned or is *about* to return is unclear: most of the verbs in lines 4–10 are in the present tense, and the repeated use of *iam* (4x) also points toward the present, but the future tense predominates in the rest of the poem.

[74] Among the candidates suggested are the child of Pollio (Gatz, *Weltalter*, 103), of Antony and Octavia (Du Quesnay, "Virgil's Fourth *Eclogue*," 34), and of Octavian (Inez Scott Ryberg, "Vergil's Golden Age," *TAPA* 89 [1958]: 116 n. 15). Due in part to the inability to reach agreement, the most common view is that the child is merely a symbol of the birth of the new age; so Paul J. Alpers (*The Singer of the Eclogues: A Study of Virgilian Pastoral* [Berkeley: University of California Press, 1979], 178), Charles Fantazzi ("Golden Age in Arcadia," *Latomus* 33 [1974]: 286), Galinsky (*Augustan Culture*, 92), Patricia A. Johnston (*Vergil's Agricultural Golden Age: A Study of the Georgics*, Mnemosyne 60 [Leiden: Brill, 1980], 42 n. 3), and Perutelli ("*Bucolics*," 61).

[75] ille deum vitam accipiet divisque videbit/permixtos heroas et ipse videbitur illis,/pacatumque reget patriis virtutibus orbem.

[76] cedet et ipse mari vector, nec nautica pinus/mutabit merces; omnis feret omnia tellus./non rastros patietur humus, non vinea falcem;/robustus quoque iam tauris iuga solvet arator.

The idea in *Ecl.* 4 that an individual might effect a return of the Golden Age is ripe for political appropriation, but Virgil's commendation of Octavian in his later works should not be imported back into this poem. The fourth *Eclogue*'s addressee, Pollio, was a partisan of Antony rather than Octavian, making praise of the latter unlikely here.[77]

The first appearance of common property in the Golden Age myth occurs in Virgil's next work, the *Georgics*, completed in 29 BCE soon after Octavian's victory over Antony at Actium. After an opening entreaty to various gods and the triumphant Octavian, "who will soon have a place on some undetermined council of the gods" (*Georg.* 1.24–25), Virgil turns to a description of farming. Acknowledging hazards such as floods, birds, and weeds, Virgil explains why such obstacles exist:

> The Father himself willed that the agricultural life should be by no means easy, and he was the first to disturb the fields by art, sharpening mortal hearts with cares, and he did not allow his kingdom to lie inactive in heavy lethargy. Before Jove, no farmers used to plow the fields: not even marking or dividing the open field with a boundary was allowed. They used to seek the common good, and the earth itself used to produce all things more freely when no one was demanding it. (*Georg.* 1.121–128)[78]

The location of this pre-agricultural time "before Jove," the absence of plowing, and the earth's spontaneous fertility mark this as a Golden Age account. Virgil also adds two new characteristics: no private possession of fields, which is the first extant assertion that the Golden Age lacked private property, and pursuit of the common good.[79] Given Virgil's frequent interactions with Lucretius in both this passage and the *Georgics* as a whole, both of these features should likely be read with *De rerum natura* in mind.[80] Presenting a rosier picture of primeval humanity, Virgil takes up Lucretius' idea that divided fields belong to a later stage of development

---

[77] So Du Quesnay, "Virgil's Fourth *Eclogue*," 29. R. J. Tarrant ("Poetry and Power: Virgil's Poetry in Contemporary Context," in *The Cambridge Companion to Virgil*, ed. Charles Martindale, Cambridge Companions to Literature [Cambridge: Cambridge University Press, 1997], 174) correctly observes that "nothing as clear-cut as a political stance can be made out" in the fourth *Eclogue*.

[78] pater ipse colendi/haud facilem esse viam voluit, primusque per artem/movit agros, curis acuens mortalia corda,/nec torpere gravi passus sua regna veterno./ante Iovem nulli subigebant arva coloni:/ne signare quidem aut partiri limite campum/fas erat; in medium quaerebant, ipsaque tellus/ omnia liberius nullo poscente ferebat.

[79] For the lack of bounded fields as a statement of the absence of private property, see Gatz, *Weltalter*, 229; Kubusch, *Aurea saecula*, 94; Roger A. B. Mynors, ed., *Georgics* (Oxford: Clarendon, 1990), 27; Christine Perkell, *The Poet's Truth: A Study of the Poet in Vergil's* Georgics (Berkeley: University of California Press, 1989), 94–5; Andrew Wallace-Hadrill, "The Golden Age and Sin in Augustan Ideology," *Past & Present* 95 (1982): 23.

[80] Monica Gale (*Virgil on the Nature of Things: The* Georgics, Lucretius, *and the Didactic Tradition* [Cambridge: Cambridge University Press, 2000], 17) sees Lucretius along with Hesiod as "the main models" in this section, and W. Y. Sellar (*The Roman Poets of the Augustan Age: Virgil* [Oxford: Clarendon, 1883], 199) claimed that "the direct and indirect, exercised by Lucretius on the thought, composition and even the diction of the *Georgics* was perhaps stronger than that ever exercised, before or since, by one poet on the work of another."

(*Rer.* 5.1108–1111) while rejecting his assertion that early humans "were not able to look to the common good" (*Rer.* 5.958).

Virgil next describes the development of primitive arts in the present Age of Jupiter, culminating with the statement that "labor overcame all things, wicked labor" (*Georg.* 1.145–146, *labor omnia vicit/improbus*), and concludes with a sobering warning:

> Now, unless you pursue weeds with incessant hoes, terrify birds with a din, prune shadows with a sickle, and summon rain with votive offerings, alas, you will look on the great stockpile of another and relieve your hunger by shaking an oak tree in the woods. (*Georg.* 1.155–159)[81]

The climactic image of a hungry man shaking trees for sustenance while looking at the surplus of his neighbor serves as a photographic negative of the community-minded Golden Age, highlighting contemporary inequality and lack of care for one's neighbor.[82]

Although Octavian appears in the *Georgics* often and in a consistently positive light, Virgil never credits him (or anyone else) with bringing about a renewed Golden Age. Virgil does finally connect Octavian with a returning Golden Age in the *Aeneid*, published a few years after the poet's death in 19 BCE. This lofty function fits with Octavian's solidification of political power in this period, during which the Senate granted him the title "Augustus." Augustus' first appearance in the *Aeneid* mentions his role of inaugurator of a better age, as Jupiter tells Venus about the Trojans' future glories:

> From a noble lineage will be born a Trojan Caesar, who will bound his empire with the ocean and his fame with the stars, Julius, a name descended from great Julus. One day you will serenely receive this one into heaven, loaded with Eastern spoils; this one also will be called upon in prayer. Then the harsh ages will grow mild when wars have been put to rest. (*Aen.* 1.286–291)[83]

The subject of this passage is most likely Augustus, at least in the latter part.[84] The softening of the "harsh ages" seems to allude to the Golden Age myth, and this renewal is linked to the return of peace attributed to Augustus.[85]

---

[81] quod nisi et adsiduis herbam insectabere rastris/et sonitu terrebis aves et ruris opaci/falce premes umbras votisque vocaveris imbrem,/heu magnum alterius frustra spectabis acervum/concussaque famem in silvis solabere quercu.

[82] Perkell (*Poet's Truth*, 97–8) grasps the import of the image. Richard Jenkyns ("*Labor Improbus*," *CIQ* 43 [1993]: 248) does not take it seriously, calling it "quaint and bantering."

[83] nascetur pulchra Troianus origine Caesar,/imperium Oceano, famam qui terminet astris,/Iulius, a magno demissum nomen Iulo./hunc tu olim caelo, spoliis Orientis onustum,/accipies secura; vocabitur hic quoque votis./aspera tum positis mitescent saecula bellis.

[84] Whether the passage describes the dictator Julius Caesar, the emperor Augustus, or both is unclear. The name "Julius" seems to point to the former, but the references to "Eastern spoils" and closing the gates of war (*Aen.* 1.294) almost certainly refer to Augustus, and the majority view is that Augustus is the object of the entire description; see Roland G. Austin, ed., *Aeneidos: liber primus* (Oxford: Clarendon, 1971), 109; Egil Kraggerud, "Which Julius Caesar? On *Aen.* 1, 286–296," *SO* 67 (1992): 104 n. 2.

[85] So John Conington and Henry Nettleship (eds., *The Works of Virgil* [Hildesheim: Olms, 1963], 2:36) and Robert D. Williams (ed., *Aeneid: Books I–VI* [London: Macmillan, 1972], 181).

The implicit crediting of Augustus with bringing about a return of the Golden Age becomes explicit in *Aen.* 6, as Anchises describes the future glories of Aeneas' progeny:

> This man, this is the one whom you have quite often heard promised to you, Augustus Caesar, the child of a god, who will establish the golden ages again in Latium throughout fields formerly ruled by Saturn, who will extend his empire beyond both the Garamantes and the Indians. (*Aen.* 6.791–795)[86]

Anchises directly links Augustus' restoration of the Golden Age to his role as princeps, and he concludes his speech to Aeneas by reemphasizing the importance of Roman *imperium*. In direct opposition to Lucretius' opinion that "it is much better to submit quietly than to rule affairs with dominion [*regere imperio res*] and to possess kingdoms" (*Rer.* 5.1129–1130), Anchises commands Aeneas, "You, Roman, do not fail to rule the peoples with dominion" (*Aen.* 6.851, *regere imperio populos*).

In *Aen.* 8, Evander describes the first Golden Age, ruled by Saturn, that Augustus is destined to reestablish:

> First from heavenly Olympus came Saturn, fleeing the weapons of Jove, an exile from a kingdom that had been taken away. He brought together a race that was ignorant and scattered on high mountains and gave laws …. What they call the golden ages happened under that ruler, in such gentle peace did he rule the peoples, until little by little a worse and degenerate age took its place, the fury of war and the lust for possession. (*Aen.* 8.319–327)[87]

The characteristics of the Golden Age in this description are typical: divine care and human concord. Evander also describes a following "worse and degenerate age" that contrasts with the Age of Gold: war replaces peace, and "lust for possession" invades a society that, according to *Georg.* 1, formerly lacked private property.

For the purposes of this study, Virgil's principal contributions to the trajectory of the Golden Age myth consist in the following: (1) Virgil is the first author to speak of a return of the Golden Age, doing so in both *Ecl.* 4 and the *Aeneid*. (2) By attributing this return to Augustus in the *Aeneid*, Virgil makes the Golden Age a potent political symbol for both Augustus and subsequent emperors. (3) Virgil's characterization of the Age of Saturn as a time when land was not privately possessed marks the first entrance of common property into the Golden Age myth, and his connection of the end of this age with "lust for possession" (*Aen.* 8.327) further links the myth with concerns about property and greed.

---

[86] hic vir, hic est, tibi quem promitti saepius audis,/Augustus Caesar, divi genus, aurea condet/ saecula qui rursus Latio regnata per arva/Saturno quondam; super et Garamantas et Indos/proferet imperium.

[87] primus ab aetherio venit Saturnus Olympo/arma Iovis fugiens et regnis exsul ademptis./is genus indocile ac dispersum montibus altis/composuit legesque dedit … aurea quae perhibent illo sub rege fuere/saecula: sic placida populos in pace regebat,/deterior donec paulatim ac decolor aetas/et belli rabies et amor successit habendi.

The Golden Age Myth in Ovid

Among Roman authors, Ovid's use of the Golden Age myth merits special attention, being unparalleled in both its quantity and influence.[88] While he avoids Virgil's notion of a returning Golden Age associated with Augustus, Ovid does take up the ideas that common property marked the Golden Age and that greed accompanied its end. Ovid emphasizes this latter aspect even more than Virgil, and he repeatedly invokes the Golden Age to contrast with the selfishness and obsession with wealth that mark the present.

Ovid's first reference to the myth occurs in his first set of poems, the *Amores*, published shortly before the turn of the era.[89] Much of the work revolves around the speaker's mistress Corinna, and *Am*. 3.8 complains about her preference for wealthy lovers and the current obsession with money, contrasting this with the simplicity and contentment that characterized the Golden Age:

> But when aged Saturn had sovereignty in heaven, the deep soil covered all riches with darkness .... But it was giving greater gifts, without a curved plowshare: produce, fruits, and honey found in the hollow oak. And no one was cutting the earth with a stout plow, nor did the surveyor mark out the ground with a boundary line, nor did they scour the sea, torn by an oar; at that time, the shore was the end of the road for a mortal. (*Am*. 3.8.35–44)[90]

In contrast to the serene and gold-free Age of Saturn, the speaker laments that men now "place weapons in discordant [*discordes*] hands" (*Am*. 3.8.48) and that money controls everything: "The Senate-house is closed to the poor—it is wealth that gives honors" (*Am*. 3.8.55). The absence of private property in the Golden Age fits with the poem's emphasis on the differing attitudes toward wealth in the present and in the ideal past.

Ovid's next book of love poetry, the *Ars amatoria*, also uses the Golden Age theme to comment on attitudes toward wealth in present-day Rome.[91] Mirroring complaints

---

[88] Karl Galinsky, "Some Aspects of Ovid's Golden Age," *Grazer Beiträge* 10 (1981): 193; Arthur O. Lovejoy and George Boas, *Primitivism and Related Ideas in Antiquity* (Baltimore: Johns Hopkins University Press, 1935), 49.

[89] The *Amores* were published in the last decade BCE, but the opening lines claim that the work is a revision of an earlier collection. Taking Ovid at his word, Ian M. le M. Du Quesnay ("The *Amores*," in *Ovid*, ed. J. W. Binns, Greek and Latin Studies [London: Routledge & Kegan Paul, 1973], 3–4) places the first edition between 25 and 15 BCE and the revised edition in the last decade BCE. Barbara Weiden Boyd (*Ovid's Literary Loves: Influence and Innovation in the* Amores [Ann Arbor: University of Michigan Press, 1997], 146) suspects that the reference to a revised edition may be nothing more than a literary conceit.

[90] at cum regna senex caeli Saturnus haberet,/omne lucrum tenebris alta premebat humus/ ... at meliora dabat—curvo sine vomere fruges/pomaque et in quercu mella reperta cava./nec valido quisquam terram scindebat aratro,/signabat nullo limite mensor humum,/non freta demisso verrebant eruta remo;/ultima mortali tum via litus erat.

[91] Ovid published the *Ars amatoria* between 2 BCE and 2 CE (Gareth Williams, "Politics in Ovid," in *Writing Politics in Imperial Rome*, ed. William J. Dominik, John Garthwaite, and Paul A. Roche [Leiden: Brill, 2009], 208).

from *Am.* 3.8 about the outsized influence of money, the teacher of the titular art sarcastically labels the current age "golden": "Now is truly the Golden Age: by means of gold, honor comes to many; by means of gold, love is gained" (*Ars* 2.277–278);[92] "Before there was rough simplicity; now Rome is golden, and it possesses the great wealth of a vanquished world" (*Ars* 3.113–114).[93]

Ovid's most extensive interaction with the myth of the ages comes in his *Metamorphoses*.[94] After describing the creation of the world, the speaker turns to human origins:

> Golden was the first race begotten .... Not yet had the felled pine descended from its mountains into the flowing waters to behold a foreign world, and mortals knew no shores beyond their own. Not yet did precipitous trenches surround towns. There was no straight war-trumpet, no curved horn of bronze, no helmets, and no sword; the untroubled peoples were leading lives of pleasant leisure with no need of a soldier. The earth itself, free and untouched by a plow, unwounded by any plowshares, also was giving all things of its own accord. (*Metam.* 1.89–102)[95]

This picture resembles that of the fourth *Eclogue*: fortifications, warfare, and plowing are rejected, and the earth's spontaneous fertility is repeatedly stressed. The complete absence of all things military is also emphasized.

The Silver Race is sketched more briefly, being marked by a change of climate and the introduction of agriculture. Ovid spends even less time on the more warlike "yet not wicked" (*Metam.* 1.127) Bronze Race before detailing the horrors of the Iron Race:[96]

> Immediately, every abomination rushed into this age of a more wicked vein. Modesty, truth, and faithfulness fled, and in their place followed deceit, guile, artifice, force, and pernicious lust for possession. They gave sails to the winds, although the sailor as yet was not well-acquainted with them, and the keels that previously stood on the mountain heights leapt on the unknown waves. And the careful surveyor marked out with a long boundary line the ground, which previously was common like sunlight and air ... And now there appeared harmful iron and gold, more harmful than iron. War appeared, which fights by means of both, and shook clattering arms with its bloody hand. People lived off of plunder. A guest was not safe from his host, nor a father-in-law from his son in law, and the

---

[92] aurea sunt vere nunc saecula: plurimus auro/venit honos: auro conciliatur amor.

[93] simplicitas rudis ante fuit: nunc aurea Roma est,/et domiti magnas possidet orbis opes.

[94] Ovid's *Metamorphoses* were written and circulated at Rome before his exile in 8 CE (William S. Anderson, ed., *Ovid's* Metamorphoses: *Books 1–5* [Norman: University of Oklahoma Press, 1997], 4–5).

[95] aurea prima sata est aetas ... nondum caesa suis, peregrinum ut viseret orbem,/montibus in liquidas pinus descenderat undas,/nullaque mortales praeter sua litora norant;/nondum praecipites cingebant oppida fossae;/non tuba derecti, non aeris cornua flexi,/non galeae, non ensis erat: sine militis usu/mollia securae peragebant otia gentes./ipsa quoque inmunis rastroque intacta nec ullis/saucia vomeribus per se dabat omnia tellus.

[96] Ovid makes no reference to Hesiod's Heroic Race; Gatz (*Weltalter*, 71) posits that this may be due to a desire to present a picture of a continuous decline.

love of brothers was rare as well. A husband longed for the death of his wife, and she for her husband's .... Piety lay overthrown, and the maiden Astraea, the last of the deities, abandoned lands dripping with murdered blood. (*Metam.* 1.128–150)[97]

The comment that this race saw the entrance of "pernicious lust for possession" (*Metam.* 1.131, *amor ... habendi*) alludes to Virgil's statement in *Aen.* 8 that the "degenerate age" was marked by "lust for possession" (*Aen.* 8.327, *amor ... habendi*), and it continues Ovid's practice of emphasizing the issues of greed and property in his references to the myth. Ovid's description of the privatization of land here is almost a quotation of his earlier remarks in *Am.* 3.8, with the addition that land used to be "common like sunlight and air" (*Metam.* 1.135), traditional examples of entities rightly considered to be common property.[98]

Ovid's final reference to the Golden Age appears in his *Fasti*.[99] Janus, explaining why gifts of money are given during his festival, cites the example of the Age of Saturn:

> Even when Saturn was reigning, I scarcely saw anyone whose heart did not find wealth sweet. Lust for possession grew with time and now has the highest place. (*Fast.* 1.193–195)[100]

Janus' claim that wealth was prized even during the reign of Saturn is surprising, but his assessment that avarice has increased and dominates the present fits with other statements in Ovid about the differences between the Golden Age and contemporary society. The signature phrase "lust for possession" (*Fast.* 1.196, *amor ... habendi*) recurs, and Janus describes its current effects: "Now it is money that has value: wealth grants honors, wealth gives friendships. The poor man is despised everywhere" (*Fast.* 1.217–218). This echoes complaints elsewhere in Ovid that wealth buys honor and affection (*Am.* 3.8.55; *Ars* 2.277–278), while poverty brings exclusion (*Am.* 3.8.55).

---

[97] protinus inrupit venae peioris in aevum/omne nefas: fugere pudor verumque fidesque;/in quorum subiere locum fraudesque dolusque/insidiaeque et vis et amor sceleratus habendi./vela dabant ventis nec adhuc bene noverat illos/navita, quaeque prius steterant in montibus altis,/fluctibus ignotis insultavere carinae,/communemque prius ceu lumina solis et auras/cautus humum longo signavit limite mensor/ ... iamque nocens ferrum ferroque nocentius aurum/prodierat, prodit bellum, quod pugnat utroque,/sanguineaque manu crepitantia concutit arma./vivitur ex rapto: non hospes ab hospite tutus,/non socer a genero, fratrum quoque gratia rara est;/inminet exitio vir coniugis, illa mariti/ ... victa iacet pietas, et virgo caede madentis/ultima caelestum terras Astraea reliquit.

[98] Anderson, *Ovid's* Metamorphoses, 165.

[99] The extant version discusses the first six months of the Roman calendar, but Ovid claims to have written twelve books covering all twelve months (*Trist.* 2.549). No trace of the last six survives, if they ever even existed (see John F. Miller, "The *Fasti*: Style, Structure, and Time," in *Brill's Companion to Ovid*, ed. Barbara Weiden Boyd [Leiden: Brill, 2002], 167). The *Fasti* was written prior to Ovid's exile in 8 CE, although he seems to have revised the poem during this time (Steven J. Green, Fasti 1: *A Commentary*, Mnemosyne 251 [Leiden: Brill, 2004], 15–18). Ovid's exile was apparently due to two reasons: immoral aspects of his *Ars amatoria* and an unnamed offense that may have involved Julia, the granddaughter of Augustus (Peter White, "Ovid and the Augustan Milieu," in Boyd, *Brill's Companion to Ovid*, 16–17).

[100] vix ego Saturno quemquam regnante videbam,/cuius non animo dulcia lucra forent./tempore crevit amor, qui nunc est summus, habendi.

Ovid's overall treatment of the Golden Age myth is solidly traditional. Ovid portrays the Golden Age as a time free from any trace of war or discord. Relative to his predecessors, he particularly emphasizes the divergent attitudes of the past and present ages toward money and property. In his two major accounts, Ovid makes the Golden Age a time of common property, and he repeatedly contrasts its conditions with the "lust for possession" and the influence of money that mark contemporary society. The absence of any idea of a return is the most surprising aspect of Ovid's presentation. Outside of a sarcastic remark that the power of wealth makes the present "truly the Golden Age" (*Ars* 2.277), Ovid's poetry never declares, implies, or even openly wishes for a return of the Golden Age.

Since Ovid fails to announce a return of the Golden Age, he necessarily also fails to credit Augustus with bringing about such a return. This accords with the common view that Ovid's works show some resistance to Augustus. Ovid's love poetry fits awkwardly with Augustus' moral legislation;[101] the *Metamorphoses* seems mostly uninterested in the emperor;[102] the *Fasti* extols Augustus, but most interpreters find the praise perfunctory, even subversive.[103] Ovid's use of the myth to attack the greed of the present by contrasting it with the unselfishness of the Golden Age, manifested in common ownership of the land, is Ovid's most significant contribution for this study.

Common Property and the Golden Age in Other Sources

Having examined the most influential individual contributors to the Golden Age tradition, I will now more briefly survey a selection of other accounts from the early Empire that convey the idea that property was held in common during the Golden Age. This group contains most of the major appearances of the myth during this period, which is itself an important observation: during the first century CE, common property became a central feature of literary descriptions of the Golden Age.[104] A second major finding is that some Golden Age accounts, such as those of Trogus, Seneca, and the *Octavia*, expand the restricted claims of Virgil and Ovid that the Golden Age lacked divided fields into general assertions that all property was held in common.

---

[101] The *lex Iulia de maritandis ordinibus* was issued in 18 BCE and the *lex Iulia de adulteriis* a year later. John A. Barsby (*Ovid*, Greece & Rome: New Surveys in the Classics 12 [Oxford: Clarendon, 1978], 11, 21) finds the *Amores* and *Ars amatoria* "clearly flying in the face of Augustus' attempts to reform marriage," and "clearly in conflict with Augustus' attempts to encourage marriage." Peter J. Davis (*Ovid and Augustus: A Political Reading of Ovid's Erotic Poems* [London: Duckworth, 2006], 82) is even more emphatic, judging that "mockery of the Julian law on adultery could hardly be more explicit."

[102] Barsby (*Ovid*, 33) and Douglas Little ("The Non-Augustanism of Ovid's 'Metamorphoses,'" *Mnemosyne* 25 [1972]: 393) both point out the dearth of references to Rome and Augustus.

[103] Elain Fantham ("Ovid's *Fasti*: Politics, History, and Religion," in Boyd, *Brill's Companion to Ovid*, 209) notes that "a subversive reading of *Fasti* has almost become the new orthodoxy."

[104] The major omission from this survey would seem to be Horace, whose *Carmen saeculare* is often seen as heralding the dawn of a new Golden Age (see, e.g., Johnston, *Vergil's Agricultural Golden Age*, 78–9). Horace, however, seems to intentionally avoid language specific to the Golden Age myth; for an argument that Horace is actually "taking a stance against Virgil's idea of a recurring Golden Age," see Andreas T. Zanker, "Late Horatian Lyric and the Virgilian Golden Age," *AJP* 131 (2010): 498.

Tibullus, a first-century BCE elegiac poet, supplies the first mention of common property in the Golden Age after that of Virgil in the *Georgics*.[105] In *El.* 1.3, the speaker, seriously ill and unable to return to his lover, laments his absence and extolls a simpler time:

> How well they used to live when Saturn was king, before the earth was opened up to long journeys! Not yet had the pine defied the dark waves and offered its spread sail to the winds, nor had the roving sailor, bringing profit back from unknown lands, loaded his vessel with foreign goods .... No house had doors, no stone was fixed in the fields to mark out farmland with fixed boundaries. (*El.* 1.3.36–44)[106]

Tibullus' poem invokes the Golden Age primarily as a contrast with the current era of sea travel, which has led to the speaker's separation from his lover.[107] He links sailing, and thus the present, to a profit motive, and Tibullus elsewhere defines the Iron Age by its desire for "plunder" (*El.* 2.3.36, *praeda*), giving the myth a financial aspect. Like Virgil and Ovid, Tibullus indicates the lack of private property in the Golden Age by the absence of bounded fields.[108]

Little is known about Pompeius Trogus, the author of a universal history entitled *Historiae Philippicae*. A Roman citizen from Gaul, Trogus likely wrote under Augustus, but his work is extant only in an epitome from at least a century later by an equally obscure author, Justin.[109] Toward the end of his work, Trogus turns to the early days of Rome, when Saturn ruled as king after being expelled from Mount Olympus:

> The first inhabitants of Italy were the Aborigines, whose king, Saturn, is said to have been so just that no one was enslaved during his time or possessed any private

---

[105] There is general agreement that Tibullus published *El.* 1 around 27 BCE; so Robert Maltby, *Tibullus: Elegies: Text, Introduction and Commentary*, ARCA Classical and Medieval Texts, Papers, and Monographs 41 (Cambridge: Cairns, 2002), 40; Paul Murgatroyd, *Tibullus I: A Commentary on the First Book of the Elegies of Albius Tibullus* (Pietermaritzburg: University of Natal Press, 1980), 4, 11–12; Michael C. J. Putnam, *Tibullus: A Commentary*, American Philological Association Series of Classical Texts (Norman: University of Oklahoma Press, 1973), 3.

[106] quam bene Saturno vivebant rege, priusquam/tellus in longas est patefacta vias!/nondum caeruleas pinus contempserat undas,/effusum ventis praebueratque sinum,/nec vagus ignotis repetens compendia terris/presserat externa navita merce ratem/ ... non domus ulla fores habuit, non fixus in agris,/qui regeret certis finibus arva, lapis.

[107] So Maltby (*Tibullus*, 195), Murgatroyd (*Tibullus I*, 111), and Putnam (*Tibullus*, 79).

[108] Maltby (*Tibullus*, 198) takes this as signifying that "there was no private property in the Golden Age," and Murgatroyd (*Tibullus I*, 114) that "all property and possessions were shared in the Golden Age."

[109] J. M. Alonso-Núñez ("An Augustan World History: The 'Historiae Philippicae' of Pompeius Trogus," *GR* 34 [1987]: 56) and John C. Yardley and Waldemar Heckel (eds., *Epitome of the Philippic History of Pompeius Trogus*, Clarendon Ancient History Series [Oxford: Clarendon, 1997], 5) place the writing under Augustus. Robert Develin (introduction to *Epitome of the Philippic History of Pompeius*, ed. John C. Yardley, Classical Resources 3 [Atlanta: Scholars Press, 1994], 3) thinks that it could date to "as late as AD 20." Suggested dates for Justin's writing vary widely. R. B. Steele ("Pompeius Trogus and Justinus," *AJP* 38 [1917]: 41) suggests "144 or 145 AD," while Ronald Syme ("The Date of Justin and the Discovery of Trogus," *Historia* 37 [1988]: 365) argues for "the vicinity of 390." Alonso-Núñez ("Augustan World History," 56), Develin (introduction, 4), and Yardley and Heckel (*Epitome*, 13) all propose the late second or early third century.

property. But all things were common and undivided to all persons, as though a single inheritance for everyone together. (*Ep.* 43.1.3)[110]

Trogus is especially significant for being the earliest source to attribute to the Golden Age the practice of common possession of property in general rather than in solely agricultural terms. The lack of slavery, a particular form of private possession, fits with this theme.

Germanicus' *Aratea*, a Latin translation of Aratus' *Phaenomena*, is of special interest for two reasons. First, Germanicus' Greek exemplar is extant, allowing precise identification of how he redacted his material. Second, the author was a member of the Julio-Claudian dynasty, being the adopted son and heir of Tiberius.[111] The poem was likely written between Tiberius' accession in 14 CE and Germanicus' death in 19.[112]

Germanicus' account of the Golden Age adds a few details to his source:

> Rage had not yet bared savage swords, and discord among brothers was not known. Sea voyages were also unknown, and one's private land was pleasing and sufficient …. The peaceful earth gave its fruits to the farmer spontaneously, and no boundary line of a small field kept lands firmly secure for their owners by a mark. (*Arat.* 112-119)[113]

Germanicus intensifies the theme of the absence of war and discord present in Aratus, and the denial of boundary lines is an outright addition. Some commentators interpret this as asserting a lack of private property. Given that Germanicus also states that "one's private land was pleasing and sufficient," however, he seems to allow for private

---

[110] Italiae cultores primi Aborigines fuere, quorum rex Saturnus tantae iustitiae fuisse dicitur, ut neque servierit quisquam sub illo neque quicquam privatae rei habuerit, sed omnia communia et indivisa omnibus fuerint, veluti unum cunctis patrimonium esset.

[111] The *Aratea* nowhere identifies its author, but Lactantius and Jerome attribute it to "Germanicus Caesar." This is usually taken to refer to Germanicus Julius Caesar, the nephew and adopted son of Tiberius, but since Tiberius was himself called Germanicus at times (Dio Cassius, *Hist. rom.* 57.8.2), it is also possible that this ascription could apply to him. D. B. Gain (ed., *The Aratus Ascribed to Germanicus Caesar*, Classical Studies 8 [London: Athlone, 1976], 20) thinks that "the evidence does not allow one to say whether the author was Tiberius or Germanicus," but most judge Germanicus Julius Caesar to be the author; so André Le Boeuffle (ed., *Les Phénomènes d'Aratos*, Collection des universités de France [Paris: Belles Lettres, 1975], vii), Gregor Maurach (*Germanicus und sein Arat. Eine vergleichende Auslegung von V. 1-327 der Phaenomena*, Wissenschaftliche Kommentare zu griechischen und lateinischen Schriftstellern [Heidelberg: Winter, 1978], 13), Peter Steinmetz ("Germanicus, der römische Arat," *Hermes* 94 [1966]: 455), Ludwig Voit ("Die geteilte Welt. Zu Germanicus und den augusteischen Dichtern," *Gymnasium* 94 [1987]: 502) and Mark D. Possanza (*Translating the Heavens: Aratus, Germanicus, and the Poetics of Latin Translation*, Lang Classical Studies 14 [New York: Lang, 2004], 235).

[112] Possanza (*Translating the Heavens*, 234) sets the writing of the poem between 4 and 7 CE, but it is more commonly dated between 14 and 19; so S. Franchet D'Espèrey ("Les Métamorphoses d'Astrée," *Revue des Études Latines* 75 [1997]: 175) Le Boeuffle (*Phénomènes*, ix), and Maurach (*Germanicus*, 21).

[113] nondum vesanos rabies nudaverat ensis/nec consanguineis fuerat discordia nota,/ignotique maris cursus, privataque tellus/grata satis … fructusque dabat placata colono/sponte sua tellus nec parvi terminus agri/praestabat dominis, sine eo tutissima, rura.

ownership of land in the Golden Age, denying only the need for visible borders.[114] The fact that Germanicus nevertheless adds the assertion of a lack of boundary lines is evidence that this motif had become a standard feature of the myth.

Seneca provides two descriptions of the Golden Age in different literary genres. The first is in the tragedy *Phaedra*, which Seneca wrote during the 50s CE while still Nero's tutor or advisor.[115] In the second act, Hippolytus defends his ascetic lifestyle as natural, comparing it to that of the Golden Age:

> Indeed, I think that this is the way that those whom the first age produced, who mingled with gods, used to live. They had no blind passion for gold, and no sacred stone in the plain divided the fields as an arbiter between peoples ... no soldier prepared savage arms for his hand. (*Phaed.* 526–533)[116]

According to Hippolytus, "this agreement was destroyed by wicked madness for gain" (*Phaed.* 540, *impius lucri furor*). Hippolytus' self-justifying invocation of the Golden Age myth may be ironic in context, but it testifies again to the common ideas that this age was marked by a lack of private property and was brought to an end by greed.

In the years prior to his death in 65 CE, Seneca composed the *Epistulae morales*, styled as a series of letters to Lucilius, the procurator of Sicily.[117] In *Ep.* 90, Seneca discusses the development of civilization, contrasting his own view with that of the Stoic Posidonius, who attributed the invention of arts to philosophers.[118] Expounding his position, Seneca describes the conditions of "that age, which they call golden" (*Ep.* 90.5):

> Those were fortunate times, when the benefits of nature lay open for the community, to be used in common, before avarice and luxury estranged mortals and taught them to leave the community and run after plunder .... What people were happier than that race? They enjoyed the nature of things in common; it sufficed as a parent for the care of all: this was the secure possession of public

---

[114] Gatz (*Weltalter*, 67) sees here "the lack of private property" (das Fehlen des Privateigentums), and Steinmetz ("Germanicus," 459) describes this Golden Age as a time of "no property" (kein Eigentum), but Gain (*Aratus*, 86) correctly notes "a reference to private ownership of land in the Golden Age," as does Maurach (*Germanicus*, 149).

[115] Michael Coffey and Roland Mayer (eds., *Phaedra*, Cambridge Greek and Latin Classics [Cambridge: Cambridge University Press, 1990], 4–5) propose a date toward the end of Claudius' reign.

[116] hoc equidem reor/vixisse ritu prima quos mixtos deis/profudit aetas. nullus his auri fuit/caecus cupido, nullus in campo sacer/divisit agros arbiter populis lapis/ ... non arma saeva miles aptabat manu.

[117] Charles D. N. Costa (ed., *17 Letters*, Classical Texts [Warminster: Aris & Phillips, 1988], 2) considers the letters "probably not a real correspondence." He dates the work to 63–4.

[118] So G. R. Boys-Stones, *Post-Hellenistic Philosophy: A Study of Its Development from the Stoics to Origen* (Oxford: Oxford University Press, 2001), 18–20; Garnsey, *Thinking about Property*, 123–5. Peter van Nuffelen and Lieve van Hoof ("Posidonius and the Golden Age: A Note on Seneca, *Epistulae morales* 90," *Latomus* 72 [2013]: 186–95) aim to complicate the contrast between the two philosophers.

property. Why should I not call that the wealthiest race of mortals, in which you would not be able to find a poor person? (*Ep.* 90.36–38)[119]

The most important feature of Seneca's depiction of the Golden Age in *Ep.* 90 is the quantity and scope of his statements about common property; like Trogus, Seneca does not limit his claim to a lack of boundaries between fields but asserts a wide-ranging practice. Seneca attributes the end of this practice to the intrusion of avarice:

> Avarice invaded these conditions that had been perfectly arranged, and, while it desired to set something apart and make it one's own, it made all things someone else's and reduced itself from boundlessness to need. Avarice caused poverty and lost many things by desiring everything. (*Ep.* 90.38–39)[120]

Like the *Phaedra*, this passage draws a causal relation between greed, private property, and the end of the Golden Age, making it one of the few accounts to explicitly identify a reason for the decline.[121] Seneca now returns to describing the Golden Age:

> It was not possible for anyone to have too much or too little: everything was divided among those of the same mind. Not yet had the stronger laid hands on the weaker, not yet had the greedy, secreting away for himself what lay unused, cut off another from what that one needed as well; each cared for the other as much as for himself. Arms lay unused. (*Ep.* 90.40–41)[122]

Again, several common Golden Age themes are drawn into an apparently causal connection: the *concordia* present in the Golden Age is linked to a community of property, and this harmony is responsible for the lack of warfare posited afterward.

The tragedy *Octavia*, likely written in the decade following Nero's death in 68 CE, was often ascribed to Seneca in antiquity, but its author is unknown.[123] In Act Two, the

---

[119] sicutaut fortunata tempora, cum in medio iacerent beneficia naturae promiscue utenda, antequam avaritia atque luxuria dissociavere mortales et ad rapinam ex consortio discurrere … quid hominum illo genere felicius? in commune rerum natura fruebantur; sufficiebat illa ut parens ita tutela omnium, haec erat publicarum opum secura possessio. quidni ego illud locupletissimum mortalium genus dixerim, in quo pauperem invenire non posses?

[120] inrupit in res optime positas avaritia et, dum seducere aliquid cupit atque in suum vertere, omnia fecit aliena et in angustum se ex inmenso redegit. avaritia paupertatem intulit et multa concupiscendo omnia amisit.

[121] Garnsey, *Thinking about Property*, 124; Kubusch, *Aurea saecula*, 79.

[122] nec ulli aut superesse poterat aut deesse; inter concordes dividebatur. nondum valentior inposuerat infirmiori manum, nondum avarus abscondendo quod sibi iaceret, alium necessariis quoque excluserat; par erat alterius ac sui cura. arma cessabant.

[123] The play was ascribed to Seneca at some point in its transmission, but the modern consensus is for non-Senecan, unknown authorship; see Timothy D. Barnes, "The Date of the *Octavia*," *Museum Helveticum* 39 (1982): 215; Anthony J. Boyle, ed., *Octavia: Attributed to Seneca* (Oxford: Oxford University Press, 2008), xvi; Rolando Ferri, ed., *Octavia: A Play Attributed to Seneca*, Cambridge Classical Texts and Commentaries 41 (Cambridge: Cambridge University Press, 2003), 5. The two most popular suggestions for the date of the *Octavia* are the reign of Galba (68–9) and the early years of Vespasian (69–mid-70s). Composition under Galba is held by Barnes (ibid., 216) and Patrick Kragelund (*Prophecy, Populism, and Propaganda in the* Octavia, Opuscula Graecolatina

character Seneca anticipates "new and better progeny," as when "Saturn had dominion in heaven" (*Oct.* 394–396):

> The peoples did not know wars, the harsh roars of war trumpets, or arms, nor were they accustomed to surround their cities with walls. The road was open to all, and the use of all things was common. (*Oct.* 400–403)[124]

After briefly describing a series of inferior ages, Seneca arrives at the nadir:[125]

> But a worse age entered into the innards of its parent: it dug out heavy iron and gold and then armed savage hands. It placed boundaries and established kingdoms …. The virgin Astraea, great ornament of the stars, disregarded, fled the earth and the savage behavior of humanity, with hands polluted by bloody gore. Lust for war and hunger for gold grew throughout the whole world. (*Oct.* 416–426)[126]

Again, the general nature of the claim regarding common property is noteworthy. A second important aspect is the political use of the myth. The author uses the Golden Age idea to criticize not just contemporary culture in general but the previous emperor in particular. Nero's reign had itself been promoted as a return to the Golden Age, but the *Octavia* upends this propagandistic use by casting the present as instead the Iron Age.[127]

Common property continues to characterize the Golden Age myth in second-century accounts. Juvenal pokes fun at this motif in the comic portrait of the Golden Age that opens his sixth Satire.[128] The speaker describes the "reign of Saturn" as a time when people would live in a "cold cave," enclosed in a "common shadow" (*Sat.* 6.1–4, *communi … umbra*).[129] The absence of land boundaries is reduced to a claim that the

---

25 [Copenhagen: Museum Tusculanum, 1982], 52), while Boyle (ibid., xvi) argues for the reign of Vespasian. Ferri (ibid., 96) is one of the few to propose a later origin, dating the play to the 90s.

[124] non bella norant, non tubae fremitus truces,/non arma gentes, cingere assuerant suas/muris nec urbes; pervium cunctis iter,/communis usus omnium rerum fuit.

[125] Whether Seneca presents four or five ages is unclear. Ferri (*Octavia*, 236) counts four; Boyle (*Octavia*, 176) counts five while allowing that "arguments can be advanced for each position."

[126] sed in parentis viscera intravit suae/deterior aetas: eruit ferrum grave/aurumque, saevas mox et armavit manus./partita fines regna constituit … Astraea virgo, siderum magnum decus./cupido belli crevit atque auri fames/totum per orbem.

[127] The *Octavia*'s ironic use of Neronian propaganda in its Golden Age account is widely recognized; see Boyle, *Octavia*, lxvi, 180; Kragelund, *Prophecy*, 49; Oliver Schwazer, "The Pseudo-Senecan *Seneca* on the Good Old Days: The Motif of the Golden Age in the *Octavia*," *Scripta Classica Israelica* 36 (2017): 2–13.

[128] Based on Juvenal's mention of a comet in conjunction with Trajan's campaign in Armenia and Parthia (*Sat.* 6.407–11), Edward Courtney (*A Commentary on the Satires of Juvenal* [London: Athlone, 1980], 1) and Lindsay Watson and Patricia Watson (eds., *Juvenal: Satire 6*, Cambridge Greek and Latin Classics [Cambridge: Cambridge University Press, 2014], 2) give a *terminus post quem* of 116 and 117 CE respectively for *Sat.* 6. Juvenal provides another humorous portrait of the Golden Age at *Sat.* 13.38–59.

[129] Watson and Watson (*Satire 6*, 79) identify this as an "allusion to the belief that, in the Golden Age, everything was held in common."

Golden Age was a time "when no one feared that a thief would steal his cabbages and apples, but people lived with their gardens unfenced" (*Sat.* 6.17-18, *aperto viveret horto*).[130] Befitting its satirical genre, this depiction of the Golden Age spoofs traditional imagery, but it again points to the association of the Golden Age with common rather than private possession.[131]

Though written in Greek, a contemporary Golden age reference made by Plutarch, a Roman citizen from Boeotia, also deserves mention here.[132] Praising the Athenian statesman Cimon, Plutarch invokes the Golden Age solely due to its association with the motif of common property:

> He made his house a town hall that was common to the citizens, and on his land he allowed strangers to take and use the first fruits that were ready and all the fine things that the seasons bring, and in a way he brought the fabled community of goods [κοινωνία] of the time of Cronus back to life again. (*Cim.* 10.6-7)[133]

The meaning of κοινωνία as "community of goods" is clear in context, and translators mostly render it in some such way.[134] Plutarch's statement is valuable for three reasons. First, it indicates that common property was considered as not only a typical but also a *defining* feature of the Golden Age, such that the mention of common property, even in isolation, brought the Golden Age myth to mind. Second, Plutarch here seems to have considered the Golden Age the preeminent example of common property; he did not, for instance, claim that Cimon brought back the "fabled community of goods of Pythagoras." Finally, this passage shows that the specific term κοινωνία could be used to describe common property in the context of the Golden Age myth.[135]

---

[130] Again, Watson and Watson (*Satire 6*, 82) see this as an allusion to "the topos of the absence of boundaries ... which symbolises the communality of life in the Golden Age," as does Yvan Nadeau (*A Commentary on the Sixth Satire of Juvenal*, Collection Latomus 329 [Brussels: Latomus, 2011], 55).

[131] Commentators agree that Juvenal's depiction of the Golden Age is a humorous and deflating one, but the author's evaluation of the primitive past is debated. Three main positions may be discerned: (a) Juvenal is showing his preference for the present over the idealized past (David Singleton, "Juvenal VI. 1-20 and Some Ancient Attitudes to the Golden Age," *GR* 19 [1972]: 164; Martin M. Winkler, *The Persona in Three Satires of Juvenal*, Altertumswissenschaftliche Texte und Studien 10 [Hildesheim: Olms, 1983], 30); (b) the description of the Golden Age contains no evaluation but is merely "a burlesque, meant to be amusing" (Nadeau, *Sixth Satire*, 18); (c) Juvenal prefers the Golden Age while still poking fun at it (Courtney, *Satires*, 31; Maria Plaza, *The Function of Humour in Roman Verse Satire: Laughing and Lying* [Oxford: Oxford University Press, 2006], 326).

[132] The exact date of the *Cimon* is unknown; C. P. Jones ("Towards a Chronology of Plutarch's Works," *JRS* 56 [1966]: 70-2) locates it somewhere between 96 and 114.

[133] ὁ δὲ τὴν μὲν οἰκίαν τοῖς πολίταις πρυτανεῖον ἀποδείξας κοινόν, ἐν δὲ τῇ χώρᾳ καρπῶν ἑτοίμων ἀπαρχὰς καὶ ὅσα ὧραι καλὰ φέρουσι χρῆσθαι καὶ λαμβάνειν ἅπαντα τοῖς ξένοις παρέχων, τρόπον τινὰ τὴν ἐπὶ Κρόνου μυθολογουμένην κοινωνίαν εἰς τὸν βίον αὖθις κατῆγεν.

[134] Bernadotte Perrin (LCL) translates κοινωνία here as "communism," Arthur Hugh Clough (ed., *The Lives of the Noble Grecians and Romans* [New York: Modern Library, 1992], 1:651) as "community of goods," and Robert Flacelière, Emile Chambry, and Marcel Juneaux (eds., *Plutarque: Vies*, Collection des universités de France [Paris: Belles Lettres, 1964-1983], 7:28) as "la communauté des biens."

[135] This is significant because Acts 2:42 refers to the κοινωνία of the Jerusalem believers.

Table 2.1 summarizes the descriptions of common property surveyed in this chapter. The data support five conclusions. (1) The inclusion of common property in the Golden Age myth begins in the Roman imperial period; its absence from

Table 2.1 Common Property in Greek and Latin Golden Age Texts

Author/Date	English Translation	Original Latin/Greek
Virgil 29 BCE	Not even marking or dividing the open field with a boundary was allowed (*Georg.* 1.126–127).	ne signare quidem aut partiri limite campum/fas erat
Tibullus 27 BCE	No stone was fixed in the fields to mark out farmland with fixed boundaries (*El.* 1.3.43–44).	non fixus in agris,/qui regeret certis finibus arva, lapis
Ovid 10–1 BCE	Nor did the surveyor mark out the ground with a boundary line (*Am.* 3.8.41–42).	signabat nullo limite mensor humum
Trogus 20 BCE–20 CE	No one … possessed any private property. But all things were common and undivided to all persons (*Ep.* 43.1.3).	neque quicquam privatae rei habuerit, sed omnia communia et indivisa omnibus fuerint
Ovid 8 CE	And the careful surveyor marked out with a long boundary line the ground, which previously was common like sunlight and air (*Metam.* 1.135–136).	communemque prius ceu lumina solis et auras/cautus humum longo signavit limite mensor
Germanicus 14–19 CE	No boundary line of a small field kept lands firmly secure for their owners by a mark (*Arat.* 118–119).	nec parvi terminus agri/praestabat dominis, signo tutissima, rura
Seneca 50–60 CE	No sacred stone in the plain divided the fields as an arbiter between peoples (*Phaed.* 528–529).	nullus in campo sacer/divisit agros arbiter populis lapis
Seneca 63–64 CE	The benefits of nature lay for the community, to be used in common (*Ep.* 90.36).	in medio iacerent beneficia naturae promiscue utenda
Seneca 63–64 CE	They enjoyed the nature of things in common … the secure possession of public property (*Ep.* 90.38).	in commune rerum natura fruebantur … publicarum opum secura possessio
Seneca 63–64 CE	Everything was divided among those of the same mind (*Ep.* 90.40).	inter concordes dividebatur
Unknown 68–75 CE	The use of all things was common (*Oct.* 403).	communis usus omnium rerum fuit
Plutarch 96–114 CE	He brought the fabled community of goods of the time of Cronus back to life again (*Cim.* 10.6–7).	τὴν ἐπὶ Κρόνου μυθολογουμένην κοινωνίαν εἰς τὸν βίον αὖθις κατῆγεν

Greek accounts before Virgil clearly contrasts with its widespread appearance afterward. (2) Common property is a standard feature of the Golden Age myth in this period. While it is not found in every version, it occurs in Virgil, Ovid, and the majority of the other major retellings of the myth in the first century CE. (3) Common property originally appears in the Golden Age myth in the form of the absence of bounded fields. This is how Virgil presents the motif, and he is followed by Tibullus, Ovid, Germanicus, and Seneca. (4) By the end of the first century CE, more general assertions of a community of property predominate in the Golden Age myth (though Trogus offers an Augustan instance as well). Seneca's *Ep.* 90, the *Octavia*, and Plutarch's *Cimon* exemplify this trend. (5) No account dives into specifics about the property arrangements; it is the general idea of common property that is important, not the practical details.

Political Applications of the Golden Age Myth in Other Sources

The second specific focus of this chapter is political applications of the Golden Age myth. Assertions of the frequent use of this motif in imperial panegyric are widespread, and in this section I examine examples from the reign of Augustus through that of Antoninus Pius.[136] This closer look both establishes the frequency of the myth's political employment and displays the variety of ways in which the Golden Age idea could be invoked to praise, or occasionally even criticize, Roman emperors.

Most of the scholarly attention given to Roman political use of the Golden Age myth has centered on the Augustan period.[137] The announcements of the return of the Golden Age in Virgil's *Ecl.* 4 and *Aen.* 6 are the fundamental witnesses, but several other pieces of evidence are commonly cited. The Ara Pacis, a monument to Augustus commissioned by the Senate and completed in 9 BCE, is often thought to display Golden Age symbolism.[138] Specific images that purportedly recall the myth include floral friezes and swans, which were traditional companions of Apollo.[139] Horace's *Carmen saeculare*,

---

[136] For typical claims of the recurrent political use of the Golden Age myth in the first century CE and beyond, see Galinsky, *Augustan Culture*, 100; Gatz, *Weltalter*, 142; Henk S. Versnel, *Transition and Reversal in Myth and Ritual*, vol. 2 of *Inconsistencies in Greek and Roman Religion*, Studies in Greek and Roman Religion 6 (Leiden: Brill, 1994), 199 n. 213; Wallace-Hadrill, "Golden Age and Sin," 22.

[137] Two of the most influential treatments of Augustan appearances of the Golden Age theme are Paul Zanker, *The Power of Images in the Age of Augustus*, trans. Alan Shapiro, Jerome Lectures Series 16 (Ann Arbor: University of Michigan Press, 1988) and Galinsky, *Augustan Culture*, 90–121.

[138] David Castriota (*The Ara Pacis Augustae and the Imagery of Abundance in Later Greek and Early Roman Imperial Art* [Princeton: Princeton University Press, 1995], 124–5) calls this "accepted opinion." This assessment seems correct: Golden Age symbolism on the Ara Pacis is also asserted by Evans (*Utopia Antiqua*, 21), Kubusch (*Aurea saecula*, 152–3), John Pollini (*From Republic to Empire: Rhetoric, Religion, and Power in the Visual Culture of Ancient Rome*, Oklahoma Series in Classical Culture 48 [Norman: University of Oklahoma Press, 2012], 285), Richard F. Thomas (*Virgil and the Augustan Reception* [Cambridge: Cambridge University Press, 2001], 2), and Zanker (*Power of Images*, 181–2).

[139] The floral imagery is claimed as Golden Age imagery by Castriota (*Ara Pacis*, 124–5), Evans (*Utopia Antiqua*, 21–2), Pollini (*From Republic to Empire*, 285), and Zanker (*Power of Images*, 181–2); Pollini (ibid., 288) and Zanker (ibid., 182) argue that the swans on the Ara Pacis refer to Virgil's connection of Apollo to the return of the Golden Age in *Ecl.* 4.10.

written for the celebration of the *Ludi saeculares* in 17 BCE, is also often seen as a poem that "celebrates the achievement under Augustus of a Golden Age."[140]

The idea that a returning Golden Age was "a staple of Augustan propaganda" has been challenged in recent years.[141] Duncan Barker notes that "there is no unambiguous reference to the Golden Age either in the *Carmen saeculare* itself, or in ... the ritual of the *Ludi saeculares*," and that "explicit proclamations of its return are restricted to two passages from a single poet," referring to Virgil.[142] Andreas Zanker goes even farther, arguing that Horace saw Virgil's Golden Age announcement as a "misstep" that he "sought to rectify in his *Carmen saeculare*" by studiously avoiding any mention of the myth.[143] Zanker also contends that Golden Age interpretations of the Ara Pacis are insufficiently grounded.[144]

The cautions of Barker and Zanker are a useful check against overinterpreting generic images of peace and fertility as references to the Golden Age myth specifically, even if their skepticism extends too far. For this study, which is primarily interested in the use of the Golden Age myth in the late first and early second centuries CE, the more important question is how the Augustan Age was characterized in retrospect. Seneca the Elder's *Controversiae*, compiled in the late 30s CE, reports that the Augustan rhetorician Latro referred to his own time as an "exceedingly happy and, as they say, Golden Age" (*Contr.* 2.7.7, *aureo ... saeculo*).[145] The pseudo-Ovidian *Consolatio ad Liviam*, likely written in the mid-first century CE, also refers to the time of Augustus as "the Golden Age" (*Cons. Liv.* 343–344, *aurea ... aetas*).[146] Even leaving aside disputed cases, the reign of Augustus was explicitly described as a Golden Age by some at the time and continued to be characterized as such afterward.

The reign of the following emperor, Tiberius (r. 14–37 CE), likely saw the publication of one of the Golden Age texts previously examined, Germanicus' *Aratea*. While this work is pro-imperial, Suetonius claims that Tiberius' contemporaries invoked the Golden Age myth to criticize the emperor: "You have altered the golden ages of Saturn, Caesar, for as long as you are still alive they will always be iron" (*Tib.* 59.1).[147] In his

---

[140] Johnston, *Vergil's Agricultural Golden Age*, 78. So also J. K. Newman, "*Saturno Rege*: Themes of the Golden Age in Tibullus and Other Augustan Poets," in *Candide iudex: Beiträge zur augusteischen Dichtung*, ed. Anne-Ilse Radke (Stuttgart: Steiner, 1998), 238.

[141] Duncan Barker ("'The Golden Age Is Proclaimed'? The 'Carmen Saeculare' and the Renascence of the Golden Race," *ClQ* 46 [1996]: 434), presenting the common opinion.

[142] Barker, "Golden Age," 435, 437.

[143] Zanker, "Late Horatian Lyric," 495.

[144] Ibid., 512. Galinsky (*Augustan Culture*, 106) more generally notes "the paucity of representations" of the Golden Age in Augustan art.

[145] Miriam T. Griffin ("The Elder Seneca and Spain," *JRS* 62 [1972]: 4) places the writing of the *Controversiae* somewhere between 37 and 40, and Lewis A. Sussman (*The Elder Seneca*, Mnemosyne 51 [Leiden: Brill, 1978], 92) between 37 and 41. Latro died in 4 BCE.

[146] Henk Schoonhoven (ed., *The Pseudo-Ovidian* Ad Liviam de morte Drusi [Consolatio ad Liviam, Epicedium Drusi]: *A Critical Text with Introduction and Commentary* [Groningen: Forsten, 1992], 26–37) dates the *Consolatio ad Liviam*, which purports to be addressed to Livia on the death of her son Drusus in 9 BCE, to 54 CE, immediately following Nero's accession.

[147] aurea mutasti Saturni saecula, Caesar; incolumi nam te ferrea semper erunt.

Legatio ad Gaium, Philo reports that the next emperor of Rome, Gaius (r. 37–41), was thought to have brought a return to the Golden Age at his accession; this passage will be examined in detail in Chapter 3.

These references indicate that the Golden Age motif continued to be applied to the present time and to the emperor himself after the reign of Augustus, and the post-Augustan highpoint of this trend in the first century occurs in the reign of Nero (r. 54–68). Several texts make more or less explicit claims that Nero's accession constituted a return of the Golden Age. Seneca's *Apocolocyntosis*, written toward the end of 54, proclaims that, as the Fates spin the years of Nero, "golden ages descend the beautiful thread" (*Apoc.* 4.1).[148] Writing a year or so later, Seneca again makes use of the Golden Age to praise Nero, now lauding the emperor's clemency as "worthy of the common innocence of the human race, for which that ancient age should return" (*Clem.* 2.1.4).[149]

Two texts that even more clearly invoke the Golden Age most likely stem from the early years of Nero's reign, although the dating of both is disputed. The *Eclogues* of Calpurnius Siculus borrow from Virgil and praise the present as a Golden Age on several occasions.[150] In the first *Eclogue*, the shepherd Ornytus proclaims that "the Golden Age is reborn with untroubled peace" (*Ecl.* 1.42) and announces "a second reign of Saturn in Latium" (*Ecl.* 1.64).[151] The fourth *Eclogue* opens with another shepherd, Corydon, searching for verses that "can celebrate the golden ages, which sing of the god himself who rules peoples, cities, and toga-clad peace" (*Ecl.* 4.6–8), with "the god" being Nero.[152] The proclamation of the Golden Age in these texts appears to serve as straightforward praise of the new emperor.[153]

---

[148] aurea formoso descendunt saecula filo. Susanna Braund (ed., *Seneca: De clementia* [Oxford: Oxford University Press, 2009], 14) and Ruurd R. Nauta ("Seneca's *Apocolocyntosis* as Saturnalian Literature," *Mnemosyne* 40 [1987]: 54) both date the *Apocolocyntosis* to 54 and connect it specifically to the Saturnalia in December of that year.

[149] generis humani innocentia dignam, cui redderetur antiquum illud saeculum. A date of 55 or 56 for the *De clementia* is given by Miriam T. Griffin (*Seneca: A Philosopher in Politics* [Oxford: Clarendon, 1976], 133) and Braund (*Seneca*, 16). That Seneca is here referring to the Golden Age myth is accepted by Braund (ibid., 385–6), Gatz (*Weltalter*, 136), and Wallace-Hadrill ("Golden Age and Sin," 30–1), who claims that this text "is the first work to articulate the Golden Age ideology systematically as a whole."

[150] Beatrice Martin ("Calpurnius Siculus' 'New' *Aurea Aetas*," *Acta Classica* 39 [1996]: 18) supports a Neronian date and judges this to be the consensus opinion; she is joined in this dating by Braund (*Seneca*, 12), Eleanor Winsor Leach ("Corydon Revisited: An Interpretation of the Political Eclogues of Calpurnius Siculus," *Ramus* 2 [1973]: 90 n. 4), Arnaldo Momigliano ("Literary Chronology of the Neronian Age," *ClQ* 38 [1944]: 97), John P. Sullivan (*Literature and Politics in the Age of Nero* [Ithaca, NY: Cornell University Press, 1985], 51), Timothy P. Wiseman ("Calpurnius Siculus and the Claudian Civil War," *JRS* 72 [1982]: 57), and Roland Mayer ("Latin Pastoral after Virgil," in *Brill's Companion to Greek and Latin Pastoral*, ed. Marco Fantuzzi and Theodore D. Papanghelis [Leiden: Brill, 2006], 454–6). Mayer provides a helpful summary of the dispute, concluding that "a Calpurnius writing later than the reign of Nero is inexplicable." A post-Neronian date is asserted by Edward Champion (first in "The Life and Times of Calpurnius Siculus," *JRS* 68 [1978]: 95–110), and Feeney (*Caesar's Calendar*, 136).

[151] aurea secura cum pace renascitur aetas; altera Saturni … Latialia regna.

[152] aurea possint/saecula cantari, quibus et deus ipse canatur,/qui populos urbesque regit pacemque togatam.

The *Einsiedeln Eclogues*, two fragmentary poems rediscovered in the nineteenth century, present similar dating challenges. As with Calpurnius' *Eclogues,* majority opinion places these early in Nero's reign.[154] In the second *Eclogue*, the shepherd Mytes proclaims the return of the Golden Age: "Certainly the stolid herd does not deny to this age the golden reigns? The days of Saturn have returned and Astraea the Maiden, and secure ages have returned to the ancient ways" (2.22–24).[155] Despite its laudatory tone, this poem is often interpreted as less than optimistic about Nero.[156] In any case, it is another witness to the use of the Golden Age myth to characterize the emperor.

Of course, Nero's tenure failed to live up to the high hopes expressed by these authors, and by the time of Vespasian (r. 69–79) the *Octavia* was using the Golden Age myth to criticize Nero's reign. Under Domitian (r. 81–96), poets again took up the idea of a returning Golden Age, drawing particularly from Virgil's fourth *Eclogue*, to praise the emperor and his family. In Martial's sixth book of epigrams, published ca. 90, the poet predicts the birth of a son to Domitian in language borrowed from Virgil's poem.[157]

Statius twice brings the Golden Age theme into his praises of Domitian, although both cases are somewhat at odds with traditional uses of the myth. The speaker in *Silv.* 1.6 praises the abundant food and gifts provided by Domitian to celebrate the Saturnalia as *preferable* to the bounty of the Golden Age: "Come now, Antiquity, compare the ages of ancient Jove and the golden time: wine did not flow so freely then, nor did the crop fill the late year" (*Silv.* 1.6.39–42).[158] Statius refers to the myth again in *Silv.* 4.3, which celebrates the

---

[153] So Braund (*Seneca*, 13), D'Espèrey ("Métamorphoses," 187), Martin ("Calpurnius Siculus," 19), and Sullivan (*Literature and Politics*, 51). Leach ("Corydon Revisited," 87–8) argues that the poems are actually "a chronicle of disappointment," seeing a downward trajectory over the course of the *Eclogues*.

[154] These poems (which may not be by the same author) are assigned to the time of Nero by Thomas K. Hubbard (*The Pipes of Pan: Intertextuality and Literary Filiation in the Pastoral Tradition from Theocritus to Milton* [Ann Arbor: University of Michigan Press, 1998], 140), Mayer ("Latin Pastoral," 464), Momigliano ("Literary Chronology," 98), and Sullivan (*Literature and Politics*, 57). Dietmar Korzeniewski ("Die 'Panegyrische Tendenz' in den Carmina Einsidlensia," *Hermes* 94 [1966]: 359) interprets the poems as anti-Neronian and concludes that this erodes any support for an early date.

[155] et negat huic aevo stolidum pecus aurea regna?/Saturni rediere dies Astraeaque virgo/tutaque in antiquos redierunt saecula mores.

[156] Hubbard (*Pipes of Pan*, 143) finds "a strong sense of ambiguity and uncertainty" in the poem, while Sullivan (*Literature and Politics*, 56) thinks its intention "is to cast doubt on the propaganda themes sounded by Calpurnius, the return of the Golden Age with peace, justice, and prosperity established again on earth under Nero-Apollo." D'Espèrey ("Métamorphoses," 187) sees only straightforward praise of Nero.

[157] John Garthwaite ("Martial, Book 6, on Domitian's Moral Censorship," *Prudentia* 22 [1990]: 14) dates Book 6 to 90. Martial states that the recently deified Julia "will draw golden threads for you with a snow-white thumb" (*Ep.* 6.3.5), which Ruurd R. Nauta (*Poetry for Patrons: Literary Communication in the Age of Domitian*, Mnemosyne Supplements 206 [Leiden: Brill, 2002], 434) interprets as a combination of "the Virgilian motifs of Golden Age and the spinning Parcae."

[158] i nunc, saecula compara, Vetustas,/antiqui Iovis aureumque tempus:/non sic libera vina tunc fluebant/nec tardum seges occupabat annum. Both Nauta (*Poetry for Patrons*, 399) and Carole E. Newlands (*Statius' Silvae and the Poetics of Empire* [Cambridge: Cambridge University Press, 2002], 245) interpret "ancient Jove" as a reference to Saturn; Nauta compares it to Statius' description of Neptune as a *secundus Jupiter*.

construction of the Via Domitiana in 95.¹⁵⁹ Mimicking Virgil's fourth *Eclogue*, Statius has the Sibyl promise Domitian that "a great series of ages awaits you!" (*Silv.* 4.3.147, *magnus te manet ordo saeculorum*).¹⁶⁰ Statius takes up the tradition of using the Golden Age in imperial panegyric but focuses on the material and technological achievements of the Empire.

Trajan's reign (98–117) was the setting for the Golden Age reference of Plutarch mentioned earlier, and under the following emperor Hadrian (r. 117–138) the use of the Golden Age in imperial propaganda peaked again.¹⁶¹ In 121, Hadrian issued an aureus featuring a standing figure holding a globe, on which stood a phoenix, a symbol of renewal.¹⁶² Lest the symbolism be missed, the legend stated openly, "SAEC AVR," an abbreviation of *saeculum aureum* ("Golden Age").

The Greek orator Aelius Aristides supplies the final example examined here. In a speech given in Rome during the reign of Antoninus Pius (r. 138–161), Aristides asserts that Hesiod would have altered his myth had he foreseen the glory of Rome:¹⁶³

> He would not, as he does now, begin to trace the generations from the Golden Race ... but when your leadership and empire should be established, then he would say that the Iron Race would cease to be on the earth, and then he would concede that Justice and Reverence would return to humanity. (*Or.* 26.106)¹⁶⁴

---

¹⁵⁹ Kathleen M. Coleman (ed., *Silvae IV* [Oxford: Clarendon, 1988], xix–xxi) dates all of Book 4 to 95, and 4.3 specifically to early in the summer of 95.

¹⁶⁰ Cf. Virgil's *magnus ab integro saeclorum nascitur ordo* (*Ecl.* 4.5). This is recognized as a Golden Age, and specifically Virgilian, allusion by Coleman (*Silvae IV*, 133), Nauta (*Poetry for Patrons*, 390), and Newlands (*Statius' Silvae*, 317).

¹⁶¹ Heinz Bellen ("SAEculum AURreum: das Säkularbewusstsein des Kaisers Hadrian im Spiegel der Münzen," in *Politik, Recht, Gesellschaft: Studien zur alten Geschichte*, ed. Leonhard Schumacher, Historia Einzelschriften 115 [Stuttgart: Steiner, 1997], 136) states that Hadrian surrounded his reign with the "sheen of the Golden Age" (Glanz des goldenen Zeitalters) more than any other emperor after Augustus; see also Evan Haley, "Hadrian as Romulus or the Self-Representation of a Roman Emperor," *Latomus* 64 (2005): 969–80.

¹⁶² *RIC* II, p. 356, no. 136. For a discussion of the symbolism of the phoenix, see Evans, *Utopia Antiqua*, 10–14.

¹⁶³ Three dates have been suggested for the delivery of this speech: 143 CE (Richard Klein, "Zur Datierung der Romrede des Aelius Aristides," *Historia* 30 [1981]: 349; James Oliver, *The Ruling Power: A Study of the Roman Empire in the Second Century after Christ through the Roman Oration of Aelius Aristides*, TAPS 43 [Philadelphia: American Philosophical Society, 1953], 887), 144 CE (Francesca Fontanella, "The Encomium on Rome as a Response to Polybius' Doubts about the Roman Empire," in *Aelius Aristides between Greece, Rome, and the Gods*, ed. William V. Harris and Brooke Holmes, Columbia Studies in the Classical Tradition 33 [Leiden: Brill, 2008], 203; Laurent Pernot, *Éloges grecs de Rome: Discours*, Roue à livres 32 [Paris: Belles Lettres, 1997], 163–70; Peter van Nuffelen, *Rethinking the Gods: Philosophical Readings of Religion in the Post-Hellenistic Period*, Greek Culture in the Roman World [Cambridge: Cambridge University Press, 2011], 122), and 155 CE (Charles A. Behr, ed., *P. Aelius Aristides: The Complete Works* [Leiden: Brill, 1981], 2:373). The year 144 has enjoyed the most support recently on the strength of Pernot's analysis.

¹⁶⁴ αὐτὸς οὐκ ἂν ὥσπερ νῦν ἀπὸ χρυσοῦ γένους ἀρξάμενος γενεαλογεῖν ... ἀλλ' ἡνίκ' ἂν ἡ ὑμετέρα προστασία τε καὶ ἀρχὴ κατασταῇ, τότ' ἂν φάναι φθαρῆναι τὸ σιδηροῦν φῦλον ἐν τῇ γῇ, καὶ Δίκη δὲ καὶ Αἰδοῖ τότ' ἂν ἀποδοθῆναι κάθοδον εἰς ἀνθρώπους.

Aristides specifically praises Rome for having brought about "great and becoming equality" (*Or.* 26.39) and for "giving a common share of all things" (*Or.* 26.65).¹⁶⁵ Near the end of his oration, Aristides even claims that Rome has satisfied the ancient longing for a common earth, although he attributes this idea specifically to Homer:¹⁶⁶

> And that which was said by Homer, that "the earth was common to all," you have done in fact, measuring out all the inhabited world, joining riverbanks with all sorts of bridges, cutting down mountains to be fit for horse-travel, filling up desolate places with post-stations, and civilizing everything. (*Or.* 26.101)¹⁶⁷

This text is exceptional insofar as it claims that the Golden Age condition of a common earth has actually become a present reality. To do so, Aristides alters the meaning of the concept, reducing the idea of common possession to that of general accessibility.

Examples of similar invocations of the Golden Age myth to praise later Roman emperors could be multiplied down to Justin II (r. 565–578), under whom the poet Corippus claimed, "Now the iron ages are passing away, and the golden ages arise!" (*Laud. Just.* 3.78).¹⁶⁸ This brief survey of Golden Age language in political discourse has confirmed the assertions of scholars that such application of the myth was "ubiquitous" and "recurrent."¹⁶⁹ Furthermore, the distribution of its uses, from coinage to authors famous and forgotten, supports Bodo Gatz's conclusion that the politicization of the myth was not confined to the minds of a few poets but was widespread in the popular imagination.¹⁷⁰ One additional observation that is particularly important is that imperial applications of the Golden Age myth were closely bound with the idea of a *return* of this age. Not every mention of the Golden Age in the early Empire was explicitly or even implicitly political. Following Virgil's attribution of a return to Augustus, however, almost every early imperial mention of a new Golden Age credited this to the emperor.¹⁷¹ In the early Empire, speaking of the Golden Age's return would call to mind the repeated claims that the Roman emperor was the one bringing such a return about.

Finally, despite claims that the Golden Age idea after Augustus was reduced to "a rather empty form of flattery," the instances noted here show a variety of possible political applications of the myth.¹⁷² Pure flattery is certainly common, but critical uses of the myth also appear. For deceased emperors, criticism could be open, as was Suetonius' accusation that Tiberius brought back the Iron Age. Yet even living

---

¹⁶⁵ πολλὴ καὶ εὐσχήμων ἰσότης; ἅπαντα εἰς τὸ μέσον καταθέντες.
¹⁶⁶ Oliver (*Ruling Power*, 947) observes that Aristides' quotation of Homer "gives it a deliberately different meaning"; in *Il.* 15.193, the expression describes the gods' shared rule over the earth.
¹⁶⁷ καὶ τὸ Ὁμήρῳ λεχθὲν "Γαῖα δ' ἔτι ξυνὴ πάντων" ὑμεῖς ἔργῳ ἐποιήσατε, καταμετρήσαντες μὲν πᾶσαν τὴν οἰκουμένην, ζεύξαντες δὲ παντοδαπαῖς γεφύραις ποταμοὺς, καὶ ὄρη κόψαντες ἱππήλατον γῆν εἶναι, σταθμοῖς τε τὰ ἔρημα ἀναπλήσαντες, καὶ ... πάντα ἡμερώσαντες.
¹⁶⁸ ferrea nunc abeunt atque aurea saecula surgunt. West (*Hesiod*, 177) counts sixteen different Roman emperors under whom the Golden Age was said to have been returning.
¹⁶⁹ Versnel, *Transition and Reversal*, 199 n. 213; Wallace-Hadrill, "Golden Age and Sin," 22.
¹⁷⁰ Gatz, *Weltalter*, 142.
¹⁷¹ Seneca the Elder's quotation of Latro's reference to the present as a "Golden Age" (*Contr.* 2.7.7) is perhaps the only exception, along with the Sibylline Oracles, which Chapter 3 treats.
¹⁷² Blundell, *Origins of Civilization*, 158.

emperors may have been the target of Golden Age–based critiques, as in the cases of Nero and Domitian.[173] The widely known imperial associations of the myth made the Golden Age motif a useful vehicle for commentary on the emperor, positive or negative, open or hidden.

Summary: The Golden Age Myth in Greek and Latin Sources

Although he may have borrowed from an existing version, Hesiod's presentation of the myth of the ages is the earliest extant form, and little can be ascertained about the details of any possible antecedents. The major Greek accounts, those of Hesiod, Plato, and Aratus, all describe a past idyllic Golden Age, usually marked by a lack of toil and strife (στάσις) and by close communion with deities. A series of declining ages leads to the present (the "Iron Race" in Hesiod), which suffers under the opposite conditions of labor and disharmony.

Latin accounts maintain this same basic outline. The Golden Age continues to be associated with the presence of deities, and Latin authors emphasize the *concordia* that characterized the Golden Age and the *discordia* that accompanied its end. At the same time, the presentation of the myth changes in four important ways. The first change regards the frequency of the Golden Age's literary use: at the time of Octavian's rise to power, the popularity of the myth explodes, and it continues to be as, if not even more, popular throughout the first century CE. Feeney labels the myth of the Golden Age "*the* great Roman myth," and its ubiquity was recognized in antiquity as well.[174] The *Aetna*, likely written in the late first century CE, presents the Golden Age myth as an example of a shopworn story: "Who does not know of the golden ages of the tranquil king?" (*Aetn.* 9).[175] With regard to the role of this chapter in the study as a whole, the criterion of "availability" has been more than amply satisfied; in the late first or early second century CE, an educated author such as Luke clearly would have been aware of, and thus able to allude to, the Golden Age myth.

The remaining three Latin innovations all begin with Virgil. First, Virgil's fourth *Eclogue* contains the first explicit announcement that the Golden Age will return, and the present or imminent advent of this age is regularly proclaimed in subsequent texts. Second, Virgil is also a pioneer in connecting this return with the figure of the emperor: in the *Aeneid*, Anchises credits Augustus with bringing back the Golden Age, and the same achievement is repeatedly ascribed to other Roman emperors by later authors. In fact, a returning Golden Age is almost never mentioned *without* crediting this return to the emperor. Virgil's third and final innovation is the attribution of a form of common property to the Golden Age. Virgil introduces this idea in the *Georgics*, and

---

[173] For Nero, see Sullivan, *Literature and Politics*, 56; for Domitian, see Garthwaite, "Martial," 21–2.
[174] Feeney, *Caesar's Calendar*, 112.
[175] aurea securi quis nescit saecula regis. Katharina Volk ("*Aetna* oder Wie man ein Lehrgedicht schreibt," in *Die Appendix Vergiliana: Pseudepigraphen im literarischen Kontext*, ed. Niklas Holzberg, Classica Monacensia 30 [Tübingen: Narr, 2005], 70) gives the majority dating for the poem as between 65 and 79 CE.

it becomes a standard feature of the myth almost immediately. Common property is so associated with the Golden Age by the end of the first century CE that, when searching for a useful analogy to a historical figure's radical sharing, Plutarch chooses the "fabled community of goods of the time of Cronus" (*Cim.* 10.6–7). Closely connected with this motif is the idea that greed, the desire "to set something apart and make it one's own" (Seneca, *Ep.* 90.38), accompanied or even caused the end of the Golden Age.

While the popularity of the Golden Age myth among Latin poets has been established, Luke was no Latin poet, nor can it be presumed that he was literate in Latin.[176] Certain relevant texts may have been available in Greek; writing during the 40s CE, Seneca refers to a Greek translation of the *Aeneid* already made by Polybius.[177] However knowledge of Latin versions of the Golden Age myth may have passed to Greek authors, it is clear that it did. As the next chapter will show, Jews and Christians of the first and second centuries who wrote in Greek did incorporate elements of the Roman Golden Age myth, including the motif of common property, into their writings.

---

[176] While any Latin competence on Luke's part must remain hypothetical, Dennis R. MacDonald (*Luke and Vergil: Imitations of Classical Greek Literature*, The New Testament and Greek Literature 2 [Lanham: Rowman & Littlefield, 2015], 4) is somewhat optimistic, noting that "many educated Greek speakers, like Luke, could read Latin." James N. Adams (*Bilingualism and the Latin Language* [New York: Cambridge University Press, 2003], 15) similarly observes that "there is abundant evidence for Greeks learning Latin" and that "Latin in particular was widely known"; for extensive documentation, see Bruno Rochette, *Le latin dans le monde grec: Recherches sur la diffusion de la langue et des lettres latines dans les provinces hellénophones de l'Empire romain*, Collection Latomus 233 (Brussells: Latomus, 1997).

[177] *Polyb.* 8.2, 11.5–6. For Greek knowledge of Virgil in general, see Johannes Irmscher, "Vergil in der griechischen Antike," *Klio* 67 (1985): 281–5.

3

The Golden Age Myth in Jewish and Christian Sources

This chapter shifts focus from appearances of the Golden Age myth in Greek and Latin literature in general to its use by Jewish and Christian authors specifically. Since the ultimate goal is to shed light on a possible Golden Age allusion in Acts, I examine texts that date from the same general period, the first and second centuries CE.[1] The two most prominent Jewish authors to make Golden Age allusions are Philo and Josephus, while the most extensive and interesting interactions with the myth, both Jewish and Christian, occur in the Sibylline Oracles. Three aspects stand out in these authors' interactions with the Golden Age myth. First, common property is an important feature of the Golden Age, particularly in the Sibylline Oracles. Second, Golden Age imagery tends to be employed in eschatological passages. Third, all of these Jewish and Christian allusions to "*the* great Roman myth" occur in works oriented in some way toward Rome, and the myth itself is sometimes used to comment on the Empire.[2] More generally, this chapter demonstrates that authors similar to Luke in certain respects, Jews and Christians of the first two centuries CE with a special interest in Rome, alluded to the Golden Age myth, satisfying the optional criterion of "occurrence in other authors."

The Golden Age Myth in Philo of Alexandria

Philo of Alexandria alludes to the Golden Age myth in at least one, and perhaps two, of his treatises. In the *Legatio ad Gaium*, Philo reports that this emperor's accession was a time of such joy and abundance that it was thought to be a return of the fabled "life of Cronus," although this hopeful expectation turned out to be quite ill-founded. In *De praemiis et poenis*, Philo arguably employs Golden Age imagery as well, including the motif of common property, in his description of the righteous who enjoy eschatological

---

[1] I consider the reign of Trajan (r. 98–117) to be the most likely period for the writing of Acts; see Richard I. Pervo, *Dating Acts: Between the Evangelists and the Apologists* (Santa Rosa, CA: Polebridge, 2006) for arguments supporting a date in this range. As Chapter 2 showed, however, the Golden Age myth was a frequent literary motif throughout the first and early second centuries CE. As a result, the argument of this study does not depend on what specific date is assigned to Acts.
[2] Feeney, *Caesar's Calendar*, 112.

peace. Philo thus provides a clear example of a first-century Jewish reference to the myth, and he is implicitly critical of those who place Golden Age hopes in a merely human ruler.

Philo's treatise *Legatio ad Gaium*, written ca. 41 CE, contains his only explicit mention of the Golden Age myth.[3] The work blames the recently deceased Gaius for attacks on Jews in Alexandria in 38 CE and recounts the experiences of the Jewish embassies subsequently sent to this emperor.[4] Following an introductory reflection on divine providence (*Legat.* 1–7), Philo begins to discuss the emperor Gaius, claiming an unprecedented level of excitement among the Roman populace at his accession:

> For who, seeing Gaius when he had received the rule of the entire earth and sea, well-ordered and free from discord ... unified in the participation in and enjoyment of peace, would not have been amazed and astounded at the extraordinary prosperity, beyond any description? (*Legat.* 8–9)[5]

This excitement manifested itself in universal celebration, resulting in conditions that brought to mind tales of the Golden Age:

> At that time, the rich did not surpass the poor, nor the reputable the disreputable; lenders were not above debtors, nor were masters above slaves. The time provided equal opportunity, so that the life of Cronus recorded by poets was no longer believed to be a mythical fiction, on account of the abundance and prosperity, the freedom from pain and fear, and the festivities occurring throughout houses and cities, day and night. (*Legat.* 13)[6]

---

[3] The *Legatio* was written after the death of Gaius and the accession of Claudius in January 41 (*Legat.* 107, 206); Per Bilde ("Philo as a Polemist and a Political Apologist: An Investigation of His Two Historical Treatises *Against Flaccus* and *The Embassy to Gaius*," in *Alexandria: A Cultural and Religious Melting Pot*, ed. Per Bilde and Minna Skafte Jensen, Aarhus Studies in Mediterranean Antiquity [Santa Barbara: Aarhus University Press, 2010], 112) suggests that Philo wrote the work later that same year.

[4] For more information on the situation in Alexandria and the events of 38 CE, see Mary E. Smallwood, ed., *Legatio ad Gaium* (Leiden: Brill, 1961), 3–36; Sandra Gambetti, *The Alexandrian Riots of 38 C.E. and the Persecution of the Jews: A Historical Reconstruction*, Supplements to the Journal for the Study of Judaism 135 (Leiden: Brill, 2009). The *Legatio* is most commonly thought to have been addressed primarily to non-Jews; so Ray Barraclough ("Philo's Politics: Roman Rule and Hellenistic Judaism," ANRW 21.2:446), Bilde ("Polemist," 110), E. R. Goodenough (*The Politics of Philo Judaeus: Practice and Theory* [New Haven: Yale University Press; London: Oxford University Press, 1938], 19), André Pelletier (ed., *Legatio ad Caium* [Paris: Cerf, 1972], 17), and Torrey Seland ("'Colony' and 'Metropolis' in Philo: Examples of Mimicry and Hybridity in Philo's Writing Back from the Empire?" *Études Platoniciennes* 7 [2010]: 19).

[5] τίς γὰρ ἰδὼν Γάιον ... παρειληφότα τὴν ἡγεμονίαν πάσης γῆς καὶ θαλάσσης ἀστασίαστον καὶ εὔνομον ... συμφρονήσαντος εἰς μετουσίαν καὶ ἀπόλαυσιν εἰρήνης—οὐκ ἐθαύμασε καὶ κατεπλάγη τῆς ὑπερφυοῦς καὶ παντὸς λόγου κρείττονος εὐπραγίας;

[6] τότε οὐ πλούσιοι πενήτων προύφερον, οὐκ ἔνδοξοι ἀδόξων, οὐ δανεισταὶ χρεωστῶν, οὐ δεσπόται δούλων περιῆσαν, ἰσονομίαν τοῦ καιροῦ διδόντος, ὡς τὸν παρὰ ποιηταῖς ἀναγραφέντα Κρονικὸν βίον μηκέτι νομίζεσθαι πλάσμα μύθου διά τε τὴν εὐθηνίαν καὶ εὐετηρίαν τό τε ἄλυπον καὶ ἄφοβον καὶ τὰς πανοικίας ὁμοῦ καὶ πανδήμους μεθ' ἡμέραν τε καὶ νύκτωρ εὐφροσύνας.

In addition to the general conditions of peace and concord, the two specific features that prompt Golden Age comparisons are equality and abundance. Equality between people of different statuses fits with the general idea of a common life in the Golden Age and with the annual celebration of Cronus' rule in the feast of the Saturnalia, when "everyone, both slave and free, has equal privilege" (Lucian, *Sat.* 7).[7] Philo is likely mirroring actual accession rhetoric here; given the regular use of the myth in imperial panegyric, the fact that Philo's only explicit Golden Age reference occurs in a description of the accession of a Roman emperor is unlikely to be a coincidence.[8]

A small but significant detail in Philo's phrasing is that he does not state that the beginning of Gaius' reign, propitious as it may have been, *was* like a return to the Golden Age, but rather that it was "believed" (νομίζεσθαι) to be so. Before narrating Gaius' final downturn, Philo breaks in to criticize these shortsighted judgments, which he attributes to "ignorance of the truth" (*Legat.* 21):

> For the human mind is blind as far as the perception of what is truly advantageous and is able to use conjecture and guesswork more than knowledge. In this case, after a short time the one who had been believed [νομισθείς] to be the savior and benefactor ... changed to savagery, or rather, displayed the cruelty that he had hidden behind a hypocritical fiction. (*Legat.* 21–23)[9]

The opening of the *Legatio* propounds this same theme. Philo describes humans as "infants," because "we believe that the most unstable thing, fortune, is the steadiest, while we think that the most certain thing, nature, is the most unreliable" (*Legat.* 1).[10] Since here "nature is primarily identifiable with God," the major contrast that Philo is drawing is one between proper confidence in God and improper confidence in less predictable aspects of human life, such as the consistent beneficence of any given political ruler.[11]

---

[7] ἰσοτιμία πᾶσι καὶ δούλοις καὶ ἐλευθέροις. Versnel (*Transition and Reversal*, 191) observes that the feast was "generally conceived as an imitation of this Golden Age," and Lucian compares the temporary social equality observed during the Saturnalia to the conditions of the reign of Cronus (*Sat.* 7). For more on the Saturnalia, see Versnel, ibid., 136–227.

[8] Barraclough ("Philo's Politics," *ANRW* 21.2:456 n. 327) and Pelletier (*Legatio*, 72 n. 2) suggest that Philo's description intentionally recalls contemporary political discourse.

[9] τυφλώττει γὰρ ὁ ἀνθρώπινος νοῦς πρὸς τὴν τοῦ συμφέροντος ὄντως αἴσθησιν εἰκασίᾳ καὶ στοχασμῷ μᾶλλον ἢ ἐπιστήμῃ χρῆσθαι δυνάμενος. εὐθὺς γοῦν οὐκ εἰς μακρὰν ὁ σωτὴρ καὶ εὐεργέτης εἶναι νομισθεὶς ... μεταβαλὼν πρὸς τὸ ἀτίθασον, μᾶλλον δὲ ἣν συνεσκίαζεν ἀγριότητα τῷ πλάσματι τῆς ὑποκρίσεως ἀναφήνας.

[10] νήπιοι, νομίζοντες τὸ μὲν ἀσταθμητότατον, τὴν τύχην, ἀκλινέστατον, τὸ δὲ παγιώτατον, τὴν φύσιν, ἀβεβαιότατον. David T. Runia ("Philo of Alexandria, 'Legatio ad Gaium' 1–7," in *Neotestamentica et Philonica: Studies in Honor of Peder Borgen*, ed. David E. Aune, Torrey Seland, and Jarl Henning Ulrichsen, NovTSup 106 [Boston: Brill, 2003], 368) notes that the Romans' fluctuating belief regarding Gaius in *Legat.* 8–21 "is meant as a paradigm case of the failure of understanding postulated in §§1–2."

[11] Ibid., 358. Charles A. Anderson (*Philo of Alexandria's Views of the Physical World*, WUNT 2/309 [Tübingen: Mohr Siebeck, 2011], 149) concludes that, in many places, "Philo does employ φύσις as metonymy for God so that, in certain circumstances, it is appropriate to identify them with each other."

To summarize, in *Legat.* 1–21, Philo contrasts those who place confidence in matters of fortune with those who trust in the providence of God. Misplaced hope is exemplified by the Roman people's exuberance at the accession of Gaius: thinking that they had secured abundance and happiness, they believed that the life of the Golden Age had returned.[12] Although Gaius was an unusually poor object of such hope, Philo sees this as not merely an isolated misjudgment but part of a more universal problem. Philo is not denigrating Roman emperors in general: he praises Augustus and Tiberius and hopes for better treatment from Claudius.[13] Nevertheless, assuming that anything contingent would provide lasting happiness was a category error, showing that "the human mind is blind as far as the perception of what is truly advantageous" (*Legat.* 21).

This Golden Age reference in *Legat.* 1–21 should also be brought into conversation with Philo's eschatological discussion in *De praemiis et poenis*. Peder Borgen argues that this latter treatise is closely tied to the *Legatio* and has significant "common phraseology" with *Legat.* 3–7 in particular; more importantly, *Praem.* 87–88 also contains a possible use of Golden Age imagery.[14] Gudrun Holtz argues for the presence of several Golden Age motifs throughout the second half of *De praemiis*, but the most relevant instance occurs at the beginning of Philo's eschatological reflections.[15] Discussing the enmity between animals and humans, Philo details the steps required to ultimately resolve this conflict:

> No mortal is able to stop this war; only the Uncreated can stop it, when he judges worthy of salvation certain people, who have a peaceful disposition, who embrace concord and fellowship, in whom envy has never been present or has quickly left, as they have determined to present their goods to the community, for common enjoyment and advantage. (*Praem.* 87–88)[16]

---

[12] Erik M. Heen ("The Role of Symbolic Inversion in Utopian Discourse: Apocalyptic Reversal in Paul and in the Festival of the Saturnalia/Kronia," in *Hidden Transcripts and the Arts of Resistance: Applying the Work of James C. Scott to Jesus and Paul*, ed. Richard A. Horsley, Semeia 48 [Atlanta: Society of Biblical Literature, 2004], 138) similarly argues that "Philo's usage of these tropes is highly ironic … Philo's depiction of the incarnation of the golden age that occurred with the accession of Gaius was exactly what the text's narrator claimed it was not—a poetic creation."

[13] Augustus: *Legat.* 143–149; 309–310; 318; Tiberius: *Legat.* 33, 141–142. Goodenough (*Politics*, 19) spoke of "Philo's hatred of the Empire" and famously opined that Philo "loved the Romans no more than the skipper of a tiny boat loves a hurricane" (ibid., 7). The majority view of more recent scholarship, however, is that Philo had a general appreciation for the benefits provided by the Roman Empire, although he was quick to protest injustice toward the Jewish people; so Barraclough ("Philo's Politics," *ANRW* 21.2:452), Katell Berthelot ("Philo's Perception of the Roman Empire," *JSJ* 42 [2011]: 168), and Mireille Hadas-Lebel ("L'évolution de l'image de Rome auprès des Juifs en deux siècles de relations judéo-romaines—164 à +70," *ANRW* 20.2:785). Exceptions to this consensus are Bilde ("Polemist," 112) and Seland ("Colony," 29), who see barely disguised threats to Rome in the *Legatio*.

[14] Peder Borgen, *Philo of Alexandria: An Exegete for His Time*, NovTSup 86 (Leiden: Brill, 1997), 182. Use of the Golden Age myth here by Philo is posited by Gerald Downing ("Common Strands in Pagan, Jewish and Christian Eschatologies in the First Century," *TZ* 51 [1995]: 209) and Gudrun Holtz (*Damit Gott sei alles in allem: Studien zum paulinischen und frühjüdischen Universalismus*, BZNW 149 [Berlin: de Gruyter, 2007], 141).

[15] Holtz, *Damit Gott*, 147–9.

[16] πόλεμος οὗτος … θνητὸς μὲν οὐδεὶς δυνατὸς καθαιρεῖν, ὁ δ' ἀγένητος μόνος καθαιρεῖ, ὅταν κρίνῃ τινὰς σωτηρίας ἀξίους, εἰρηνικοὺς μὲν τὸ ἦθος, ὁμοφροσύνην δὲ καὶ κοινωνίαν ἀσπαζομένους, οἷς φθόνος ἢ συνόλως οὐκ ἐνῴκησεν ἢ τάχιστα μετανέστη τὰ ἴδια προφέρειν εἰς μέσον ἀγαθὰ διεγνωκόσιν εἰς κοινὴν μετουσίαν καὶ ἀπόλαυσιν.

Gerald Downing claims that this "willingness to share possessions clearly echoes Golden Age tradition," as does Holtz.[17] While the motif of common property on its own does not necessarily indicate a Golden Age allusion, the context supports this identification. The eschatological peace between humans and animals mirrors the situation at creation, when the animals were "tame toward humanity" (*Opif.* 84), showing a correspondence between protological and eschatological conditions.[18] As such, Philo is describing, whether literally or figuratively, a future return of original conditions for nature and humanity, characterized by peace, concord, and common property. In this context, the motif of common property does point toward a specifically Golden Age allusion.

If such an allusion is accepted, it strengthens the implicit contrast between *Legat.* 1–21 and the eschatological portrait in *De praemiis*. In the *Legatio*, Philo criticizes the blindness of the Roman people who thought that Gaius' accession had secured peace and abundance, a veritable return of the life of the Golden Age. In Philo's eyes, such hope should only be placed in the providence of God. In *De praemiis*, Philo sketches the *true* "Golden Age" that God will oversee, describing conditions of peace, abundance, and communality. This contrast in no way constitutes an open challenge to Roman rule. Nevertheless, to the extent that Rome and its emperors make claims proper only to God, such as divinity or the provision of eschatological beatitude, Philo demurs.

For this study, the most important observations regarding Philo's use of the Golden Age idea are the following. (1) Philo provides a clear example of a Golden Age reference by a first-century CE Jewish author. (2) This example occurs in the context of Roman politics; not only does it appear in one of Philo's two political treatises, but the reference is specifically associated with the accession of the emperor Gaius. (3) The conditions that prompt the Golden Age comparison are peace, concord, equality, and abundance. (4) Philo undercuts the hopes expressed in this Golden Age language; they are placed not only on a singularly unfit object, Gaius, but ultimately in the wrong sphere entirely, the instability of fortune rather than the certainty of God. (5) Finally, the illusory hopes in Gaius contrast with the firm expectations of eschatological beatitude depicted in *De praemiis*. These conditions are described in language that may reflect Golden Age influence, including, most importantly, the language of common property.

The Golden Age Myth in Josephus

A half century after Philo's *Legatio*, Josephus provides another instance of a Jewish author making use of the Golden Age myth. Unlike Philo and the Sibylline Oracles, Josephus does not employ this myth in an eschatological setting or in a way that is explicitly or even implicitly critical of Rome. Josephus is, however, another witness to the inclusion of common property as a feature of the Golden Age myth.

---

[17] Downing, "Common Strands," 209; Holtz, *Damit Gott*, 142.
[18] Borgen, *Exegete*, 281; Holtz, *Damit Gott*, 167.

Written in the early 90s during Josephus' residence in Rome, the *Jewish Antiquities* traces Jewish history from creation to the start of the Jewish War.[19] The first eleven books retell biblical events, purportedly "without adding or omitting anything" (*A.J.* 1.17), although Josephus does not strictly abide by this claim.[20]

Several scholars argue that the first book of the *Antiquities*, which covers Gen 1–35, utilizes elements of the Golden Age myth in its retellings of the banishment from Eden and the story of Cain.[21] Louis Feldman's 1968 study "Hellenizations in Josephus' Portrayal of Man's Decline" is the most thorough exploration of the parallels between Golden Age accounts and Josephus' additions to the biblical text. Others, however, attribute some of these supposedly "Golden Age" details solely to Josephus' exegesis of Genesis; H. W. Basser, for instance, argues that Josephus "adds nothing significant to the text which cannot be justified by an exegesis of some passage or other" in the story of the expulsion from the garden.[22] Establishing the influence of the Golden Age myth thus demands more than a mere compiling of parallels; whether Josephus' additions could plausibly be derived solely from the biblical text itself must also be considered.

When Josephus describes God's visit to Adam, "who had previously frequented God's company" (*A.J.* 1.45), he adds a speech detailing the conditions that Adam and Eve would have enjoyed had they not disobeyed:

> God said, "Yet I had determined that you would live a life that was happy and unaffected by any evil, with your soul untroubled by any care. All things that

---

[19] The standard date given for the *Antiquities* is 93/94; see Per Bilde, *Flavius Josephus between Jerusalem and Rome: His Life, His Works and Their Importance*, JSPSup 2 (Sheffield: JSOT Press, 1988), 104; Steve Mason, introduction to *Judean Antiquities 1–4*, ed. Louis H. Feldman, Flavius Josephus Translation and Commentary 3 (Leiden: Brill, 2004), xvii. The primary intended audience of the *Antiquities* was almost certainly non-Jewish, as Josephus declares in the opening of the book; see Harold W. Attridge, *The Interpretation of Biblical History in the* Antiquitates Judaicae *of Flavius Josephus*, HDR 7 (Missoula, MT: Scholars Press, 1976), 65; Bilde, *Flavius Josephus*, 93; Arthur J. Droge, *Homer or Moses? Early Christian Interpretations of the History of Culture*, HUT 26 (Tübingen: Mohr Siebeck, 1989), 41; Louis H. Feldman, "Hellenizations in Josephus' Portrayal of Man's Decline," in *Religions in Antiquity: Essays in Memory of Erwin Ramsdell Goodenough*, ed. Jacob Neusner, SHR 14 (Leiden: Brill, 1968), 336 n. 1; Peter Höffken, "Überlegungen zum Leserkreis der 'Antiquitates' des Josephus," *JSJ* 38 (2007): 332; Steve Mason, "'Should Any Wish to Enquire Further' (*Ant.* 1.25): The Aim and Audience of Josephus's *Judean Antiquities/Life*," in *Understanding Josephus: Seven Perspectives*, ed. Steve Mason, JSPSup 32 (Sheffield: Sheffield Academic, 1998), 66–7; Gregory E. Sterling, *Historiography and Self-Definition: Josephos, Luke-Acts, and Apologetic Historiography*, NovTSup 64 (Leiden: Brill, 1991), 298.

[20] οὐδὲν προσθεὶς οὐδ' αὖ παραλιπών. For a survey of attempts to understand Josephus' claim to reproduce the scriptures unaltered, see Louis H. Feldman, *Josephus's Interpretation of the Bible*, HCS 27 (Berkeley: University of California Press, 1998), 37–46. Feldman's solution is that Josephus saw himself as carrying on "the Septuagint's tradition of liberal clarification" (ibid., 46) and thus not truly altering the Bible.

[21] So René S. Bloch, *Moses und der Mythos: Die Auseinandersetzung mit der griechischen Mythologie bei jüdisch-hellenistischen Autoren*, Supplements to the Journal for the Study of Judaism 145 (Leiden: Brill, 2011), 193; Droge, *Homer or Moses*, 36; Feldman, "Hellenizations," 341–50; John R. Levison, *Portraits of Adam in Early Judaism: From Sirach to 2 Baruch*, JSPSup 1 (Sheffield: JSOT Press, 1988), 107; Étienne Nodet, "Flavius Josèphe: Création et histoire," *RB* 100 (1993): 19–20. Attridge (*Interpretation*, 123) notes unspecified "parallels in Hellenistic descriptions of human devolution."

[22] H. W. Basser, "Josephus as Exegete," *JAOS* 107 (1987): 30. Thomas W. Franxman (*Genesis and the "Jewish Antiquities" of Flavius Josephus*, BibOr 35 [Rome: Biblical Institute Press, 1979], 61) similarly suggests that Josephus' additions in this story "could be drawn" from the biblical text.

contribute to enjoyment and pleasure would have sprung up for you spontaneously without toil and hardship on your part, according to my providence. In these circumstances, old age would not have come upon you very quickly, and your life would have been long." (A.J. 1.46–47)[23]

In terms of Golden Age characteristics, the earth's spontaneous production is the most striking detail, and Josephus repeats it in his presentation of the curses decreed by God:

The land will no longer give forth to them spontaneously, but it will provide some things to those who work hard and are worn out by their labors, while others it will not deem worthy. (A.J. 1.49)[24]

In addition to spontaneous production, Feldman identifies three other Golden Age motifs in Josephus' version: (1) "close contact and friendship with the gods," (2) life "free from evils and toil," and (3) the absence or suspension of old age.[25]

All four of these motifs appear in Golden Age accounts; the question is whether these parallels between Josephus' account and the Golden Age myth are sufficient to indicate dependence. Basser argues that many of these details could be "inferred from the biblically stated punishment," since "they are, in effect, the mere reverse of what the curses against Adam and Eve entail."[26] This claim is correct: although Golden Age parallels are certainly present, and although the language of spontaneity is particularly suggestive, this passage on its own does not contain enough non-biblical details from the myth to conclude that Josephus here necessarily made use of the Golden Age tradition.

The second passage in the *Antiquities* in which Feldman identifies Golden Age language is the story of Cain in Gen 4. The first possible Golden Age detail that Josephus adds is the invention of plowing, which he attributes to Cain:

But Cain was especially wicked and paid attention only to gain, and he was the first to conceive of plowing the earth. (A.J. 1.53)[27]

---

[23] εἶπεν ὁ θεός, "ἔγνωστο περὶ ὑμῶν, ὅπως βίον εὐδαίμονα καὶ κακοῦ παντὸς ἀπαθῆ βιώσετε μηδεμιᾷ ξαινόμενοι τὴν ψυχὴν φροντίδι, πάντων δ' ὑμῖν αὐτομάτων ὅσα πρὸς ἀπόλαυσιν καὶ ἡδονὴν συντελεῖ κατὰ τὴν ἐμὴν ἀνιόντων πρόνοιαν χωρὶς ὑμετέρου πόνου καὶ ταλαιπωρίας, ὧν παρόντων γῆράς τε θᾶττον οὐκ ἂν ἐπέλθοι καὶ τὸ ζῆν ὑμῖν μακρὸν γένοιτο."

[24] τὴν γῆν οὐκέτι μὲν οὐδὲν αὐτοῖς ἀναδώσειν αὐτομάτως ... πονοῦσι δὲ καὶ τοῖς ἔργοις τριβομένοις τὰ μὲν παρέξειν, τῶν δ' οὐκ ἀξιώσειν.

[25] Feldman, "Hellenizations," 341. For spontaneous production, see Germanicus, *Arat.* 117–118; Hesiod, *Op.* 117–118; *Oct.* 404–405; Ovid, *Metam.* 1.102; Plato, *Pol.* 271d; Seneca, *Phaed.* 537; Tibullus, *El.* 1.3.45–46; Virgil, *Ecl.* 4.18; *Georg.* 1.127–128. For divine/human fellowship, see Aratus, *Phaen.* 100–101; Hesiod, *Op.* 120; *Oct.* 397–399; Plato, *Pol.* 271e; Seneca, *Phaed.* 527; Virgil, *Ecl.* 4.15–16. A life free from toil is present in essentially every account examined here; see Hesiod, *Op.* 112–113, 115 and Ovid, *Metam.* 1.100 for two of many examples. Unlike the other three motifs, the absence of old age appears almost nowhere in the Golden Age tradition outside of Hesiod (*Op.* 113–114).

[26] Basser, "Exegete," 27; Franxman (*Genesis*, 60) makes the same argument. Feldman ("Hellenizations," 341), on the other hand, assumes dependence, stating that Josephus "followed a tradition found in many authors from Hesiod on ... the Golden Age."

[27] Κάϊς δὲ τά τε ἄλλα πονηρότατος ἦν καὶ πρὸς τὸ κερδαίνειν μόνον ἀποβλέπων γῆν τε ἀροῦν ἐπενόησε πρῶτος.

Moving on to the sacrifices of Cain and Abel, Josephus explains God's preference for Abel's offering by once again invoking the idea of spontaneous production:

> But God was more pleased with this sacrifice, because he values things that are produced spontaneously and according to nature, but not those brought forth forcibly according to the design of a greedy person. (*A.J.* 1.54)[28]

The greatest concentration of Golden Age parallels occurs in Josephus' description of Cain following his banishment for the murder of Abel:

> Increasing his estate by a mass of goods gotten by robbery and force, he incited to pleasure and robbery those he met, becoming for them a teacher of wicked practices. By the invention of weights and measures, he took away the quiet life that humans used to live together, turning their way of life, which had been pure and generous, away from the ignorance of these things toward wickedness. He was the first to place boundaries on land, to build a city, and to fortify it with walls. (*A.J.* 1.61–62)[29]

The Golden Age parallels in these passages present a stronger case for the myth's influence. Josephus could have derived the idea that Cain "paid attention only to gain" from interpreting the name "Cain" as "possession" (*A.J.* 1.52, κτῆσιν).[30] Nevertheless, the strong emphasis on greed in Josephus is not present in the biblical story of Cain, but it fits well with the prominent role played by avarice in Latin versions of the Golden Age myth.[31] The claim that Cain "was the first to conceive of plowing the earth" also has potential grounding in Genesis' statement that Cain was "a tiller [LXX: ἐργαζόμενος] of the ground" (Gen 4:2), but the biblical text does not mention plowing specifically, much less claim it as an invention of Cain. Again, this detail fits better with Latin versions of the myth, which frequently locate the invention of plowing in the Iron Age.[32]

Other statements in Josephus' description of Cain have even less of a basis in Genesis. The two most significant additions are found in *A.J.* 1.62: Cain "was the first to place boundaries on land" and, having built a city, "to fortify it with walls." The role of bounded fields in the Golden Age myth has been thoroughly explored in the previous

---

[28] ὁ δὲ θεὸς ταύτῃ μᾶλλον ἥδεται τῇ θυσίᾳ, τοῖς αὐτομάτοις καὶ κατὰ φύσιν γεγονόσι τιμώμενος, ἀλλ' οὐχὶ τοῖς κατ' ἐπίνοιαν ἀνθρώπου πλεονέκτου [καὶ] βίᾳ πεφυκόσιν.

[29] αὔξων δὲ τὸν οἶκον πλήθει χρημάτων ἐξ ἁρπαγῆς καὶ βίας πρὸς ἡδονὴν καὶ λῃστείαν τοὺς ἐντυγχάνοντας παρακαλῶν διδάσκαλος αὐτοῖς ὑπῆρχε πονηρῶν ἐπιτηδευμάτων, καὶ τὴν ἀπραγμοσύνην, ᾗ πρότερον συνέζων οἱ ἄνθρωποι, μέτρων ἐπινοίᾳ καὶ σταθμῶν μετεστήσατο ἀκέραιον αὐτοῖς ὄντα τὸν βίον ἐκ τῆς τούτων ἀμαθίας καὶ μεγαλόψυχον εἰς πανουργίαν περιαγαγών, ὅρους τε γῆς πρῶτος ἔθετο καὶ πόλιν ἐδείματο καὶ τείχεσιν ὠχύρωσεν.

[30] This interpretation also appears in Philo (*Cher.* 52) and comes from Gen 4:1, where Cain's name is explained by Eve: "I have acquired [LXX: ἐκτησάμην] a man by means of God."

[31] Greed is instrumental in the decline from the Golden Age in Germanicus, *Arat.* 116–117; *Oct.* 425–426; Ovid, *Metam.* 1.131; Seneca, *Ep.* 90.36; *Phaed.* 527–528; Tibullus, *El.* 1.3.39; Virgil, *Aen.* 8.327.

[32] *Oct.* 413–414; Ovid, *Am.* 3.8.41; *Metam.* 1.101; Virgil, *Ecl.* 4.40; *Georg.* 1.125.

chapter, and city walls were a common feature of the Iron Age starting with Virgil's fourth *Eclogue*.[33] Neither detail occurs in the biblical text.

Taken together, these elements do indicate a borrowing from the Golden Age myth by Josephus in his retelling of this portion of scripture. With this established, the parallels in the story of the banishment from Eden, even if insufficiently distinctive on their own, can also be plausibly attributed to Golden Age influence. While Feldman thinks that Josephus "may well have had Hesiod's passage in mind while writing his own description", the most distinctive Golden Age details in Josephus' story of Cain—the invention of plowing, land boundaries, and fortifications—are all absent from Hesiod but common in Latin accounts.[34] No single primary source can be specified, but Josephus was certainly influenced by Latin versions of the myth.

Why did Josephus introduce these elements from the Golden Age myth? The most common suggestion is that this and other instances of "Hellenizing" made his work "comprehensible" and "intelligible" to a non-Jewish audience.[35] This broad explanation is insufficient for the passages considered here, however: the stories of Eden and Cain would have been equally comprehensible to a non-Jewish audience absent the Golden Age details. One function that the myth does perform is that of helping to explain God's rejection of Cain's sacrifice. By adopting the Golden Age myth's evaluation of spontaneous production as superior to agriculture, Josephus is able to "solve" the problem of God's refusal of Cain's offering. Finally, Josephus may have incorporated elements of the Golden Age myth into the early chapters of Genesis to make the historicity of the biblical story more credible. Josephus' one explicit mention of Hesiod in the *Antiquities* (1.108) is to serve as a corroborating witness to the long lifespans recorded in Genesis, so that "no one should think that the things written about them are false" (*A.J.* 1.105). By assimilating parts of the prehistory of Genesis to a widely known primeval account, Josephus may not be making the biblical story more "intelligible" so much as more believable.[36]

The results of this section may now be summarized. (1) Josephus provides a second example of first-century Jewish literary use of the Golden Age myth. (2) As in Philo, Josephus' reference to the myth occurs in a Roman context, here in a work written from Rome and primarily directed toward a non-Jewish Roman audience. (3) Also like Philo, Josephus emphasizes the economic aspects of the myth. The clearest use of Golden Age motifs appears in the story of Cain, whose dominant characteristic is greed. (4) In line with many Roman authors, Josephus locates the institution of private property in the Iron Age, as Cain is the "first to place boundaries on land"

---

[33] Land boundaries as a post–Golden Age development appear in Germanicus, *Arat.* 118–119; Ovid, *Am.* 3.8.41–42; *Metam.* 1.135–136; Seneca, *Phaed.* 528–529; Tibullus, *El.* 1.2.43–44; Virgil, *Georg.* 1.126–127. Fortifications are found in *Oct.* 401–402; Ovid, *Metam.* 1.97; Seneca, *Phaed.* 531–532; Virgil, *Ecl.* 4.32–33. Gen 4:17 does state that Cain "built a city," but it says nothing about walls or fortifications.

[34] Feldman, "Hellenizations," 342. Feldman concludes this from three verbal parallels: "toil" (*Op.* 113; *A.J.* 1.46, πόνου), "old age" (*Op.* 114; *A.J.* 1.46, γήρας), and "spontaneously" (*Op.* 118, αὐτομάτη; *A.J.* 1.46, αὐτομάτων). This opinion is seconded by Bloch (*Moses und der Mythos*, 193) and Droge (*Homer or Moses*, 37).

[35] Attridge, *Interpretation*, 17; Droge, *Homer or Moses*, 37; Feldman, "Hellenizations," 339.

[36] This fits Josephus' general approach in *A.J.* 1–11, where he "buttresses the reliability of his text by quoting from pagan authors who confirm the account" (Sterling, *Historiography*, 295).

(*A.J.* 1.62). (5) While Philo adopts a somewhat critical stance toward the Golden Age myth, or at least to its overly enthusiastic political application, the myth is purely useful for Josephus, allowing him to explain the rejection of Cain's sacrifice and bolster the credibility of the biblical account.

Excursus: The Essenes in Philo and Josephus

The practice of common property in Philo and Josephus can scarcely be treated without mentioning the Essenes.[37] This group, discussed by both Philo and Josephus and mentioned briefly by Pliny the Elder, is commonly identified with the Qumran community.[38] In Philo's two accounts of the Essenes (*Prob.* 75–91; *Hypoth.* 11.1–18), the primary focus is on their economic arrangements, especially their practice of common property. This has naturally drawn the attention of Acts scholars, but no firm historical or literary connection is identifiable between the Essenes and the community described in Acts 2:42–47 and 4:32–35. Philo does, however, seem to present the Essenes as a historical foreshadowing of the eschatological lifestyle described in *De praemiis*, and in doing so he bolsters the link between common property and the eschaton found in *De praemiis* and the Sibylline Oracles.

Four types of relationship between the Essenes and the Jerusalem community have been proposed. (1) Capper argues for a *direct historical* relationship: based on "close terminological and administrative parallels" and a hypothesized geographical proximity between Christians and Essenes in Jerusalem, he concludes that "the property-sharing which took place in the earliest Christian community … was probably modelled upon Essene practice."[39] (2) Others see an *indirect historical*

---

[37] Although the Essenes are usually identified with the Qumran community, this study engages only with the Essene accounts of Philo and Josephus and not with the Dead Sea Scrolls, since only the former would have been available to Greek and Roman readers. Furthermore, the Dead Sea Scrolls show no signs of interaction with the Golden Age myth.

[38] A few scholars have challenged this identification. Florentino García Martinez and A. S. van der Woude ("A 'Groningen' Hypothesis of Qumran Origins and Early History," *RevQ* 14 [1990]: 537) have proposed that the Qumran community was an offshoot from a broader Essene movement, while Eyal Regev (*Sectarianism in Qumran: A Cross-Cultural Perspective*, Religion and Society 45 [Berlin: de Gruyter, 2007], 264) suggests the opposite, that the Essenes were an offshoot of the Qumran movement. Steve Mason (*Josephus, Judea, and Christian Origins: Methods and Categories* [Peabody: Hendrickson, 2009], 276) rejects the identification, based on discrepancies between the descriptions of the two groups.

[39] Capper, "Palestinian Cultural Context," 335. Capper bases his claim of geographical proximity on the work of Bargil Pixner ("An Essene Quarter on Mount Zion?" in *Studia Hierosolymitana: In onore del P. Bellarmino Bagatti*, ed. Ignacio Mancini, Michele Piccirillo, and Emmanuele Testa, Collectio Maior 22 [Jerusalem: Franciscan, 1976], 1:245–84) and Rainer Riesner ("Das Jerusalemer Essenerviertel und die Urgemeinde: Josephus, Bellum Judaicum V 145; 11QMiqdasch 46,13–16; Apostelgeschichte 1–6 und die Archäologie," *ANRW* 26.2:1775–922). Joseph A. Fitzmyer ("Jewish Christianity in Acts in Light of the Qumran Scrolls," in *Studies in Luke-Acts*, ed. Leander E. Keck and J. Louis Martyn [Nashville: Abingdon, 1966], 244) also sees "an imitation of Qumran practices" among the Jerusalem believers, and both Klauck ("Gütergemeinschaft," 99) and Herbert Braun (*Qumran und das Neue Testament* [Tübingen: Mohr, 1966], 1:148) assume some unspecified Qumran/Essene influence.

relationship, considering the Essenes and the Jerusalem community to be roughly parallel phenomena. These scholars use Essene and Qumran texts to argue for the historicity of the Acts summaries, as these writings indicate that some in the region did practice a community of property and show that idealizing descriptions do not preclude a historical kernel.[40]

More relevant for this study are claims of a literary relationship between the Essenes accounts and the Acts summaries. (3) Hans Conzelmann proposes a *direct literary* relationship: doubting the historicity of the summaries, he suggests that Luke modelled his description on accounts of Qumran and the Essenes.[41] (4) Finally, Sterling claims an *indirect literary* relationship, arguing that the Acts summaries, if not directly based on the Essene accounts, represent parallel instances of the same literary genre.[42] Another option, of course, is to deny any relationship altogether, which is not uncommon.[43]

Though direct historical influence cannot be ruled out, insufficient evidence exists for a positive claim.[44] The geographical proximity claimed by Capper is uncertain and, in any case, not probative, and the proposed terminological parallels do not stand up to examination.[45] The common argument that Qumran proves that idealized descriptions are not incompatible with historical substance is true as far as it goes, although it hardly counts as positive evidence for the historicity of Acts. *Pace* Conzelmann, there is no good reason to see the Essene accounts in particular as models for Luke, as the parallels in vocabulary are no closer than those with several other traditions examined in Chapter 1.[46] Finally, Sterling's arguments for placing the Acts summaries in the same genre as the descriptions of the Essenes have already been critiqued.

---

[40] Barrett, *Acts*, 1:168; Bartchy, "Community of Goods," 311; Klauck, "Gütergemeinschaft," 76; Marguerat, *Actes*, 107; Mealand, "Community of Goods," 99; Theissen, "Urchristlicher Liebeskommunismus," 704.

[41] Conzelmann, *Acts*, 24.

[42] Sterling, "Athletes of Virtue," 688.

[43] Haenchen (*Acts*, 234), Johnson (*Literary Function*, 4), Alan C. Mitchell ("'Greet the Friends by Name': New Testament Evidence for the Greco-Roman *Topos* on Friendship," in *Greco-Roman Perspectives on Friendship*, ed. John T. Fitzgerald, RBS 34 [Atlanta: Scholars Press, 1997], 242 n. 66), and Richard I. Pervo (*Acts: A Commentary*, Hermeneia [Minneapolis: Fortress, 2009], 90 n. 21) fall into this category.

[44] For critical analysis of the hypothesis of direct historical influence, see Richard Bauckham, "The Early Jerusalem Church, Qumran, and the Essenes," in *The Dead Sea Scrolls as Background to Postbiblical Judaism and Early Christianity: Papers from an International Conference at St. Andrews in 2001*, ed. James R. Davila, STDJ 46 (Leiden: Brill, 2003), 63–89; Jörg Frey, "The Impact of the Dead Sea Scrolls on New Testament Interpretation: Proposals, Problems, and Further Perspectives," in *The Scrolls and Christian Origins*, ed. James H. Charlesworth, vol. 3 of *The Bible and the Dead Sea Scrolls*, ed. James H. Charlesworth (Waco: Baylor University Press, 2006), 406–71; Hays, *Luke's Wealth Ethics*, 196–200.

[45] Bauckham ("Early Jerusalem Church," 72) thinks geographic proximity probable but notes that this "in itself establishes no presumption of influence or meaningful contact." Frey ("Impact," 433) and Hays (*Luke's Wealth Ethics*, 197 n. 24) are more uncertain about the proposed proximity. Both Bauckham (ibid., 85–8) and Hays (ibid., 199) persuasively argue against taking the phrase ἐπὶ τὸ αὐτό in Acts 2:44, 47 as equivalent to the Qumran community's self-designation יחד, one of Capper's main pieces of evidence.

[46] The terms κοινός and κοινωνία constitute the only significant shared vocabulary.

While certain parallels exist between the descriptions of the Essenes and the Golden Age myth, they are insufficient to conclude that the myth exercised any influence on the Essene portrayals.[47] Most importantly, there is no notion in these texts that the Essenes mark the dawn of a new age. Both Philo and Josephus present the Essenes as a longstanding segment of Jewish society, making it difficult to see their presence as signaling a return of the Golden Age. Yet while the Essenes are not directly styled as a "Golden Race," Philo does seem to view them as a foreshadowing of an eschatological community, insofar as they enact the conditions that will more widely characterize the Messianic Age. While any pair of idealizing depictions by the same author may be expected to show some overlaps, the parallels between Philo's description of the men who will usher in the Messianic Age in *Praem.* 87–88 and his Essene accounts are extensive enough to merit attention (Table 3.1). Almost every phrase in the former has a parallel in the latter.

Table 3.1 Philo's Descriptions of the Messianic Age and the Essenes

Description of the Messianic Age (*Praem.* 87–88)	Description of the Essenes (*Prob.* 75–91; *Hypoth.* 11.1–18)
• "who have a peaceful [εἰρηνικοὺς] disposition"	• "others pursue crafts that assist with peace" (*Prob.* 76, εἰρήνης) • "no one … pursues anything associated with war" (*Prob.* 78)
• "who embrace concord and fellowship" (κοινωνίαν)	• "their fellowship [κοινωνίαν] … is beyond words" (*Prob.* 85) • "their fellowship [κοινωνίαν] … is beyond words" (*Prob.* 91) • "Our lawgiver spurred great numbers of pupils toward fellowship [κοινωνίαν]; they are called Essenes" (*Hypoth.* 11.1)
• "in whom envy [φθόνος] has never been present or has quickly left"	• "for care of the sick … they spend without any fear from ungrudging stores" (*Prob.* 87, ἀφθονωτέρων) • "the elderly … are cared for ungrudgingly" (*Prob.* 88, ἀφθονίᾳ) • "the steward … supplies ungrudging [ἀφθόνους] food" (*Hypoth.* 11.10)
• "as they have determined to present their goods to the community" (εἰς μέσον)	• "their wages … they bring forward for the community" (*Prob.* 86, εἰς μέσον) • "they put all their things together for the community" (*Hypoth.* 11.4, εἰς μέσον)
• "for common [κοινὴν] enjoyment and advantage"	• "No one's house … is not common [κοινήν] to all" (*Prob.* 85) • "they all have … common [κοιναί] expenditures, common [κοιναί] clothes, and common [κοιναί] food" (*Prob.* 86) • "they provide a common [κοινήν] benefit" (*Prob.* 86) • "they have things for the care of the sick in readiness from the common [κοινῶν] stock" (*Prob.* 87) • "they … enjoy the common [κοινήν] benefit" (*Hypoth.* 11.4) • "Not only is their table common [κοινή] but also their clothing" (*Hypoth.* 11.12) • "anyone who is sick is tended from the common [κοινῶν] stock" (*Hypoth.* 11.13)

---

[47] In addition to common property, the Essenes are characterized by peace (*Prob.* 76), lack of commerce (*Prob.* 78) and slaves (*Prob.* 79), a simple existence, and long lives (*B.J.* 2.151), all of which are features of various Golden Age accounts.

In conclusion, no strong connection is demonstrable between the Essenes and the Jerusalem community in Acts. Despite some overlapping details, there is also no compelling case for seeing specifically Golden Age influence on the descriptions of the Essenes in Philo and Josephus; most significantly, the Essenes are not presented as in any way signaling the advent of a new age. For Philo, however, the Essenes' lifestyle, including their practice of common property, does seem to provide a foretaste of the conditions that will more widely mark the Messianic Age, understood figuratively or literally. This reinforces the emphasis that Philo places on common property, the dominant feature of Philo's accounts of the Essenes, as a sign of eschatological blessedness in *De praemiis*.

The Golden Age Myth in the Sibylline Oracles

The Sibylline Oracles consist of fourteen books compiled over several centuries by a series of unknown authors, often of unknown provenance.[48] To make matters more difficult, many of the individual books have had a complicated redaction history, and some include both Jewish and Christian layers. Despite the uncertainties involved, the Sibylline Oracles are well worth examining, since they feature the most sustained engagement with the Golden Age myth in any Jewish or Christian text prior to the fourth century CE. Furthermore, the portions that most extensively interact with the Golden Age motif (books 1, 2, and 8) date to the first and second centuries CE, making the Sibylline Oracles a suitable comparison for the late first- or early second-century book of Acts.[49] Three specific aspects of the Oracles' use of the myth are particularly important. First, Golden Age imagery is applied mostly to eschatological descriptions. Second, the Sibylline Oracles employ the Golden Age motif to criticize the Roman Empire. Third, common property is a central feature of the Oracles' Golden Age.

The Jewish and Christian Sibylline Oracles purport to contain the utterances of the Sibyl, a prophetess with a long history in the Greco-Roman world. The earliest mention of the Sibyl occurs in a quotation preserved by Plutarch from the sixth-century BCE philosopher Heraclitus: "The Sibyl, uttering grave, unembellished, and rough things with her frenzied mouth, reaches for thousands of years with her voice because of the god" (*Pyth. orac.* 397a–b).[50] By the early fifth century BCE, the Romans had compiled a collection of the Sibyl's oracles, which apparently consisted of instructions for performing appropriate rituals in response to various disasters or signs.[51] While

---

[48] In this study, "Sibylline Oracles" will refer to the extant collection of Jewish and Christian writings; the Greek and Roman oracles attributed to the Sibyl will be otherwise designated.

[49] See note 1 in this chapter.

[50] Σίβυλλα δὲ μαινομένῳ στόματι ... ἀγέλαστα καὶ ἀκαλλώπιστα καὶ ἀμύριστα φθεγγομένη, χιλίων ἐτῶν ἐξικνεῖται τῇ φωνῇ διὰ τὸν θεόν.

[51] Herbert W. Parke, *Sibyls and Sibylline Prophecy in Classical Antiquity*, Croom Helm Classical Studies (London: Routledge, 1988), 137. David Potter ("Sibyls in the Greek and Roman World," *JRA* 3 [1990]: 476) puts the first attestation of the Roman books at 496 BCE based on Dionysius of Halicarnassus.

some passages in the Sibylline Oracles may have been borrowed from these pagan sources, almost no comparative evidence exists to verify such a claim.[52] In any case, the Jewish and Christian books, "which typically predict disasters rather than prescribe solutions," seem to have differed considerably from their Greco-Roman antecedents.[53] This study examines three of the Sibylline Oracles that make use of the Golden Age myth: books 1–2, 8, and 14.[54]

The Golden Age in Books 1–2 of the Sibylline Oracles

The Golden Age myth plays a central role in Sib. Or. 1–2, with elements of it appearing in various parts of the ten-generation scheme that forms the books' main structure. Golden Age imagery is predominately employed in eschatological passages, and the motif of common property is prominent in these descriptions.

Though labeled as two separate books, Sib. Or. 1–2 form a single, albeit multilayered, work.[55] The extant text is thought to consist of a base text and a later revision. The main indication is a sharp break at 1.323, where a review of the generations following creation is suddenly interrupted by an account of Christ's life, death, and resurrection. The generational scheme then reappears in Sib. Or. 2.6–33. At a minimum, 1.1–323 and 2.6–33 are assigned to a base text and 1.324–400 to a later revision.[56] The most common hypothesis is that the base text of Sib. Or. 1–2 is Jewish and the revision

---

[52] Parke (*Sibyls*, 4–5) states that such borrowing "is impossible to prove" but finds "a number of passages in the *Oracula Sibyllina* where the style and subject matter strongly suggest verbal borrowing from a classical original." These classical oracles were associated by some with the idea of a new age; Virgil describes the returning Golden Age as "the last age of the Cumaean song" (*Ecl.* 4.4, *ultima Cumaei ... carminis aetas*), referring to the Cumaean Sibyl, and Horace opens his *Carmen saeculare*, written to celebrate a new *saeculum*, with a mention of "the Sibyl's verses" (*Saec.* 5, *Sibyllini ... versus*).

[53] John J. Collins, *Seers, Sibyls and Sages in Hellenistic-Roman Judaism*, Supplements to the Journal for the Study of Judaism 54 (Leiden: Brill, 1997), 183. Elsewhere, Collins ("The Development of the Sibylline Tradition," *ANRW* 20.1:424) also notes that the pagan oracles do not seem to have contained anything like "the attempted prophecy of the entire course of history" that appears in the Sibylline Oracles.

[54] Valentin Nikiprowetzky (*La troisième Sibylle*, Etudes juives 9 [Paris: Mouton, 1970], 102) argues that Sib. Or. 3, dating from the second or first century BCE, also contains allusions to "the Golden Age and the fateful race of the Iron Age" (l'âge d'or et la funeste race de l'âge de fer). The best evidence for an allusion is Sib. Or. 3.263, which describes the fertility of the "wheat-giving earth" (ζείδωρος ἄρουρα). Hesiod uses this same phrase three times, once each in his accounts of the Golden Race (*Op.* 117), the Race of Heroes (*Op.* 173), and the City of the Just (*Op.* 237). This expression is not limited to Hesiod, however; Homer also employs it on four occasions. On the whole, the case for an allusion to the Golden Age myth in book 3 is inconclusive: the author may have had Hesiod in mind at times, but the evidence does not allow for a definite conclusion.

[55] The clearest indicator of the connection between the two books is that the sequence of generations in Sib. Or. 1.1–323 is continued at 2.6–33. For more arguments for the unity of books 1–2, see Olaf Wassmuth, *Sibyllinische Orakel 1–2: Studien und Kommentar*, AGJU 76 (Leiden: Brill, 2011), 56–9.

[56] Even Jane L. Lightfoot (*The Sibylline Oracles: With Introduction, Translation, and Commentary on the First and Second Books* [Oxford: Oxford University Press, 2007], 99, 103), who thinks a unified composition to be possible, accepts that there are "two main compositional units" and that "the rupture at 1.323 ... is obvious."

Christian.⁵⁷ The Christian nature of 1.324–400 is obvious, while a Jewish origin for the base text is presumed due to its lack of Christian elements, its positive references to "the Hebrews," and its use of a local Noah tradition from Apamea Kibotos, which seems to have had a sizable Jewish community.⁵⁸ These indications are admittedly not demonstrative, but the internal evidence does point toward books 1–2 being a composite text, and a Jewish origin for the base text is more likely than not.⁵⁹

This base text is commonly dated to the first century CE.⁶⁰ No decisive evidence demands this time frame, but parallels to other eschatological descriptions, the lack of any reference to the destruction of Jerusalem, and use by subsequent texts support this dating.⁶¹ The Christian revision is post-70 CE, since Sib. Or. 1.393 describes the destruction of the Temple. The redactor also knows at least some of the Gospels, and Olaf Wassmuth suggests that he or she may show knowledge of 1 Peter as well.⁶² At the other end, portions of Sib. Or. 8 that likely date to the third century are probably

---

⁵⁷ This is the position of Bloch (*Moses und der Mythos*, 160), Wilhelm Bousset ("Sibyllen und Sibyllinische Bücher," *RE* 18:273), Collins ("Development," *ANRW* 20.1:441), Johannes Geffcken (*Komposition und Entstehungszeit der Oracula Sibyllina* [Leipzig: Hinrichs, 1902], 48), Parke (*Sibyls*, 171 n. 5), Aloisius Rzach ("Sibyllinische Orakel," *Realencyclopädie der classischen Altertumswissenschaft* 2:2146), and Wassmuth (*Sibyllinische Orakel 1–2*, 466). Both Wassmuth (ibid., 55–6), who accepts this view, and Lightfoot (*Sibylline Oracles*, 97), who questions it, identify it as the consensus position.

⁵⁸ Wassmuth, *Sibyllinische Orakel 1–2*, 467–8; John J. Collins, "Sibylline Oracles," in *The Old Testament Pseudepigrapha*, ed. James H. Charlesworth (Peabody: Hendrickson, 2009), 1:330. Sib. Or. 1.261–265 locates the resting place of Noah's ark in Phrygia, at "the springs of the great river Marsyas." Several third-century coins from this location, Apamea Kibotos, depict Noah's ark, and Cicero (*Flac.*, 67–68) reports that Apamea sent nearly one hundred pounds of gold to Jerusalem each year, which would seem to indicate the presence of a sizable Jewish community in the region. For further discussion of the evidence regarding Apamea, see Lightfoot, *Sibylline Oracles*, 99–102; Pieter van der Horst, "The Jews of Ancient Phrygia," *European Journal of Jewish Studies* 2 (2008): 283–92; Wassmuth, ibid., 475–85.

⁵⁹ Martin Goodman ("Jewish Writings under Gentile Pseudonyms," in *The History of the Jewish People in the Age of Jesus Christ*, ed. Emil Schürer, rev. and ed. Géza Vermès, Fergus Millar, and Martin Goodman [Edinburgh: T&T Clark, 1986], 3:645) argues against an early Jewish layer based on the absence of any pre-Constantinian citations of the work. Jörg-Dieter Gauger (*Sibyllinische Weissagungen: griechisch-deutsch*, Sammlung Tusculum [Düsseldorf: Artemis & Winkler, 1998], 438) and Lightfoot (*Sibylline Oracles*, 99–104) are open to the possibility of books 1–2 being a unified Christian composition.

⁶⁰ Collins ("Sibylline Oracles," 1:331) and Alfons Kurfess ("Oracula Sibyllina I/II," *ZNW* 40 [1941]: 162) date the base layer to around the turn of the era, Bousset ("Sibyllen," 18:274) to before 70 CE, and Wassmuth (*Sibyllinische Orakel 1–2*, 487) to the first or possibly the early second century CE. Parke (*Sibyls*, 171 n. 5) places it in the second century CE but gives no reason why. Geffcken (*Komposition*, 52) argues for a third century CE date, but Collins (ibid.) effectively refutes his arguments for this position.

⁶¹ Kurfess ("Oracula Sibyllina I/II," 161–2) sees parallels to Pseudo-Phocylides in particular. Collins ("Development," *ANRW* 20.1:442) argues from the lack of references to Jerusalem's destruction and the return of Nero. The controlling subsequent text is Sib. Or. 8.

⁶² Wassmuth, *Sibyllinische Orakel 1–2*, 501. Kurfess ("Oracula Sibyllina I/II," 165) thinks the redactor knows Revelation and the Gospel of John. A further possible literary antecedent is the Apocalypse of Peter, which Lightfoot (*Sibylline Oracles*, 104) argues is a source for much of Sib. Or. 2. Similarities are certainly present; Wassmuth (ibid., 440) thinks that direct dependence is unlikely, suggesting that a common source is more probable. If the Christian revision of books 1–2 is dependent on the Apocalypse of Peter, then this revision occurred is no earlier than the middle of the second century CE.

dependent on the revised version of books 1–2.[63] The Christian revision thus belongs in or close to the second century CE.[64] The provenance of the Jewish base text is presumably Phrygian, based on the Apamea Kibotos tradition, while that of the Christian revision is unclear.[65]

The First Race: Sib. Or. 1.65–86

After retelling Genesis' accounts of creation, Adam's sin, and the expulsion from the garden, the Jewish author of Sib. Or. 1–2 introduces a generation labelled the "first race" (Sib. Or. 1.86, πρῶτον γένος) of humans. The description clearly borrows from Hesiod, but the portrait is mixed, combining elements from different Hesiodic races:[66]

> They furnished all kinds of houses, and they also began to build cities and walls, skillfully and well. He granted them a long-lasting day for a very lovely life; for they did not die oppressed by sorrow, but as though overcome by sleep. Happy were those great-hearted men! God, the king, the immortal savior, loved them. But even they sinned, dominated by folly. For they laughed shamelessly and dishonored their fathers and mothers, and they did not recognize those they knew, plotting against their brothers. And so they were defiled, glutted with men's blood, and they made wars. (Sib. Or. 1.67–78)[67]

The statement that "they did not die [θνῆσκον] oppressed by sorrow, but as though overcome by sleep" (Sib. Or. 1.70–71, ὡς δεδμημένοι ὕπνῳ) is the clearest allusion to Hesiod's Golden Race, which "died as though overcome by sleep" (*Op.* 116, θνῆσκον δ' ὥσθ' ὕπνῳ δεδμημένοι). Yet the depiction quickly turns negative, employing motifs from the Bronze and Iron Races.[68] The allusions to Hesiod situate the account in a Golden Age myth framework, but the reader is denied an initial Golden Age. As it happens, this denial is only temporary; the sixth race enjoys the Golden Age that is withheld from the first.

---

[63] Kurfess ("Oracula Sibyllina I/II," 151–65) argues in detail for the priority of books 1–2 over book 8, and this is accepted as probable by Collins ("Sibylline Oracles," 1:332) and Wassmuth (*Sibyllinische Orakel 1–2*, 487).

[64] Kurfess ("Oracula Sibyllina I/II," 165) and Wassmuth (*Sibyllinische Orakel 1–2*, 487) locate the Christian revision in the mid-second century, and Collins ("Development," ANRW 20.1:444) states that "it can hardly be later than 150 CE." Geffcken (*Komposition*, 52) dates the revision to the third century CE, but this is based on the assumption of the priority of book 8 over books 1–2, which has fallen out of favor.

[65] Collins, "Sibylline Oracles," 1:332.

[66] The Hesiodic coloring of this passage is widely recognized; see Collins, "Sibylline Oracles," 1:336; Alfons Kurfess, "Homer und Hesiod im 1. Buch der Oracula Sibyllina," *Philologus* 100 (1956): 147–53; Lightfoot, *Sibylline Oracles*, 348–52; Wassmuth, *Sibyllinische Orakel 1–2*, 172.

[67] οἴκους δὲ μὲν ἐξήσκησαν/παντοίους ἠδ' αὖτε πόλεις καὶ τείχε' ἐποίουν/εὖ καὶ ἐπισταμένως· οἷσιν πολυχρόνιον ἦμαρ/ὤπασεν εἰς ζωὴν πολυήρατον· οὐ γὰρ ἀνίαις/τειρόμενοι θνῆσκον, ἀλλ' ὡς δεδμημένοι ὕπνῳ·/ὄλβιοι οἱ μέροπες μεγαλήτορες, οὓς ἐφίλησεν/σωτὴρ ἀθάνατος βασιλεὺς θεός. ἀλλὰ καὶ αὐτοί/ἥλιτον ἀφροσύνῃ βεβολημένοι. οἳ γὰρ ἀναιδῶς/ἐξέγελων πατέρας καὶ μητέρας ἠτίμαζον,/γνωστοὺς δ' οὐ γίνωσκον ἀδελφειῶν ἐπίβουλοι./ἦσαν δ' ἄρ μιαροὶ κεκορεσμένοι αἵματι φωτῶν/καὶ πολέμους ἐποίουν.

[68] The martial activity recalls Hesiod's Bronze Race, while the dishonoring of father and mother suggests the Iron Race, who "will dishonor their aged parents" (*Op.* 185).

The Sixth Race: Sib. Or. 1.283–306

After second, third, and fourth races that follow a declining pattern, God creates a fifth, "much worse" (Sib. Or. 1.120) race. These people are destroyed in the flood, after which a new series of five races begins, commencing now with a genuine Golden Age:

> Then in turn a new race of humanity arose, the first golden one, the best, which was the sixth from when the first-formed man came into being. Its name will be "heavenly," because God will take care of everything .... Time will be at its midpoint. There will be a royal, kingly rule; for three great-hearted kings, most just men, will destroy portions. They will rule for many years, distributing what is just to men who have given care to toil and lovely deeds. The earth will once again exult, springing up with many spontaneous fruits, producing for the race beyond measure. The laborers will be ageless for all their days, and they will die stricken by sleep, far from terrible, chilling diseases. (Sib. Or. 1.283–301)[69]

Far more than the first, the Oracle's sixth race is clearly modeled on Hesiod's Golden Race: this race is explicitly labelled "golden," lacks any negative traits, and includes the signal motif of spontaneous fertility, absent in the first race.

By calling the post-Flood generation the "first golden" race, the Sibyl makes it plain that the post-Eden "first race" was *not* a true Golden Race.[70] Yet these two races, the first and the sixth, are structurally parallel. By placing the sixth at the "midpoint" of time, the author points toward a two-cycle structure for the historical overview. History is divided into two five-race, Hesiodic cycles. The first begins after creation and culminates in destruction by the flood; the second starts after the flood with the sixth race and concludes in the eschatological events described in book 2.[71]

The most difficult phrase in the passage occurs at the end of Sib. Or. 1.294, the assertion that the three kings "will destroy portions."[72] The manuscript reading is μοίρας δέ τε δηλήσονται, but a variety of emendations and interpretations have

---

[69] ἔνθ' αὖτις βιότοιο νέη ἀνέτειλε γενέθλη/χρυσείη πρώτη, ἥτις πέλεθ' ἕκτη, ἀρίστη,/ἐξότε πρωτόπλαστος ἀνὴρ γένετ'· οὔνομα δ' αὐτῇ/οὐρανίη, ὅτι πάντα θεῷ μεμελημένη ἔσται/ ... μεσάσει δὲ χρόνος· βασιλήιον ἀρχήν/σκηπτροφόρον δ' ἕξει. τρεῖς γὰρ βασιλεῖς μεγάθυμοι,/ἄνδρε δικαιότατοι, μοίρας δέ τε δηλήσονται·/πουλυετῆ δ' ἄρξουσι χρόνον τὰ δίκαια νέμοντες/ἀνδράσιν, οἷσι μέμηλε πόνος καὶ ἔργ' ἐρατεινά./γαίη δ' αὖ καρποῖς ἐπαγάλλεται αὐτομάτοισιν/φυομένη πολλοῖσιν, ὑπερσταχυοῦσα γενέθλη./οἱ δὲ τιθηνευτῆρες ἀγήραοι ἤματα πάντα/ἔσσονται, νόσφιν νούσων κρυερῶν μαλεράων/θνήξονται ὕπνῳ βεβολημένοι.

[70] Wassmuth, *Sibyllinische Orakel 1–2*, 166.

[71] Collins ("Development," *ANRW* 20.1:426) thinks that the ten-race scheme borrows from the pagan Sibyl: Servius (*Ecl.* 4.4), commenting on Virgil's fourth *Eclogue*, states that the last age is the tenth. Wassmuth (ibid., 170–1) believes the number ten comes from combining a two-cycle structure of history with Hesiod's five-race scheme.

[72] The "three great-hearted kings" who will destroy these portions are usually identified as Noah's sons (Collins, "Sibylline Oracles," 1:341; Wassmuth, *Sibyllinische Orakel 1–2*, 179–80); cf. the description in LAB 5.1 of a time when the sons of Ham, Japheth, and Shem chose three rulers, under whom "everyone came together in one placed and lived harmoniously, and the earth was peaceful" (convenirent omnes in unum et habitaverunt unanimes, et erat terra pacifica).

been proposed.⁷³ While none is entirely satisfactory, Wassmuth's suggestion that the expression may be linked to the statement in a later Golden Age depiction that wealth will be "undivided" (Sib. Or. 2.321, ἄμοιρος) is promising.⁷⁴ In light of the parallel, Wassmuth interprets the phrase in book 1 as describing the abolition of current land allotments in service of a more just redistribution. While this is a reasonable possibility, the difficulty of the expression precludes a definitive claim that the sixth race was characterized by property redistribution. A clear assertion of common property must await the next Golden Age portrait in Sib. Or. 1–2, the picture of paradise associated with the tenth race.

The Tenth Race: Sib. Or. 2.6–33

The description of the tenth race in Sib. Or. 2.6–33, which rejoins the sequence of races disrupted by the Christian interpolation beginning at 1.324, almost certainly stems from the same Jewish author as 1.1–323.⁷⁵ Predicting various disasters, the Sibyl announces that "a tenth race of men will appear after these things," when God "will shake the people of seven-hilled Rome" (Sib. Or. 2.15–18).⁷⁶ Although most humans will be destroyed, the pious that remain will enjoy an Arcadian existence:

> Then the great God who dwells in heaven will again become the savior of pious men in every way. Then there will also be abundant peace and unity, and the fruitful earth will again bear more produce, not being divided and no longer enslaved. Every harbor, every anchorage will be free for people, as it was before, and shamelessness will cease. (Sib. Or. 2.27–33)⁷⁷

The general Golden Age themes of divine favor, peace, unity, and agricultural fertility are present, and the cessation of "shamelessness" (Sib. Or. 2.33, ἀναιδείη) may refer back to the first, abortive "golden" race of 1.65–86, who "laughed shamelessly"

---

⁷³ In addition to Wassmuth's interpretation, approaches to this phrase include the following: (1) Collins ("Sibylline Oracles," 1:341) translates μοίρας as "fates," so that the three kings "will destroy the fates." (2) Lightfoot (*Sibylline Oracles*, 414) presumes that the verse should state that "the three kings share the world" but is skeptical that such an emendation can be justified. (3) Alfons Kurfess ("Ad oracula Sibyllina," SO 28 [1950]: 96) does emend the verse, adopting the reading μοίρας διακληρώσονται, "will now distribute lots" (werden nun die Lose verteilen). Wassmuth (*Sibyllinische Orakel 1–2*, 180) understands this as equivalent to his own interpretation, although Wassmuth does not emend the verse.

⁷⁴ Wassmuth, *Sibyllinische Orakel 1–2*, 180.

⁷⁵ So Bousset ("Sibyllen," 18:273), Collins ("Development," *ANRW* 20.1:441), Geffcken (*Komposition*, 48), and Rzach ("Sibyllinische Orakel," 2:2146). Wassmuth (ibid., 471) suggests a Jewish layer behind 2.6–26 that was revised and expanded to 2.6–33 by the Christian redactor.

⁷⁶ δεκάτη γενεὴ μετὰ ταῦτα φανεῖται/ἀνθρώπων ... λαόν τε τινάξει/Ῥώμης ἑπταλόφοιο.

⁷⁷ τότε δ' αὖτε μέγας θεὸς αἰθέρι ναίων/ἀνδρῶν εὐσεβέων σωτὴρ κατὰ πάντα γένηται./καὶ τότε δ' εἰρήνη τε βαθεῖα τε σύνεσις ἔσται,/καὶ γῆ καρποφόρος καρποὺς πάλι πλείονας οἴσει/οὐδὲ μεριζομένη οὐδ' εἰσέτι λατρεύουσα./πᾶς δὲ λιμήν, πᾶς ὅρμος ἐλεύθερος ἀνθρώποισιν/ἔσσεται, ὡς πάρος ἦεν, ἀναιδείη τ' ἀπολεῖται.

(Sib. Or. 1.74, ἀναιδῶς).⁷⁸ Most notable is the theme of common property, expressed here in the typical Golden Age modality of an unbounded earth.⁷⁹

Finally, the Golden Age character of this text is reinforced by its protological orientation: the earth "will again" be fertile, and access to earth and sea will be common, "as it was before" (Sib. Or. 2.30, 33).⁸⁰ Although the overview of history would now seem to be wrapped up, Sib. Or. 2 adds a second eschatological portrait of the righteous, in which common property appears even more prominently.

The Blessings of the Righteous: Sib. Or. 2.313–338

The origin of the second passage in which Sib. Or. 2 depicts the eschatological rewards of the righteous is unclear; disagreement persists as to which layer it belongs to.⁸¹ In either case, the Golden Age character of the account is unmistakable:

> The earth will be equally shared with all, not divided by walls or fences, and it will then bear more produce spontaneously. Property will be common and wealth undivided. In that place there will not be poor or rich, tyrant or slave; there will no longer be someone great or small, no kings and no leaders. Everyone will be together in common. (Sib. Or. 2.319–324)⁸²

Though the sixth race's explicit label of "golden" is missing, the use of a Golden Age model is clear. The most obvious Golden Age motifs here are the earth's spontaneous fertility and common property, and both are phrased in ways typical of the myth. This passage also has parallels with earlier Golden Age depictions in Sib. Or. 1–2; the closest verbal echo occurs in the descriptions of the undivided earth's production in the tenth race (Sib. Or. 2.30–31, καρποὺς πάλι πλείονας οἴσει οὐδὲ μεριζομένη) and in the present section (Sib. Or. 2.319–320, οὐ ... διαμεριζομένη καρποὺς τότε πλείονας οἴσει).

---

⁷⁸ This passage is classified as a specifically Golden Age description by Lightfoot (*Sibylline Oracles*, 414), Parke (*Sibyls*, 21 n. 28), and Wassmuth (*Sibyllinische Orakel 1–2*, 238).

⁷⁹ Identifying the undivided earth as a Golden Age reference is supported by the use of a parallel expression in 2.321, which is clearly a Golden Age portrait; see Wassmuth, *Sibyllinische Orakel 1–2*, 275. Interestingly, the usual motif of common access to the earth expands to include common access to the sea; this stands in contrast to the standard claim in Latin versions that the first age was free of all sea travel; see, for example, Ovid, *Metam.* 1.94–96; Tibullus, *El.* 1.3.37–40; Virgil, *Ecl.* 4.38–39.

⁸⁰ Lightfoot (*Sibylline Oracles*, 449) sees here a reversion to a "prelapsarian state." See also Wassmuth, *Sibyllinische Orakel 1–2*, 275, who describes it as an "original state theory" (Urstandstheorie).

⁸¹ Wassmuth (*Sibyllinische Orakel 1–2*, 443) thinks that this passage is Jewish because he sees it as the conclusion of the ten-generation scheme. More commonly, Sib. Or. 2.6–33, which explicitly mentions the tenth race, is thought to complete the original sequence. Geffcken (*Komposition*, 51) claims this section as part of the Christian revision due to his minority view that parts of book 2 are derived from book 8. Bousset ("Sibyllen," 18:273), Collins ("Development," *ANRW* 20.1:442), Alfons Kurfess ("Christian Sibyllines," in *New Testament Apocrypha*, ed. Edgar Hennecke and Wilhelm Schneemelcher, trans. Robert McLachlan Wilson [Philadelphia: Westminster, 1965], 1:707), and Rzach ("Sibyllinische Orakel," 2:2150) refuse to assign the passage to either layer.

⁸² γαῖα δ' ἴση πάντων οὐ τείχεσιν οὐ περιφραγμοῖς/διαμεριζομένη καρποὺς τότε πλείονας οἴσει/ αὐτομάτη, κοινοί τε βίοι καὶ πλοῦτος ἄμοιρος./οὐ γὰρ πτωχὸς ἐκεῖ, οὐ πλούσιος, οὐδὲ τύραννος,/ οὐ δοῦλος, οὐδ' αὖ μέγας, οὐ μικρός τις ἔτ' ἔσται,/οὐ βασιλεῖς, οὐχ ἡγεμόνες· κοινῇ δ' ἅμα πάντες.

The focus on common property here is noteworthy. Like Sib. Or. 2.27–33 and many Latin versions of the myth, this passage includes the motif of an undivided earth, but it restates the idea of commonality several times for emphasis: "equally shared," "not divided," "common," "undivided," "together in common." Wassmuth asserts that these verses contain the clearest extant expression of a Jewish expectation of a community of goods; if one grants Jewish authorship of this section, this assessment is correct.[83]

Summary: The Golden Age in Books 1–2 of the Sibylline Oracles

Sib. Or. 1–2 make the Golden Age myth a major structural principle, using the motif to link the beginning, middle, and end of the historical review with the conclusion of the eschatological section. The primary use of the myth is eschatological.[84] References to Hesiod's Golden Race do appear in the Oracle's description of the "first race," but a mix of negative motifs indicates that it is no true Golden Age. This is found instead at the end of history, as described in Sib. Or. 2.27–33 and 313–338, as well as in the sixth race. Even the sixth race can be seen as figuratively eschatological, occurring as it does after the catastrophe of the flood.[85] Common property is also an eschatological concept in books 1–2, and its prominence grows as the work proceeds toward its eschatological conclusion. Completely absent from the spurious Golden Age of the first race, common property is arguably hinted at in the account of the sixth race, clearly appears in the brief eschatological portrait in 2.27–33, and finally becomes a major characteristic of eschatological blessedness in 2.313–338.

Rome has not appeared in this discussion of the Golden Age in Sib. Or. 1–2, an absence corresponding to the relative lack of interest that these books show in Rome. In the next text to be examined, Sib. Or. 8, the situation changes dramatically: book 8 not only takes up the Golden Age theme but also contains some of the most intense anti-Roman polemic of the entire collection.

The Golden Age in Book 8 of the Sibylline Oracles

Like the first two books, Sib. Or. 8 applies Golden Age imagery in eschatological descriptions and makes common property a central theme of these passages. In addition, the idea of common property informs a major contrast that runs throughout book 8: the inequality of the present age versus the equality of the eschaton. This contrast functions as part of a polemic against Rome, and the most important aspect of Sib. Or. 8 for this study is that it contains the clearest example of an empire-critical use of the Golden Age theme in general and of the motif of common property in particular.

---

[83] Wassmuth, *Sibyllinische Orakel 1–2*, 455.
[84] Ibid., 167.
[85] Ibid., 166, 168.

Even more than the first two books of the Sibylline Oracles, book 8 is almost universally acknowledged to be a composite work.[86] The two main sections discernable are vv. 1–216, which consist mostly of politically oriented oracles directed primarily against Rome, and vv. 217–500, which contain Christian reflections on subjects such as the incarnation and idolatry. Although various parts of Sib. Or. 8.1–216 have been assigned to pagan or Christian authors, the origin of most of this section is usually thought to be Jewish.[87] John J. Collins and Aloisius Rzach argue that the polemic against Hadrian in vv. 50–59 is best read as a Jewish response to the suppression of the Bar Kokhba revolt, and the Christian elements ubiquitous in vv. 217–500 are absent from this earlier section.[88] Despite occasional dissent, Collins' judgment that Jewish authorship for most of Sib. Or. 8.1–216 enjoys "a slight balance of probability" is correct.[89]

The date of the first part of book 8 can be specified within a couple of decades. Verses 68–72 predict a return of Nero during the reign of Marcus Aurelius (r. 161–180 CE), making 180 the *terminus ante quem* for the writing of the Jewish layer.[90] The Christian redaction obviously postdates the original Jewish composition, and portions of the revision are quoted by Lactantius; a third-century date is therefore most likely.[91] The provenance of both the base text and the Christian revision is unclear.[92]

A Condemnation of Greed: Sib. Or. 8.17–36

The polemic against greed in Sib. Or. 8.17–36 belongs to the late second-century Jewish layer of book 8. This passage follows an announcement of "God's wrath towards the last age" (Sib. Or. 8.2), which is dominated by "the famous unlawful kingdom of the Italians" (Sib. Or. 8.9). This kingdom "will show forth many evils to mortals" (Sib. Or. 8.10), and vv. 17–36 attack greed specifically as the "beginning of evils":

---

[86] Bousset, "Sibyllen," 18:275; Collins, "Sibylline Oracles," 1:415; Gauger, *Sibyllinische Weissagungen*, 457–8; Geffcken, *Komposition*, 41–2; Goodman, "Jewish Writings," 645 n. 248; Arnaldo Momigliano, "From the Pagan to the Christian Sibyl: Prophecy as History of Religion," in *Nono contributo alla storia degli studi classici e del mondo antico*, ed. Riccardo Di Donato, Storia e letteratura 180 (Rome: Edizioni di storia e letteratura, 1992), 732; Parke, *Sibyls*, 171 n. 5; Rzach, "Sibyllinische Orakel," 2:2144.

[87] Collins, "Sibylline Oracles," 1:416; Gauger, *Sibyllinische Weissagungen*, 458; Goodman, "Jewish Writings," 645 n. 248; Momigliano, "From the Pagan to the Christian Sibyl," 732; Parke, *Sibyls*, 175 n. 1; Rzach, "Sibyllinische Orakel," 2:2143–44.

[88] Collins, "Sibylline Oracles," 1:416; Rzach, "Sibyllinische Orakel," 2:2143. Collins (ibid.) and Rzach (ibid., 2:2144) also find Jewish elements in the discussion of Nero's return (Sib. Or. 8.139–150).

[89] Collins, "Sibylline Oracles," 1:416. Bousset ("Sibyllen," 18:277), Geffcken (*Komposition*, 44), and Kurfess ("Christian Sibyllines," 1:707) suggest a Christian origin for all of book 8, although none makes any compelling arguments for this position.

[90] Collins, "Sibylline Oracles," 1:416; Gauger, *Sibyllinische Weissagungen*, 457–8; Geffcken, *Komposition*, 41; Kurfess, "Christian Sibyllines," 1:707; Rzach, "Sibyllinische Orakel," 2:2143. Based on a prediction of the destruction of Rome in 195 (Sib. Or. 8.148–150), Momigliano ("From the Pagan to the Christian Sibyl," 732) and Parke (*Sibyls*, 1) give the latest date of Jewish layer as 195 CE.

[91] The Christian revision of book 8 is dated to the third century by Bousset ("Sibyllen," 18:275), Gauger (*Sibyllinische Weissagungen*, 458), Geffcken (*Komposition*, 46), Momigliano ("From the Pagan to the Christian Sibyl," 732), and Rzach ("Sibyllinische Orakel," 2:2146).

[92] Collins, "Development," *ANRW* 20.1:447; Gauger, *Sibyllinische Weissagungen*, 457–8.

> The beginning of evils for all will be love of money and folly, for there will be desire for deceitful gold and silver. For mortals have preferred nothing before these …. It is a fount of impiety and a harbinger of disorder, an engine of war, a hostile bane of peace that makes parents hateful to children and children to parents. (Sib. Or. 8.17–26)[93]

This description recalls aspects of the Iron Age, particularly as presented by Ovid in the *Metamorphoses*: Ovid portrays this age as seized by "lust for possession" (*Metam.* 1.131), and he identifies gold as the means of warfare (*Metam.* 1.145–148) and links it to strife between family members (*Metam.* 1.142). The similarities increase as the Oracle turns to the theme of private property:

> The earth will have boundaries, and the whole sea guards, being deceitfully divided between all those who possess gold. As though wanting to possess forever the earth, which feeds many, they will plunder the poor so that they may enslave them and acquire more land by pretense. If the enormous earth did not have its throne far away from the sparkling heaven, men would not have an equal share of light, but the rich would have bought it with gold. (Sib. Or. 8.28–35)[94]

Like Ovid, Sib. Or. 8 regards land boundaries as a marker of decline (cf. *Metam.* 1.136), and Ovid also compares previously common land to sunlight (*Metam.* 1.135).[95] The combination of a bounded earth and a divided sea also recalls the Golden Age description of Sib. Or. 2.29–33, which pairs an undivided earth with free access to the sea.

This attack on unrestrained privatization forms part of a larger polemic against Rome.[96] Anti-Roman prophecies immediately precede and follow Sib. Or. 8.17–36, and the theme of Rome's wealth and greed continues in the subsequent sections. The Oracle says to "haughty Rome" that its "wealth will be lost" (Sib. Or. 8.37, 40), that Hadrian, although "having abundant gold and silver," will still "gather more" (Sib. Or. 8.54–55), and that Marcus Aurelius "will guard and shut up all the money of the world in his halls" (Sib. Or. 8.69–70). Verses 17–36 thus criticize Rome specifically for its avarice and especially for its immoderate desire to possess what should be common property.

---

[93] ἀρχὴ πᾶσι κακῶν φιλοχρημοσύνη καὶ ἄνοια./χρυσοῦ γὰρ δολίοιο καὶ ἀργυρίου πόθος ἔσται./ οὐδὲν γὰρ τούτων θνητοὶ μεῖζον προέκριναν/ … πηγὴ δυσσεβίης καὶ ἀταξίης προοδηγός,/μηχανίη πολέμων, εἰρήνης ἐχθρὰ ἀνία/ἐχθραίνουσα τέκνοις γονέας καὶ τέκνα γονεῦσιν.
[94] γαῖά θ' ὅρους ἕξει καὶ φρουροὺς πᾶσα θάλασσα/πᾶσι μεριζομένη δολίως τοῖς χρυσὸν ἔχουσιν·/ ὡς αἰῶσι θέλοντες ἔχειν πολυθρέμμονα γαῖαν/πορθήσουσι πένητας, ἵν' αὐτοὶ πλείονα χῶρον/ προσπορίσαντες ἀλαζονίῃ καταδουλώσωσιν./κεὶ μὴ γαῖα πέλωρος ἀπ' οὐρανοῦ ἀστερόεντος/τὸν θρόνον εἶχε μακρήν, οὐκ ἦν ἴσον ἀνδράσι φέγγος,/ἀλλ' ἀγοραζόμενον χρυσῷ πλουτοῦσιν ὑπῆρχεν.
[95] The shared themes between the *Metamorphoses* and Sib. Or. 8 are not specific enough to posit direct dependence, but they do indicate how well this passage fits with explicitly Golden Age accounts.
[96] Collins ("Sibylline Oracles," 1:417) and Geffcken (*Komposition*, 42) both see 8.17–36 as directed against Rome specifically.

Equality in Hades: Sib. Or. 8.107-121

Book 8's assault on the Empire continues in Sib. Or. 8.73-106. These verses tell of God's "inexorable wrath" against Rome, which "will be utterly destroyed and will be burning ash forever" (Sib. Or. 8.93, 103-104). The Oracle eventually places Rome in Hades and then describes the conditions there, emphasizing the equality of its inhabitants:

> Night is equally shared by all together, by those who have wealth and by the poor .... No one is a slave there, no master, no tyrant, no kings, no leaders with great affectation .... There is no strife, no manifold wrath, and no sword at the side of the perishing, but the age is common to all. (Sib. Or. 8.107-121)[97]

This is certainly no Golden Age portrait, but it has parallels with the accounts of the eschaton in books 2 and 8 that are colored by the myth. In the end-time Golden Age of the righteous, "there will not be poor or rich, tyrant or slave, there will no longer be someone great or small, no kings and no leaders" (Sib. Or. 2.322-324). Just as the age "is common to all" here in Hades, so in paradise "everyone will be together in common" (Sib. Or. 2.324), and "property and wealth will be common to all" (Sib. Or. 8.208).

This picture of Hades thus serves as a photographic negative of the images of the Golden Age of the righteous in the Sibylline Oracles: just as the righteous will enjoy an eschatological equality, sharing God's bounty, so Rome will experience a leveling in Hades, an equality through deprivation. Like Sib. Or. 8.17-36, this passage is part of a larger critique of Rome. The description of Hades is the culmination of a prophecy of Rome's destruction, and the equality that Rome will experience in the eschaton contrasts with the inequality it has created through unrestrained acquisition.

The Blessings of the Righteous: Sib. Or. 8.205-212

The authorship of the third and last passage from book 8 to be considered here, Sib. Or. 8.205-212, is less certain than that of the remaining portions of the book. Some scholars assign it to the earlier layer along with the rest of vv. 1-216, to which it belongs thematically.[98] Redaction by a later, Christian author, however, is more likely.[99] Collins argues that Sib. Or. 8.196-197, which speaks of a "holy child" who will "utterly destroy the baleful abyss," depends on Rev 20.[100] Furthermore, the prediction of healing in 8.205-207 shares language with and is almost certainly derived from a Christian portion of

---

[97] πᾶσιν ὁμοῦ νύξ ἐστιν ἴση τοῖς πλοῦτον ἔχουσιν/καὶ πτωχοῖς ... οὐδεὶς δοῦλος ἐκεῖ, οὐ κύριος, οὐδὲ τύραννος,/οὐ βασιλεῖς, οὐχ ἡγεμόνες μάλα τῦφον ἔχοντες/ ... οὐκ ἔρις, οὐκ ὀργὴ πολυποίκιλος, οὐδὲ μάχαιρα/ἔστι παρὰ φθιμένοις, ἀλλ' αἰὼν κοινὸς ἅπασιν.
[98] Geffcken, *Komposition*, 41; Rzach, "Sibyllinische Orakel," 2:2144. Geffcken thinks that 8.1-216 is itself a composite of two Christian layers, but he assigns vv. 169-216 to the earlier of these.
[99] Bousset, "Sibyllen," 18:277; Collins, "Sibylline Oracles," 1:416.
[100] Collins, "Sibylline Oracles," 1:416.

book 1 (vv. 353–355).¹⁰¹ Whether Sib. Or. 8.205–212 is an original Christian composition or a Christian redaction of a Jewish eschatological account is unclear; as a result, the date of writing for the common property claims in 8.207–210 cannot be narrowed beyond a range that includes both layers of the text, the late second or third century CE.

The eschatological description that concludes Sib. Or. 8.1–216 continues themes from earlier in the book. Rome is still a special object of focus, as it is the only specific place mentioned in the passage (Sib. Or. 8.171). Immoderate acquisition is highlighted once again: the wicked "will not be sated with wealth but will shamelessly gather more" (Sib. Or. 8.188–189). Recalling the ten races of books 1–2, the climax of the account occurs "when the tenth race [ἡ δεκάτη γενεή] is in the house of Hades" (Sib. Or. 8.199). After the earth has been laid waste, resurrection will be followed by a Golden Age:

> There will be a rising of the dead and the swiftest running of the lame. The deaf will hear, the blind will see, and those not speaking will speak. Property and wealth will be common to all. And the earth will be equally shared with all, not divided by walls or fences, and it will then bear more produce and give springs of sweet wine, milk, and honey. (Sib. Or. 8.205–212)¹⁰²

Like the previous two passages from book 8 examined here, this description has parallels with Sib. Or. 2. The clearest borrowing occurs in the statement, "and the earth will be equally shared with all, not divided by walls or fences, and it will then bear more produce," which shares twelve of thirteen Greek words with Sib. Or. 2.319–320. The remarks that "property and wealth will be common to all" and that the earth will "give springs of sweet wine, milk, and honey" differ slightly more in wording from their counterparts in book 2, but Sib. Or. 2.313–338 is likely their source as well.

Summary: The Golden Age in Book 8 of the Sibylline Oracles

While the Golden Age myth is not as structurally central for Sib. Or. 8 as for books 1–2, the motif of common property does play an important role in the anti-Roman polemic that pervades Sib. Or. 8.1–216.¹⁰³ One major point of attack against Rome is its greed and, more specifically, its attempt to privatize what is properly common.¹⁰⁴

---

¹⁰¹ Collins (ibid.) thinks that 8.205–207 "probably depends on Matthew 11:5," although he allows that it might also come from Sib. Or. 1.353–355. The latter option is preferable, as Sib. Or. 1.353–355 and 8.205–207 have instances of identical wording that are absent from Matt 11:5: νεκρῶν δ' ἐπανάστασις ἔσται (Sib. Or. 1.355; 8.205) and λαλήσουσ' οὐ λαλέοντες (Sib. Or. 1.354; 8.207).

¹⁰² νεκρῶν δ' ἐπανάστασις ἔσται·/καὶ χωλῶν δρόμος ὠκύτατος καὶ κωφὸς ἀκούσει/καὶ τυφλοὶ βλέψουσι, λαλήσουσ' οὐ λαλέοντες,/καὶ κοινὸς πάντεσσι βίος καὶ πλοῦτος ἐσεῖται./γαῖα δ' ἴση πάντων οὐ τείχεσιν οὐ περιφραγμοῖς/διαμεριζομένη καρποὺς ποτε πλείονας οἴσει,/πηγὰς δὲ γλυκεροῦ οἴνου λευκοῦ τε γάλακτος/καὶ μέλιτος δώσει.

¹⁰³ Collins ("Sibylline Oracles," 1:417) identifies "the coming destruction of Rome" as the "main theme" of the Jewish layer and draws attention to 8.1–216 as "a striking example of anti-Roman prophecy." See also Kurfess, "Christian Sibyllines," 1:707; Momigliano, "From the Pagan to the Christian Sibyl," 732; Geffcken, *Komposition*, 41.

¹⁰⁴ "The explicit basis for this polemic is not, as we might expect, Rome's violation of the sovereignty of any particular people (even the Jews) but rather her greed and social injustice (vss. 18–36)" (Collins, "Sibylline Oracles," 1:417).

Common property is the primary motif that connects the Golden Age eschatology of 8.205–212 with the preceding polemics: the community of property that exists in paradise contrasts with Rome's attempt to privatize earth and sea, and it is the positive counterpart to the leveling that Rome will experience in Hades. The intersection here of Golden Age eschatology, the motif of common property, and criticism of Rome makes Sib. Or. 8 a most valuable example for this study.

The Golden Age in Book 14 of the Sibylline Oracles

The last appearance of Golden Age–inflected eschatology in the Sibylline Oracles may be treated more briefly, as it adds nothing substantial to the texts already surveyed. Nevertheless, the fact that a portrait of a Golden Age of common property forms the coda to the entire sibylline corpus, appearing in the concluding passage of the final book, is noteworthy. Book 14 may have been compiled as early as the latter half of the third century CE, but it is often dated later.[105] Jewish authorship is commonly supposed.[106]

Whatever the date of the final version of book 14, both Collins and Walter Scott suggest that its eschatological coda, Sib. Or. 14.351–361, was written much earlier and appended to successive revisions.[107] The Golden Age coloring is by now quite familiar:

> There will no longer be deceitful gold or silver, no possession of the earth, no toilsome slavery, but one friendship and one way of life for a cheerful people. All things will be common, and one light will be equally shared with humankind. (Sib. Or. 14.351–354)[108]

The statement "all things will be common" recalls the predictions of common property in the eschatological descriptions of Sib. Or. 2.313–338 and 8.205–212, but this passage also seems to be dependent on the condemnation of greed in 8.17–36. The absence here of "deceitful gold" contrasts with the "desire for deceitful gold" in Sib. Or. 8.18, while the remark that "one light will be equally shared" recalls the claim in 8.34 that, if the rich could buy access to it, "men would not have an equal share of light."

The uncertainty regarding the date of Sib. Or. 14.351–361 limits its value as evidence. Nevertheless, these verses are an additional, conspicuously placed witness to the importance of the Golden Age myth in general and the common property motif in particular for the authors of the Sibylline Oracles, especially in eschatological contexts.

---

[105] Bousset ("Sibyllen," 18:279) dates book 14 to the late third century CE, while Geffcken (*Komposition*, 67) and Rzach ("Sibyllinische Orakel," 2:2165) place it in the fourth century or later.
[106] Collins, "Development," *ANRW* 20.1:452; Geffcken, *Komposition*, 68; Rzach, "Sibyllinische Orakel," 2:2165; Scott, "Last Sibylline Oracle," 144. Bousset ("Sibyllen," 18:279) is alone in considering book 14 a Christian work. Collins ("Sibylline Oracles," 1:459) and Scott (ibid.) think the book was written in Alexandria, although Rzach ("Sibyllinische Orakel," 2:2165) disputes this.
[107] Collins, "Development," *ANRW* 20.1:452; Scott, "Last Sibylline Oracle," 145.
[108] οὐκέτι γὰρ δόλιος χρυσὸς οὐδ' ἄργυρος ἔσται,/οὐ κτῆσις γαίης, οὐ δουλείη πολύμοχθος·/ἀλλὰ μίη φιλότης τε καὶ εἷς τρόπος εὔφρονι δήμῳ·/κοινὰ δὲ πάντ' ἔσται καὶ φῶς ἴσον ἐν βιότοιο.

Summary: The Golden Age Myth in the Sibylline Oracles

The Sibylline Oracles provide the best evidence regarding Jewish and Christian usage of the Golden Age myth in the first two centuries CE. The most relevant observations follow. (1) The Sibylline Oracles demonstrate extensive Jewish and Christian literary use of the Golden Age myth in the first and second centuries CE. In Sib. Or. 1–2, Hesiod's myth is a central structuring principle, and elements of the myth appear multiple times in the eighth book. (2) The primary application of the Golden Age myth is in eschatological descriptions. The "first race" in book 1 is conspicuously *not* a Golden Race; the post-flood generation, a type of the post-judgment righteous, is instead the first race to be labelled "golden." All the remaining Golden Age passages in the Sibylline Oracles are eschatological. (3) In book 8, the Golden Age myth is used in anti-Roman polemic. Rome is condemned for its greed and excessive privatization, in stark contrast with the Golden Age of the righteous portrayed at the end of book 8, when "property and wealth will be common to all" (Sib. Or. 8.208). (4) In the Sibylline Oracles, common property becomes perhaps the most characteristic feature of the Golden Age. The eschatological Golden Ages of books 2, 8, and 14 all feature a community of property, and common property connects the concluding eschatological portrait of book 8 to the preceding polemics against Rome.

Summary: The Golden Age Myth in Jewish and Christian Sources

In the overall argument of this study, the main role of the current chapter is to evaluate whether the supplementary criterion of "occurrence in other authors" is satisfied for a possible Lukan allusion to the Golden Age myth. The evidence presented in this chapter fulfills this criterion. In the first and second centuries CE, Jewish and Christian authors such as Philo, Josephus, and multiple writers and redactors of the Sibylline Oracles made use of the Golden Age myth for their own literary purposes.

Three further observations about Jewish and Christian uses of the Golden Age myth are of value for this study, and these correspond to the three innovations of Virgil identified in Chapter 2. First, the Golden Age motif often appears in eschatological depictions. This fits with Virgil's idea of a future return of the Golden Age. Sibylline Oracles 2 makes this notion of a returning age explicit when it states that the eschaton will produce Golden Age conditions "again" and "as it was before" (Sib. Or. 2.30, 33).

Second, most of the Jewish and Christian Golden Age references examined in this chapter occur in texts linked more or less closely to Rome. Philo's *Legatio* focuses on the misbehavior of a Roman emperor, Josephus' *Antiquities* is written from Rome, and the Sibylline Oracles adopt as a mouthpiece a prophetess strongly associated with Rome. Furthermore, Sib. Or. 8.1–216 is shot through with anti-Roman invective, and elements of the Golden Age myth are used to advance the book's polemic. While the attitudes displayed toward the Empire in these texts are often strongly at odds with those presented in Virgil's works, it is the close connection between the Golden Age theme and Rome, inaugurated in the fourth *Eclogue* and the *Aeneid*, that is likely responsible for the fact that Jewish and Christian authors employ this myth in texts oriented toward Rome.

Third, the motif of common property, which Virgil first inserts into the myth, is central to Jewish and Christian use of the Golden Age idea. Philo, Josephus, and all four of the eschatological Golden Age passages in the Sibylline Oracles employ this motif. The appearances of common property surveyed in this chapter are summarized in Table 3.2.

With the relevant Jewish and Christian texts now compiled, the Latin and Greek vocabulary for the Golden Age motif of common property can be compared. Boundaries and the act of dividing typify the Iron Age, while the Golden Age is characterized by property being common rather than private.

Table 3.2 Common Property in Jewish and Christian Golden Age Texts

Author/Date	English Translation	Original Greek
Philo 37–41 CE	They have determined to present their goods to the community, for common enjoyment and advantage (*Praem.* 87–88).	τὰ ἴδια προφέρειν εἰς μέσον ἀγαθὰ διεγνωκόσιν εἰς κοινὴν μετουσίαν καὶ ἀπόλαυσιν
Unknown 0–70 CE	The fruitful earth will again bear more produce, not being divided and no longer enslaved. Every harbor, every anchorage will be free for people, as it was before (Sib. Or. 2.30–33).	γῆ καρποφόρος καρποὺς πάλι πλείονας οἴσει/οὐδὲ μεριζομένη οὐδ' εἰσέτι λατρεύουσα./πᾶς δὲ λιμήν, πᾶς ὅρμος ἐλεύθερος ἀνθρώποισιν/ ἔσσεται, ὡς πάρος ἦν.
Josephus 93–94 CE	He [Cain] was the first to place boundaries on land (*A.J.* 1.62).	ὅρους τε γῆς πρῶτος ἔθετο
Unknown 0–150 CE	Property will be common and wealth undivided…. Everyone will be together in common (Sib. Or. 2.321, 324).	κοινοί τε βίοι καὶ πλοῦτος ἄμοιρος/ … κοινῇ δ' ἅμα πάντες
Unknown 161–180 CE	The earth will have boundaries and the whole sea guards, being deceitfully divided between all those who possess gold (Sib. Or. 8.28–29).	γαῖά θ' ὅρους ἕξει καὶ φρουροὺς πᾶσα θάλασσα/πᾶσι μεριζομένη δολίως τοῖς χρυσὸν ἔχουσιν
Unknown 161–180 CE	The age is common to all (Sib. Or. 8.121).	αἰὼν κοινὸς ἅπασιν
Unknown 161–300 CE	Property and wealth will be common to all. And the earth will be equally shared with all, not divided by walls or fences (Sib. Or. 8.208–210).	κοινὸς πάντεσσι βίος καὶ πλοῦτος ἐσεῖται./γαῖα δ' ἴση πάντων οὐ τείχεσιν οὐ περιφραγμοῖς/ διαμεριζομένη
Unknown 2nd–7th c. CE	There will no longer be deceitful gold and silver, no possession of the earth…. All things will be common, and one light will be equally shared with mankind (Sib. Or. 14.351–354).	οὐκέτι γὰρ δόλιος χρυσὸς οὐδ' ἄργυρος ἔσται,/οὐ κτῆσις γαίης … κοινὰ δὲ πάντ' ἔσται καὶ φῶς ἴσον ἐν βιότοιο

The main words for "common" in these descriptions are *communis* in Latin and κοίνος in Greek, along with derivative words that share these roots. Trogus and Philo provide the contrary Latin and Greek terms, *privatus* and ἴδιος. While this language is not peculiar to descriptions of the Golden Age or even common property in general, what Table 3.3 does indicate is that words like κοίνος and κοινωνία would constitute common, perhaps even standard, terminology for Greek-language Golden Age accounts.

Chapter 2 showed that early imperial versions of the Golden Age myth (1) commonly predicted the advent of a new age, figured as the return of a primeval Golden Age of peace and divine presence, (2) were often used to comment, positively and even occasionally negatively, on Rome and the emperor, and (3) regularly included the motif of common property. Chapter 3 has indicated that Jewish and Christian allusions to the Golden Age from this period also (1) often appeared in descriptions of a coming age of human concord and divine care, sometimes conceived of as a return to primeval conditions, (2) occurred in works with some Roman orientation and were at times used to criticize Rome, and (3) regularly included the motif of common property.

Table 3.3 Property Language in Golden Age Accounts

Concept	Latin Terms		Greek Terms	
Boundary (noun)	*limes*	Virgil, *Georg.* 1.126 Ovid, *Am.* 3.8.42 Ovid, *Metam.* 1.136	ὅρος	Josephus, *A.J.* 1.62 Sib. Or. 8.28
	finis	Tibullus, *El.* 1.3.44 Seneca, *Ep.* 90.39		
	terminus	Germanicus, *Arat.* 118		
To divide (verb)	*partio* *divido*	Virgil, *Georg.* 1.126 Seneca, *Phaed.* 529	μερίζω	Sib. Or. 2.31 Sib. Or. 8.29
			διαμερίζω	Sib. Or. 2.320 Sib. Or. 8.210
Private (adjective)	*privatus*	Trogus, *Ep.* 43.1.3	ἴδιος	Philo, *Praem.* 87
Common (adjective)	*communis*	Trogus, *Ep.* 43.1.3 Ovid, *Metam.* 1.135 *Oct.* 403	κοίνος	Philo, *Praem.* 88 Plutarch, *Cim.* 10.6 Sib. Or. 2.321
	publicus	Seneca, *Ep.* 90.38		Sib. Or. 8.121 Sib. Or. 8.208 Sib. Or. 14.354
			ἴσος	Sib. Or. 2.319 Sib. Or. 8.107 Sib. Or. 8.209 Sib. Or. 14.354
In common/for the community (adverb)	*in medium* *in medio* *promiscue* *in commune*	Virgil, *Georg.* 1.127 Seneca, *Ep.* 90.36 Seneca, *Ep.* 90.36 Seneca, *Ep.* 90.38	εἰς μέσον κοινῇ	Philo, *Praem.* 88 Sib. Or. 2.324
Commonality (abstract noun)	—		κοινωνία	Philo, *Praem.* 87 Plutarch, *Cim.* 10.7

In Chapter 4, I turn to Luke-Acts itself. The presence of the common property motif in Acts 2:42–47 and 4:32–35 is obvious; I will argue that the other two characteristics of Jewish and Christian use of the Golden Age motif that have been highlighted here also fit with a proposed Golden Age allusion in the Acts summaries. First, due to the eschatological nature of the Spirit's coming in Acts, the summaries, which directly follow outpourings of the Spirit, can be considered as eschatological depictions. Second, Luke not only shows a strong interest in Rome but even employs imperial language on occasion to make supra-imperial claims for Christ.

4

Preliminaries to a Golden Age Reading of the Acts Summaries

With the basic features and functions of the Golden Age myth in Greek, Roman, Jewish, and Christian sources now established, I now turn my focus to Luke-Acts. Prior to the focused exegesis of Acts 2:42–47 and 4:32–35 that will occupy Chapter 5, this chapter treats three broader aspects of Luke's writings that are important preliminaries for a Golden Age interpretation of these summaries. First, I argue that Luke presents Acts 2:42–47 and 4:32–35 as descriptions of an eschatological lifestyle. As such, these passages are of the sort most likely to use Golden Age imagery, per the findings of Chapter 3. Second, this chapter manifests Luke's interest in Rome, again with an eye to the observation in Chapter 3 that Jewish and Christian uses of Golden Age imagery often occur in works concerned with Rome. Third, claims that Luke refers to Golden Age ideology in his infancy narrative are examined and judged to be inconclusive. While Luke does employ imperial language more than once, a specific use of the Golden Age myth in Luke 2 remains unproven and the optional criterion of "recurrence in the same author" unfulfilled.

Acts 2:42–47 and 4:32–35 as Eschatological Descriptions

Chapter 3 showed that Jewish and Christian uses of the Golden Age myth often occurred in eschatological depictions, and in this section I establish that Luke presents the summaries in Acts 2:42–47 and 4:32–35 as descriptions of an eschatological lifestyle. After an overview of perspectives on Lukan eschatology, I examine Luke's redaction of Joel 3:1 LXX in Acts 2:17. This passage interprets the coming of the Spirit as an event marking "the last days," designating the present time as a new age and marking phenomena associated with the Spirit as eschatological in nature. Next, I show that the summaries are portraits of a way of life that directly results from outpourings of the Spirit. As a result, the summaries' portrayal of a Spirit-filled lifestyle constitutes a sort of eschatological description.

Eschatology in Luke-Acts: Conzelmann and His Responders

Since the mid-1950s, debates about Luke's eschatology have mostly consisted of responses to the thesis of Conzelmann, who argues that the driving factor for Luke's eschatological stance is "the delay of the parousia."¹ Due to this delay, Luke has "abandoned belief in the early expectation," pushing Jesus' return to a distant, indefinite future time.² In place of imminent eschatology, Luke offers a scheme of salvation history, an "outline of the successive stages in redemptive history."³ This scheme has three main phases: the "period of Israel," the "period of Jesus," and the "period of the Church and of the Spirit."⁴ Since the present age of the Spirit lacks any imminent expectation, Conzelmann argues that the "Spirit Himself is no longer the eschatological gift, but the substitute in the meantime for the possession of ultimate salvation."⁵

Conzelmann's proposals have been accepted by some; Ernst Haenchen, for instance, agrees that Luke "denied the imminent expectation" and presented instead a "history of salvation" in "three periods."⁶ Disagreement has been more common. A few scholars, such as Andrew Mattill and John Nolland, assert the contrary to Conzelmann's position, denying the premise that Luke rejected imminent eschatology.⁷ Most often, an intermediate approach is adopted that recognizes in Luke-Acts both a delay motif and aspects of realized or imminent eschatology.⁸ Among these authors, Luke's emphasis is commonly thought to be on the present stage, "on the reality of the present fulfilment of eschatological hopes."⁹

The thesis that Luke-Acts contains elements of both present and future eschatology is correct.¹⁰ Luke's focus on present eschatology appears quite clearly in Acts 2:17–21, a passage that is particularly relevant here: Acts 2:17–21 is the eschatological text in closest proximity to the summary in Acts 2:42–47, and it includes the most explicit claim that the present is itself an eschatological age.

---

1. Hans Conzelmann, *The Theology of St. Luke*, trans. Geoffrey Buswell (New York: Harper, 1961) 97; originally published in German in 1954.
2. Ibid., 135.
3. Ibid.
4. Ibid., 150.
5. Ibid., 95.
6. Haenchen, *Acts*, 96.
7. Andrew Jacob Mattill Jr., "Naherwartung, Fernerwartung, and the Purpose of Luke-Acts: Weymouth Reconsidered," *CBQ* 34 (1972): 285, 292–3; John Nolland, "Salvation-History and Eschatology," in *Witness to the Gospel: The Theology of Acts*, ed. I. Howard Marshall and David Peterson (Grand Rapids: Eerdmans, 1998), 65.
8. Darrell L. Bock, *A Theology of Luke and Acts*, Biblical Theology of the New Testament (Grand Rapids: Zondervan, 2012), 399; E. Earle Ellis, *Eschatology in Luke*, FBBS 30 (Philadelphia: Fortress, 1972), 13; Beverly Roberts Gaventa, "The Eschatology of Luke-Acts Revisited," *Enc* 43 (1982): 38, 42; William Kurz, "Acts 3:19–26 as a Test of the Role of Eschatology in Lukan Christology," *SBLSP* 16 (1977): 311–13; S. G. Wilson, "Lukan Eschatology," *NTS* 16 (1969–1970): 345, 347; Witherington III, *Acts*, 186.
9. Robert L. Maddox, *The Purpose of Luke-Acts*, FRLANT 126 (Göttingen: Vandenhoeck & Ruprecht, 1982), 145. That Luke's emphasis falls on present eschatological fulfillment is also asserted by Bradley J. Chance (*Jerusalem, the Temple, and the New Age in Luke-Acts* [Macon, GA: Mercer University Press, 1988], 140), Fred O. Francis ("Eschatology and History in Luke-Acts," *JAAR* 37 [1969]: 62), Keener (*Acts 1:1–2:47*, 686), and I. Howard Marshall (*Luke: Historian and Theologian*, 3rd ed. [Grand Rapids: Academie, 1989], 134).
10. Commonly cited instances of present and imminent eschatology include Luke 11:20 ("The kingdom of God has come to you") and Luke 21:31–32 ("When you see these things taking place, you know that the kingdom of God is near. Truly I tell you, this generation will not pass away until all things have taken place"). Examples of future eschatology include Luke 19:11, where Luke identifies the parable of the Minas as a corrective for those who "supposed the kingdom of God was to appear immediately," and multiple redactions in Luke 21:5–36 to Mark 13 aimed at an "eschatological phase clarification" that "accommodates a delay in the completion of the eschatological scenario" (John T. Carroll, *Response to the End of History: Eschatology and Situation in Luke-Acts*, SBLDS 92 [Decatur, GA: Scholars Press, 1988], 108, 110).

Realized Eschatology in Acts 2:17–21

Acts 2:14–40 presents Peter's speech following the manifestation of the Spirit on Pentecost. To explain the events, Peter quotes Joel 3:1–5 LXX; most significantly for the eschatology of Luke-Acts, the quotation locates the gift of the Spirit "in the last days":

> In the last days it will be, God declares, that I will pour out my Spirit upon all flesh, and your sons and your daughters shall prophesy, and your young men shall see visions, and your old men shall dream dreams. (Acts 2:17)

This is the only place where Luke uses the adjective ἔσχατος ("last") temporally, and it seems to be a Lukan redaction. Joel 3:1 LXX locates the outpouring of the Spirit "after these things" (μετὰ ταῦτα), but Luke's quotation, per the NA[28], replaces this phrase with "in the last days" (ἐν ταῖς ἐσχάταις ἡμέραις). This reading has not gone unchallenged; Codex Vaticanus and a handful of other manuscripts read μετὰ ταῦτα along with Joel, and Haenchen, Eldon J. Epp, and Richard Pervo accept μετὰ ταῦτα as original in Acts 2:17. This study defends the NA[28]'s reading ἐν ταῖς ἐσχάταις ἡμέραις and argues that Luke thereby presents the Spirit's coming as marking the dawn of a new, eschatological age.

The Text-Critical Debate Regarding ἐν ταῖς ἐσχάταις ἡμέραις in Acts 2:17

The external witnesses for ἐν ταῖς ἐσχάταις ἡμέραις are stronger than those for μετὰ ταῦτα, and the latter reading is easily explicable as a conformation to the text of the Septuagint.[11] Furthermore, the great majority of those who have evaluated the text-critical problem support the reading of the NA[28], ἐν ταῖς ἐσχάταις ἡμέραις.[12] Nevertheless, the proponents of μετὰ ταῦτα muster the following arguments:

(1) *"In the last days" does not fit Lukan theology*: Haenchen's main objection to ἐν ταῖς ἐσχάταις ἡμέραις is its incongruity with his understanding of Luke's eschatology, which is similar to that of Conzelmann: "In Lucan theology the last days do not begin as soon as the Spirit has been outpoured."[13]
(2) *The D-variants in Acts 2:17–21 show a distinctive, anti-Jewish bias*: Epp thinks that the D-text's variants here stem from an anti-Jewish perspective and thus are secondary: "The significance of the D-variants is clear: the D-text is here far more universalistic and, in by-passing Judaism, more anti-Judaistic than the B-text."[14]

---

[11] For ἐν ταῖς ἐσχάταις ἡμέραις: ℵ A D E I P S 462 vg syr Irenaeus Hilary Macarius Chrysostom Augustine; for μετὰ ταῦτα: B 076 cop[sa] Cyril of Jerusalem.

[12] Many commentators accept ἐν ταῖς ἐσχάταις ἡμέραις without comment; those who explicitly favor it include Barrett (*Acts*, 1:136), Darrell L. Bock (*Acts*, BECNT [Grand Rapids: Baker Academic, 2007], 137), Carroll (*Response*, 136), Conzelmann (*Acts*, 19), Fitzmyer (*Acts*, 252), Francis ("Eschatology and History," 51 n. 11), Gaventa ("Eschatology," 38 n. 40), Bruce M. Metzger (*A Textual Commentary on the Greek New Testament*, 2nd ed. [Stuttgart: Deutsche Bibelgesellschaft; United Bible Societies, 1998], 256), Franz Mussner ("'In den letzten Tag' [Apg 2,17a]," *BZ* 5 [1961]: 265), David Peterson (*The Acts of the Apostles*, Pillar New Testament Commentary [Grand Rapids: Eerdmans; Nottingham: Apollos, 2009], 141 n. 43), and Stanley E. Porter ("Scripture Justifies Mission: The Use of the Old Testament in Luke-Acts," in *Hearing the Old Testament in the New Testament*, ed. Stanley E. Porter, McMaster New Testament Studies [Grand Rapids: Eerdmans, 2006], 122).

[13] Haenchen, *Acts*, 179.

(3) *Luke usually reproduces the Septuagint's text*: Pervo's "chief rationale" for his textual decisions in Acts 2:17–21, including his preference for μετὰ ταῦτα, is Luke's usual quotation practice: "Since Luke tends to handle quotation from the LXX conservatively, readings that conform to the Septuagint should enjoy a certain preponderance of probability."[15]

None of these arguments is compelling. Haenchen's objection (1) relies on the sort of thoroughgoing non-eschatological reading of Luke that has been generally rejected. Furthermore, the rest of the Joel-quotation includes material that is clearly eschatological, regardless of whether ἐν ταῖς ἐσχάταις ἡμέραις or μετὰ ταῦτα is accepted in v. 17.[16]

Epp's contention (2) that certain variants in the D-text of Acts 2:17–21 reflect an anti-Jewish tendency typical of Codex Bezae may be granted for the sake of argument. This admission, however, does not necessitate the conclusion that μετὰ ταῦτα is original; both Darrell Bock and Bruce Metzger accept that some variants in this passage show the D-text's "anti-Jewish bias" but still consider ἐν ταῖς ἐσχάταις ἡμέραις the correct reading in v. 17.[17] Even Epp admits that ἐν ταῖς ἐσχάταις ἡμέραις is not itself anti-Jewish and "may be only an attempt to adapt the quotation to the present situation."[18] Furthermore, most of the other variants in Acts 2:17–21 appear only in D and a few related Western manuscripts, while ἐν ταῖς ἐσχάταις ἡμέραις boasts a variety of Western and Alexandrian witnesses.

Finally, Pervo's argument (3) from Luke's conservative quotation style is weak. Pervo himself accepts the presence in this passage of "three or four changes that quite probably go back to Luke"; if so, there is no good reason to deny the possibility of one further Lukan change here.[19] Given the weakness of the counterarguments, the weight of the external evidence, along with the greater ease in explaining a secondary corruption to μετὰ ταῦτα, solidly supports the NA[28]'s reading in Acts 2:17, ἐν ταῖς ἐσχάταις ἡμέραις.

Eschatology and the New Age in Acts 2:17–21

The reading just established for Acts 2:17, "in the last days," is the most important feature of the Joel-quotation for this study. First, the phrase is likely a Lukan redaction

---

[14] Eldon J. Epp, *Tendency of Codex Bezae Cantabrigiensis in Acts*, SNTSMS 3 (Cambridge: Cambridge University Press, 1966), 69–70.

[15] Pervo, *Acts*, 77, 79. Pervo attributes the omission of ἐν ταῖς ἡμέραις ἐκείναις in D (v. 18) to this text's insertion of ἐν ταῖς ἐσχάταις ἡμέραις in v. 17, and he notes that Luke does not use ἔσχατος to modify ἡμέρα elsewhere but does use μετὰ ταῦτα several times.

[16] Carroll (*Response*, 136) points out that Luke chose to cite Joel 3:4 LXX, "which speak[s] directly of end-time events." Mussner ("In den letzten Tag," 263) was the first to argue that both variants give an eschatological meaning to the quotation, invalidating Haenchen's argument.

[17] Darrell L. Bock, *Proclamation from Prophecy and Pattern: Lucan Old Testament Christology*, JSNTSup 12 (Sheffield: JSOT Press, 1987), 158; Metzger, *Textual Commentary*, 255.

[18] Epp, *Tendency*, 67.

[19] Pervo, *Acts*, 79.

and thus reveals the author's own perspective.[20] Second, this redaction explicitly characterizes the outpouring of the Spirit as an eschatological event, one that signals the dawning of a new age.[21] Although commentators rarely mention the Golden Age myth in association with Pentecost, they do recognize that Luke sees the coming of the Spirit as marking the birth of "the new age," "a new age," "the new era," "the age to come," "the eschatological time," or "the eschatological age."[22] This idea is widely accepted and independent of any posited Golden Age allusion in the summaries.

The specific phenomenon that marks the last days, according to Luke's quotation, is God pouring out his Spirit. The next step in the argument is showing the relationship between the activity of the Spirit and the summaries in Acts 2:42–47 and 4:32–35.

The Pneumatological Context of Acts 2:42–47 and 4:32–35

The eschatological character of Pentecost, explicitly affirmed by Luke's insertion of "in the last days" in Acts 2:17, is generally recognized. The summary in Acts 2:42–47 that immediately follows Peter's Pentecost sermon, however, is sometimes analyzed in isolation from its context, as is the summary in Acts 4:32–35.[23] Yet while the Spirit is not mentioned in either Acts 2:42–47 or 4:32–35, context indicates that both summaries describe a way of life specifically resulting from the outpouring of the Spirit.

The pneumatological framing of the summaries is more often recognized in the case of Acts 2:42–47.[24] At the end of his Pentecost sermon, which opens with the Joel-quotation discussed above, Peter announces that the same eschatological gift of the

---

[20] Due to the lack of evidence for Luke's use of a traditional form here and the explicability of the alterations as adaptations to the context in Acts, most commentators attribute the insertion of "in the last days" to Luke: so Barrett, *Acts*, 1:129; Carroll, *Response*, 137; Fitzmyer, *Acts*, 252; Gaventa, "Eschatology," 38; Holladay, *Acts*, 101; Johnson, *Acts*, 49; Keener, *Acts 1:1–2:47*, 875; Maddox, *Purpose*, 137; Marguerat, *Actes*, 88; Metzger, *Textual Commentary*, 256.

[21] Several commentators note the presence of this same idea in Judaism. James D. G. Dunn (*Baptism in the Holy Spirit: A Re-Examination of the New Testament Teaching on the Gift of the Spirit in Relation to Pentecostalism Today*, SBT 15 [Naperville, IL: Allenson, 1970], 46) states that in "Jewish eschatology the gift of the Spirit was one of the decisive marks of the new age," citing Isaiah and Ezekiel. Barrett (*Acts*, 1:137) observes that this text from Joel in particular "was taken up in Judaism and understood to refer to an outpouring of the Spirit in the age to come"; Chance (*Jerusalem*, 79) cites Midr. Ps. 14:6 and Num. Rab. 15:25 in support of this claim.

[22] "The new age": C. M. Blumhofer, "Luke's Alteration of Joel 3.1–5 in Acts 2.17–21," *NTS* 62 (2016): 510; F. F. Bruce, *The Acts of the Apostles: The Greek Text with Introduction and Commentary*, 3rd ed. (Grand Rapids: Eerdmans, 1990), 121; Dunn, *Baptism*, 43; Johnson, *Acts*, 50; Maddox, *Purpose*, 139; "a new age": Fitzmyer, *Acts*, 250; Eduard Schweizer, "πνεῦμα, πνευματικός," *TDNT* 6:411; William H. Shepherd, *The Narrative Function of the Holy Spirit as a Character in Luke-Acts*, SBLDS 147 (Atlanta: Scholars Press, 1994), 164; "the new era": Bock, *Acts*, 113; Holladay, *Acts*, 133; "the age to come": Barrett, *Acts*, 1:137; "the eschatological time": Keener, *Acts 1:1–2:47*, 880; "the eschatological age": Witherington III, *Acts*, 140.

[23] As noted (and criticized) by Marguerat (*Actes*, 100) and Pesch (*Apostelgeschichte*, 129).

[24] A causal relationship between the giving of the Spirit promised in Acts 2:38 and the summary in 2:42–47 is recognized by, among others, Bartchy ("Community of Goods," 316), Bruce (*Acts*, 132), Hume (*Early Christian Community*, 91), Johnson (*Literary Function*, 184–5), Keener (*Acts 1:1–2:47*, 1000), Klauck ("Gütergemeinschaft," 74), Marguerat (*Actes*, 97), Pesch (*Apostelgeschichte*, 129), Peterson (*Acts*, 61 n. 28), Schnabel (*Acts*, 182), Schneider (*Apostelgeschichte*, 1:364), Shepherd (*Narrative Function*, 167), and Thompson (*One Lord, One People*, 89).

Spirit is available to his hearers: "Repent and be baptized every one of you in the name of Jesus Christ so that your sins may be forgiven; and you will receive the gift of the Holy Spirit" (Acts 2:38). Acts 2:41 then reports that three thousand people respond and are baptized, presumably receiving the promised Spirit as a result. The summary follows immediately. Furthermore, these two sections are not merely adjacent but also share the same grammatical subject: "So those who welcomed his message were baptized, and that day about three thousand persons were added. They devoted themselves to the apostles' teaching and fellowship, to the breaking of bread and the prayers" (Acts 2:41–42).[25] Finally, the fact that the related summary in 4:32–35 also immediately follows an outpouring of the Spirit (4:31) makes it unlikely that this juxtaposition is coincidental in both places.[26]

The pneumatological context of Acts 4:32–35 is highlighted less often, although not infrequently.[27] When Peter and John are released by the Jerusalem authorities, they return to "their friends" (Acts 4:23, τοὺς ἰδίους); this group is not specified further but is most commonly understood as referring to the Jerusalem believers in general.[28] In 4:31, "all" of those present are "filled with the Holy Spirit." The second summary immediately follows. Again, in isolation the placement of this summary adjacent to an outpouring of the Spirit could be considered a coincidence, but the "conspicuous proximity" of both these summaries to "major Spirit-events" indicates that the juxtapositions are intentional.[29] The summaries display the "life of this community created by the Spirit."[30]

Conclusion: The Eschatological Character of Acts 2:42–47 and 4:32–35

The logic of this section's argument is straightforward. The major premise is that Luke characterizes the outpouring of the Spirit as an eschatological event marking a new age. The minor premise is that the summaries describe the life of the Jerusalem believers as

---

[25] Marguerat, *Actes*, 100; Matthias Wenk, *Community-Forming Power: The Socio-Ethical Role of the Spirit in Luke-Acts* (Sheffield: Sheffield Academic, 2000), 262. Marguerat (ibid.) also points out that vv. 41 and 42 are linked by a μέν ... δέ pairing.

[26] Keener, *Acts 1:1–2:47*, 1003; Aaron Kuecker, *The Spirit and the "Other": Social Identity, Ethnicity and Intergroup Reconciliation in Luke-Acts*, LNTS 444 (London: T&T Clark, 2011), 126; Max Turner, *Power from on High: The Spirit in Israel's Restoration and Witness in Luke-Acts* (Sheffield: Sheffield Academic, 1996), 414; Wenk, *Community-Forming Power*, 265.

[27] The connection with the filling by the Spirit in 4:31 is observed by Haenchen (*Acts*, 232), Keener (*Acts 1:1–2:47*, 1003), Klauck ("Gütergemeinschaft," 74), Kuecker (*Spirit and the "Other,"* 127), Marguerat (*Actes*, 168), Peterson (*Acts*, 61 n. 28), Schneider (*Apostelgeschichte*, 1:364), Shepherd (*Narrative Function*, 170–1), Thompson (*One Lord, One People*, 89), Turner (*Power from on High*, 415), Steve Walton ("Primitive Communism in Acts? Does Acts Present the Community of Goods [2:44–45; 4:32–35] as Mistaken?" *EvQ* 80 [2008]: 105), and Wenk (*Community-Forming Power*, 270).

[28] Johnson (*Literary Function*, 193) argues that the phrase refers to the apostles specifically, but the passage does not state or imply this, and most commentators reject limiting the reference to this extent; so Barrett (*Acts*, 1:242–43), Fitzmyer (*Acts*, 307), Haenchen (*Acts*, 226), Pesch (*Apostelgeschichte*, 175), Schneider (*Apostelgeschichte*, 1:356), and Witherington III (*Acts*, 201 n. 6).

[29] Kuecker, *Spirit and the "Other,"* 126.

[30] Johnson, *Literary Function*, 184–5.

flowing from outpourings of the Spirit in Acts 2:41 and 4:31. Both premises are widely accepted and support the conclusion that the summaries serve as an eschatological portrait, "an ideal picture of the Spirit-endowed community of the new age."[31]

While demonstrating the eschatological character of the summaries in no way proves a Golden Age allusion, it fits with the observation from Chapter 3 that Jewish and Christian texts often use this myth in eschatological depictions. In the next section I argue for a second agreement between these Golden Age texts and Luke-Acts: interest in Rome.

Luke-Acts and Rome

A second observation from Chapter 3 was that Jewish and Christian Golden Age allusions typically appear in texts concerned with Rome. While Luke's perspective on the Empire is debated, his interest in Rome is generally not. Many claim Luke to be the most Rome-focused Gospel, and Acts the most Rome-focused book, in the NT.[32] The basis for these judgments goes far beyond tabulations of vocabulary, but a few lexical observations may serve as quick indications: five of the eight NT uses of Ῥώμη (Rome) and eleven of the twelve NT uses of Ῥωμαῖος (Roman) are found in the book of Acts;[33] seventeen of the twenty-nine NT uses of Καῖσαρ (Caesar) occur in Luke-Acts;[34] Luke is the only NT book to name a Roman emperor, doing so twice (Augustus and Tiberius);[35] Acts contains the only three NT instances of the imperial title σεβαστός (Augustus).[36]

After surveying scholarly perspectives on Luke's view of Rome, I argue that Luke on occasion mimics imperial discourse in order to set up a supra-imperial contrast between Christ and the Roman emperor. This closely parallels the function that Chapter 5 will propose for Luke's allusion to the Golden Age myth.

---

[31] Bruce, *Acts*, 132.

[32] For Luke as the Gospel most concerned with Rome, see Virginia Burrus, "The Gospel of Luke and the Acts of the Apostles," in *A Postcolonial Commentary on the New Testament*, ed. Fernando F. Segovia and Rasiah S. Sugirtharajah, Bible and Postcolonialism 13 (London: T&T Clark, 2009), 134; Pyung Soo Seo, *Luke's Jesus in the Roman Empire and the Emperor in the Gospel of Luke* (Eugene, OR: Pickwick, 2015), 2; Steve Walton, "The State They Were In: Luke's View of the Roman Empire," in *Rome in the Bible and the Early Church*, ed. Peter Oakes (Grand Rapids: Baker Academic, 2002), 16. For Acts, see Gary Gilbert, "Luke-Acts and Negotiations of Authority and Identity in the Roman World," in *The Multivalence of Biblical Texts and Theological Meanings*, ed. Christine Helmer, SymS 37 (Atlanta: SBL Press, 2006), 84; Brigitte Kahl, "Acts of the Apostles: Pro(to)-Imperial Script and Hidden Transcript," in *In the Shadow of Empire: Reclaiming the Bible as a History of Faithful Resistance*, ed. Richard A. Horsley (Louisville: Westminster John Knox, 2008), 142.

[33] Ῥώμη: Acts 18:2; 19:21; 23:11; 28:14, 16; elsewhere Rom 1:7, 15; 2 Tim 1:17. Ῥωμαῖος: Acts 2:10; 16:21, 37, 38; 22:25, 26, 27, 29; 23:27; 25:16; 28:17; elsewhere: John 11:48.

[34] Luke 2:1; 3:1; 20:22, 24, 25 (2x); 23:2; Acts 17:7; 25:8, 10, 11, 12 (2x), 21; 26:32; 27:24; 28:19; elsewhere: Matt 22:17, 21 (3x); Mark 12:14, 16, 17 (2x); John 19:12 (2x), 15; Phil 4:22.

[35] Luke 2:1; 3:1.

[36] Acts 25:21, 25; 27:1.

Luke-Acts and Rome: Major Approaches

Over the past four centuries, the dominant understanding of Luke's approach to the Roman Empire has been that Luke's aim was to show to Roman officials the compatibility of Christianity with Rome, presenting an apology for the church. Adherents include some of the most important Lukan scholars of the twentieth century, such as F. F. Bruce, Conzelmann, Joseph Fitzmyer, and Haenchen, and it is still often claimed to be the majority position.[37] The main evidence is that Roman officials repeatedly find Jesus and Paul innocent, a potentially useful feature for securing toleration for the Christian movement in Luke's time.[38] Bruce also argues that "Luke's attitude to the imperial authorities throughout the provinces is quite positive."[39]

This supposedly majority position has attracted more criticism than support in recent years, with opponents highlighting several potential problems. (1) While Paul and Jesus may have been found innocent, the narrative shows that their activities repeatedly led to public disturbances, a trend that would not have recommended Christianity to Roman authorities.[40] (2) Despite Bruce's claim regarding the "quite positive" attitude toward the Roman authorities, Luke's depictions of these officials contain a fair amount of negative material, unsuitable for currying Roman favor.[41] (3) Luke's argument is seen as far too subtle and/or theological to function as an effective apology for a Roman audience.[42] C. K. Barrett's withering dismissal is regularly cited: "No Roman official would ever have filtered out so much of what to him would be theological and ecclesiastical rubbish in order to reach so tiny a grain of relevant apology."[43]

---

[37] Bruce, *Acts*, 24; Conzelmann, *Theology*, 137–8; Joseph A. Fitzmyer, *The Gospel according to Luke I–IX: A New Translation with Introduction and Commentary*, AB 28 (New Haven: Yale University Press, 2009), 10; Haenchen, *Acts*, 106. The apologetic view is described as the current majority opinion by Yong-Sung Ahn (*The Reign of God and Rome in Luke's Passion Narrative: An East Asian Global Perspective*, BibInt 80 [Leiden: Brill, 2006], 72–3), Raymond Pickett ("Luke and Empire: An Introduction," in *Luke-Acts and Empire: Essays in Honor of Robert L. Brawley*, ed. David Rhoads, David Esterline, and Jae-won Lee, Princeton Theological Monograph Series 151 [Eugene, OR: Pickwick, 2011], 5), and C. Kavin Rowe (*World Upside Down: Reading Acts in the Graeco-Roman Age* [New York: Oxford University Press, 2009], 53–4).

[38] Bruce, *Acts*, 24; Conzelmann, *Theology*, 140.

[39] Bruce, *Acts*, 24–5.

[40] Loveday Alexander, "The Acts of the Apostles as an Apologetic Text," in *Apologetics in the Roman Empire: Pagans, Jews and Christians*, ed. Mark Edwards, Martin Goodman, and Simon Price (Oxford: Oxford University Press, 1999), 34; Richard J. Cassidy, *Society and Politics in the Acts of the Apostles* (Maryknoll, NY: Orbis Books, 1983), 149; Alexandru Neagoe, *The Trial of the Gospel: An Apologetic Reading of Luke's Trial Narratives*, SNTSMS 116 (Cambridge: Cambridge University Press, 2002), 181.

[41] Christopher Bryan, *Render to Caesar: Jesus, the Early Church, and the Roman Superpower* (Oxford: Oxford University Press, 2005), 96; Burrus, "Gospel of Luke," 140; Cassidy, *Society and Politics*, 152; Jacob Jervell, *The Theology of the Acts of the Apostles*, New Testament Theology (Cambridge: Cambridge University Press, 1996), 103; Rubén Muñoz-Larrondo, *A Post-Colonial Reading of the Acts of the Apostles*, StBibLit 147 (New York: Lang, 2012), 232; Neagoe, *Trial*, 181–2; Pickett, "Luke and Empire," 6; Seo, *Luke's Jesus*, 4; Walton, "State They Were In," 30.

[42] Alexander, "Acts," 24; Jervell, *Theology*, 103; Maddox, *Purpose*, 96; Neagoe, *Trial*, 10; Walton, "State They Were In," 30.

[43] C. K. Barrett, *Luke the Historian in Recent Study*, A. S. Peake Memorial Lecture 6 (London: Epworth, 1961), 63.

In an attempt to counter these objections, some scholars have reversed the direction of the apology: instead of defending the church before Rome, Luke is defending Rome before the church.[44] While this variation avoids some of the objections raised against the aforementioned interpretation, it too struggles to explain why Luke would portray Roman officials in a somewhat negative light. A third view, proposed by Philip Esler and Sterling, holds that Luke presents a rosy picture of Christianity's relationship with Rome to allow Christians to understand their own position within the Roman Empire in a positive way.[45] Yet this still fails to explain the elements in Luke-Acts that are critical of Rome or indicate the likelihood of conflict.[46]

Unsurprisingly, the longstanding dominance of the pro-Roman reading has produced a counter-reaction, and over the past few decades several interpreters have argued that Luke presents Jesus as "a serious threat to the Roman empire" and "in direct confrontation with the emperor."[47] The (at least partially) negative depictions of Pilate and other Roman officials are taken as evidence for this position, but perhaps the most common type of argument for anti-imperial interpretations centers on Luke's purported mimicry of Roman propaganda.[48] According to this view, Luke's frequent use of imperial titles (such as "savior," "lord," and "son of god") and concepts to describe Jesus amounts to "a counterclaim of authority that challenged the existing world political order."[49] But, just as in the case of the apologetic interpretations, opponents of the anti-imperial view object that this position fails to take into account the full body of evidence from Luke and Acts, such as the repeated verdicts of innocence given by Roman officials and certain positive aspects of their behavior in Luke's presentation.[50]

---

[44] Paul W. Walaskay (*"And So We Came to Rome": The Political Perspective of St. Luke*, SNTSMS 49 [Cambridge: Cambridge University Press, 1983], 13, 64) is the exegete most often identified with this position, arguing that Luke "was decidedly pro-Roman" and "consciously presented an *apologia pro imperio* to his church." Other proponents include Maddox (*Purpose*, 97) and Daniel Marguerat (*The First Christian Historian: Writing the "Acts of the Apostles,"* trans. Ken McKinney, Gregory J. Laughery, and Richard Bauckham, SNTSMS 121 [Cambridge: Cambridge University Press, 2002], 77).

[45] Philip Francis Esler, *Community and Gospel in Luke-Acts: The Social and Political Motivations of Lucan Theology*, SNTSMS 57 (Cambridge: Cambridge University Press, 1987), 210; Sterling, *Historiography*, 385–6.

[46] So Walton, "State They Were In," 31–2; Joshua P. Yoder, *Representatives of Roman Rule: Roman Provincial Governors in Luke-Acts*, BZNW 209 (Berlin: de Gruyter, 2014), 24–5.

[47] Richard J. Cassidy, *Jesus, Politics, and Society: A Study of Luke's Gospel* (Maryknoll, NY: Orbis Books, 1983), 78; Richard A. Horsley, *The Liberation of Christmas: The Infancy Narratives in Social Context* (New York: Crossroad, 1989), 33. See also Gary Gilbert, "The List of Nations in Acts 2: Roman Propaganda and the Lukan Response," *JBL* 121 (2002): 528; Muñoz-Larrondo, *Post-Colonial Reading*, 231; Seo, *Luke's Jesus*, 16; Kazuhiko Yamazaki-Ransom, *The Roman Empire in Luke's Narrative*, LNTS 404 (London: T&T Clark, 2010), 201.

[48] Gary Gilbert has argued often for reading such mimicry as anti-imperial ("List of Nations," 518–19; "Roman Propaganda and Christian Identity in the Worldview of Luke-Acts," in *Contextualizing Acts: Lukan Narrative and Greco-Roman Discourse*, ed. Todd Penner and Caroline Vander Stichele, SymS 20 [Atlanta: SBL Press, 2003], 255; "Luke-Acts and Negotiations of Authority," 87), and he is joined by Horsley (*Liberation of Christmas*, 33), Muñoz-Larrondo (*Post-Colonial Reading*, 198), and Yamazaki-Ransom (*Roman Empire*, 83).

[49] Yamazaki-Ransom, *Roman Empire*, 86.

[50] Sterling, *Historiography*, 382; Walton, "State They Were In," 32.

Since both the thoroughgoing pro-Roman and anti-Roman interpretations explain part of the material of Luke-Acts but fit awkwardly with other elements, most recent interpreters have adopted an intermediate stance. These readers find "ambiguity," "ambivalence," or even "contradiction" in Luke's perspective on Rome.[51] The major pieces of evidence on both sides of the ledger, pro-Roman and anti-Roman, have already been noted: Roman authorities repeatedly declare Jesus and Paul to be innocent, but these same officials are also depicted at times as weak and corrupt. Like proponents of a thoroughly anti-Roman interpretation, many of these interpreters also highlight Luke's use of language associated with Augustan ideology, seeing this as an indication of an intentional contrast between Caesar and Jesus to the detriment of the former.[52] Due to the prominence of this type of evidence in the debate over Luke's perspective on Rome, as well as its bearing on Luke's possible appropriation of imperial mythology in the Acts summaries, I will examine the relevant data and their possible interpretations in detail.

Establishing Luke's Use of Imperial Language

This section presents evidence that Luke intentionally applies imperial titles and concepts to describe Christ in both Luke and Acts. The likeliest instances occur in Luke's infancy narrative and Acts 10:36. The relevant terms are εἰρήνη, κύριος, and σωτήρ in the infancy narrative and εἰρήνη and κύριος in Acts 10:36.

The most frequently cited pagan parallel to Luke's language is an inscription from Priene in Ionia, with other copies at Apameia and Eumeneia. Made in 9 BCE, this inscription commemorates the adoption of Augustus' birthday as the first day of the year:

---

[51] "Ambiguity": Burrus ("Gospel of Luke," 133), John T. Carroll (*Luke: A Commentary*, NTL [Louisville: Westminster John Knox, 2012], 399), Kahl ("Acts of the Apostles," 138); "ambivalence": Ahn (*Reign of God*, 218), Carroll (ibid.); "contradiction": John Moles ("Accommodation, Opposition or Other? Luke-Acts' Stance towards Rome," in *Roman Rule in Greek and Latin Writing: Double Vision*, ed. Jesper Majborn Madsen and Roger Rees, Impact of Empire [Leiden: Brill, 2014], 102). Others who fall into this general category include Eric D. Barreto ("Crafting Colonial Identities: Hybridity and the Roman Empire in Luke-Acts," in *An Introduction to Empire in the New Testament*, ed. Adam Winn, RBS 84 [Atlanta: SBL Press, 2016], 110), Jervell (*Theology*, 106), Amanda C. Miller (*Rumors of Resistance: Status Reversals and Hidden Transcripts in the Gospel of Luke* [Minneapolis: Fortress, 2014], 255), Pickett ("Luke and Empire," 7), Dean Pinter ("The Gospel of Luke and the Roman Empire," in *Jesus Is Lord, Caesar Is Not: Evaluating Empire in New Testament Studies*, ed. Scot McKnight and Joseph Modica [Downers Grove, IL: InterVarsity Press, 2013], 104), Rowe (*World Upside Down*, 4), Seo (*Luke's Jesus*, 129), Walton ("State They Were In," 35), and Yoder (*Representatives*, 336).

[52] Bradley Billings, "'At the Age of 12': The Boy Jesus in the Temple (Luke 2:41–52), the Emperor Augustus, and the Social Setting of the Third Gospel," *JTS* 60 [2009]: 85), Allen Brent ("Luke-Acts and the Imperial Cult in Asia Minor," *JTS* 48 [1997]: 420–9), Raymond E. Brown (*The Birth of the Messiah: A Commentary on the Infancy Narratives in the Gospels of Matthew and Luke*, ABRL, [New York: Doubleday, 1993], 415), Bryan (*Render to Caesar*, 99), Carroll (*Luke*, 401), Joel B. Green (*The Gospel of Luke*, NICNT [Grand Rapids: Eerdmans, 1997], 122), Kahl ("Acts of the Apostles," 149), Seyoon Kim (*Christ and Caesar: The Gospel and the Roman Empire in the Writings of Paul and Luke* [Grand Rapids: Eerdmans, 2008], 80–1), Miller (*Rumors of Resistance*, 114), and Walton ("State They Were In," 27–8).

Since the providence that has divinely ordered our life, employing zeal and ambition, adorned our life with the most perfect good by bringing Augustus, whom it filled with virtue for the benefaction of humankind, as though granting us and our descendants a savior who brought an end to war and arranged peace; and since when Caesar appeared, he exceeded the hopes of all those who had anticipated good news, not only surpassing those who were born before him but not even leaving for those in the future hopes of surpassing him; and since the birthday of the god made a beginning of good news for the world. (*OGIS* 458I:32–41)[53]

Citing the "astonishing number of words in this inscription [that] are used in Luke-Acts," Kazuhiko Yamazaki-Ransom concludes that "Luke consciously uses the language of imperial ideology in his narrative."[54] Three words or phrases commonly identified as Lukan allusions to imperial ideology appear in this passage: "peace" (εἰρήνη), "savior" (σωτήρ), and "god" (θεός), which Yamazaki-Ransom associates with Luke's use of the title "Son of God" (υἱὸς θεοῦ).[55] Although it does not occur here, the term "lord" (κύριος) is also often claimed as an imperial allusion. The following pages examine the appearances of these four expressions in imperial discourse and in Luke-Acts.

The role of peace in imperial propaganda is well known (Table 4.1).[56] While Luke-Acts does not use the term εἰρήνη more frequently than the rest of the NT, two facts make an imperial allusion more plausible.[57] First, the three texts in Table 4.1 tie the idea of peace to the presence of Jesus; neither Matthew nor Mark does this explicitly. Second, all three appear in a Roman or imperial context: Luke 1:79 and 2:14 bracket the NT's only mention of Augustus by name (Luke 2:1), and the addressee in Acts 10:36 is a Roman centurion.

The evidence for κύριος as an imperial title is equally plentiful (Table 4.2).[58] Luke's use of the word is again proportional to that of the rest of the NT, although his Gospel does use κύριος more often than its three canonical counterparts.[59] However, some individual instances are promising candidates for being allusions to imperial discourse. The three

---

[53] ἐπειδὴ ἡ θείως διατάξασα τὸν βίον ἡμῶν πρόνοια σπουδὴν εἰσενενκαμένη καὶ φιλοτιμίαν τὸ τελητότατον τῶι βίωι διεκόσμησεν ἀγαθὸν ἐνενκαμένη τὸν Σεβαστόν, ὃν εἰς εὐεργεσίαν ἀνθρώπων ἐπλήρωσεν ἀρετῆς, ὥσπερ ἡμεῖν καὶ τοῖς μεθ' ἡμᾶς σωτῆρα χαρισαμένη τὸν παύσαντα μὲν πόλεμον, κοσμήσοντα δὲ εἰρήνην, ἐπιφανεὶς δὲ ὁ Καῖσαρ τὰς ἐλπίδας τῶν προλαβόντων εὐαγγέλια πάντων ὑπερέθηκεν, οὐ μόνον τοὺς πρὸ αὐτοῦ γεγονότας εὐεργέτας ὑπερβαλόμενος, ἀλλ' οὐδ' ἐν τοῖς ἐσομένοις ἐλπίδα ὑπολιπὼν ὑπερβολῆς, ἦρξεν δὲ τῶι κόσμωι τῶν δι' αὐτὸν εὐαγγελίων ἡ γενέθλιος ἡμέρα τοῦ θεοῦ.

[54] Yamazaki-Ransom, *Roman Empire*, 83.

[55] "Good news" (here, εὐανγέλια) is also claimed as imperial language by Billings ("At the Age of 12," 86), Green (*Luke*, 123), Kim (*Christ and Caesar*, 79), and Yamazaki-Ransom (*Roman Empire*, 83), but the Packard Humanities Institute's inscriptions database indicates that εὐαγγέλ- vocabulary appears in conjunction with imperial titles much less often than the other expressions examined here.

[56] For examples, see Klaus Wengst, *Pax Romana and the Peace of Jesus Christ*, trans. John Bowden (Philadelphia: Fortress, 1987), 7–54.

[57] Yamazaki-Ransom (*Roman Empire*, 83) notes that Luke-Acts contains 23% of the NT uses of εἰρήνη. Given that Luke-Acts accounts for 27% of the NT, however, εἰρήνη is actually *under*-represented.

[58] For further examples, see C. Kavin Rowe, "Luke-Acts and the Imperial Cult: A Way through the Conundrum?" *JSNT* 27 (2005): 292–3.

[59] Luke: 104x; Matthew: 80x; Mark: 16x; John: 52x. Luke-Acts accounts for 29% of the uses of κύριος in the NT, which is unremarkable given that Luke-Acts represents 27% of the NT by word count.

Table 4.1 Examples of "Peace" (εἰρήνη) in Imperial Texts and in Luke-Acts

Source	Text
Inscription at Pergamum Post-9 BCE	To the Emperor Caesar, god, son of god, Augustus, because of the Augustan Peace (*IMT* 834:3–5, Αὐτοκράτορι Καίσαρι θεῷ, υἱῷ θεοῦ, Σεβαστῷ, ὑπὲρ Εἰρήνης Σεβαστῆς)
Res Gestae 14–19 CE	When the whole land under the Romans and the sea was brought to peace (*Res gest. divi Aug.* 13, εἰρηνευομένης τῆς ὑπὸ Ῥωμαίοις πάσης γῆς τε καὶ θαλάσσης)
Philo's *Legatio ad Gaium* 41 CE	Augustus ... dispensed peace on every side, through earth and sea even to the ends of the world (*Legat.* 309–310, Σεβαστὸς ... τὴν εἰρήνην διαχέας πάντη διὰ γῆς καὶ θαλάττης ἄχρι τῶν τοῦ κόσμου περάτων)
Inscription at Dendera 42 CE	Because of the peace and concord of Tiberius Claudius Caesar Augustus Germanicus, Emperor (*OGIS* 663:1–2, ὑπὲρ τῆς Τιβερίου Κλαυδίου Καίσαρος Σεβαστοῦ Γερμανικοῦ Αὐτοκράτορος εἰρήνης)
Bronze Coin of Trajan 98–117 CE	Augustan Peace (*RPC* III 1101, εἰρήνη σεβαστή)
Luke 1:79	To guide our feet into the way of peace (εἰρήνης)
Luke 2:14	On earth peace [εἰρήνη] among those whom he favors
Acts 10:36	You know the message he sent to the people of Israel, preaching peace [εἰρήνην] by Jesus Christ—he is Lord of all

Table 4.2 Examples of "Lord" (κύριος) in Imperial Texts and in Luke-Acts

Source	Text
Philo's *Legatio ad Gaium* 41 CE	Lord Gaius (*Legat.* 356, κύριε Γάιε)
Inscription at Akraiphia 67 CE	Nero, the lord of the whole world (*IG* VII 2713:31, ὁ τοῦ παντὸς κόσμου κύριος Νέρων)
Inscription at Delphi 90 CE	Our lord, the most divine Emperor Domitian Caesar (*SIG* 821D:1, τοῦ κυρίου ἡμῶν θειοτάτου Αὐτοκράτορος Δομετιανοῦ Καίσαρος)
Epictetus' *Dissertationes* 108 CE	Caesar, the lord of all (*Diatr.* 4.1.12–13, ὁ πάντων κύριος Καῖσαρ)
Inscription at Tralles 117–138 CE	The lord Caesar Trajan Hadrian Augustus (*CIG* 2927:5–6, τοῦ κυρίου Καίσαρος Τραϊανοῦ Ἀδριανοῦ Σεβαστοῦ)
Luke 1:76	You will go before the Lord [κυρίου] to prepare his ways
Luke 2:11	A Savior, who is the Messiah, the Lord (κύριος)
Acts 10:36	Preaching peace by Jesus Christ—he is Lord [κύριος] of all

examples given above, Luke 1:76, 2:11 and Acts 10:36, all occur in the same imperial contexts noted in the discussion of εἰρήνη above. Furthermore, each of these uses of κύριος appears in close proximity to other words with imperial connotations: εἰρήνη in Luke 1:79 and Acts 10:36, and σωτήρ (savior) in Luke 2:11, to be discussed next.

Beyond the Priene inscription, numerous other examples testify to the application of the title "savior" (σωτήρ) to Augustus and later Roman emperors (Table 4.3). Luke uses the word four times in his writings, three times as a title for Jesus.[60] This is more noteworthy in comparison to the other Gospels: neither Matthew nor Mark uses the term at all, and John does so on only one occasion (John 4:42). The most significant Lukan instance is found in Luke 2:11, since this verse both closely follows the reference to Augustus in 2:1 and occurs in conjunction with the title "lord" (κύριος), another common imperial honorific.

As was the case for the previous three terms examined, the evidence for the application of θεοῦ υἱός, the Greek equivalent of *divi filius*, to various Roman emperors is ample (Table 4.4).[61] Out of forty-five NT variations of the phrase, however, Luke contains six and Acts only one, less than both Matthew and John.[62] As to the form of the expression, Robert Mowery points out that Matthew, not Luke, is the only Gospel to reproduce the usual imperial order of υἱὸς θεοῦ.[63] Finally, Luke never joins this phrase to any of the terms examined above, and only Luke 1:35 can make a plausible case for having an imperial context, preceding (by fifty-six verses) the reference to Augustus in Luke 2:1. The evidence for understanding Luke's use of υἱὸς θεοῦ as an imperial allusion is weaker than that for the previous three words.

The data indicate that three terms in particular, εἰρήνη, κύριος, and σωτήρ, present solid initial cases for being allusions to imperial language. Although interpreters often move directly from the fact of parallel terminology to claims that Luke intentionally appropriated imperial themes and titles, others recently have raised methodological objections to such an inference. Several have noted correctly that the mere existence of parallel language does not indicate automatically that a comparison was intended by the author or understood by the reader.[64] More specifically, Joel White argues for an alternate source for these expressions, pointing out that much of the purportedly imperial terminology "has a rich Septuagintal tradition."[65] That is certainly the case for

---

[60] The other instance is in the Magnificat (Luke 1:47). Luke-Acts uses σωτήρ more than the other Gospels, but not disproportionately often relative to the NT as a whole (4/24x).

[61] Further first-century examples may be found in Robert L. Mowery, "Son of God in Roman Imperial Titles and Matthew," *Bib* 83 (2002): 101–5.

[62] Luke-Acts accounts for 16% of the NT uses, less than for each of the three previous terms.

[63] Mowery, "Son of God," 101.

[64] Bryan, *Render to Caesar*, 90; Christoph Heilig, *Hidden Criticism? The Methodology and Plausibility of the Search for a Counter-Imperial Subtext in Paul*, WUNT 2/392 (Tübingen: Mohr Siebeck, 2015), 143; Kim, *Christ and Caesar*, 28; Anders Klostergaard Petersen, "Imperial Politics in Paul: Scholarly Phantom or Actual Textual Phenomenon?" in *People under Power: Early Jewish and Christian Responses to the Roman Empire*, ed. Michael Labahn and Outi Lehtipuu, Early Christianity in the Roman World 1 (Amsterdam: Amsterdam University Press, 2015), 111; Rowe, "Luke-Acts and the Imperial Cult," 284–5.

[65] Joel White, "Anti-Imperial Subtexts in Paul: An Attempt at Building a Firmer Foundation," *Bib* 90 (2009): 309.

Table 4.3 Examples of "Savior" (σωτήρ) in Imperial Texts and in Luke-Acts

Source	Text
Inscription at Athens 27 BCE–14 CE	Emperor Caesar, savior, Augustus (SEG 29:168:1–3, Αὐτοκράτορα Καίσαρα σωτῆρα Σεβαστόν)
Philo's *In Flaccum* 40–41 CE	The savior and benefactor Augustus (*Flacc.* 74, ὁ σωτὴρ καὶ εὐεργέτης Σεβαστός)
Inscription from Attica 49–53 CE	Tiberius Claudius Caesar Augustus Germanicus, emperor, savior of the world (*IG* II² 3273:49–53, Τιβέριον Κλαύδιον Καίσαρα Σεβαστὸν Γερμανικὸν αὐτοκράτορα σωτῆρα τοῦ κόσμου)
Inscription at Talei 60–61 CE	To Nero Claudius Caesar Augustus Germanicus, Emperor, the savior and benefactor of the world (*OGIS* 668:1–5, Νέρωνι Κλαυδίωι Καίσαρι Σεβαστῶι Γερμανικῶι Αὐτοκράτορι, τῶι σωτῆρι καὶ εὐεργύτηι τῆς οἰκουμένης)
Inscription at Laodicea 84–85 CE	To the greatest God, Savior, and Emperor Domitian Caesar Augustus Germanicus (*CIG* 3949:2, Διὶ Μεγίστωι Σωτῆρι καὶ Αὐτοκράτορι Δομιτιανῶι Καίσαρι Σεβαστῶι Γερμανικῶι)
Luke 2:11	To you is born this day in the city of David a Savior [σωτήρ], who is Christ the Lord
Acts 5:31	God exalted him at his right hand as Leader and Savior (σωτῆρα)
Acts 13:23	God has brought to Israel a Savior [σωτῆρα], Jesus

Table 4.4 Examples of "Son of God" (υἱὸς θεοῦ) in Imperial Texts and in Luke-Acts

Source	Text
Inscription at Chondria 27 BCE–14 CE	Emperor Caesar, son of god, god Augustus (*CIL* III 7113:8–9, Αὐτοκράτωρ Καῖσαρ θεοῦ υἱὸς θεὸς Σεβαστός)
Inscription at Delphi 14–27 CE	Tiberius Caesar, son of God, Augustus, Savior, Benefactor (*FD* III 1:529:2–4, Τιβέριον Καίσαρα, Θεοῦ υἱόν, Σεβαστόν, Σωτῆρα, Εὐεργέταν)
Inscription from Attica 61–62 CE	The greatest Emperor Nero Caesar Claudius Augustus Germanicus, son of god (*IG* II² 3277:2–4, Αὐτοκράτορα μέγιστον Νέρωνα Καίσαρα Κλαύδιον Σεβαστὸν Γερμανικὸν θεοῦ υἱόν)
Inscription from Cyprus 84 CE	Emperor Domitian Caesar Augustus, son of god, Germanicus (SEG 23:631:1–2, Αὐτοκράτορα Δομιτιανὸν Καίσαρα Σεβαστὸν θεοῦ υἱὸν Γερμανικόν)
Inscription from Attica Post-113 CE	Emperor Caesar Nerva Trajan Augustus Germanicus Dacicus, god, unconquered son of god (*IG* II² 3284:1–3, Αὐτοκράτορα Καίσαρα Νερούαν Τραιανὸν Σεβαστὸν Γερμανικὸν Δακικὸν θεὸν θεοῦ υἱὸν ἀνείκητον)
Luke 1:35	The child to be born will be holy; he will be called Son of God (υἱὸς θεοῦ)
Acts 9:20	And immediately he began to proclaim Jesus in the synagogues, saying, "He is the Son of God" (ὁ υἱὸς τοῦ θεοῦ)

the three words highlighted above: σωτήρ appears more than forty times in the LXX, εἰρήνη more than two hundred, and κύριος more than eight thousand!

Nevertheless, as Christoph Heilig points out, even if one grants a Septuagintal origin for certain language, "this does not mean that the resulting proposition does not evoke implications for the Roman sphere nor that it is neutral with regard to Roman ideology."[66] In fact, most of those recommending caution still accept that the terms in question do, in certain instances, intentionally mirror imperial discourse. To distinguish accidental from intentional parallels, Heilig identifies certain "stylistic devices" that an author can use for "making clear that he was evoking imperial associations."[67]

One such device is the immediate context. Heilig's example is 1 Cor 8:6, in which the application of the title "Lord" (κύριος) to Christ is contrasted with the existence of "many lords" (κύριοι) in the previous verse.[68] Another device is clustering, using multiple terms with imperial resonance in close conjunction. White, for instance, judges Phil 3:20 to be "the clearest example of a remark in Paul that is undeniably set against an imperial background" based on the joint appearance of πολίτευμα, κύριος, and σωτήρ.[69]

Both indicators appear in two of the passages highlighted above. Acts 10:36 contains two of the significant terms: "peace" (εἰρήνη) and "lord" (κύριος). Furthermore, C. Kavin Rowe argues that the context, Peter's conversation with a Roman centurion, "create[s] an ethos in which the presence of the Roman Empire is keenly felt."[70] As a result, Rowe, who is generally skeptical of imperial parallels, judges that in this verse "the juxtaposition of the κύριοι ... is too obvious to be missed, and it is too potent to be accidental."[71]

The case for an intentional use of imperial language in Luke 1:76–2:14 is even stronger. Zechariah prophesies that John "will go before the Lord" (1:76, κυρίου), who will "guide our feet into the way of peace" (1:79, εἰρήνης). An angel then announces to the shepherds the birth of a "Savior [σωτήρ], who is the Messiah, the Lord" (2:11, κύριος), before proclaiming "peace [εἰρήνη] among those whom he favors" (2:14). Even more important is what stands in the center of this cluster of imperial terminology: the only mention of Augustus by name in the entire NT (Luke 2:1).[72] Again, even some of the more hesitant interpreters acknowledge that Luke here makes a contrast between Jesus and Augustus "unmistakably clear."[73]

---

[66] Heilig, *Hidden Criticism*, 145.
[67] Ibid., 144.
[68] Ibid.
[69] White, "Anti-Imperial Subtexts," 314.
[70] Rowe, "Luke-Acts and the Imperial Cult," 292.
[71] Ibid., 297.
[72] This is the only use of the transliteration Αὔγουστος in the NT. The title "Augustus" (σεβαστός) is used three times in the NT, all in Acts, but each refers to later emperors. That this explicit reference to Augustus is intended to set up a contrast between Christ and Caesar is widely held: so Billings ("At the Age of 12," 85), Christian Blumenthal ("Augustus' Erlass und Gottes Macht: Überlegungen zur Charakterisierung der Augustusfigur und ihrer erzählstrategischen Funktion in der lukanischen Erzählung," *NTS* 57 [2011]: 4), François Bovon (*Luke 1: A Commentary on the Gospel of Luke 1:1–9:50*, trans. Christine M. Thomas, Hermeneia [Minneapolis: Fortress, 2002], 83), Brent ("Luke-Acts," 430), Brown (*Birth of the Messiah*, 415), Fitzmyer (*Luke I–IX*, 394), and Green (*Luke*, 58).
[73] Kim, *Christ and Caesar*, 87. So too Bryan, *Render to Caesar*, 99.

Interpreting Luke's Use of Imperial Language

The previous section has shown that at least two passages in Luke-Acts contain recognizable appropriations of imperial language. Opinions on the import of the shared language range from Richard Horsley's claim that "Luke clearly understands Jesus to be in direct confrontation with emperor" to Bradley Billings' suggestion that Luke is assimilating Jesus to a figure that is "culturally and socially appealing" to his non-Jewish audience.[74] Given the mixed evidence regarding Luke-Acts' perspective on Rome, I adopt neither a thoroughly pro- nor a wholly anti-imperial interpretation of Luke's use of imperial titles and concepts. Instead, I understand the function of this appropriation to be "supra-imperial," a term recently coined by the classicist Karl Galinsky. Galinsky suggests that the common description of Paul as "anti-imperial" should be replaced by a more accurate term: "Paul's message is not *anti*-imperial, but *supra*imperial: the emperor and the dispensations of empire go only so far. They are surpassed, in a far more perfect way, by God and the kingdom of heaven."[75] The expression "supra-imperial" connotes a claim of superiority that stops short of outright hostility, and it has since been adopted by others to characterize the attitudes present in Paul, Hebrews, and Q.[76] This term also accurately describes the position of many interpreters of Luke-Acts who do not use it explicitly.[77]

In light of the entirety of the evidence, a supra-imperial interpretation of Luke-Acts as a whole and of its use of imperial vocabulary in particular is the most plausible, and this reading is provisionally accepted here. As is widely acknowledged, Luke never displays open hostility toward Rome, but his application of imperial titles to Jesus in Rome-centered contexts implies a contrast in which Jesus is clearly the superior party. This conclusion is especially valuable insofar as it indicates that Luke makes use of terms and concepts commonly found in imperial propaganda in a way that subverts the absolute nature of these claims. In other words, Luke employs the same literary strategy elsewhere that this study posits is at work in the Acts summaries.

---

[74] Horsley, *Liberation of Christmas*, 33; Bradley Billings, "At the Age of 12," 89.

[75] Karl Galinsky, "In the Shadow (or Not) of the Imperial Cult: A Cooperative Agenda," in *Rome and Religion: A Cross-Disciplinary Dialogue on the Imperial Cult*, ed. Jeffrey Brodd and Jonathan L. Reed, WGRWSup 5 (Atlanta: SBL Press, 2011), 222.

[76] Paul: Heilig, *Hidden Criticism*, 133; Harry O. Maier, "Colossians, Ephesians, and Empire," in *An Introduction to Empire in the New Testament*, ed. Adam Winn, RBS 84 (Atlanta: SBL Press, 2016), 201; Todd D. Still and Bruce W. Longenecker, *Thinking through Paul: A Survey of His Life, Letters, and Theology* (Grand Rapids: Zondervan, 2014), 343. Hebrews: Jason A. Whitlark, *Resisting Empire: Rethinking the Purpose of the Letter to "the Hebrews,"* LNTS 484 (London: Bloomsbury, 2014), 98. Q: John S. Kloppenborg, "The Power and Surveillance of the Divine Judge in the Early Synoptic Tradition," in *Christ and the Emperor: The Gospel Evidence*, ed. Gilbert van Belle and Jozef Verheyden, BTS 20 (Leuven: Peeters, 2014), 184.

[77] Readings that may be classified as supra-imperial include those of Blumenthal ("Augustus' Erlass," 19), Brent ("Luke-Acts," 438), Brown (*Birth of the Messiah*, 415), Bryan (*Render to Caesar*, 99), Fitzmyer (*Luke I–IX*, 394), Rowe ("Luke-Acts and the Imperial Cult," 298), Seo (*Luke's Jesus*, 129), and Walton ("State They Were In," 34).

Previous Claims of Lukan Allusions to the Golden Age Myth

Allen Brent, Michael Wolter, and Schreiber go beyond the conclusion of the previous section, that Luke appropriates Augustan themes in general, and argue further that Luke's infancy narrative alludes to the Golden Age myth in particular. A positive evaluation of these arguments would mean that the supplementary criterion of "recurrence in the same author" would be satisfied. Yet while these authors successfully demonstrate Luke's use of imperial discourse, reinforcing the findings already reached by this study, none makes a compelling case for a Lukan allusion to the Golden Age myth specifically.

Allen Brent on Luke-Acts and the Golden Age

In his article "Luke-Acts and the Imperial Cult in Asia Minor" and in two subsequent books, Brent argues that Luke-Acts should be understood "against the backcloth of the concept of a *saeculum aureum*" and that Luke's work presents "a refashioned Christian version of the Augustan *saeculum aureum*."[78] Brent primarily supports this by pointing to parallels between the Golden Age myth and Luke's infancy narrative. The roles of the Magnificat and the Benedictus in Luke 1 are compared to "the announcement of the Golden Age ... through the medium of hymns," specifically Horace's *Carmen saeculare*.[79] Brent also connects the idea that the unnamed boy in Virgil's *Ecl.* 4 "will receive the life of the gods" (*Ecl.* 4.15) with what he sees as Luke's particular emphasis on Jesus being "Son of God already by conception," and he links the virgin birth in Luke with the "divine child born of a Virgin" in Virgil's poem.[80]

Brent's treatment of the Golden Age myth suffers from two related shortcomings. First, while Brent repeatedly refers to the Golden Age motif, his engagement with the literary tradition of this myth is quite limited. The only Golden Age text that he mines for parallels is Virgil's fourth *Eclogue*, while the Golden Age accounts of Hesiod, Plato, Aratus, Ovid, Seneca, and the other authors surveyed in Chapter 2 are almost completely ignored. This provides a very sparse basis for comparisons between the myth and Luke. Second, Brent identifies the Golden Age idea so closely with the imperial cult and Augustan ideology in general that he can consider a reference to any part of this ideology as a Golden Age reference. Brent justifies this move by claiming sources such as Lucan's *De bello civili*, Horace's *Carmen saeculare*, the imagery of the Ara Pacis, and especially the Priene inscription as examples of Golden Age ideology.[81] Unfortunately, none of these are versions of or even make clear references to the myth.

---

[78] Brent, "Luke-Acts," 414, 419; the two books referred to are *The Imperial Cult and the Origins of Church Order: Concepts and Images of Authority in Paganism and Early Christianity before the Age of Cyprian*, Supplements to Vigiliae Christianae 45 (Leiden: Brill, 1999) and *A Political History of Early Christianity* (London: T&T Clark, 2009).

[79] Brent, "Luke-Acts," 420.

[80] Ibid., 423–4; Brent, *Imperial Cult*, 54.

[81] Lucan: Brent, *Political History*, 122; Horace: Brent, "Luke-Acts," 420; the Ara Pacis: Brent, *Imperial Cult*, 60; the Priene inscription: Brent, *Imperial Cult*, 84.

The problems with considering the *Carmen saeculare* and the Ara Pacis as Golden Age representations have already been discussed in Chapter 2, and neither Lucan nor the Priene inscription refers to the myth in any recognizable way.[82]

As such, the vast majority of the parallels that Brent adduces to illuminate Luke's "Christian version of the Augustan *saeculum aureum*" have no direct connection with the Golden Age myth itself. To whatever extent Brent may be successful in showing a connection between Luke and Augustan propaganda in general, most of the evidence he presents cannot be construed as proof of an allusion to the Golden Age myth in particular. As for the few parallels to Luke that Brent does draw from an actual Golden Age text, Virgil's fourth *Eclogue*, none is compelling enough to indicate a specific allusion.[83]

Michael Wolter on Luke-Acts and the Golden Age

Wolter's essay "Die Hirten in der Weihnachtsgeschichte" focuses on the shepherds' role in Luke's infancy narrative.[84] Taking up a suggestion of Johannes Geffcken, Wolter argues that the shepherds' appearance is due to their connection with the Golden Age in Roman bucolic poetry.[85] Noting that shepherds are linked with an announcement of the Golden Age in all three extant works of bucolic poetry from the early Empire (the *Eclogues* of Virgil and Calpurnius and the anonymous *Einsiedeln Eclogues*), Wolter chooses Calpurnius' *Ecl.* 1 as his basis of comparison with Luke.[86]

Wolter supports his claim with three types of evidence. The first and most obvious is a list of parallels between Calpurnius' first *Eclogue* and Luke 2. Wolter identifies seven specific similarities: (1) shepherds receive an announcement of salvation; (2) the shepherds are called to be joyful; (3) universal peace is proclaimed; (4) shepherds are the first addressees; (5) the perspective is subsequently expanded to the whole world; (6) the announcement of salvation is connected with a specific individual; (7) the shepherds proclaim the message they have received.[87]

---

[82] See Barker, "Golden Age," 434–46 on the *Carmen saeculare* and Zanker, "Late Horatian Lyric," 505–13 on the *Carmen saeculare* and the Ara Pacis.

[83] The parallels between the "divine child" of Virgil's *Ecl.* 4 and Luke's designation of Christ as the Son of God are far too inexact to posit an allusion to the poem. Brent's claim (*Imperial Cult*, 54, 97) that *Ecl.* 4 features a virgin birth is far from obvious: the figure of the Virgin (*Ecl.* 4.6) is borrowed from Aratus' version of the myth (*Phaen.* 97, 136), where she does not play any maternal role, and Virgil's *Eclogue* never implies that the Virgin is the mother of the child described in the poem. The presence of hymns in Luke 1 is insufficient on its own to posit a link to the Golden Age tradition.

[84] Michael Wolter, "Die Hirten in der Weihnachtsgeschichte (Lk 2,8–20)," in *Religionsgeschichte des Neuen Testaments: Festschrift für Klaus Berger zum 60. Geburtstag*, ed. Axel von Dobbeler, Kurt Erlemann, and Roman Heiligenthal (Tübingen: Francke, 2000), 501–17.

[85] Ibid., 505–8; Johannes Geffcken, "Die Hirten auf dem Felde," *Hermes* 49 (1914): 321–51.

[86] Wolter, "Die Hirten," 509–10. A Neronian date for both Calpurnius Siculus and the *Einsiedeln Eclogues* is likely but disputed; see the relevant sections in Chapter 2 for more information. Wolter (ibid., 509) claims that in Virgil's *Eclogue* the dawning of the Golden Age is sung by shepherds, but the identity of the speaking voice is unclear; Brian W. Breed (*Pastoral Inscriptions: Reading and Writing Virgil's Eclogues*, Classical Literature and Society [London: Bloomsbury Academic, 2012], 136) judges that "the speaker of the poem bears no apparent signs of being a shepherd himself." The speakers in the *Einsiedeln Eclogues* are clearly shepherds.

[87] Wolter, "Die Hirten," 512.

Next, Wolter argues for the existence of a general topos of Golden Age announcements to shepherds by appealing to the Sibylline Oracles. Interpreting Sib. Or. 3.367–370 as a Golden Age description, Wolter translates v. 372 as "there would be a proclamation by blessed ones, as among shepherds."[88] Wolter understands the last phrase to indicate that the idea of divine pronouncements to shepherds was a commonplace. Finally, Wolter suggests that this Golden Age shepherd topos can explain why Luke specifies that the shepherds were "keeping watch over their flock by night" (Luke 2:8). Wolter connects this with Ornytus' description of Golden Age shepherding in Calpurnius' first *Eclogue*:

> The whole herd may wander while their keeper is carefree, and the shepherd might not close the fold at night with a barrier of ash-wood; yet no robber will set any ambush for the sheep. (*Ecl.* 1.37–41)[89]

Luke's mention of the shepherds watching their flock at night, then, may be interpreted as a contrast to the Golden Age insouciance that they were about to experience.

Wolter's best evidence consists in the thematic parallels between Calpurnius' *Ecl.* 1 and Luke 2: in both cases, shepherds are the first recipients of an announcement that a time of joy and peace is dawning. The attempt to demonstrate a general topos using Sib. Or. 3.372 is less successful. The main problem is that Wolter's interpretation relies on an emendation of the text, originally proposed by Geffcken, that is not universally accepted.[90] Collins does adopt Geffcken's emendation for v. 372, μακάρων κεν ἔῃ φάτις ὡς ἐν ἀγραύλοις, translating it as "there will be report of the blessed ones, as among countryfolk."[91] Both Rieuwerd Buitenwerf and Valentin Nikiprowetzky, however, retain the manuscript reading, μακάρων κενεήφατος ὅσσον ἄγραυλος.[92] With this reading, any notion of an announcement to shepherds disappears.[93] Wolter's final argument, that the use of a bucolic Golden Age tradition explains the detail of the shepherds keeping watch, is neither conclusive nor implausible and thus does not add much to his overall case.[94]

---

[88] Ibid., 513; "es wäre eine Verkündigung von Seligen, wie unter Hirten."

[89] licet omne vagetur/securo custode pecus nocturnaque pastor/claudere fraxinea nolit praesepia crate:/non tamen insidias praedator ovilibus ullas/afferet. Wolter (ibid., 515) also points to Tibullus, who describes the ideal past as a time when "the leader of the flock would seek sleep among various sheep without a care" (*El.* 1.10.9–10).

[90] Geffcken, *Komposition*, 14.

[91] Collins, "Sibylline Oracles," 1:370.

[92] Rieuwerd Buitenwerf, *Book III of the Sibylline Oracles and Its Social Setting*, SVTP 17 (Leiden: Brill, 2003), 225; Nikiprowetzky, *La troisième Sibylle*, 308. Buitenwerf (ibid.) offers as a possible translation, "any insignificant peasant will belong among the blessed ones."

[93] A separate problem is Wolter's identification ("Die Hirten," 513) of Sib. Or. 3.367–370 as a description of the Golden Age. These lines certainly predict a return of ideal conditions, but no distinctive features of the Golden Age myth are present that would justify the claim of a reference to this specific literary tradition.

[94] There is no indication that the shepherds would permanently cease to watch their flocks after the angelic pronouncement, and the parallel with Calpurnius is quite general. On the other hand, alternative explanations for this detail also lack force. Fitzmyer (*Luke I–IX*, 409) suggests only that the night setting serves as a contrast to the glory of the Lord, while Bovon (*Luke 1*, 87) sees the activity as intentionally "familiar and banal" to contrast with the sudden divine appearance.

Commentators often summarily dismiss suggestions that the shepherds should be interpreted through the bucolic tradition, but these dismissals tend to be poorly grounded.[95] First, some reject such an allusion based on the assumption that no connection exists with bucolic poetry "save for a generic reference to shepherds."[96] Dismissals of this sort fail to deal with the array of parallels that Wolter identifies. The other main objection stems from the idea that "Luke's narrative is firmly centred in the stories of the history of Israel rather than Greco-Roman allusions."[97] This both begs the question and ignores the mention of Caesar Augustus by name just a few verses prior.

On the whole, Wolter's argument that the shepherds in Luke 2 function as a metonym for the idea of the Golden Age is plausible, but it falls short of being persuasive. Unlike Brent, Wolter primarily draws on a genuine Golden Age text, and the parallels he highlights between Calpurnius and Luke are noteworthy, even if the other evidence he presents is less compelling. The main weakness in Wolter's case is the limited supply of evidence. Geffcken's emendation to Sib. Or. 3.372 is doubtful, which means that Wolter can muster only one example of shepherds as recipients of a Golden Age announcement: Calpurnius' *Ecl.* 1. Wolter does not argue for a specific allusion to this poem, and this single text is insufficient to support the claim of a more widespread topos.

Stefan Schreiber on Luke-Acts and the Golden Age

Schreiber's monograph *Weihnachtspolitik: Lukas 1–2 und das Goldene Zeitalter* was prompted by and expands upon the essay of Wolter examined above.[98] Drawing upon a wider selection of texts and artifacts, Schreiber argues that Luke includes Golden Age imagery in his infancy narrative in order to contrast Jesus and Caesar, using the myth to engage in political criticism of Rome. As such, Schreiber's work represents a close analogue to the present study in both its approach and its conclusion.

Schreiber's survey of the Golden Age tradition, especially its instantiations during the reigns of Augustus and Nero, is fairly thorough. After briefly noting the Greek accounts of Hesiod, Plato, and Aratus, Schreiber examines the myth's appearances under Augustus, focusing on the poetry of Horace and Virgil, the Priene inscription, the reliefs on the Ara Pacis, and a statue of Augustus from Prima Porta.[99] Moving to the time of Nero, Schreiber considers four works: Seneca's *Apocolocyntosis*, Calpurnius' *Eclogues*, Lucan's *De bello civili*, and the *Einsiedeln Eclogues*.[100] Schreiber then catalogues the fundamental elements of the Golden Age concept using the same base

---

[95] Bovon (*Luke 1*, 87) and Wolfgang Wiefel (*Das Evangelium nach Lukas*, THKNT 3 [Berlin: Evangelische Verlagsanstalt, 1988], 71) are open to at a least a secondary reference to Greco-Roman poetry, although neither explores the issue further.

[96] Fitzmyer, *Luke I–IX*, 395; so also Sarah Harris, *The Davidic Shepherd King in the Lukan Narrative*, LNTS 558 (New York: T&T Clark, 2016), 60; Marshall, *Luke*, 108.

[97] Harris, *Davidic Shepherd King*, 60; so also Brown, *Birth of the Messiah*, 421.

[98] Schreiber, *Weihnachtspolitik*, 9.

[99] Ibid., 29–44.

[100] Ibid., 46–53.

text as Wolter, the first *Eclogue* of Calpurnius. Cross-referencing this poem with other accounts, Schreiber identifies five basic Golden Age themes: peace, justice, world rule, restoration of ancient order, and carefree enjoyment of nature's bounty.[101]

Turning to Luke, Schreiber begins by arguing that the mention of Augustus in Luke 2:1 is an "unveiled reception signal," indicating that Augustan ideology and terminology may constitute a proper interpretive lens for Luke's narrative.[102] Schreiber discerns in Luke's infancy narrative four "noticeable correspondences" with "Golden Age topoi."[103] First, he notes that Golden Age themes appear in "the literary form of songs."[104] Second, the new rule comes with divine backing: Jesus' reign is announced by prophecies, and he himself is titled the "Son of God."[105] Third, Schreiber agrees with Wolter that the announcement of salvation to shepherds parallels bucolic accounts of the Golden Age.[106] Finally, Schreiber points to "politically charged terms" in Luke 1–2, specifically noting the words οἰκουμένη, εὐαγγελίζομαι, σωτήρ, and κύριος.[107] Having laid out these parallels, Schreiber expresses confidence that Luke's audience would have immediately recognized and understood them as claiming for Jesus "the divinely legitimated lordship over the whole world."[108] In Schreiber's estimation, this message ultimately makes Luke-Acts into "a piece of subversive underground literature."[109]

Since Schreiber's focus is on the political significance of the Golden Age idea, he primarily engages with texts that approach the myth from a political angle. While this is understandable, it results in two potential weaknesses in his survey of the Golden Age tradition. First, several Golden Age accounts or references from the early Empire are left untreated, including Trogus' *Historiae*, Germanicus' *Aratea*, Seneca's *Phaedra*, and the *Octavia*.[110] Even the poetry of Ovid, perhaps the most influential Golden Age author of the period, is given short shrift.[111] Second, like Brent, Schreiber gives center stage to several texts or artifacts that make no explicit or clear implicit use of the Golden Age myth. Four of Schreiber's five main Augustan examples of Golden Age ideology fall into this category: the poetry of Horace, the Ara Pacis, the Prima Porta statue, and the Priene inscription. As a result, the overall portrait painted by Schreiber is not so much one of the Golden Age myth specifically as it is of Augustan ideology more generally.[112]

---

[101] Ibid., 58–62.
[102] Ibid., 63; "unverhülltes Rezeptionssignal."
[103] Ibid., 64; "auffällige Entsprechungen"; "Topik des Goldenen Zeitalters."
[104] Ibid., 64–5; "die literarische Form des Liedes."
[105] Ibid., 65.
[106] Ibid.
[107] Ibid., 66; "politisch aufgeladene Begriffe."
[108] Ibid., 67; "die göttliche legitimierte Herrschaft über die ganze Welt."
[109] Ibid., 80; "einem Stück subversiver Untergrundliteratur."
[110] The *Phaedra* and the *Octavia* are cited only in a single footnote (ibid., 26 n. 4), while Trogus and Germanicus are not mentioned at all.
[111] Schreiber mentions Ovid on only three pages (ibid., 27, 45, 61).
[112] Schreiber is aware of this potential problem, as he notes Galinsky's objections to characterizing Horace's *Carmen saeculare*, the Ara Pacis, and the Prima Porta statue as Golden Age sources (ibid., 30 n. 16, 35 n. 35, 41).

Schreiber does use a genuine Golden Age text to organize his catalogue of fundamental Golden Age motifs: Calpurnius' *Ecl*. 1. The five motifs vary in their distinctiveness and thus in their usefulness for detecting a Golden Age allusion.[113] The themes of peace and justice certainly do appear in Golden Age texts, but these ideas are quite general and widespread outside of the myth. The notions of a new world rule and the restoration of ancient order come much closer to the specific concept of a returning Golden Age, although these also appear often in non-Golden Age texts, as Schreiber's own citations indicate.[114] The final Golden Age feature that Schreiber discerns, the spontaneous fruitfulness of nature, is the one most distinctive of the myth.

Moving on to Luke, some of the Golden Age parallels that Schreiber highlights in the infancy narrative are clearly not Golden Age-specific, such as the use of political vocabulary and Jesus' divine mandate. The two specific features that might point toward this myth in particular are the presentation of this message in the form of songs and the presence of the shepherds, which were also highlighted by Brent and Wolter respectively. As to the most distinctive of the Golden Age motifs identified, spontaneous fruitfulness, Schreiber admits that, "in contrast to the conception of the Golden Age, Luke nowhere speaks about the superabundance of nature."[115] There may be good reasons for this omission, as Schreiber argues, but the absence of a distinctive Golden Age feature such as this makes Schreiber's case less compelling.[116]

Schreiber persuasively argues that Luke intentionally appropriates of elements of imperial ideology, and he has many excellent insights into the purpose of this appropriation. Furthermore, Schreiber helpfully details the ways in which the Golden Age idea was incorporated into Augustan ideology. Unfortunately, however, his arguments for an allusion to the specific concept of the Golden Age in Luke's infancy narrative do not advance much beyond those of Wolter. Schreiber's case for an allusion to the Golden Age in Luke 1–2 too falls short of being conclusive.[117]

---

[113] Schreiber (ibid., 27) also recognizes that common property appears in Golden Age accounts of the period, citing Virgil, Tibullus, Ovid, and Seneca to this effect. Yet Schreiber fails to classify this as one of the fundamental motifs of the Golden Age. This is likely due to his predominant focus on Golden Age references that are explicitly political, which results in Schreiber giving little attention to many of the Golden Age texts that mention common property, including Germanicus' *Aratea*, Seneca's *Phaedra*, the *Octavia*, and Plutarch's *Cimon*. As a result, the prevalence of the common property motif in early imperial Golden Age accounts does not fully emerge in Schreiber's study.

[114] Schreiber cites many non-Golden Age texts containing these motifs, such as Horace's *Carmen saeculare*, the Priene inscription, Velleius Paterculus' *Historiae Romanae*, and Lucan's *De bello civili*.

[115] Ibid., 75; "im Gegensatz zur Konzeption vom Goldenen Zeitalter spricht Lukas nirgends von der Überfülle der Natur."

[116] Schreiber (ibid., 75) attributes this omission to Luke's desires to criticize the Empire for its false promises and to concentrate on social justice issues.

[117] F. Gerald Downing (review of *Weihnachtspolitik: Lukas 1–2 und das Goldene Zeitalter*, by Stefan Schreiber, *JSNT* 33 [2011]: 68–9) gives a more positive evaluation, judging that "overall the case is persuasive."

Summary: Preliminaries to a Golden Age Reading of the Acts Summaries

In this chapter, I have arrived at three main conclusions on issues relevant to the Golden Age reading of the Acts summaries that will take place in Chapter 5. (1) The summaries in Acts 2:42–47 and 4:32–35 portray an eschatological lifestyle. Acts 2:17 characterizes the gift of the Spirit as an eschatological event, and both of these summaries depict the way of life that follows from outpourings of the Spirit in the immediately preceding verses, Acts 2:41 and 4:31. This fits with the finding in Chapter 3 that Jewish and Christian uses of the Golden Age myth often occur in eschatological contexts.

(2) Luke-Acts not only shows a special interest in Rome but even adopts imperial language, most notably in the infancy narrative and in Peter's speech to Cornelius in Acts 10. Again, this matches with the observation in Chapter 3 that Jewish and Christian references to the Golden Age appear in works concerned with Rome. Furthermore, it indicates that the appropriation of imperial discourse is one of Luke's literary strategies. The preliminary assessment of the function of this appropriation is that it is supra-imperial: Luke is not openly hostile toward Rome, but he sets up an implicit contrast in which Rome and its emperor are inferior to Christ and his kingdom. (3) Although a few authors have argued that Luke uses Golden Age imagery in his infancy narratives, the evidence presented is insufficient to assent fully to this claim. The authors in question have demonstrated that Luke makes use of Augustan discourse, of which the Golden Age myth is a part; nevertheless, the cases made for a specifically Golden Age reference are not conclusive as they stand.

In Chapter 5, I will argue that a stronger case for a Golden Age allusion can be made for the Acts summaries. In addition to the general parallels that this chapter has drawn between Luke-Acts and other Jewish and Christian texts that refer to the myth, I will present more specific correspondences that link the Acts summaries and Golden Age accounts. I will also offer two interpretations of this allusion: Luke's use of Golden Age imagery characterizes the Spirit's coming as both an eschatological and a universal event, and at the same time it presents Christ rather than Caesar as one able to effect a restoration of human concord and divine blessing.

5

Reading Acts 2:42–47 and 4:32–35 as Golden Age Allusions

The previous chapters have investigated instances of the Golden Age myth from Hesiod to the Sibylline Oracles along with aspects of Luke-Acts that are relevant to the central thesis of this study, that the common property motif in Acts 2:42–47 and 4:32–35 serves as an allusion to the Golden Age tradition. The fruits of these investigations can now be brought to bear on the summaries themselves. In this chapter I interpret these two passages in three steps. First, I examine the main exegetical issues in the summaries to establish what these texts actually say. Second, I argue that the Acts summaries are distinctive in their context and contain sufficient correspondences with the Golden Age myth such that they can be read as alluding to this tradition. Third, I propose two distinct but complementary interpretations of this allusion: Luke's use of Golden Age themes both signifies that the Spirit's coming inaugurates a universal and eschatological restoration and makes a supra-imperial claim for Christ over against Caesar, showing Christ to be the only "savior" who can bring about such a restoration.

Five Exegetical Issues

Before any claims are made regarding the presence or meaning of a Golden Age allusion in the Acts summaries, what these passages actually say must be determined. This section addresses five disputed exegetical issues: (1) the meaning of κοινωνία in Acts 2:42; (2) the meaning of ἐπὶ τὸ αὐτό in Acts 2:44, 47; (3) the meaning of ἀφελότης in Acts 2:46; (4) the meanings of ἔχειν χάριν πρός in Acts 2:47 and of χάρις in Acts 4:33; (5) the nature of the property arrangements described in Acts 2:44–45 and 4:32, 34–35.

The Meaning of κοινωνία in Acts 2:42

In Acts 2:42, Luke states that the converts at Pentecost "devoted themselves to the apostles' teaching and fellowship [τῇ κοινωνίᾳ], to the breaking of bread and the prayers." The basic lexical meaning of κοινωνία is "(the) having *something* in common with *someone*."[1] When the word is used absolutely, as in Acts 2:42, Frederick Hauck gives three possible meanings: (1) "fellowship," (2) "a contract of partnership," or (3) "community of possession or communal possession."[2] Most commentators adopt the first interpretation for Acts 2:42, taking κοινωνία as "an abstract and spiritual term for the fellowship of brotherly concord."[3] Pervo, for example, argues that the other practices mentioned in v. 42 (teaching, breaking bread, and praying) are spiritual ones, making "'spiritual' togetherness" the most likely meaning for κοινωνία here.[4] Conversely, J. Y. Campbell and Reta Finger contend that the three other elements listed in 2:42 each denotes "a manifestation of fellowship" and "an *activity*," indicating that κοινωνία refers to something more concrete than a mere feeling of fellowship.[5] Moreover, Julien Ogereau concludes from his survey of the word κοινωνία in documentary sources that the meaning of "spiritual communion/fellowship" appears "seldom, if ever" in these materials.[6]

While this is Luke's only use of the term κοινωνία, κοιν-rooted words with related meanings do appear twice elsewhere in Acts (κοινά in 2:44; 4:32), and both describe the believers' community of property.[7] Given that κοινωνία can denote a community of goods (cf. Plutarch, *Cim.* 10.6–7, treated in Chapter 2), that the other two similar uses of κοιν-language in Acts refer to this arrangement, and that one of these occurs just two verses later, interpreting κοινωνία in Acts 2:42 as primarily referring to the practice of common property is preferable.

The Meaning of ἐπὶ τὸ αὐτό in Acts 2:44, 47

In the first summary, Luke states that "all who believed were together" (Acts 2:44, ἐπὶ τὸ αὐτό), and the same phrase appears in the concluding verse: "and day by day the Lord added to their number [ἐπὶ τὸ αὐτό] those who were being saved" (2:47). Unlike

---

[1] J. Y. Campbell, "KOINΩNIA and Its Cognates in the New Testament," *JBL* 51 (1932): 356. A wealth of extra-biblical comparative material is available: Plato, Aristotle, and Philo each use the term more than eighty times. For surveys of κοινωνία in literary sources, see Campbell, ibid., 352–80; Norbert Baumert, *KOINONEIN und METECHEIN—synonym? Eine umfassende semantische Untersuchung*, SBB 51 (Stuttgart: Katholisches Bibelwerk, 2003). For κοινωνία in documentary sources, see Julien M. Ogereau, *Paul's Koinonia with the Philippians: A Socio-Historical Investigation of a Pauline Economic Partnership*, WUNT 2/377 (Tübingen: Mohr Siebeck, 2014), 151–219.

[2] Frederick Hauck, "κοινωνία," *TDNT* 3:798.

[3] Hauck, *TDNT* 3:809. Others supporting a primary meaning of "fellowship" include Barrett (*Acts*, 1:163), Baumert (*KOINONEIN*, 172), Bock (*Acts*, 149), Bruce (*Acts*, 131–2), Hays (*Luke's Wealth Ethics*, 191), Hume (*Early Christian Community*, 102), Keener (*Acts 1:1–2:47*, 1002–3), Klauck ("Gütergemeinschaft," 73), Georg Panikulam (*Koinōnia in the New Testament: A Dynamic Expression of Christian Life*, AnBib 85 [Rome: Biblical Institute Press, 1979], 124), and Pervo (*Acts*, 92–3).

[4] Pervo, *Acts*, 92.

[5] Campbell, "KOINΩNIA," 374; Reta Finger, *Of Widows and Meals: Communal Meals in the Book of Acts* (Grand Rapids: Eerdmans, 2007), 227. Both identify the referent of κοινωνία as the practice of common property, as do Cerfaux ("La première communauté," 26), Dupont ("Community of Goods," 87), and Johnson (*Acts*, 58).

[6] Julien M. Ogereau, "A Survey of Κοινωνία and Its Cognates in Documentary Sources," *NovT* 57 (2015): 293.

[7] The word κοινωνία appears nineteen times in the NT but is used absolutely only twice outside of this verse (Gal 2:9; Heb 13:16). It occurs only three times in the LXX (Lev 5:21; Wis 8:18; 3 Macc 4:6). Luke also uses κοιν-rooted words six times in Acts with the meaning of "profane."

κοινωνία, the expression ἐπὶ τὸ αὐτό has a sizeable Septuagintal and Lukan pedigree.[8] In the LXX, ἐπὶ τὸ αὐτό can mean "at the same time," "at the same place," or "together" in the sense of being a unified body.[9] In addition, Metzger argues that the NT contains a more specific variant of the third, unitive sense, stating that "ἐπὶ τὸ αὐτό ... acquired a quasi-technical meaning in the early church" that "signifies the union of the Christian body, and perhaps could be rendered 'in church fellowship.'"[10]

In Luke's writings, the expression seems to have a spatial sense in Luke 17:35 but a nonspatial, unitive one in Acts 4:26. The two closest parallels are in Acts 1:15 and 2:1, both of which describe the gathered community of believers in Jerusalem: "there was a group of about one hundred and twenty persons in the one place" (1:15, ἐπὶ τὸ αὐτό), and "they were all in one place together" (2:1, ὁμοῦ ἐπὶ τὸ αὐτό). Although the NRSV translates ἐπὶ τὸ αὐτό spatially in both places, the unitive sense is also possible.[11]

Given that ἐπὶ τὸ αὐτό clearly does not have a primarily spatial meaning in Acts 2:47, a nonspatial sense is preferable in 2:44 as well.[12] Luke seems to emphasize here the unity of the community more than the location of its members in the same physical place. Acts 2:44 may be suitably rendered as "all who believed were one community" and 2:47 as "the Lord added to the community those who were being saved."

The Meaning of ἀφελότης in Acts 2:46

Toward the end of the first summary, Luke reports that the believers "ate their food with glad and generous hearts" (Acts 2:46, ἐν ... ἀφελότητι καρδίας). The word ἀφελότης, translated by the NRSV as "generous," appears nowhere else in the NT or the LXX; in fact, there is no attestation of it at all prior to Luke. The second century provides only limited evidence: the astronomer Vettius Valens uses ἀφελότης twice to mean something like "simplemindedness," while Melito of Sardis repeats Luke's phrase, wishing "peace ... to those who love the Lord ἐν ἀφελότητι καρδίας" (*Pasch.* 826).[13]

The word ἀφελότης shares a root with ἀφέλεια, which means "simplicity," and Barrett and Johnson argue that it is used in Acts 2:46 in place of ἁπλότης, an unrelated noun

---

[8] Nearly half of the extant occurrences of ἐπὶ τὸ αὐτό prior to the NT occur in the LXX, which uses the expression fifty-one times. It appears six times in Luke-Acts.

[9] Takamitsu Muraoka, "ἐπί," GELS 267.

[10] Metzger, *Textual Commentary*, 265; cf. Bruce, *Acts*, 108; Everett Ferguson, "'When You Come Together': Epi To Auto in Early Christian Literature," *ResQ* 16 (1973): 207.

[11] Keener (*Acts 1:1–2:47*, 795) sees the emphasis of ἐπὶ τὸ αὐτό in Luke-Acts as usually "not so much on their common location ... as on their concerted activity or unity." A. A. Vazakas ("Is Acts I–XV.35 a Literal Translation from an Aramaic Original?" *JBL* 37 [1918]: 107–8) identifies Acts 1:15 and 2:1 as verses in which ἐπὶ τὸ αὐτό "signifies the union of the Christian body," as does Metzger (*Textual Commentary*, 265).

[12] Although Bock (*Acts*, 152) and Schneider (*Apostelgeschichte*, 1:287) adopt a spatial reading of ἐπὶ τὸ αὐτό in Acts 2:44, most commentators seem to prefer a nonspatial interpretation: so Johnson, *Literary Function*, 186–7; Marguerat, *Actes*, 105; Schnabel, *Acts*, 181; Walton, "Primitive Communism," 103; Witherington III, *Acts*, 161.

[13] Vettius states that his mystical style is not due to "malice or simplemindedness" (*Anth.* 3.10 [145,29 Pingree = 3.13 (153,30 Kroll)], ἀφελότητι) and later refers to a person who is "betrayed by his simplemindedness" (*Anth.* 6 Preface [230,12–13 Pingree = 240,15 Kroll], ἀφελότητος).

that also means "simplicity, sincerity, uprightness."[14] The parallel phrase ἐν ἁπλότητι καρδίας occurs twice in the NT and in the LXX and four times in the Testaments of the Twelve Patriarchs.[15] In all eight cases, ἁπλότης is best translated as "sincerity," "integrity," or "simplicity." Some propose that ἀφελότης means "generosity" in Acts 2:46, but the support for this view is weak.[16] "Simplicity" is closer to the root meaning of the term, and most instances of ἐν ἁπλότητι καρδίας do not appear in contexts that imply a specific reference to generosity.[17] Interpreting the expression in Acts 2:46 as meaning "in simplicity of heart" is preferable to the NRSV's "with … generous hearts."

The Meanings of ἔχειν χάριν πρός in Acts 2:47 and of χάρις in Acts 4:33[18]

Near the end of the first summary, Luke describes the believers as "having the favor of all the people" (Acts 2:47, ἔχοντες χάριν πρὸς ὅλον τὸν λαόν). The word χάρις reappears in the second summary: between references to the community's property arrangement, Acts 4:33 declares that "great favor was upon them all" (χάρις τε μεγάλη ἦν ἐπὶ πάντας αὐτούς). The interpretations of both verses are disputed.

Most commentators understand Acts 2:47 as the NRSV renders it, as stating that the community found favor in the eyes of the people.[19] Others, however, have followed T. David Andersen, who argues that the Greek construction χάρις πρός denotes showing favor *toward* rather than finding favor *with*.[20] The context seems to support the majority position: the idea that the community was held in esteem by the people fits well with the second half of Acts 2:47 ("day by day the Lord added to their number") and with similar comments elsewhere in the early chapters of Acts (4:21; 5:13–16, 26). Yet Andersen contends that in all nine instances of the construction χάρις πρός in Philo and Josephus the object of πρός is the recipient of favor rather than the giver.[21]

Andersen, however, overstates the evidence from Philo and Josephus. Two of the occurrences of χάρις πρός in Josephus describe a reciprocal relationship of favor, so that the object of πρός is a giver of favor no less than a recipient.[22] In two other cases,

---

[14] BDAG, "ἁπλότης," 104; Barrett, *Acts*, 1:171; Johnson, *Acts*, 59.

[15] Eph 6:5; Col 3:22; 1 Chr 28:17 LXX; Wis 1:1 LXX; T. Reu. 4.1; T. Iss. 3.8; 4.1; 7.7.

[16] "Generosity" is suggested by Bock (*Acts*, 154), Bruce (*Acts*, 133), and Conzelmann (*Acts*, 24).

[17] The one exception is T. Iss. 3.8, where the phrase could refer to simplicity or generosity.

[18] For a slightly expanded version of this argument, see Joshua Noble, "The Meaning of ἔχοντες χάριν πρός in Acts 2:47: Resolving Some Recent Confusion," *NTS* 64 (2018): 573–9.

[19] Barrett, *Acts*, 1:171; Bock, *Acts*, 154; Bruce, *Acts*, 133; Fitzmyer, *Acts*, 272; Haenchen, *Acts*, 193; Holladay, *Acts*, 108; Keener, *Acts 1:1–2:47*, 1073; Schneider, *Apostelgeschichte*, 1:289.

[20] T. David Andersen, "The Meaning of ΕΧΟΝΤΕΣ ΧΑΡΙΝ ΠΡΟΣ in Acts 2,47," *NTS* 34 (1988): 604–10. This same position was argued more briefly by F. P. Cheetham, "Acts ii. 47: ἔχοντες χάριν πρὸς ὅλον τὸν λαόν," *ExpTim* 74 (1963): 214–15. Marguerat (*Actes*, 108–9) adopts Andersen's position, while Pervo (*Acts*, 94–5), Pesch (*Apostelgeschichte*, 132), and Peterson (*Acts*, 164) acknowledge its strength.

[21] Andersen, "Meaning," 607.

[22] In *A.J.* 14.146, Jewish envoys request a renewal of "goodwill and friendship with the Romans" (πρὸς Ῥωμαίους χάριτας καὶ τὴν φιλίαν), and the Romans agree to a relationship of "friendship and goodwill with them" (φιλίαν καὶ χάριτας πρὸς αὐτούς) in *A.J.* 14.148.

the object of πρός may actually designate the giver of favor instead of the recipient.[23] Most importantly, Andersen does not note the existence of more precise parallels to Acts 2:47. At least three instances of the construction ἔχειν χάριν πρός + acc. are extant outside of this verse, and in all three cases the expression clearly means "to find favor with."[24] For example, Plutarch, recounting Demosthenes' early frustrations, remarks that the orator "found no favor with the people [χάριν οὐκ ἔχει πρὸς τὸν δῆμον], but drunks, sailors, and ignorant people were listened to and held the stage, while he himself was disregarded" (*Dem.* 7.2).[25] In light of the parallels, the contextually favored interpretation of Acts 2:47, that the community found favor in the eyes of the people, is almost certainly correct.

Disagreement about the meaning of χάρις in Acts 4:33 centers on whether the term refers to divine grace or human favor. The former is supported by a large majority of commentators, who often point to the parallel construction in Luke 2:40:[26]

Luke 2:40	Acts 4:33
καὶ χάρις θεοῦ ἦν ἐπ᾽ αὐτό.	χάρις τε μεγάλη ἦν ἐπὶ πάντας αὐτούς.
And the favor of God was upon him.	And great favor was upon them all.

Fitzmyer is almost alone in taking the referent of χάρις in Acts 4:33 to be human favor, but this interpretation also has reasonable textual support, in this case from parallel expressions of the people's esteem for the community in the other two summaries:[27]

---

[23] Christopher Begg (ed., *Judean Antiquities Books 5-7*, Flavius Josephus Translation and Commentary 4 [Leiden: Brill, 2005], 122) translates ἕνεκα … χάριτος τῆς πρὸς ἄλλους in *A.J.* 6.86 as "[to win] favor with others," and the Loeb translation of Philo, *Conf.* 116 renders χάριτος ἕνεκα τῆς πρὸς τοὺς ἐπιεικεστέρους as "to keep the goodwill of the more decent sort" (Colson and Whitaker).

[24] In addition to the occurrence in Plutarch mentioned above, the construction appears twice in the Greek magical text known as the *Cyranides* to describe the effects of talismans: "you will not be drunk, and you will find favor with everyone" (*Cyr.* 1.8.27, πρὸς πάντας χάριν ἔχων); "he will find favor with all men and with all women" (*Cyr.* 3.9.15–16, ἕξει δὲ χάριν πρὸς πάντας ἀνθρώπους καὶ πάσας γυναῖκας). One further instance of this construction is in Aristotle's *Politics*, in the description of a nose that is "beautiful and graceful to look at" (*Pol.* 1309b25–26, καλὴ καὶ χάριν ἔχουσα πρὸς τὴν ὄψιν). This is not an exact parallel, as the object of πρός is not a personal agent. Nonetheless, the general meaning is in agreement with that in the other three examples: the subject that has χάριν is viewed favorably by others.

[25] Giuseppe Gamba ("Significato letterale e portata dottrinale dell'inciso participiale di Atti 2,47b: ἔχοντες χάριν πρὸς ὅλον τὸν λαόν," *Salesianum* 43 [1981]: 58–9 n. 29) argues that the sense of χάρις is different in the two texts, being objective in *Dem.* 7.2 and subjective in Acts 2:47, and that this parallel is thus not interpretively significant. This dismissal is unsatisfactory for three reasons: (1) the identification of χάρις in *Dem.* 7.2 as objective is questionable and disagrees with the *LSJ*'s analysis of this text; (2) even if χάρις is objective here, the direction of the potential favor is still relevant; (3) the two passages from the *Cyranides* mentioned in the note above are clearly subjective and therefore immune to Gamba's objection.

[26] Bock, *Acts*, 214; Haenchen, *Acts*, 231; Johnson, *Acts*, 86; Keener, *Acts: An Exegetical Commentary*. 3:1–14:28 (Grand Rapids: Baker Academic, 2013), 1177; Marguerat, *Actes*, 170; Pervo, *Acts*, 127; Schneider, *Apostelgeschichte*, 1:364.

[27] Fitzmyer, *Acts*, 313–14. Pierre Benoit ("Remarques sur les 'sommaires' de Actes 2.42 à 5," in *Aux sources de la tradition chrétienne: Mélanges offerts à M. Maurice Goguel à l'occasion de son soixante-dixième anniversaire*, ed. P. H. Menoud and Oscar Cullmann [Neuchâtel: Delachaux & Niestlé, 1950], 6) also holds this position.

Acts 2:47	Acts 4:33	Acts 5:13
ἔχοντες χάριν πρὸς ὅλον τὸν λαόν.	χάρις τε μεγάλη ἦν ἐπὶ πάντας αὐτούς.	ἀλλ' ἐμεγάλυνεν αὐτοὺς ὁ λαός.
Having the favor of all the people.	And great favor was upon them all.	But the people esteemed them greatly.

Given the many parallels between these three summaries, the claims of the people's favor in the other two summaries using related language (χάρις, μεγαλύνω//χάρις ... μεγάλη) constitute strong evidence for reading Acts 4:33 in a similar way.[28] The most likely meaning of Acts 4:33 is that the community enjoyed great favor in the eyes of the people.

The Nature of the Property Arrangements in Acts 2:44–45 and 4:32, 34–35

Specifying the nature of the property arrangement(s) that Luke describes is the interpretive crux for the first two summaries. The aim of this section is not to determine either the historical *realia* behind or the literary function of these accounts but merely to clarify what Luke actually asserts regarding the sharing of property. The first issue is whether the two passages portray the same or different arrangements. Setting the two descriptions side-by-side reveals a number of structural, thematic, and lexical parallels:

Acts 2:44b–45	Acts 4:32b, 34–35
	καὶ οὐδὲ εἷς τι τῶν ὑπαρχόντων αὐτῷ ἔλεγεν ἴδιον εἶναι (4:32b)
καὶ εἶχον ἅπαντα κοινά (2:44b)	ἀλλ' ἦν αὐτοῖς ἅπαντα κοινά (4:32c)
	οὐδὲ γὰρ ἐνδεής τις ἦν ἐν αὐτοῖς (4:34a)
καὶ τὰ κτήματα καὶ τὰς ὑπάρξεις ἐπίπρασκον (2:45a)	ὅσοι γὰρ κτήτορες χωρίων ἢ οἰκιῶν ὑπῆρχον, πωλοῦντες (4:34b)
	ἔφερον τὰς τιμὰς τῶν πιπρασκομένων καὶ ἐτίθουν παρὰ τοὺς πόδας τῶν ἀποστόλων (4:34c–35a)
καὶ διεμέριζον αὐτὰ πᾶσιν καθότι ἄν τις χρείαν εἶχεν. (2:45b)	διεδίδετο δὲ ἑκάστῳ καθότι ἄν τις χρείαν εἶχεν. (4:35b)
	And no one claimed private ownership of any possessions, (4:32b)
And [they] had all things in common; (2:44b)	but all things were common to them. (4:32c)
	There was not a needy person among them, (4:34a)
they would sell their possessions and goods (2:45a)	for as many as owned lands or houses sold them (4:34b)
	and brought the proceeds of what was sold. They laid it at the apostles' feet, (4:34c–35a)
and distribute the proceeds to all, as any had need. (2:45b)	and it was distributed to each as any had need. (4:35b)

---

[28] For a detailed examination of the interrelations, see Co, "Major Summaries," 67–81.

Each clause from Acts 2:44b–45 has a close parallel in Acts 4:32, 34–35; the question is whether the additional comments in the second summary describe aspects of the property arrangement that have changed since the first summary.

The first addition, "no one claimed private ownership of any possessions," is the negative counterpart to the following statement, "all things were common to them"; it does not indicate any change in situation from the first summary. The second addition is the claim that "there was not a needy person among them." Again, this seems not to be a new development but rather an explication of the effects of the selling of property described in both summaries.[29] The most substantial addition is Acts 4:34c–35a, which explains that the proceeds from the sold property were brought to the apostles prior to distribution. Does this imply a change from the arrangement in 2:44–45, when the proceeds were perhaps dispensed by the individual sellers?[30] This is not implausible, but, given the general pattern of elaboration between the first and second summaries, 4:34c–35a may be reasonably seen as filling a gap in the description of 2:44–45, clarifying the middle step between the selling of property and the distribution of proceeds. Given that Luke does not hint at any change in the arrangement, Acts 2:44–45 and 4:32, 34–35 are most naturally read as two descriptions of the same phenomena.

Read synoptically, the two accounts present the community's practices regarding property in four main steps:

(1) General claim that the believers have "all things in common" (2:44b; 4:32b–c)
(2) Statement about the selling of property (2:45a; 4:34b)
(3) Description of placing the proceeds at the feet of the apostles (4:34c–35a)
(4) Explanation of how the money was distributed (2:45b; 4:35b)

These steps will now be examined individually to clarify their meaning.

"And [they] had all things in common" (2:44b); "and no one claimed private ownership of any possessions, but all things were common to them" (4:32c)

As noted in Chapter 1, the expression "all things in common" (ἅπαντα/πάντα κοινά) could be applied to various forms of property sharing. Aristotle uses it to describe friends who share goods that each continues to possess privately, Strabo to characterize the Scythian practice of predominately common ownership (excepting only cups and swords), and Iamblichus to label the Pythagoreans' complete pooling of possessions.[31] As such, this phrase does not specify the Jerusalem community's practice beyond a general notion of extraordinary communality. The added statement in Acts 4:32, that "no one claimed private ownership of any possessions," is merely a denial of the

---

[29] This statement (οὐδὲ γὰρ ἐνδεής τις ἦν ἐν αὐτοῖς) is likely an allusion to Deut 15:4 LXX: "There will not be a needy person among you" (οὐκ ἔσται ἐν σοὶ ἐνδεής).
[30] So, for example, Theissen, "Urchristlicher Liebeskommunismus," 693–4.
[31] Aristotle, *Eth. nic.* 1159b32; Strabo, *Geogr.* 7.3.7; Iamblichus, *Vit. pyth.* 168.

contrary and does not provide any further information.[32] The most significant aspect of these statements is the universality of Luke's claims: "all things"; "no one."

"They would sell their possessions and goods" (2:45a); "for as many as owned lands or houses sold them" (4:34b)

Four words denote the items that were sold. The first term in Acts 2:45, κτήματα, can refer to possessions in general or to land in particular, while the second, ὑπάρξεις, is a generic name for property.[33] Whether by addition or repetition, therefore, Acts 2:45 uses language that is broad in scope to describe the types of property that were liquidated. Acts 4:34, by contrast, presents more specific, limited objects of sale: lands (χωρία) and houses (οἰκίαι). While a few suggest that the different terminology marks a change in the practice depicted, the increased specificity in Acts 4:34 is consistent with the expanded nature of the second summary's description.[34] The first summary notes that the believers sold their property; the second spells out the most important kinds of property that were sold.[35]

Many commentators assert that the use of progressive tenses in these verses indicates that "members periodically sold their goods when needs arose, rather than immediately on entering the community."[36] The progressive aspect of the verbs could be due to a variety of practices, however: (1) members did not sell all their saleable property upon entering the community, but did so periodically, as needs arose;[37] (2) members did sell all their saleable property upon entering the community but then sold or donated other goods that they acquired while being members; (3) members sold all their saleable property upon entering the community, but new members were continually joining (cf. Acts 2:47; 4:4), leading to repeated acts of selling. Philo and Josephus use progressive tenses to describe practices similar to (2) and (3) respectively

---

[32] Johnson (*Acts*, 86) and Taylor ("Community of Goods," 152) argue that the mention of individual possessions indicates that the private property was retained. This is a possible interpretation, but the verse may rather explain that the members of the community were willing to sell everything that they had *previously* possessed as private property, since they no longer regarded them as personal possessions.

[33] Those who distinguish κτῆμα from ὕπαρξις refer the latter to personal property and the former to real property, which finds support in the use of κτῆμα in Acts 5:1 to denote the land sold by Ananias.

[34] Pervo (*Acts*, 127), for instance, sees the specification of lands and houses as marking a shift "from the ideal … to the reality: the needy received support from contributions of those with more means."

[35] The D-text of Acts 2:45 brings the wording more in line with that of 4:34, stating that "as many as had possessions or goods" (ὅσοι κτήματα εἶχον ἢ ὑπάρξεις) would sell them, implying that not all the members of the community possessed the type of property that would be sold under this arrangement.

[36] Keener, *Acts 1:1–2:47*, 1026. This same interpretation is given by Bock (*Acts*, 153), Haenchen (*Acts*, 231), Hays (*Luke's Wealth Ethics*, 198–9), Peterson (*Acts*, 163), and Witherington III (*Acts*, 162). "Would sell" (2:45, ἐπίπρασκον) and "owned" (4:34, κτήτορες … ὑπῆρχον) are imperfect verbs, while "sold" (4:34, πωλοῦντες) is a present participle; all three are progressive in aspect, as are the verbs that describe the distribution of the proceeds.

[37] "Saleable" refers to the sort of property Luke presents as typically sold: "lands or houses."

in the case of the Essenes.[38] Therefore, the imperfect tense in the Acts summaries does not demonstrate that members retained some or all of their saleable property until occasional, specific needs arose, although it is compatible with this interpretation.

Due to the general nature of the statement "all things in common" and the lack of specificity regarding the logistics of property divestiture, accusations of internal inconsistency in the Acts summaries are misplaced.[39] Again, the universal nature of the claims is noteworthy. While not every early believer would have owned houses or lands, Acts 4:34 asserts that all those who did (ὅσοι) sold these pieces of property.

"And [they] brought the proceeds of what was sold. They laid it at the apostles' feet" (4:34c–35a)

Those who sold lands and houses handed over all the proceeds (there is no hint of a partial donation) to the apostles. The expression "to lay at the feet" (τιθέναι παρὰ τοὺς πόδας) seems to signify a transfer; Luke repeats it twice in the immediately following stories of Barnabas (4:37, with πρός in place of παρά) and Ananias and Sapphira (5:2). Similar though not identical expressions appear in Cicero, Josephus, and Lucian.[40]

"And [they would] distribute the proceeds to all, as any had need" (2:45b); "and it was distributed to each as any had need" (4:35b)

The persons responsible for distributing the donated proceeds are not explicitly identified in either summary. Since Acts 4:35a states that the money was deposited with the apostles, they are the implied distributors in the second summary. The most recent grammatical subject in the first summary is πάντες … οἱ πιστεύοντες in 2:44; as noted above, some have taken this to indicate that the first summary describes a distribution by individual members rather than the apostles. On the synoptic reading preferred here, however, the second summary enlarges rather than contradicts the first account, so that the apostles are presumably the unspecified distributors in the first summary as well.

---

[38] Philo: "They do not keep their wages as private, but they bring them forward for the community, providing a common benefit" (*Prob.* 86, ὅσα γὰρ ἂν μεθ' ἡμέραν ἐργασάμενοι λάβωσιν ἐπὶ μισθῷ, ταῦτ' οὐκ ἴδια φυλάττουσιν, ἀλλ' εἰς μέσον προτιθέντες κοινὴν τοῖς ἐθέλουσι χρῆσθαι τὴν ἀπ' αὐτῶν παρασκευάζουσιν ὠφέλειαν); Josephus: "For it is law to confiscate for the order the property of those entering into the sect" (*B.J.* 2.122, νόμος γὰρ τοὺς εἰς τὴν αἵρεσιν εἰσιόντας δημεύειν τῷ τάγματι τὴν οὐσίαν).

[39] Those who see inconsistencies between Acts 4:32 and 4:34 in particular include Barrett (*Acts*, 1:252), Fitzmyer (*Acts*, 313), Haenchen (*Acts*, 233), Marguerat (*Actes*, 161), Taylor ("Community of Goods," 154), and Theissen ("Urchristlicher Liebeskommunismus," 703).

[40] Cicero, *Flac.* 68: "At Apamea, a little less than a hundred pounds of gold that had been openly seized was laid out before the feet of the praetor in the forum" (Apameae manifesto comprehensum ante pedes praetoris in foro expensum est auri pondo c paulo minus); Josephus, *B.J.* 2.625: "Three thousand immediately deserted, and when they arrived they threw their weapons at his feet" (τρισχιλίους μὲν ἀπέστησεν εὐθέως, οἳ παραγενόμενοι τὰ ὅπλα παρὰ τοῖς ποσὶν ἔρριψαν αὐτοῦ); Lucian, *Dial. meretr.* 14.3: "Did I not place a silver drachma before the feet of Aphrodite for your sake?" (οὐχὶ δραχμὴν ἔθηκα πρὸ τοῖν ποδοῖν τῆς Ἀφροδίτης σοῦ ἕνεκεν ἀργυρᾶν).

In Acts 4:35, the expression καθότι ἄν τις χρείαν εἶχεν clearly modifies (only) the verb διεδίδετο, specifying that the distribution was done iteratively, "as any had need."[41] Maria Anicia Co suggests that in Acts 2:45, on the other hand, καθότι ἄν τις χρείαν εἶχεν modifies *both* διεμέριζον *and* ἐπίπρασκον, indicating that particular acts of selling were done only to meet specific needs.[42] Given that the identical phrase occurs in the second summary and there modifies only the verb of distribution, however, it is likely that it does so in the first summary as well.[43] If so, this clause provides no further information about the extent and timing of the property sales described in Acts 2:45a and 4:34.

Summary: The Nature of the Property Arrangement

Due to the parallel structures of the property descriptions in Acts 2:44–45 and 4:32–35, the shared concepts and vocabulary, and the absence of any clearly indicated change, these passages are best read as two accounts of the same property arrangement, with the second being an expanded version of the first. Luke initially characterizes the economic practices of the community with the phrase ἅπαντα κοινά ("all things in common"), an expression that could be applied to a wide variety of communal situations. He then gives a more detailed account of the believers' communality: whoever had property (specifically, lands or houses) would sell it and hand the proceeds over to the apostles. These in turn would distribute it to any member of the community who had need of it. The passage does not explicitly state whether the believers sold their property upon joining the community or only as need arose. Luke's assertion that "as many as owned lands or houses sold them" does, however, seem to fit better with the former. Universalizing language is prominent throughout the property descriptions of both summaries: "all things" (2:44), "to all" (2:45), "no one," "everything" (4:32), "as many as" (4:34), "to each" (4:35).

Identifying Acts 2:42–47 and 4:32–35 as Golden Age Allusions

With the main individual exegetical issues dealt with, attention now can turn to the interpretation of Acts 2:42–47 and 4:32–35 as a whole. The central thesis of this study is that these summaries may be profitably read as allusions to the myth of the Golden Age. In Chapter 1, three criteria were proposed as necessary in order to posit an allusion: "availability," "markedness," and "sense." Chapters 2 and 3 have already shown the criterion of "availability" to be amply satisfied. Regarding the latter two criteria, Don Fowler summarizes the burden on the interpreter: "We ask: show me that this is not common, and tell me something interesting."[44] The remainder of this

---

[41] Imperfect + ἄν is used in Hellenistic Greek to indicate "repetition in past time" (BDF 367).
[42] Co, "Major Summaries," 72–3. Co operates on the assumption that the added information in the second summary indicates a substantive change from the conditions of the first summary rather than merely an expanded description.
[43] So also Schneider, *Apostelgeschichte*, 1:288.
[44] Fowler, "On the Shoulders of Giants," 20.

chapter takes up the task of doing just that. The current section tackles the criterion of "markedness" in two steps. First, I show that the summaries in Acts 2:42–47 and 4:32–35, and particularly their claims about communal property, are "not common": these passages stand out from their immediate contexts, from Luke-Acts as a whole, and from the entirety of the HB and the rest of the NT. This is not to say that the summaries appear as foreign bodies in the text of Acts; as will be argued below, they have thematic ties with several nearby passages. Nevertheless, the summaries are distinct in several ways, and this distinctiveness justifies the concentrated attention given here to these texts, as it suggests that Luke's literary purposes in the summaries go beyond mere historical description. Second, I make the case for seeing an allusion specifically to the Golden Age myth in these two passages, based on the characteristics of the myth and of Luke-Acts that have been elucidated in previous chapters.

The Distinctiveness of Acts 2:42–47 and 4:32–35

The summaries in Acts 2:42–47 and 4:32–35 are distinctive in three respects. First, the vocabulary in these summaries is often peculiar, appearing (sometimes multiple times) in these passages but rarely elsewhere in Luke-Acts or the NT. Second, the summaries' claims regarding common property are often seen as inconsistent with their immediate contexts, particularly with the stories of Barnabas and of Ananias and Sapphira that immediately follow Acts 4:32–35. Third, and most importantly, the practice of common property asserted by the summaries is an outlier both in Luke-Acts and in the biblical canon as a whole.

The Use of Distinctive Vocabulary in Acts 2:42–47 and 4:32–35

Based on the high volume of "unusual vocabulary and turns of phrase" that he catalogued in the summaries (and in Acts 2:41–5:42 more broadly), Cerfaux concluded that "Luke has used a written source."[45] The summaries are now widely held to be Luke's own compositions, but Cerfaux correctly pointed out the presence of several Lukan and NT *hapax legomena*.[46] The words κτῆμα, ὕπαρξις, and πιπράσκω occur nowhere else in Luke-Acts outside of these summaries and the closely related story of Ananias and Sapphira that follows (Acts 5:1–11). Even rarer are ἐνδεής and κτήτωρ, which are NT *hapax legomena*. Perhaps the most conspicuous vocabulary in both Acts 2:42–47 and 4:32–35 is the κοιν-rooted language used to describe the community's economic practice: κοινωνία in 2:42 and κοινά in 2:44 and 4:32. Again, in Luke-Acts this terminology is peculiar to the summaries. The word κοινωνία does not appear elsewhere in Luke's writings. As for κοινός, while Luke does use the term in three other places (Acts 10:14, 28; 11:8), in each case it has the meaning of "ceremonially impure"; in Luke-Acts, κοινός in the sense of "communal" occurs only in these two summaries.

---

[45] Cerfaux, "La première communauté," 30; "vocabulaire et des tournures inusités"; "Luc s'est servi d'une documentation écrite."

[46] Co ("Major Summaries," 54) categorically asserts that "no scholar now would deny the Lukan authorship of the summaries." Of course, this does not necessarily mean that Luke did not rely on one or several traditions; for a summary of different approaches to this issue, see Marguerat, *Actes*, 101.

Additionally, this language, although unusual for Luke, is emphasized through repetition. The most conspicuous expression in the summaries, ἅπαντα κοινά, is repeated verbatim (2:44; 4:32), as is καθότι ἄν τις χρείαν εἶχεν (2:45; 4:35). The word πιπράσκω ties both summaries to the story of Ananias and Sapphira (2:45; 4:34; 5:4) but appears nowhere else in Luke-Acts. The summaries are further linked by related terms: κτήματα (2:45)//κτήτορες (4:34) and ὑπάρξεις (2:45)//ὑπαρχόντων (4:32). The repeated, distinctive vocabulary of Acts 2:42–47 and 4:32–35 strongly binds the two passages together while distinguishing these summaries from the remainder of Luke's narrative.

Tensions between the Summaries and Their Immediate Contexts

While the second summary formally ends with Acts 4:35, the stories of Barnabas (4:36–37) and Ananias and Sapphira (5:1–11) are thematically connected to the preceding passage. This connection is reinforced by a high degree of shared vocabulary:

Acts 4:34-35	Acts 4:36-37	Acts 5:1-2
ὅσοι γὰρ κτήτορες χωρίων ἢ οἰκιῶν <u>ὑπῆρχον</u>, <u>πωλοῦντες</u> <u>ἔφερον</u> τὰς <u>τιμὰς</u> τῶν πιπρασκομένων καὶ <u>ἐτίθουν</u> παρὰ <u>τοὺς πόδας τῶν ἀποστόλων</u>. For as many as <u>owned</u> lands or houses <u>sold</u> them and <u>brought</u> the <u>proceeds</u> of what was sold. They <u>laid</u> it at <u>the apostles' feet</u>.	Βαρναβᾶς … <u>ὑπάρχοντος</u> αὐτῷ ἀγροῦ <u>πωλήσας ἤνεγκεν</u> τὸ χρῆμα καὶ <u>ἔθηκεν</u> πρὸς <u>τοὺς πόδας τῶν ἀποστόλων</u>. Barnabas … <u>sold</u> a field that <u>belonged</u> to him, then brought the money, and <u>laid</u> it at <u>the apostles' feet</u>.	Ἀνανίας … <u>ἐπώλησεν</u> κτῆμα καὶ ἐνοσφίσατο ἀπὸ τῆς <u>τιμῆς</u> … καὶ <u>ἐνέγκας</u> μέρος τι παρὰ <u>τοὺς πόδας τῶν ἀποστόλων</u> <u>ἔθηκεν</u>. Ananias … <u>sold</u> a piece of property … he kept back some of the <u>proceeds</u>, and brought only a part and <u>laid</u> it at <u>the apostles' feet</u>.

Although these two accounts are typically treated as positive and negative examples respectively of the communality described in Acts 4:32–35, commentators have also often seen both stories as contradicting the picture presented in this summary.

The case for contradiction based on the story of Barnabas is weak. Haenchen argues that Barnabas' donation must have been "out of the ordinary" for it to receive special mention, indicating that such actions were not practiced by "as many as owned lands or houses" (Acts 4:34).[47] Craig Keener offers a satisfactory response: noting that Luke "often mentions his characters in preliminary ways before introducing them in their primary roles," he proposes that Luke may have chosen Barnabas as an exemplar in Acts 4:36–37 in preparation for his important role later in the narrative.[48] As a result, Luke's singling out of Barnabas does not necessarily indicate anything about the prevalence of such acts of divestiture and thus does not contradict the description in Acts 4:32–35.

---

[47] Haenchen, *Acts*, 233; so too Barrett, *Acts*, 1:258; Dupont, "Community of Goods," 93.
[48] Keener, *Acts 3:1–14:28*, 1179; cf. the introductions of Stephen in Acts 6:5 and Saul in Acts 7:58. Capper ("Community of Goods," *ANRW* 26.2:1742), Klauck ("Gütergemeinschaft," 76), and Marguerat (*Actes*, 164) reject the idea that Barnabas' action was seen as exceptional for similar reasons.

The story of Ananias and Sapphira contains a more evident tension with the picture painted in the summaries. Specifically, Peter's remark to Ananias regarding his field, "While it remained unsold, did it not remain your own? And after it was sold, were not the proceeds at your disposal?" (Acts 5:4), is difficult to reconcile with Luke's claim in Acts 4:34 that "as many as owned lands or houses sold them and brought the proceeds" to the apostles. If Ananias was truly free to not sell his property or, having sold it, to not hand over the proceeds, then it would seem that doing so was not a universal practice of the community, as the second summary clearly asserts.[49]

In light of this and other indications that not all the Jerusalem believers fully divested themselves of real estate (the reference to the "house of Mary" in Acts 12:12, for example), some commentators openly accuse Luke of inconsistency in Acts 4–5.[50] More commonly, Luke's language in the summaries is described as "idealizing," "generalizing," or "hyperbole."[51] Even scholars who are deeply invested in upholding both the historicity and the consistency of Luke's account, such as Capper and Hays, acknowledge that the author has engaged in "dense literary idealizing" and has tried to "juice up his description."[52] The upshot of these various descriptors is the same: Luke's summaries stand out as apparently exaggerated when viewed next to some of the material that surrounds them. This is not a shocking observation; as Pervo notes, "even writers far more scrupulous than this one descend to an occasional hyperbole."[53] Nevertheless, Luke's universalizing claims in the summaries do stand in tension with parts of their immediate context and even with stories that seem designed to illustrate the communality asserted in the summaries, a fact that further marks Acts 2:42–47 and 4:32–35 as unusual.

The Uniqueness of the Summaries in Their Broader Context

While most commentators try to resolve discrepancies between the summaries and other material in Acts by assuming that Luke generalized a sporadic practice, Capper argues that this move "does not solve, but rather heightens, the hermeneutical problem":

> If Luke, for example, was aware that only a few isolated events of substantial charitable giving had occurred in the earliest community, but embellished these to give the impression of substantial, community-wide communal sharing ... why does he thereafter allow the theme to drop?[54]

[49] Capper ("Community of Goods," ANRW 26.2:1741–52) tries to reconcile the two passages by positing an Essene-like multistage admission procedure to the Jerusalem community. His arguments have convinced few; see Hays, *Luke's Wealth Ethics*, 196–221. Hays' own solution (ibid., 221–5), that divestiture was neither mandatory nor supererogatory, does not resolve the tension between Acts 4:34–35, which envisions no exceptions, and 5:4, which allows for them.
[50] Barrett, *Acts*, 1:253; Conzelmann, *Acts*, 36; Fitzmyer, *Acts*, 323; Johnson, *Literary Function*, 10 n. 1; Klauck, "Gütergemeinschaft," 68–9.
[51] "Idealizing": Barrett, *Acts*, 1:252; Conzelmann, *Acts*, 24; Holladay, *Acts*, 107; Horn, "Gütergemeinschaft," 381; Johnson, *Literary Function*, 5; Keener, *Acts 1:1–2:47*, 1027; Klauck, "Gütergemeinschaft," 76; Marguerat, *Actes*, 107; Schneider, *Apostelgeschichte*, 1:285; Seccombe, *Possessions and the Poor*, 209; "generalizing": Dupont, "Community of Goods," 94; Pesch, *Apostelgeschichte*, 131; "hyperbole": Bock, *Acts*, 214; Fitzmyer, *Acts*, 272; Pervo, *Acts*, 128.
[52] Capper, "Community of Goods," ANRW 26.2:1740; Hays, *Luke's Wealth Ethics*, 208.
[53] Pervo, *Acts*, 128.
[54] Capper, "Reciprocity," 503.

Capper here identifies the most curious aspect of Acts 2:42–47 and 4:32–35, and the one that most demands an explanation: the idea of having "all things in common" appears without warning in these two passages and then disappears without comment. As Johnson observes, the complete absence of this motif from the remainder of Luke-Acts is even more peculiar than the incongruities in the immediate context highlighted above:

> We are faced here not simply with the frequently noted inconsistencies in the narrative itself, but a possible conflict of ideology. It can be said with fair certainty that Luke elsewhere presents almsgiving as the ideal way of handling possessions. Yet the ideal of community possessions is in tension with, if not actually contradictory to, the ideal or practice of almsgiving.[55]

Luke's evaluation of the Jerusalem believers' community of property appears to be purely positive: he portrays it as an effect of the Spirit and a cause of great favor in the eyes of the people. Yet the theme of common property fails to resurface elsewhere in Luke-Acts, and it is absent from rest of the NT and the HB as well.

Acts 2:42–47 and 4:32–35 are therefore strongly marked in their immediate contexts, in Luke's writings more broadly, and in the entire NT and HB. The vocabulary in these passages is distinct, the descriptions stand in tension with some of the following material in Acts, and the motif of common property appears nowhere else in the biblical canon. Johnson expresses the obvious question that arises next: "Does the imagery of community possessions fulfill a function in the text which is uniquely demanded by the context and the impression the author wished to make here and only here?"[56] The following sections contend that reading these summaries against the background of the early imperial Golden Age myth can supply a satisfying response to this question.

Golden Age Features in Acts 2:42–47 and 4:32–35

In the preceding section, I showed the distinctiveness of Acts 2:42–47 and 4:32–35, particularly their claims of common property, suggesting that these summaries and this motif might have a special literary function in Luke's narrative. In this section, I argue that this special function is alluding to the myth of the Golden Age. It may be helpful here to recall some of the main characteristics of the Golden Age detailed in previous chapters.

(1) *A Lost Age and a New Age*: The first Golden Age (or Race) is lost in the mists of time, appearing at the beginning of human history as "the first race begotten" (Ovid, *Metam*. 1.89). Yet Roman texts often proclaim a return of the Golden Age in the present, as "the great series of ages is born anew" (Virgil, *Ecl*. 4.5).

---

[55] Johnson, *Literary Function*, 10. Capper ("Reciprocity," 502–3) similarly states that "after this powerfully expressed beginning, community of property as a theme receives no further mention…. Community of property appears to be replaced by the theme of almsgiving."

[56] Johnson, *Literary Function*, 10.

(2) *Blessed with Divine Favor*: Those who lived during the Golden Age were "dear to the blessed gods" (Hesiod, *Op.* 120), and "god himself tended and took care of them" (Plato, *Pol.* 271e). This is in contrast to the Iron Age, in which humanity has been "left destitute of the care of the god" (Plato, *Pol.* 274b).

(3) *Marked by Unity and Harmony*: In the Golden Age, people were "at peace" (Hesiod, *Op.* 119), "discord among brothers was not known" (Germanicus, *Arat.* 113), and all were "of the same mind" (Seneca, *Ep.* 90.40). Conversely, the decline from this age was marked by "wars and hostile bloodshed" (Aratus, *Phaen.* 125) and the breakdown of intimate relationships (Hesiod, *Op.* 182–188).

(4) *A Time When Property Was Common*: Roman authors depict the Golden Age as a time when "no one ... possessed any private property, but all things were common and undivided to all persons" (Trogus, *Ep.* 43.1.3), when "everything was divided among those of the same mind" (Seneca, *Ep.* 90.40) and "the use of all things was common" (*Oct.* 403), such that "you would not be able to find a poor person" (Seneca, *Ep.* 90.38). The Iron Age is characterized by the opposite attitude, by "wicked madness for gain" (Seneca, *Phaed.* 540) and "the lust for possession" (Virgil, *Aen.* 8.327; Ovid, *Metam.* 1.131; *Fast.* 1.196). The cardinal sin of this age is the desire "to set something apart and make it one's own," the action of "the greedy man, secreting away for himself" (Seneca, *Ep.* 90.38, 40).

(5) *Associated with Imperial Ideology*: In the *Aeneid*, Anchises attributes the Golden Age's return to the Roman emperor, "Augustus Caesar, the child of a god, who will establish the golden ages again" (*Aen.* 6.792–793), and later authors often follow suit. Seneca claims the same for Nero (*Apoc.* 4.1), as do the *Einsiedeln Eclogues* (2.22–24) and Calpurnius Siculus (*Ecl.* 1.42). This trend continues in the second century, as exemplified by Hadrian's *saeculum aureum* coins.

(6) *An Eschatological Image*: Jewish and Christian writers such as Philo and the authors of the Sibylline Oracles take up the idea of a returning Golden Age and employ it in eschatological depictions, describing a restoration of prelapsarian conditions in paradise, where "property will be common" (Sib. Or. 2.321).

The following sections present correspondences between these six Golden Age characteristics and the portraits of the Jerusalem believers in Acts 2:42–47 and 4:32–35.

The Summaries in Acts: A Lost Age and a New Age

As observed in Chapter 4, commentators often assert that Luke portrays the gift of the Spirit at Pentecost as signaling the beginning of a "new age."[57] Acts 2:42–47 describes the way of life of the three thousand who receive the Spirit on Pentecost, and Acts 4:32–35 also directly follows an outpouring of the Spirit on the community. Both summaries, therefore, depict the lifestyle resulting from the coming of the eschatological Spirit, presenting "an ideal picture of the Spirit-endowed community of the new age."[58]

---

[57] Blumhofer, "Luke's Alteration," 510; Bruce, *Acts*, 121; Dunn, *Baptism*, 43; Fitzmyer, *Acts*, 250; Johnson, *Acts*, 50; Maddox, *Purpose*, 139; Schweizer, *TDNT* 6:411; Shepherd, *Narrative Function*, 164.

[58] Bruce, *Acts*, 132.

This specific origin in time distinguishes the summaries from the accounts of the Essenes with which they are often compared. Like Luke, Philo and Josephus also describe communities that manifest social harmony and practice a community of property.[59] The Essenes, however, are presented as a perduring sect; Philo and Josephus make no mention of how or when the Essenes arose, and their existence does not signify the arrival of any particular era. The Acts summaries, on the other hand, depict a utopian lifestyle that originates at a definite time from a specific era-defining event.

Also unlike the Essene accounts, Acts 2:42–47 and 4:32–35 do not present the community's praxis as an ongoing reality.[60] Particularly with respect to the practice of common property, the summaries portray a situation that suddenly arises after Pentecost but then apparently ceases soon afterward. By the time Acts was written, some sixty to eighty-five years separated the readers/hearers from the events narrated. The summaries are not set "once upon a time," but they do describe phenomena that ceased prior to the lifetimes of most if not all of Luke's audience.[61]

Luke's summaries, therefore, describe a utopian yet ephemeral period of existence tied to the gift of the Spirit, whose arrival marked the beginning of a new age. This basic picture is quite conducive to a Golden Age reading of the summaries, fitting both with the idea of a possible return of this age in the present and with the common relegation of the Golden Age to the ancient past. In the following sections, I show that correspondences between the summaries and the myth extend to more specific details as well.

The Summaries in Acts: Blessed with Divine Favor

The connection between the gift of the Spirit and the Acts summaries also shows that the Jerusalem believers are recipients of divine favor. Acts 2:42–47 and 4:32–35 describe a group created and empowered by the Spirit, a divine "gift" (Acts 2:38). God's care is further indicated by the statement in Acts 2:47 that "day by day the Lord added to their number," asserting that the community's growth was directly caused by God. For their part, the people respond with worship, spending "much time together in the temple" and "praising God" (2:46–47). The picture is one of complete human-divine harmony. Thus, like the humans of the Golden Age, the community is presented as one which "God himself tended and took care of" (Plato, *Pol.* 271e), and the believers in turn display the sort of reverence that is conspicuously absent in descriptions of the Iron Age.

The Summaries in Acts: Marked by Unity and Harmony

Next to the motif of common property, the Jerusalem believers' unity and harmony is the dominant theme of the summaries. A variety of phrases express this characteristic, such as ἐπὶ τὸ αὐτό (2:44, 47), ὁμοθυμαδόν (2:46), and καρδία καὶ ψυχὴ μία (4:32).

---

[59] The major accounts are Josephus, *B.J.* 2.119–161; *A.J.* 18.18–22; Philo, *Prob.* 75–91; *Hypoth.* 11.1–18.

[60] Philo and Josephus use the present tense to describe the Essenes, giving no indication that they are speaking of a past phenomenon.

[61] Plümacher (*Lukas als hellenistischer Schriftsteller*, 18 n. 61) sees a significant similarity in the fact that both Luke and Greek Golden Age accounts relegate the ideal time to the past.

As argued above, ἐπὶ τὸ αὐτό has a primarily unitive sense in the first summary. Luke uses the term ὁμοθυμαδόν multiple times early in Acts to signify the believers' "unanimity of spirit."[62] The expression καρδία καὶ ψυχὴ μία "idyllically describes the unity and harmony of the Jerusalem Christians," emphasizing their "perfect concord."[63] Some manuscripts make this even more explicit, glossing "one heart and soul" with the statement "and there was no quarrel/division [D, Cyprian: διάκρισις; E: χωρισμός] among them." The community's unity is further highlighted by the κοιν-rooted vocabulary used to describe their practice of common property. Finally, the universality of the summaries' language (πᾶς/ἅπας [6x], ὅλος, οὐδὲ εἷς, οὐδέ τις, ὅσος, ἕκαστος) portrays the believers as acting in complete unison.

This accentuation of the community's unanimity corresponds to a similar emphasis in Golden Age accounts, which "present the reign of Kronos as one of absolute harmony."[64] The Golden Age was free of στάσις and *discordia*; all were "of the same mind" (Seneca, *Ep*. 90.40, *concordes*). The ostensibly unanimous community of Acts 2:42–47 and 4:32–35, which lived as though sharing "one heart and soul," is certainly "golden" in this respect.

The Summaries in Acts: A Time when Property Was Common

Acts 2:44 and 4:32 present the Jerusalem believers as selling their lands and houses and handing over the proceeds to the apostles, who then distribute the money to needy members of the community. The summaries label this practice as having "all things in common." While this expression can be used to describe a variety of forms of communality, its employment in both summaries does seem rather stretched with respect to the practice that Luke explicitly narrates, the divestiture of real estate by wealthier believers. Further, the following story of Ananias and Sapphira casts reasonable doubt on the universality of this practice even among those who did own lands or houses. The language of common property therefore appears to be hyperbolic. The degree of exaggeration may not be extreme, but the relevant point is that Luke *chooses* to frame the community's economic arrangement as one of common property in Acts 2:44 and 4:32; such a descriptor is not demanded by the procedure detailed in Acts 2:45 and 4:34–35, much less by the story of Ananias and Sapphira in 5:1–11. Yet while the idea of common property appears prominently, even pointedly, in these two summaries, Luke never again mentions this practice, nor does the rest of the NT. However one interprets Acts 2:42–47 and 4:32–35, the uniqueness of the common property motif must be accounted for.

---

[62] Johnson, *Acts*, 59. The word describes the Jerusalem believers in Acts 1:14; 2:46; 4:24; 5:12. It also appears with the same meaning but different referents in Acts 7:57; 8:6; 12:20; 15:25; 18:12; 19:29. Steve Walton ("Ομοθυμαδόν in Acts: Co-location, Common Action or 'Of One Heart and Mind'?" in *The New Testament in Its First Century Setting: Essays on Context and Background in Honour of B. W. Winter on His 65th Birthday*, ed. P. J. Williams et al. [Grand Rapids: Eerdmans, 2004], 104) concludes that "overall ὁμοθυμαδόν is used rather more with at least some sense of unity of thought or action than merely in the sense of shared location," although he judges that the latter sense is primary in Acts 2:46.

[63] Fitzmyer, *Acts*, 313; Dupont, "Community of Goods," 98.

[64] Evans, *Utopia Antiqua*, 20.

As documented in Chapter 2, Golden Age accounts from Virgil onward typically depict it as a time when property was held in common. Parallels to Luke's description of the Jerusalem community's economic arrangement are easy to find in Golden Age portraits, such as those of Trogus, Seneca, and the *Octavia*:

Acts 4:32, 34	Golden Age Accounts
Now the whole group of those who believed were of one heart and soul (καρδία καὶ ψυχὴ μία), and no one claimed private [ἴδιον] ownership of any possessions, but all things were common to them (ἅπαντα κοινά) ….	"Everything was divided among those of the same mind" (Seneca, *Ep.* 90.40, *concordes*). "No one … possessed any private [*privatae*] property" (Trogus, *Ep.* 43.1.3). "All things were common" (Trogus, *Ep.* 43.1.3, *omnia communia*). "The use of all things was common" (*Oct.* 403, *communis usus omnium rerum fuit*).
There was not a needy person [ἐνδεής] among them.	"You would not be able to find a poor person" (Seneca, *Ep.* 90.38, *pauperem*).

These parallels, of course, do not prove a Lukan Golden Age allusion; similar correspondences could doubtless be constructed from other literary traditions. For present purposes, three observations will suffice. First, both the Acts summaries and early imperial Golden Age accounts feature the idea of common property. Second, the language that Luke uses to portray the community's property arrangement would be completely at home in first- or second-century CE descriptions of the Golden Age. Third, the motif of common property is not a minor but a central, distinctive feature of both the summaries and the Golden Age myth. In the summaries, fully half of the verses are devoted to detailing the believers' property arrangement. As for the myth, Plutarch's remark that Cimon's decision to make his house and land common "in a way … brought the fabled community of goods [κοινωνίαν] of the time of Cronus back to life again" (*Cim.* 10.6–7) indicates that Plutarch considered the Golden Age to be the standard example of common property in the late first/early second century.

The Golden Age motif of common property is reinforced by two contrasting stories in Acts 1–5. The accounts of Judas in Acts 1 and of Ananias and Sapphira in Acts 5 are linked to the summaries by not only theme but also vocabulary, sharing the terms κτάομαι/κτῆμα/κτήτωρ (to acquire/property/owner) and χωρίον (field).[65] Both stories present the actions of those who separate themselves from the community as flowing from Satan rather than the Spirit and as motivated by the Iron Age vice of greed.

Judas supplies a counterexample to this generosity and sharing that mark the Jerusalem community. Luke first mentions Judas' treachery in Luke 22, giving two important details: Judas' betrayal is incited by Satan, who "entered into Judas" (Luke 22:3), and is financially rewarded, as the Jewish authorities "agreed to give him money" (Luke 22:5). In Acts 1, Peter explains what Judas did with the money: "Now

---

[65] The story of Judas in Acts 1, the summary in Acts 4, and the account of Ananias and Sapphira in Acts 5 are the only three passages in the NT in which the terms κτάομαι/κτῆμα and χωρίον appear together.

this man acquired a field [ἐκτήσατο χωρίον] with the reward of his wickedness" (Acts 1:18).⁶⁶ The contrast with the summaries' claim that "as many as owned lands [κτήτορες χωρίων] ... sold them" (Acts 4:34) is hard to miss.⁶⁷ Acts 1 then strengthens this contrast, as the communal prayer describes how Judas left his "place [τόπον] in this ministry and apostleship" and "turned aside to go to his own place" (Acts 1:25, τὸν τόπον τὸν ἴδιον). The summaries depict a community so strongly unified (ἐπὶ τὸ αὐτό, etc.) that "no one claimed private ownership [ἴδιον] of any possessions" (Acts 4:32). Acts 1 also presents a unified group of believers, again described as being ἐπὶ τὸ αὐτό in v. 15, in contrast to Judas, who buys his own field and goes "to his own [ἴδιον] place."⁶⁸ In relation to the Golden Age portrait of the summaries, Judas plays the role of a representative of the Iron Age's "lust for possession" (Virgil, *Aen.* 8.327; Ovid, *Metam.* 1.131; *Fast.* 1.196), the desire "to set something apart and make it one's own" (Seneca, *Ep.* 90.38).⁶⁹

The story of Ananias and Sapphira parallels that of Judas in several respects and is even more clearly meant as a counterpart to the summaries, as argued above. As with Judas, Ananias' sin is attributed to the fact that "Satan filled your heart" (Acts 5:3), involves a financial transaction regarding a field, and results in death.⁷⁰ Like the believers in the summaries, Ananias and Sapphira sell "a piece of property" (Acts 5:1, κτῆμα; cf. Acts 2:45), specified as "land" (Acts 5:3, χωρίου; cf. Acts 4:34). Unlike the faithful believers, however, Ananias and Sapphira "kept back [ἐνοσφίσατο] some of the proceeds" (Acts 5:2). As Ivoni Reimer observes, the verb νοσφίζομαι (*LSJ*: "to put aside for oneself") is typically used when "the action of keeping back is directed against the common property that exists also for my sake, or that belongs to a community of which I am a member."⁷¹ Supporting examples are easy to find:⁷²

---

⁶⁶ Luke's account differs from that of Matthew, who states that Judas returned the money and that the chief priests then used it to purchase a field.

⁶⁷ Johnson, *Literary Function*, 180; Hans-Josef Klauck, *Judas, ein Jünger des Herrn*, QD 111 (Freiburg: Herder, 1987), 108; Pervo, *Acts*, 53; Jesse E. Robertson, *The Death of Judas: The Characterization of Judas Iscariot in Three Early Christian Accounts of His Death*, New Testament Monographs 33 (Sheffield: Sheffield Phoenix, 2012), 101; Arie W. Zwiep, *Judas and the Choice of Matthias: A Study on Context and Concern of Acts 1:15–26*, WUNT 2/187 (Tübingen: Mohr Siebeck, 2004), 147–8.

⁶⁸ The connection between the uses of ἴδιον in Acts 1:25 and 4:32 is noted by Johnson (*Literary Function*, 181) and Klauck (*Judas*, 109); The common opinion is that Judas' "own place" is a reference to hell; so Barrett, *Acts*, 1:104; Bock, *Acts*, 89; Haenchen, *Acts* 162; Zwiep, *Judas and the Choice of Matthias*, 147. Johnson (ibid., 181–2) and Klauck (ibid., 109) see it as a reference to the field that Judas bought.

⁶⁹ "In Acts 1:18–19 ... one attribute of the mind of Judas is featured most prominently: his greed" (Robertson, *Death of Judas*, 100). Similarly DooHee Lee, *Luke-Acts and "Tragic History": Communicating Gospel with the World*, WUNT 2/346 (Tübingen: Mohr Siebeck, 2013), 228; Zwiep, *Judas and the Choice of Matthias*, 147–8.

⁷⁰ For the parallels between the two stories, see Schuyler Brown, *Apostasy and Perseverance in the Theology of Luke*, AnBib 36 (Rome: Pontifical Biblical Institute, 1969), 106–7.

⁷¹ *LSJ*, "νοσφίζω," 1182; Ivoni Richter Reimer, *Women in the Acts of the Apostles: A Feminist Liberation Perspective*, trans. Linda M. Maloney (Minneapolis: Fortress, 1995), 9.

⁷² Some see a link to the use of νοσφίζομαι in the story of Achan (Josh 7:1 LXX); for a detailed presentation of the case, see Hyung Dae Park, *Finding Herem? A Study of Luke-Acts in the Light of Herem*, LNTS 357 (London: T&T Clark, 2007): 131–45. Fitzmyer (*Acts*, 319), however, points out that "save for the verb ... there is little relation between the two accounts."

There is a great deal of property in the camp, and I am not unaware that we could take for ourselves [νοσφίσασθαι] as much as we wanted, although it belongs in common [κοινῶν] to those who seized it with us. (Xenophon, *Cyr.* 4.2.42)[73]

The people of the Vaccaei ... divide up their land and cultivate it, and they make its produce common property [κοινοποιούμενοι] and give a share to each, but to those farmers who take something for themselves [νοσφισαμένοις] they give death as the penalty. (Diodorus Siculus, *Bib. hist.* 5.34.3–4)[74]

Viriathus ... took for himself [νοσφιζόμενος] absolutely nothing from the common spoils. (Diodorus Siculus, *Bib. hist.* 33.1.5, κοινῶν)[75]

The verb νοσφίζομαι is also regularly associated with the vice of greed (πλεονεξία):

I have spoken earlier about how no one takes for himself [νοσφίζεσθαι] anything from the spoils ... the Romans are never at risk of losing everything due to greed. (Polybius, *Hist.* 10.16.6–9, πλεονεξίαν)[76]

Greed [πλεονεξίαις] ... persuades some to take for themselves [νοσφίζεσθαι] the property of others. (Philo, *Decal.* 171–172)[77]

Regarding Ananias and Sapphira, commentators sometimes argue that "it is not avarice for which they are blamed but deceit."[78] The use of the term νοσφίζομαι, however, brings in the notions of greed and the improper appropriation of what should be common property.[79] Like Judas, Ananias and Sapphira embody the Iron Age themes of "lust for possession" and the desire "to set something apart and make it one's own."

In summary, Acts 2:42–47 and 4:32–35 depict the faithful as being filled with the Spirit and living out the Golden Age ideal of common property. Those who by their actions place themselves outside of the community, on the other hand, are portrayed as being filled with Satan and characterized by the Iron Age trait of greed, particularly the desire to acquire or retain property for themselves alone.

The Summaries in Acts: Associated with Imperial Ideology

The preceding four sections have set forth the primary correspondences between the descriptions of the Jerusalem believers in Acts 2:42–47 and 4:32–35 and the Golden

---

[73] χρήματα πολλά ἐστιν ἐν τῷ στρατοπέδῳ, ὧν οὐκ ἀγνοῶ ὅτι δυνατὸν ἡμῖν κοινῶν ὄντων τοῖς συγκατειληφόσι νοσφίσασθαι ὁπόσα ἂν βουλώμεθα.

[74] τὸ τῶν Οὐακκαίων ... διαιρούμενοι τὴν χώραν γεωργοῦσι, καὶ τοὺς καρποὺς κοινοποιούμενοι μεταδιδόασιν ἑκάστῳ τὸ μέρος, καὶ τοῖς νοσφισαμένοις τι γεωργοῖς θάνατον τὸ πρόστιμον τεθείκασι.

[75] Ὑρίατθος ... οὐδὲν ἁπλῶς ἐκ τῶν κοινῶν νοσφιζόμενος.

[76] περὶ δὲ τοῦ μηδένα νοσφίζεσθαι μηδὲν ἐκ τῆς διαρπαγῆς ... εἴρηται πρότερον ἡμῖν ... οὐδέποτε κινδυνεύει Ῥωμαίοις τὰ ὅλα διὰ πλεονεξίαν.

[77] πλεονεξίαις, ὑφ' ὧν πείθονταί τινες ... τἀλλότρια νοσφίζεσθαι.

[78] Barrett, *Acts*, 1:262; so also Bruce, *Acts*, 162.

[79] The implicit greed motivating the actions of Ananias and Sapphira is recognized by Brown (*Apostasy*, 106), Holladay (*Acts*, 138), Lee (*Luke-Acts and "Tragic History,"* 228), and Alfons Weiser ("Das Gottesurteil über Hananias und Saphira: Apg 5,1–11," *TGl* 69 [1979]: 155).

Age myth presented in Chapter 2. In Chapter 3, Jewish and Christian authors were seen to have employed this myth generally in works concerned with Rome and specifically in eschatological contexts; in this and the following section, I argue that the proposed allusion to the Golden Age in Acts 2 and 4 fits these patterns as well.

Chapter 2 highlighted the regular use of the Golden Age myth to praise or even criticize Roman emperors, and Chapter 3 showed that Jewish and Christian uses of this myth tended to occur in texts with some orientation toward Rome. Chapter 4 has already established that Luke-Acts also evinces a special interest in Rome and thus is the type of work more likely to allude to the Golden Age myth. In addition, the contexts of the summaries in Acts are also conducive to seeing a reference to this imperially resonant myth.

Readers of Luke and Acts have often identified structural parallels between the two books.[80] One basic correspondence is between the birth of Jesus in Luke 1–2 and the birth of the church in Acts 1–2.[81] In the first chapter of each book, these births are associated with a promised coming of the Holy Spirit: to Mary in Luke 1:35 ("the Holy Spirit will come upon you") and to the apostles in Acts 1:8 ("when the Holy Spirit has come upon you"). The identical vocabulary strengthens the thematic parallel.

The two births are then given a worldwide, and arguably imperial, context. Both aspects are clear in Luke 2: Jesus' birth is linked with a "decree … from Emperor Augustus that all the world should be registered" (Luke 2:1), hinting "at the worldwide significance of that birth" and setting up an implicit comparison between Jesus and Augustus.[82] The universal setting of the birth of the church in Acts is also plain, as it occurs in the presence of a crowd "from every nation under heaven" (Acts 2:5), a claim that is followed by a list of the nations represented (2:9–11).[83] No explicit imperial reference appears here (though Rome is included in the list), but Gary Gilbert argues that "the list of nations in Acts 2 echoes similar lists from this period that celebrated Rome's position as ruler over the inhabited world."[84] Gilbert proposes that this echo "responds to Rome's claim of universal authority and declares that the true empire belongs not to Caesar but to Jesus," and Daniel Marguerat similarly sees Luke as challenging "the Empire's pretention of being the unifying link for the peoples under the aegis of the emperor."[85]

In Luke 2, after the universal, imperial context has been established, the newborn Jesus is announced using language often applied to the Roman emperor (σωτήρ, κύριος,

---

[80] See Charles H. Talbert, *Literary Patterns, Theological Themes, and the Genre of Luke-Acts*, SBLMS 20 (Cambridge: Society of Biblical Literature, 1974), 15–23.
[81] Brown, *Birth of the Messiah*, 243.
[82] Fitzmyer, *Luke I–IX*, 394; similarly, Brent, "Luke-Acts," 431; Green, *Luke*, 125.
[83] Brown (*Birth of the Messiah*, 415 n. 19) finds a parallel between the listing of the nations in Acts 2:5–11 and the mention of Augustus' census in Luke 2:1.
[84] Gilbert, "List of Nations," 499. Gilbert (ibid., 513) argues that "among the various methods Rome used to promote its ideology of universal rule, the listing of foreign nations or peoples proved to be one of the more frequent and effective" and provides many examples.
[85] Ibid., 499; Marguerat, *Actes*, 80; "la prétention de l'Empire d'être le lien rassembleur des peoples sous l'égide de l'empereur." Gilbert's arguments have been accepted by Bock (*Acts*, 102–3), while Holladay (*Acts*, 95 n. 49) and Keener (*Acts 1:1–2:47*, 840) are open to his proposed interpretation.

εἰρήνη). If the presence of a Golden Age allusion in Acts 2:42–47 is accepted, then the newborn church is also immediately portrayed in terms that have imperial resonance, given the regular use of the Golden Age myth to praise the emperor. My claim is that, given the parallels between Luke 1–2 and Acts 1–2, a Golden Age allusion would therefore be especially fitting precisely in the location where the first summary appears:

Parallel Features	Birth of Jesus (Luke 1–2)	Birth of Church (Acts 1–2)
Promised with coming of the Holy Spirit	"The Holy Spirit will come upon you" (1:35).	"When the Holy Spirit has come upon you" (1:8).
Set in universal, imperial context	"A decree went out from Caesar Augusts that the whole world should be enrolled" (2:1).	"Jews … from every nation under heaven … Parthians … and visitors from Rome" (2:5, 9–10).
Birth occurs	"She gave birth to her first-born son" (2:7).	"They were all filled with the Holy Spirit … and there were added that day about three thousand souls" (2:4, 41).
Described using imperial language	"A Savior … the Lord … peace" (2:10, 14).	"All who were believed were together and had all things in common" (2:44).

These structural parallels do not mandate reading Acts 2:42–47 as incorporating imperial language or themes, but they do provide further support for such an interpretation.

With regard to the second summary, Acts 4:32–35, the context is again supportive of an empire-critical reading. The passage that immediately precedes this summary, Acts 4:23–31, centers around a prayer that is explicitly political, drawing attention to "the kings of the earth … and the rulers," specifically "Herod and Pontius Pilate," who "gathered together against your holy servant Jesus" (Acts 4:26–27). Beyond its general political focus, three specific aspects of this prayer are worth highlighting here. First, by describing these rulers as merely doing "whatever your hand and your plan had predestined" (Acts 4:28), the prayer "minimize[s] the authority of earthly rulers" relative to God.[86] Second, the two Psalms that the prayer quotes also emphasize the relative impotence of human political figures. In Psalm 2, quoted in Acts 4:25–26, the psalmist warns "the rulers of the earth" to "serve the Lord with fear" (Ps 2:10–11) stating that God "has them in derision" (Ps 2:4). Psalm 146, which "is essentially cited in v. 24," warns "not to put your trust in princes" (Ps 146:3) but rather in God, "who made heaven and earth, the sea, and all that is in them" (Ps 146:6).[87] Third, it is not only generic rulers who are minimized and criticized in Acts 4 but Pilate specifically, "Caesar's agent."[88] Commentators often see Luke as minimizing Pilate's responsibility for Jesus'

---

[86] Barrett, *Acts*, 1:241–42.

[87] Pervo, *Acts*, 121 n. 8. Barrett (*Acts*, 1:244), Keener (*Acts 3:1–14:28*, 1167), and Didier Rimaud ("La première prière liturgique dans le livre des Actes," *La Maison-Dieu* 51 [1957]: 103–4) also see a use of Psalm 146 here.

[88] Keener, *Acts 3:1–14:28*, 1168.

death in his Gospel, but here in Acts he classes Pilate as an antagonist, indicating "that the Roman system is by no means guiltless."[89] Thus, Luke places a prayer immediately prior to the second summary that portrays political powers, including Roman political figures specifically, as both in opposition to Christ and inferior to God.

The imperial associations of the Golden Age myth in the early Roman Empire encourage reading the Acts summaries as alluding to this motif. Not only does Luke-Acts show general interest in Rome, but the contexts of the summaries bolster the claim that these passages specifically invoke imperial ideology. The structural parallels between Luke 1–2 and Acts 1–2 support an imperial reading of the first summary, while the politically charged prayer preceding the second summary explicitly calls attention to the hostility and ultimate impotence of Roman political figures.

The Summaries in Acts: An Eschatological Image

A final piece of evidence supporting a Golden Age interpretation of the Acts summaries is their eschatological nature. As I argued in Chapter 4, the summaries describe the lifestyle that resulted from the outpouring of the Spirit on Pentecost, an event marking "the last days" (Acts 2:17). This fits well with a Golden Age reading, since Chapter 3 showed that Jewish and Christian texts, especially the Sibylline Oracles, employ the Golden Age motif particularly in eschatological depictions. This section further specifies the parallel, arguing that both Acts and the Sibylline Oracles use Golden Age imagery to portray groups that prefigure the final eschatological restoration.

As noted in Chapter 4, Luke-Acts contains elements of not only present but also future eschatology. One of the clearest instances of the latter occurs in Acts 3:19–21, as Peter exhorts his audience to repent in anticipation of a future restoration:

> Repent therefore, and turn to God so that your sins may be wiped out, so that times of refreshing may come from the presence of the Lord, and that he may send the Messiah appointed for you, that is, Jesus, who must remain in heaven until the time of universal restoration that God announced long ago through his holy prophets.

Disputes primarily revolve around two phrases: "times of refreshing" (καιροὶ ἀναψύξεως) and "time of universal restoration" (χρόνων ἀποκαταστάσεως πάντων). The two main questions are (1) whether these expressions apply to the same time/period and (2) which specific time(s) the two phrases refer to.[90] The most common

---

[89] Walton, "State They Were In," 30.
[90] The "conventional view" (Kevin L. Anderson, *"But God Raised Him from the Dead": The Theology of Jesus' Resurrection in Luke-Acts*, Paternoster Biblical Monographs [Bletchley: Paternoster, 2001], 226) is that both phrases refer to the same time, the future eschaton; so Anderson, ibid., 227; Bock *Acts*, 178; Conzelmann, *Acts*, 29; Fitzmyer, *Acts*, 288–9; Haenchen, *Acts*, 208; Marguerat, *Actes*, 133; James Parker, *The Concept of Apokatastasis in Acts: A Study in Primitive Christian Theology* (Austin: Schola, 1978), 31; Pervo, *Acts*, 107–8; Eduard Schweizer, "ἀνάψυξις," TDNT 9:664. Barrett (*Acts*, 1:205–6) holds that the "times of refreshing" are in the present while the "universal restoration" is in the future. Both phrases are assigned to the present period by Bruce (*Acts*, 143–4), Carroll (*Response*, 148), Kurz ("Acts 3:19–26," 310–11), and Peterson (*Acts*, 180–2).

interpretation, which I adopt here, is that both designate a future, eschatological time marked by the return of Christ.[91] In any case, "the text shows that Luke, for all his emphasis on what is happening now eschatologically, has not abandoned the idea of a future eschatology."[92]

For this study, the most significant aspect of the passage is its use of the phrase "universal restoration" (ἀποκατάστασις πάντων) to characterize the eschaton. This is the only appearance of the noun ἀποκατάστασις in the NT, and the word never occurs in the LXX. The *TDNT* gives the basic sense as "restitution to an earlier state" or "restoration," and this meaning is generally accepted.[93] The question is *what* will be restored to its "earlier state"? Based on the use of the cognate verb in Acts 1:6, when the disciples ask Jesus, "is this the time when you will restore [ἀποκαθιστάνεις] the kingdom to Israel," commentators usually see Peter as referring to the restoration of Israel in 3:21. Yet most do not limit the scope of the remark to Israel alone but also find here a reference to "God's ancient plan to restore not only Israel but all creation."[94]

Expectations of a new or renewed creation appear in the HB and are common in Jewish apocalyptic, which typically anticipates a time "when God acts in a final and decisive manner to restore his creation to its original, pristine state."[95] Accordingly, the "time of universal restoration" mentioned in Acts 3:21 is regularly taken to refer to a return of the "fallen world to the purity and integrity of its initial creation," God "establishing again the original creation's pristine character," "a messianic restoral of everything to pristine integrity and harmony," "a restitution of the original order of creation," "the restitution of the integrity of creation," and "the ultimate renewal of the whole created order."[96] The correspondence of this restoration eschatology with the Golden Age-infused portraits of the end time in Sib. Or. 2 and 8 is obvious.

Although Luke presents the definitive eschatological restoration of the world as a future reality, he nonetheless characterizes the early believers in Acts as a community belonging to "the last days." As such, they can be seen as foreshadowing on a small scale

---

[91] Anderson (*But God Raised Him*, 227) succinctly presents the argument for this position: "First, the coming of the καιροὶ ἀναψύξεως and the sending of the Messiah are correlated results .... Second, heaven must receive the Messiah ἄχρι χρόνων ἀποκαταστάσεως πάντων. Both the καιροί and χρόνοι are thus related to the sending of the Messiah."

[92] Bock, *Acts*, 174.

[93] Albrecht Oepke, "ἀποκαθίστημι, ἀποκατάστασις," *TDNT* 1:389; similarly Barrett; *Acts*, 1:206; Carroll, *Response*, 146; Parker, *Concept of Apokatastasis*, 2. The suggestion of Bruce (*Acts*, 144) that ἀποκατάστασις here means "'establishment,' 'fulfilment'" has found little support.

[94] Anderson, *But God Raised Him*, 228. Keener (*Acts 3:1–14:28*, 1112) and Witherington III (*Acts*, 187) are among a minority who restrict the referent of ἀποκατάστασις to the restoration of Israel.

[95] David Aune and Eric Stewart, "From the Idealized Past to the Imaginary Future: Eschatological Restoration in Jewish Apocalyptic Literature," in *Restoration: Old Testament, Jewish, and Christian Perspectives*, ed. James M. Scott, Supplements to the Journal for the Study of Judaism 72 (Leiden: Brill, 2001), 177. The most explicit expectations in the HB are found in Isa 65:17 and 66:22, which both look forward to "new heavens" and a "new earth." Extra-biblical examples include Jub. 1:29; 4:26; 1 En. 45:4–5; 72:1; 91:16; LAB 3:10; 2 Bar. 32:6; 44:12; 57:2; 4 Ezra 8:52.

[96] C. K. Barrett, "Faith and Eschatology in Acts 3," in *Glaube und Eschatologie: Festschrift für Werner Georg Kümmel zum 80. Geburtstag*, ed. Erich Grässer and Otto Merk (Tübingen: Mohr, 1985), 16; Bock, *Acts*, 177; Fitzmyer, *Acts*, 289; Haenchen, *Acts*, 208; Marguerat, *Actes*, 133 ("la restauration de l'intégrité de la creation"); Peterson, *Acts*, 182.

the "universal restoration" still to come.⁹⁷ A sign of this incipient restoration is arguably present in the Pentecost narrative in Acts 2; commentators have often noted thematic and even lexical connections between this account and that of the Tower of Babel:

Reversed Features	Babel (Gen 11:1–9 LXX)	Pentecost (Acts 2:1–13)
Unity vs. diversity of language	"The Lord said … 'let us confuse their language'" (11:7, γλῶσσαν).	They "began to speak in other languages" (2:4, γλώσσαις).
Each does not understand vs. does understand the sound	"So that each [ἕκαστος] will not understand [ἀκούσωσιν] the sound [φωνὴν] of his neighbor" (11:7).	"At this sound [φωνῆς] the crowd gathered … 'we understand [ἀκούομεν], each [ἕκαστος], in our own native language'" (2:6, 8).
Scattering vs. gathering	"And the Lord scattered them from there over the face of all the earth" (11:8).	"Jews from every nation under heaven … gathered" (2:5–6).
Same result: confusion	"It was called 'Confusion' [Σύγχυσις] because there the Lord confused [συνέχεεν] the languages of all the earth" (11:9).	"The crowd … was confused" (2:6, συνεχύθη).

A reference to the Babel story is not universally accepted, but the parallels are sufficient to make an allusion probable.⁹⁸ Reading the Pentecost narrative as a partial reversal of Babel further encourages seeing the gift of the Spirit "as both an eschatological event of new creation and a utopian restoration of the unity of the human race."⁹⁹

In summary, Luke portrays the full eschatological renewal, the "time of universal restoration," as a future event linked with the return of Christ. This universal restoration presumably includes not just a reestablishment of Israel but also "a restitution of the original order of creation."¹⁰⁰ At the same time, Luke also characterizes the early Jerusalem believers as an eschatological community, filled with the Spirit whose arrival marks the start of "the last days." This community can therefore be understood as representing the "beginnings of the restoration."¹⁰¹ The probable allusion in Acts 2 to the Tower of Babel story also favors understanding the gift of the Spirit as an event signaling a reversal of the primeval curses against humanity. Viewed in this light, the Golden Age motif would provide eminently suitable imagery for depicting this community, which foreshadows the "messianic restoral of everything to pristine integrity and harmony."¹⁰²

---

⁹⁷ Blumhofer, "Luke's Alteration," 514; Kurz, "Acts 3:19–26," 310–11; Parker, *Concept of Apokatastasis*, 124; Wenk, *Community-Forming Power*, 272.
⁹⁸ Haenchen (*Acts*, 174) and Marguerat (*Actes*, 81) deny a reference, while Barrett (*Acts*, 1:112) and Bock (*Acts*, 101) leave the door open to an allusion but remain skeptical. Bruce (*Acts*, 119) and Holladay (*Acts*, 94) seem to lean toward accepting the presence of a reference to Babel. Keener (*Acts 1:1–2:47*, 842–4), Pervo (*Acts*, 61), Peterson (*Acts*, 136), and Wenk (*Community-Forming Power*, 256 n. 78) are fully in favor of seeing an allusion to Gen 11 in the Pentecost account.
⁹⁹ Pervo, *Acts*, 61–2.
¹⁰⁰ Haenchen, *Acts*, 208.
¹⁰¹ Blumhofer, "Luke's Alteration," 514.
¹⁰² Fitzmyer, *Acts*, 289. Cf. Capper, "Reciprocity," 511: "That a new phase of history has begun is symbolized by the momentary return of the paradisal state of the first human beings. Since the eschatological hope is hope for a return to paradise, Luke's description is also a glimpse of the eschatological future."

The fact that Sib. Or. 1–2 employs the Golden Age myth in precisely this way makes the proposed interpretation of Acts even more attractive. Sibylline Oracles 2 twice uses Golden Age imagery, including the motif of common property, in eschatological portrayals. In addition, however, the Sibyl also depicts an earlier race of humanity, the sixth, as a "golden one" (Sib. Or. 1.284), using much of the same imagery. Wassmuth argues that structurally this sixth race itself marks an "eschaton" but one that "points forward to a further 'second' or even definitive Golden Age."[103] Wassmuth labels this scheme "proto-eschatological mesology," in which the true eschatological Golden Age is prefigured in the middle of historical time by a "golden" generation that is itself in some way eschatological.[104] This corresponds closely to the interpretation of the Acts summaries proposed here: Luke uses Golden Age imagery to present the Jerusalem believers as a community that lives in historical time but foreshadows the final eschatological restoration of all creation. Based on both the internal features of Luke's narrative and the external parallel in Sib. Or. 1–2, the eschatological nature of the Jerusalem community suits a Golden Age reading of the summaries perfectly.

Summary: Identifying Acts 2:42–47 and 4:32–35 as Golden Age Allusions

Chapter 1 singled out the criterion of "markedness" as presenting the greatest hurdle for establishing a Golden Age allusion in the Acts summaries. Most literary allusions are recognized based on distinctive language shared by an alluding text and its source. The language of the Acts summaries, however, is not uniquely characteristic of any particular text or tradition; as a result, a specific allusion to the Golden Age myth (or to friendship, ideal state, or ethnographic traditions) cannot be asserted on the basis of vocabulary alone. Yet even in the absence of this sort of literary smoking gun, allusions can still be identified through a confluence of other evidence. The converging data that support a Golden Age reading of Acts 2:42–47 and 4:32–35 can now be summarized.

The most distinctive motif in the Acts summaries is that of common property. This theme occupies half of the verses in the summaries and is found nowhere in the biblical canon outside of these verses. While the language that Luke uses to describe this practice is not peculiar to the Golden Age tradition alone, this myth would have been one of the standard associations brought to mind by the mention of common property. In fact, Plutarch's reference to the Golden Age (*Cim.* 10.6–7) implies that, for at least some of Luke's contemporaries, the Golden Age would likely have been the dominant association evoked by the common property motif. The themes of divine blessing, human concord, and simplicity also connect the summaries with the Golden Age tradition. In addition to these basic thematic parallels, four additional characteristics support a Golden Age interpretation.

The first is the connection of the community with the beginning of a new age. In Acts 2, the Jerusalem community comes into being as a result of the gift of the Spirit, an

---

[103] Wassmuth, *Sibyllinische Orakel 1–2*, 57, 168; "weist auf eine weitere, 'zweite' oder eben definitive Goldene Zeit voraus."

[104] Ibid., 168; "proto-eschatologische Mesologie."

event that marks the dawning of a "new age."[105] The lifestyle of these believers, including their practice of common property, is not a timeless example of virtue but rather the direct result of a new divine dispensation. Second, the community's distinctive praxis is also ephemeral and located solidly in the past. Unlike the Essenes, whom Philo marshals as perduring Jewish "athletes of virtue" (Philo, *Prob.* 88), the Jerusalem believers' lifestyle disappears quickly from the pages of Acts, vanishing before most if not all of Luke's audience had even been born. The reason for this evanescence requires further exploration, but the point here is that this characteristic fits naturally with the idea of a transitory Golden Age.

Third, the Jerusalem community, which arises at the start of "the last days" (Acts 2:17), represents the first fruits of the ultimate "universal restoration" (Acts 3:21), the "messianic restoral of everything to pristine integrity and harmony."[106] Portraying this group using the motif of the Golden Age, the paradigmatic period of "pristine integrity and harmony," suits the community's role of offering a "glimpse of the eschatological future."[107] The fact that Sib. Or. 1-2 uses the Golden Age motif in just this way, to depict a historical generation that foreshadows the final eschatological Golden Age, makes this reading still more compelling.

Fourth, Luke's use of imperial ideology elsewhere also supports a Golden Age interpretation of the summaries. Narrating Jesus' birth in Luke 2, Luke characterizes him as "Savior," "Lord," and the bringer of "peace," three appellations commonly applied to the Roman emperor. When Luke describes the birth of the church in Acts 2, he portrays it as enjoying divine blessing, social harmony, simplicity, and common property, features of the Golden Age that the Roman emperor was supposed to be bringing about. Reading this passage as an allusion to the Golden Age motif fits both with Luke's general interest in Rome and with the specific precedent of Luke 2.

Taken together, these correspondences between Acts 2:42-47 and 4:32-35 and the Golden Age tradition form a convincing case for seeing an allusion to this myth in the summaries. Recalling the words of Fowler quoted earlier, the case for an allusion would be further strengthened if the proposed Golden Age reference could tell the reader "something interesting." In the remainder of this chapter, I explore the meanings that a Golden Age allusion might have conveyed to Luke's audience.

Interpreting Acts 2:42-47 and 4:32-35 as Golden Age Allusions

Before I consider the possible meanings of the Golden Age allusion in Acts 2:42-47 and 4:32-35, it will be helpful to establish what a satisfying interpretation would look like. First, a successful interpretation would be consistent with Luke's narrative as a whole. Second, the reason behind the choice of the *specific* referent should be clarified.

---

[105] Blumhofer, "Luke's Alteration," 510; Bruce, *Acts*, 121; Dunn, *Baptism*, 43; Fitzmyer *Acts*, 250; Johnson, *Acts*, 50; Maddox, *Purpose*, 139; Schweizer, *TDNT* 6:411; Shepherd, *Narrative Function*, 164.
[106] Fitzmyer, *Acts*, 289.
[107] Capper, "Reciprocity," 511.

This study has argued that Luke alludes to the Golden Age tradition in particular, not merely to some vague set of "Greek ideals"; as such, a satisfying interpretation would be grounded in characteristics distinctive of the Golden Age myth itself. Third, a convincing interpretation should shed some light on a puzzling issue that has emerged at several points in this study, that of the ephemeral nature of the community's praxis. Why does the motif of common property so quickly and quietly disappear after its dazzling entrance in Acts?

As an initial step toward providing a satisfying interpretation for the proposed allusion to the Golden Age, I first review previous suggestions regarding the purpose of Luke's idealizing language. I then further pursue two suggestions that hold particular promise and propose them as complementary interpretations. The first sees the Golden Age allusion as signifying the dawning of a new period of salvation history, while the second understands the use of the myth as a challenge to imperial ideology.

Suggested Reasons for Luke's Utopian Language in Acts 2:42–47 and 4:32–35

Numerous interpreters have recognized that Luke's descriptions in Acts 2:42–47 and 4:32–35 make use of "utopian" language and themes. By far the most common suggestion for the function of this utopian stylization is that it had an "apologetic" purpose, "a certain propaganda value."[108] By showing that "all the dreams and wishful ideas of Hellenistic social thought had been realized in an exemplary way in the early Christian community," Luke could "call forth the high respect" of his readers and present the early believers "in a way pleasing for his Hellenistic readers," giving them "a picture of the early church which they would understand and appreciate."[109] This proposed function is independent of any particular referent: it is advanced by scholars who see allusions to friendship, ideal state, ethnographic, and Golden Age traditions alike.[110]

Beyond the suggestion that they serve as a general apologetic flourish, there has been relatively little discussion and even less agreement as to any further function of Luke's utopian touches. Hays and a handful of others suggest that their purpose was primarily paraenetic, arguing that "any utopian resonances are to stimulate ethical response."[111] Dupertuis' hypothesis that Luke's primary referent is Plato's *Republic* leads him to propose that the goal was to provide the apostles with "impressive leadership credentials," which is similar to Johnson's interpretation of the summaries.[112]

---

[108] Dupertuis, "Summaries in Acts," 179; Witherington III, *Acts*, 156.
[109] Klauck, "Gütergemeinschaft," 73 ("all die Träume und Wunschgebilde hellenistischen Sozialdenkens in der christlichen Urgemeinde vorbildlich verwirklicht wurden"); Bartchy, "Community of Goods," 311; Keener, *Acts 1:1–2:47*, 1176; Seccombe, *Possessions and the Poor*, 207.
[110] Others who see an apologetic purpose include Dupont ("Community of Goods," 89), Haenchen (*Acts*, 233), Johnson (*Acts*, 62), Klauck ("Gütergemeinschaft," 73), Marguerat (*Actes*, 169), Mealand ("Community of Goods," 99), Pesch (*Apostelgeschichte*, 132–3), and Schreiber (*Weihnachtspolitik*, 76).
[111] Hays, *Luke's Wealth Ethics*, 209. Klauck ("Gütergemeinschaft," 74) and Mitchell ("Social Function of Friendship," 258) also see Luke's utopian language as having a hortatory function.
[112] Dupertuis, "Summaries in Acts," 173. For Acts 4:32–35 in particular, Johnson (*Acts*, 91) asserts that "the entire point ... is to show the authority of the apostles."

There is no reason to reject the idea that the function of these two summaries is partially apologetic; in both passages, Luke explicitly states that outsiders were impressed by the community's lifestyle (Acts 2:47; 4:33). Yet this explanation is not fully satisfying as it stands: it makes little use of the particulars of the Golden Age myth, and it does not help to explain why the motif of common property appears only here in Acts. If Luke formulated the community's economic arrangement as having "all things in common" for its apologetic usefulness, why did he do so only here and then never mention the idea again? The other two proposals also fail to provide a sufficient account, even if they may contain elements of truth. Luke is certainly interested in spurring generosity, but if his main goal in the summaries was to inspire almsgiving, why explicitly frame the community's practice as a community of property and a short-lived one at that?[113] And if the intention was to underscore the apostles' authority, why allude to the Golden Age myth, which typically says nothing at all about authority structures?

Two other suggested purposes for Luke's utopian language show more promise. A few interpreters propose that the first believers' distinctive yet fleeting communal lifestyle was intended as a sign that this time was unique and uniquely important, "to imply that foundation-events of unique import for world history were taking place."[114] This reading fits with the general idea of the Golden Age as a discrete, distinctive period, and its proponents also tend to be those most favorable to the idea of a Golden Age allusion.[115] This interpretation also has the advantage of potentially explaining the passing nature of the common property motif in Acts: if this motif primarily "is meant as an illustration of the uniqueness of the earliest days of the movement," then the practice of common property might not be expected to persist beyond these earliest days.[116]

A second promising suggestion regarding the use of Golden Age imagery, made by Dupertuis, is that Luke "may be trying to counter imperial claims of ushering in a new age."[117] As it happens, Dupertuis thinks that Luke's primary referent is not the Golden Age myth but rather Plato's *Republic*, and he makes this remark in passing without further explanation. Although almost no one has pursued an empire-critical reading of the Acts summaries, this interpretation takes into account a specific feature of the Golden Age myth (its imperial applications) and has potential parallels with other Lukan appropriations of imperial discourse. In the following sections, I investigate the latter two suggestions as those most likely to inform a successful interpretation of the Golden Age allusion in the Acts summaries.

---

[113] Those who see the summaries as primarily paraenetic typically think that Luke is simply "encouraging the rich to provide for the poor of his own community" (Mitchell, "Social Function of Friendship," 272), not suggesting that his readers adopt any true community of property.

[114] Capper, "Reciprocity," 509.

[115] Conzelmann (*Acts*, 24), Plümacher (*Lukas als hellenistischer Schriftsteller*, 18 n. 61), and Schreiber (*Weihnachtspolitik*, 76) give similar interpretations to that of Capper quoted above.

[116] Conzelmann, *Acts*, 24.

[117] Dupertuis, "Summaries in Acts," 179.

The Golden Age Allusion as a Sign of the Universal, Eschatological Spirit

Capper, Conzelmann, Plümacher, and Schreiber all propose that the Golden Age coloring of the Acts summaries is intended to signify that something important and/or unique is occurring in the events of Pentecost. I will develop this idea by considering three questions: (1) what specific phenomenon does the Golden Age motif characterize (i.e., what is the target of the allusion), (2) what features of the Golden Age myth might make it a fitting sign, and, as a result, (3) what function does this Golden Age allusion have in Acts? I argue that the Golden Age allusion characterizes the Spirit's coming as the beginning of an ultimate eschatological restoration that is available to all humans, both Jewish and Gentile. Interpreting the summaries in this way also helps to explain why the motif of common property does not reappear in Acts.

First, what event or object might the Golden Age motif illuminate? Based on the material presented in Chapter 4, the most likely target would seem to be the arrival of the Spirit. As argued there, the positioning of Acts 2:42–47 and 4:32–35 directly after outpourings of the Spirit (Acts 2:41; 4:31) indicates that these passages narrate the "direct and immediate result of the Spirit's coming."[118] If the summaries thus describe the effects of the Spirit, then portraying these effects in a Golden Age key would also tell Luke's audience something about the nature of the cause, Jesus, who "has poured out this that you both see and hear" (Acts 2:33).[119]

What specifically might a Golden Age allusion communicate? As Michael Leddy explains, an allusion "invokes one or more associations of ... an entity or event and brings them to bear upon a present context."[120] The next task, then, is determining what the "one or more associations" of the Golden Age myth are that would make it a fruitful image for understanding Jesus' outpouring of the Spirit on the early church. Certain aspects of the myth, although prominent in the Golden Age tradition itself, may be ruled out from being interpretively significant on the grounds that they are inconsistent with the way in which the Spirit's coming is depicted elsewhere in Acts. A clear example is the spontaneous fertility motif. Although this is one of the most distinctive features of the myth, there is no hint in the summaries or elsewhere in Acts that the Spirit has brought about an increase in agricultural productivity.[121] Similar reasoning also militates against seeing the practice of common property as an association that directly interprets the era of the Spirit. If the point of the allusion were that the gift of the Spirit brings about communities of property, why would this practice be absent from the rest of Acts? Instead, the motif of common property seems

---

[118] Dunn, *Baptism*, 51.
[119] For Jesus as the giver of the Spirit, cf. Luke 3:16; 24:49.
[120] Michael Leddy, "Limits of Allusion," *British Journal of Aesthetics* 32 (1992): 110–11.
[121] Schreiber (*Weihnachtspolitik*, 76) thinks that the community of goods described in the Acts summaries is an example of the "motif of the 'overabundance of nature'" ("Motiv des 'Überflusses der Natur'"), but the ideas of spontaneous fertility and common property are distinct in the Golden Age myth.

to serve as a means of evoking the Golden Age myth; it is not, however, one of the features of the myth that conveys meaning about the Spirit's coming.[122]

Acts itself provides an initial interpretation of Jesus' gift of the Spirit on Pentecost, as Peter quotes Joel 3:1–5 LXX to explain the event. This citation signals to the audience how the coming of the Spirit should be understood, and it thereby suggests which characteristics of the Golden Age myth might be most important for interpreting the summaries. The two most pertinent features of this quotation occur in Acts 2:17a: "'In the last days it will be,' God declares, 'that I will pour out my Spirit upon all flesh.'"

The first relevant element is Luke's redactional insertion of "in the last days," by which "the Spirit is given an eschatological function."[123] Since Luke's eschatology includes the idea of restoration (cf. Acts 3:21), the coming of the Spirit can be viewed as "the beginnings of the restoration," as "a utopian restoration of the unity of the human race."[124] The Golden Age motif was perfectly suited to signify this aspect of the Pentecost event. As detailed in Chapter 2, in the early Empire the Golden Age often was portrayed not only as a past but also as a returning reality, as the restoration of a lost utopia: "now … the reign of Saturn *returns*" (Virgil, *Ecl.* 4.6); "Augustus Caesar … will establish the golden ages *again*" (Virgil, *Aen.* 6.792–793); "the Golden Age is *reborn*" (Calpurnius Siculus, *Ecl.* 1.42); "the days of Saturn have *returned* … secure ages have *returned* to the ancient ways" (*Einsiedeln Eclogues* 2.23–24). Utopian accounts of harmony, piety, simplicity, and even common property appear in a variety of literary traditions; what is distinctive of the Golden Age tradition is the portrayal of this utopian state of affairs as (a restoration of) the conditions of primeval humanity. An allusion to the Golden Age would thus fit with and reinforce Luke's presentation of the Jerusalem community as enjoying a "restored Paradisal unity" brought about by the Spirit.[125]

The second important feature of the Joel quotation is the statement that the Spirit will come "upon all flesh." In its original context in Joel, this claim was most likely limited to the people of Israel, and commentators reasonably suggest that Peter would have shared this same understanding when quoting the passage in Acts 2.[126] Nevertheless, from Luke's standpoint, this prophecy anticipates the outpouring of the Spirit on all humanity, including Gentiles.[127] The Spirit is not only an eschatological but also a universally available gift. The Golden Age myth was a suitable vehicle for this

---

[122] This does not mean that the common property motif has no ethical import; Luke clearly contrasts the community's unselfish use of wealth with the selfish practices of Ananias and Sapphira and, arguably, Judas, upholding the community's ethic as superior. The claim here is that Luke's choice to portray their practice as specifically one of common property was due more to the sign value of this motif than to a desire to make common property an ethical paradigm for his audience.

[123] Shepherd, *Narrative Function*, 164. For more on this topic, see Chapter 4.

[124] Blumhofer, "Luke's Alteration," 514; Pervo, *Acts*, 61–2.

[125] Turner, *Power from on High*, 406.

[126] Bock, *Acts*, 113; Fitzmyer, *Acts*, 252; Johnson, *Acts*, 49; Keener, *Acts 1:1–2:47*, 881; Robert P. Menzies, *Empowered for Witness: The Spirit in Luke-Acts*, Journal of Pentecostal Theology Supplement Series 6 (Sheffield: Sheffield Academic, 1994), 188; Turner, *Power from on High*, 404.

[127] Bock, *Acts*, 113; Bruce, *Acts*, 121; Fitzmyer, *Acts*, 252; Johnson, *Acts*, 49; Keener, *Acts 1:1–2:47*, 881; Menzies, *Empowered for Witness*, 188; Shepherd, *Narrative Function*, 165–6.

idea for two reasons. First, this myth tells of a time when all humans lived together in "absolute harmony," free from the στάσις (Plato, *Pol.* 271e) and *discordia* (Germanicus, *Arat.* 113) that marked late ages. Through the gift of the Spirit, in which God "made no distinction" (Acts 15:10) between Jews and Gentiles, Acts depicts the Christian community as the new locus of harmony for all humanity. Second, characterizing the early Jewish believers by means of a tradition strongly associated with Greek and Roman writers is itself a universalizing move. By alluding to a myth that primarily non-Jewish authors such as Hesiod, Plato, Virgil, and Seneca had used to portray the ideal condition of humanity, Luke is implying that "in the new community of faith not only the biblical promises, but also the hopes of the peoples, find their fulfillment."[128]

For signaling Jesus' gift of the eschatological, universal Spirit, therefore, the Golden Age myth was an attractive and effective instrument. This interpretation has another benefit as well, as it helps to explain why the motif of common property might quickly vanish from the pages of Acts.[129] Both in Acts and elsewhere in the biblical canon, the Spirit's arrival is often marked by some initial, observable sign. When the Spirit falls on the seventy elders in Num 11 and on Saul in 1 Sam 10 and 19, for instance, they immediately begin to prophesy. In Acts, speaking in tongues accompanies the initial reception of the Spirit in chapters 2, 10, and 19. Additional indicators in Acts include "tongues of fire" in 2:3 and an earthquake in 4:31. The relevant characteristic of all of these signs is that they are temporary. This is explicit in Num 11:25: although the Spirit presumably remained on the seventy elders, after their first act of prophesying "they did not do so again." Similarly, there is no indication that the apostles, Cornelius, or the Ephesian twelve continue to speak in tongues, although they surely continue to possess the Spirit. Instead, these phenomena flare up "on occasions of intense or epochal irruptions of the Spirit."[130] If the practice of common property serves as another one of these signs of the Spirit, then it should not necessarily be expected to persist after its initial appearance. The disappearance of the common property motif does not indicate that the church has declined from some original ideal state but rather that this motif has fulfilled its role as sign.[131]

---

[128] Pesch, *Apostelgeschichte*, 182; "in der neuen Glaubensgemeinschaft nicht nur die biblischen Verheißungen, sondern auch die Hoffnungen der Völker ihre Erfüllung finden."

[129] Earlier commentators sometimes understood the disappearance as a sign that Luke regarded the community of goods as a mistake; so George Thomas Stokes, *The Acts of the Apostles*, Expositor's Bible 34–5 (New York: Armstrong, 1891), 1:197–98. More recently, the Golden Age allusion has been thought to imply that the practice was commendable but unrepeatable; so Capper, "Reciprocity," 509; Conzelmann, *Acts*, 24; Klauck, "Gütergemeinschaft," 73; Plümacher, *Lukas als hellenistischer Schriftsteller*, 18 n. 61.

[130] Turner, *Power from on High*, 357. Cf. Eduard Schweizer, *The Holy Spirit*, trans. Reginald H. Fuller and Ilse Fuller (Philadelphia: Fortress, 1980), 63: "Luke mentions such striking phenomena as speaking in tongues only where it is God's purpose to take some new extraordinary step for his people."

[131] Capper ("Reciprocity," 503) sees "the sin of Ananias and Sapphira … as a kind of fall of the first community from innocence (thereafter irretrievable)," and Marguerat (*First Christian Historian*, 175) similarly understands it as "the repetition of the original sin of Adam and Eve." Luke, however, gives no indication that Ananias and Sapphira's sin marks some sort of general decline. Instead, the stories of Judas and of Ananias and Sapphira use Iron Age motifs to depict those whose actions separate them from the community, not to convey the idea of an initial ideal period and a subsequent fall.

This section has argued that Luke's presentation of the Jerusalem believers as leading a Golden Age lifestyle serves as a sign of the Spirit's coming and highlights certain aspects of this new dispensation. Based on Peter's use of Joel 3:1–5 LXX to explain this event, the two most relevant associations of the Golden Age myth seem to be the restoration of some past, ideal state and the idea of universal harmony. By means of this allusion, Luke implies that Jesus' outpouring of the Spirit is bringing about the beginning of a "universal restoration" that will encompass all peoples. The short-lived nature of the practice of common property fits with and supports the idea that this motif functions primarily as a sign of the coming of the Spirit. Yet while this account might be sufficient on its own to explain a Golden Age allusion, Luke likely had an additional reason to portray the early community using this specific myth.

The Golden Age Allusion as a Supra-Imperial Claim

Those who have identified a reference to the Golden Age tradition in the Acts summaries have rarely noted the strong political overtones of this myth in the early Empire. In this section I argue that Luke's Golden Age allusion raises a clear if implicit critical contrast between what Jesus has accomplished through the gift of the Spirit and what the Roman emperor has failed to accomplish. First, I defend the relevance of the myth's political associations for interpreting the Golden Age allusion in Acts. Second, I establish the range of meanings that might be conveyed by the use of such a political myth. Third, I propose an empire-critical reading of the allusion: Luke's use of the Golden Age motif calls to mind claims that the Roman emperor would bring about a return of this age and implies that it is Christ, not Caesar, who is bringing about this "universal restoration," reconciliation with God and harmony among humans.

Chapter 2 detailed the political applications of the Golden Age myth in the early Empire: beginning with Virgil, "the association of the reigning emperor with a return of the Golden Age became a recurrent topic in poetry, imperial panegyric and the official coinage."[132] Still, the mere fact that this myth had imperial connotations does not imply that every Golden Age allusion would have been read as political commentary.[133] In the case of Luke, however, there are good reasons to judge that the myth's political associations are not incidental to the meaning of the allusion. First, given the prevalence of political uses of the myth, and the fact that "the political transformation of the Golden Age idea came to expression not only in the great works of poetry but rather soon also took root in the general popular belief," Luke and his audience would almost certainly have been aware of the imperial connotations of the Golden Age motif.[134] Second, while not all references to the Golden Age were political in nature, Chapter 2 showed that almost every mention of a new or returning Golden

---

[132] Wallace-Hadrill, "Golden Age and Sin," 22.
[133] Josephus' use of Golden Age themes in *A.J.* 1.46–62, for instance, shows no signs of having a political purpose.
[134] Gatz, *Weltalter*, 142; "die politische Transformation der Goldalteridee nicht nur in den großen Werken der Dichtung zum Ausdruck gelangte, sondern sehr bald auch im allgemeinen Volksglauben Wurzeln geschlagen hatte."

Age attributed this to the Roman emperor. Third, it is unlikely that the political aspects of the myth would have been irrelevant to Luke. As Chapter 4 noted, Luke shows a keen interest in Roman authorities, dating Jesus' birth and ministry to the reigns of Roman emperors and depicting encounters with an array of Roman officials. Fourth, and most important, Luke elsewhere seems to consciously incorporate elements drawn from imperial ideology into his own presentation. This phenomenon is perhaps most prominent in the infancy narrative, where Jesus' birth is both explicitly linked with the reign of Augustus and proclaimed using terms like "Lord," "savior," and "peace."

The next question is what message might have been communicated to Luke's audience by the use of such a politically resonant myth. Heilig breaks NT perspectives on the relationship between Christian and Roman claims into three categories: the Christian message can be seen as (a) complementing, (b) relativizing, or (c) denying certain imperial assertions.[135] The closest analogue in Luke-Acts to the Golden Age allusion is the use of imperial terminology in Luke 2, and suggestions as to the purpose of this borrowing span all the categories above.[136] The most widely held view, however, is that Luke's appropriation of imperial terminology to describe Jesus implies a denial of certain claims made by Rome.[137] Those who find a specific allusion to the Golden Age in Luke 2 hold a similar range of interpretations. Brent opts for a complementary reading, taking Luke to be presenting "a Christian ... counterpart to the imperial peace."[138] Wolter adopts a more relativizing approach, pointing to elements in Luke 2 that "raise Jesus far over the status of the Roman Caesar," while Schreiber sees an "indirect confrontation" that makes Luke-Acts into "a piece of subversive underground literature."[139]

Turning to the Acts summaries, no single, definitive political interpretation can be established; individual members of Luke's audience who recognized a Golden Age allusion might well have taken different meanings from it. Nevertheless, when read in the context of Luke-Acts as a whole, interpretations from the critical end of the spectrum are more probable than uncritical, complementary ones for three reasons. First, Chapter 4 argued that Luke-Acts as a whole evinces a "supra-imperial" perspective on the Roman emperor and empire: "they are surpassed, in a far more perfect way, by God and the kingdom of heaven."[140] This does not necessitate that every

---

[135] Heilig, *Hidden Criticism*, 131.

[136] Walaskay (*And So We Came to Rome*, 27) occupies the complementary end of the spectrum, arguing that Luke's point was that "the *pax Augusta* was completed (complemented) by the *pax Christi*"; Fitzmyer (*Luke I–IX*, 175) and Pinter ("Gospel of Luke," 110) may be placed in this category as well. In a slightly more critical vein, Billings ("At the Age of 12," 88) judges that while Luke's language "could not be conceived as anti-imperial," he nonetheless "presents Jesus as the superior and ultimate (eschatological) successor to the emperor," relativizing imperial ideology; cf. Bryan, *Render to Caesar*, 99.

[137] Even within this category, the degree of opposition that is posited varies widely, ranging from "gentle counterpropaganda" (Brown, *Birth of the Messiah*, 424) to "a vigorous critique of Rome and its claims" (Gilbert, "Roman Propaganda," 255). Others who see an implicit denial of Roman pretensions include Bovon (*Luke 1*, 83), Green (*Luke*, 122), Kim (*Christ and Caesar*, 80–1), Moles ("Accommodation," 87), Walton ("State They Were In," 26), and Yamazaki-Ransom (*Roman Empire*, 86).

[138] Brent, "Luke-Acts," 414.

[139] Wolter, "Die Hirten," 517; "Jesus weit über den Status des römischen Kaisers hinaus heben"; Schreiber, *Weihnachtspolitik*, 80; "indirekter Konfrontation"; "einem Stück subversiver Untergrundliteratur."

[140] Galinsky, "In the Shadow (or Not) of the Imperial Cult," 222.

Lukan reference to Rome function in precisely this way, but it does lend support to critical interpretations of the Golden Age allusion. Second, this study (and a plurality of commentators) has judged that the analogous application of imperial titles to Jesus in Luke 2 has a supra-imperial function.

Third, even apart from comparisons with Luke 2 or the perspective of Luke-Acts in general, the Golden Age allusion on its own is conducive to a critical, supra-imperial reading. Luke and many in his audience likely would have been aware of the common claim that the emperor was bringing about a return of the Golden Age. A non- or less critical interpretation of Luke's Golden Age allusion, therefore, would be complementary: the gift of the Spirit would mark the beginning of an eschatological restoration that would complement the current, earthly restoration effected by Rome. Yet even if Luke had an "informed and admiring view" of Rome's institutional and material achievements, as some assert, he nowhere indicates that the empire had brought about any sort of spiritual renewal of divine blessing and social harmony.[141] The most that could be claimed would be that Luke appreciated certain aspects of Roman society for providing "an environment in which Christian mission can progress."[142] But the restoration itself, the reconciliation of humanity with God, comes through the agency of the only true savior, Jesus Christ.

By the time that Luke is writing Acts, Roman claims of a returning Golden Age have been ongoing for over a century. Virgil's fourth *Eclogue* provides the first example circa 40 BCE, and his *Aeneid* ties the return to a specific figure: "Augustus Caesar, the child of a god, who will establish the golden ages again" (*Aen.* 6.792–793). This expectation passes on to subsequent emperors but seems never to be met. Tiberius, Augustus' successor, is criticized for presiding over an Iron rather than a Golden Age (Suetonius, *Tib.* 59.1). Philo reports that the people initially thought that the next emperor, Gaius, had brought about "the life of Cronus recorded by poets" (*Legat.* 13), but "after a short time the one who had been believed to be the savior and benefactor ... changed to savagery" (ibid., 21–2). Predictions of an emperor-led return of the Golden Age flourish again at the accession of Nero in 54 CE, with poems proclaiming that "the Golden Age is reborn" (Calpurnius, *Ecl.* 1.42) and "the days of Saturn have returned" (*Einsiedeln Eclogues* 2.23). These hopes prove to be ill-founded as well, and two decades later the *Octavia* depicts the reign of Nero as an Iron Age, "an oppressive age in which wickedness reigns and impiety raves and rages" (430–1). A similar dynamic continues through the late first and early second centuries: while Hadrian declares his reign a "Golden Age," Juvenal pokes fun at it as being "an age worse than the times of iron" (*Sat.* 13.28–29).

Against this background, Luke makes a counterclaim for the Christian community: *we* are living in the "Golden Age"! Particularly through the motif of common property, seemingly a foreign body in the narrative of Acts, Luke invokes the Golden Age myth to depict the renewal brought about by Jesus' gift of the Spirit that first appears on Pentecost. Through their reception of this same Spirit, all believers now take part in

---

[141] Marguerat, *First Christian Historian*, 76.
[142] Kim, *Christ and Caesar*, 178; cf. Marguerat, ibid.; Walaskay, *And So We Came to Rome*, 26.

the restoration of human harmony and divine blessing, one that will reach its apex at the return of Christ. Certainly, this notion is useful for the audience's "own self-understanding," providing "a positive revaluation of their social status."[143] At the same time, the implication that a Golden Age restoration has begun among the followers of Christ raises a contrast with the repeated imperial claims sketched above. What a series of Roman emperors have failed to do, to bring about a return of Golden Age unity and piety, Jesus has done by sending the Spirit.

In fact, the emphasis on the figure of the emperor specifically in contemporary Golden Age texts makes this particular myth ripe for Lukan appropriation. As Andrew Wallace-Hadrill points out, the purpose of Roman versions of the Golden Age myth was to focus attention on the unique and central role played by the emperor:

> For the Augustans its function is to put the emperor at the centre of the scheme of things. The myth does then have an ideological function: … to enforce the subjection of every Roman to the person of the emperor.[144]

Luke likewise sees the hopes of all humanity as concentrated on a single figure, Jesus, whose claims are similarly exclusive: "There is salvation in no one else, for there is no other name under heaven given among mortals by which we must be saved" (Acts 4:12).

Relative to the Jewish and Christian uses of the myth examined in Chapter 3, the political meaning conveyed by Luke's Golden Age allusion most likely falls somewhere between those in Philo and in Sib. Or. 8. Josephus' application of the Golden Age motif appears to be politically neutral; he borrows elements of the myth to depict primeval humanity, but he does not hint at a return of this age, much less suggest the presence of a contemporary or future Golden Age that might compete with the imperial one. Philo, however, indicates that the Golden Age hopes attached to the accession of Gaius were misplaced, and he borrows Golden Age language to describe a future divine restoration of peace. This could plausibly be read as an indictment of imperial claims to be bringing back the Golden Age. On the other hand, Philo is effusive in his praise of both Augustus and Tiberius, and the divine "Golden Age" that he hints at is only a future, not present, reality. In Sib. Or. 8, the anti-Roman polemic is overt: Rome is labelled "the famous unlawful kingdom" (Sib. Or. 8.9), and the Golden Age motif of common property clearly has a critical function. Rome is condemned for privatizing the earth, and its fate is depicted as an anti-Golden Age, in which darkness and death are "common to all" (Sib. Or. 8.121).

Luke is not openly hostile toward Rome in the manner of Sib. Or. 8. The portrayals of Roman officials in Luke-Acts may not be entirely positive, but neither are they uniformly negative. Relative to Philo, however, both Luke's general stance and his employment of the Golden Age motif appear to be more critical. Although Luke mentions multiple Roman emperors, he never praises them at all, much less in the

---

[143] Schreiber, *Weihnachtspolitik*, 76; "eigenen Selbstverständnis"; "eine Aufwertung ihres sozialen Status."

[144] Wallace-Hadrill, "Golden Age and Sin," 25.

extended, inflated way of the *Legatio ad Gaium*.[145] And while Philo's implicit Golden Age is only a future possibility, Luke alludes to a Golden Age in the present, one that is potentially in competition with the restoration purportedly being wrought by the emperor. Sibylline Oracles 8 is anti-imperial, while Philo is perhaps tacitly supra-imperial behind a veil of praise. Luke's presentation seems to fall more firmly into the supra-imperial category. In both Luke 2 and the Acts summaries, Luke implies that Caesar has claimed for himself titles and roles that are properly applied to Christ. Christ is Lord, Savior, and the bringer of peace, and Christ is the one who will bring about the "universal restoration" that is already beginning in the Jerusalem believers.

In addition to signifying the coming of the eschatological Spirit on all humanity, I have argued in this section that a Golden Age allusion would also have conveyed an empire-critical meaning to many in Luke's audience. Given the prevalence of imperial uses of this myth, Luke's general interest in Rome, and his appropriation of imperial language elsewhere in Luke-Acts, the political associations of the Golden Age myth are significant for interpreting a Golden Age allusion in the Acts summaries. This allusion is best read as having a supra-imperial function: Jesus is portrayed as effecting a superior restoration to anything that a Roman emperor has been able to achieve. This does not imply that Luke thinks that Rome is an illegitimate governing power or that Christians should engage in some form of political resistance to the Empire. What the Golden Age allusion does imply is both that Christ's status is superior to that of Caesar and that the emperor has improperly arrogated to himself certain claims, namely that of restoring human harmony, piety, and ultimately the entire created order.

Summary: Reading Acts 2:42–47 and 4:32–35 as Golden Age Allusions

I have argued in this chapter that the summaries in Acts 2:42–47 and 4:32–35 allude to the myth of the Golden Age and have suggested what meanings this allusion might convey in the context of Luke-Acts. As a preliminary step, I examined the principal exegetical issues in these texts. The most significant task was determining precisely what process Luke describes in his account of the property arrangement of the community. The conclusion reached here was that Acts 2:42–47 and 4:32–35 most likely depict the same practice, with the second summary providing more details than the first. Luke states that those believers who owned lands and houses sold them and gave the proceeds to the apostles, who then distributed the money to individual members according to need. The summaries do not specify or imply when property was sold; the use of imperfect verbs could be explained by a variety of situations. The most notable aspect of these accounts is the universality of the language, especially the repeated claim that the believers "had all things in common" (Acts 2:44; 4:32). Since neither the summaries themselves nor the stories that surround them fully justify this far-reaching assertion, it seems that Luke has some particular reason for emphasizing the idea of common property.

---

[145] Of course, the *Legatio* also harshly criticizes the emperor Gaius, but the praises of Augustus and Tiberius would indicate to the audience that Philo has no problem with Roman emperors per se.

Next, I showed that Acts 2:42–47 and 4:32–35 satisfy one of the necessary criteria for establishing an allusion, that of "markedness." The summaries were seen to be distinctive in their contexts, both lexically and thematically; most significantly, the idea of common property appears nowhere else in Luke-Acts or even in the entire biblical canon. I then argued that the common property motif in these passages can be satisfactorily explained as an allusion to the Golden Age myth. Five additional features of the Acts summaries support this assertion. First, other themes in these passages, such as divine blessing, simplicity, and especially the emphasis on unity and harmony, match standard features of the Golden Age myth. Second, the community's lifestyle commences at the beginning of a "new age" brought about by the Spirit. Third, as in the Golden Age, the believers' distinctive way of life is ephemeral, vanishing before the lifetimes of Luke's audience. Fourth, this community of the "last days" marks the beginning of the "universal restoration" that will culminate in the return of Christ, corresponding to the common idea of the Golden Age as a restoration of primeval bliss. Fifth, a Lukan use of this imperial myth would fit with appropriations of imperial language elsewhere in Luke-Acts. Taken together, these characteristics are sufficient to identify a Golden Age allusion in Acts 2:42–47 and 4:32–35 with some confidence.

Finally, I proposed two complementary interpretations for this allusion, explaining why Luke might have chosen to use the Golden Age myth in particular to depict the early Jerusalem community. First, this myth was well suited to signify Jesus' gift of the Spirit. The Golden Age myth told of a past time of universal harmony, and in the early Empire an imminent restoration of this utopian past was often proclaimed. Luke sees the coming of the Spirit as an event that marks the beginning of the "last days," the start of a "universal restoration" that is still to come. Further, this gift of the Spirit is universal, one that is poured out "on all flesh" as the Spirit fills both Jews and Gentiles in the narrative of Acts. The community's Golden Age property sharing is a sign of this universal, eschatological Spirit; since other signs of the Spirit are often ephemeral (prophesy, tongues, fire, etc.), the apparent temporariness of the common property arrangement is not surprising.

The second meaning that this Golden Age allusion would have conveyed was political in nature. Given the repeated claims that the Roman emperor would bring about a new Golden Age, Luke's implication that Christ was the one who had actually initiated this anticipated restoration would have suggested a contrast between the two figures. This supposition is confirmed by Luke's similar practice in Luke 2 and Acts 10, where he uses titles for Jesus that were commonly applied to the emperor. Like those passages, the Acts summaries imply that "the dispensations of empire go only so far. They are surpassed, in a far more perfect way, by God and the kingdom of heaven."[146]

---

[146] Galinsky, "In the Shadow (or Not) of the Imperial Cult," 222.

Conclusion

In this study, I have argued that Luke's descriptions of the early Jerusalem believers in Acts 2:42–47 and 4:32–35, particularly in their claims regarding common property, allude to the Golden Age myth. As told by Roman authors, this myth spoke of an initial, ideal period of human existence, when people enjoyed the favor of the gods and harmony with each other, free from war, strife, and the selfishness and greed associated with private property. In the early Empire, these authors also began to speak of a returning Golden Age, a restoration of utopian conditions that the Roman emperor would effect. By alluding to this myth in his accounts of the lifestyle practiced by the first Christians, Luke portrays the gift of the Spirit as marking the beginning of a "universal restoration" (Acts 3:21) that is available to all humanity. At the same time, Luke's invocation of this imperial myth implies that it is Christ, not Caesar, who truly brings about this restored harmony between God and humanity and among humans themselves.

Chapter 1 demonstrated that pursuing this line of interpretation would be both useful and feasible. Many scholars have recognized similarities between Luke's language in the Acts summaries and that found in various Greek and Latin descriptions of common property. I showed that while many have identified Golden Age accounts as a relevant part of this common property discourse, interpreters of Acts 2:42–47 and 4:32–35 have paid less attention to the Golden Age myth than to other common property contexts, such as ideal state discussions, ethnographic portraits, and friendship traditions. Further, the objections that have been raised against a Golden Age interpretation of the summaries were shown to be easily refuted. A review of the arguments offered for the alternative common property contexts indicated that none had a stronger prima facie case than the Golden Age myth for guiding the interpretation of Acts 2:42–47 and 4:32–35. Finally, I outlined six criteria by which an allusion to the Golden Age myth could be established. The history of scholarship showed that one of the supplementary criteria, "later recognition," was fulfilled by several scholars who had seen allusions to the Golden Age idea in these summaries.

Chapter 2 traced the Golden Age myth from its earliest extant occurrence in Hesiod's *Works and Days* through its many appearances in early imperial authors such as Virgil and Ovid. Virgil was the most important figure in this trajectory, as he introduced three important features that became standard for the Golden Age myth. First, Virgil announced an imminent return of the Golden Age: "the Iron Race will now at last cease and a Golden Race will arise in the whole world" (*Ecl.* 4.8–9).

Second, Virgil attributed this return to the emperor, to "Augustus Caesar, the child of a god, who will establish the golden ages again" (*Aen.* 6.792–793). Third, Virgil was the first to explicitly ascribe an absence of private property to the Golden Age, when "not even marking or dividing the open field with a boundary was allowed" (*Georg.* 1.126–127). Subsequent Roman authors regularly described the Golden Age as a time when "all things were common" (Trogus, *Ep.* 43.1.3), and no less than sixteen emperors were credited with bringing about a return of this age.[1] This chapter showed that the necessary criterion of "accessibility" was fully satisfied.

Chapter 3 explored the uses of this myth by Jewish and Christian authors in the early Empire. An important general conclusion was that authors such as Philo, Josephus, and the writers of the Sibylline Oracles did allude to or even openly refer to the Golden Age myth, fulfilling the supplementary criterion of "occurrence in other authors." In addition, I showed that Jewish and Christian references to the Golden Age (1) often occurred in eschatological descriptions, (2) usually included the motif of common property, and (3) appeared in works interested in Rome and were sometimes employed to criticize the Empire. Sibylline Oracles 8 provided the most explicit instance of the latter function, as Rome's practice of dividing the earth with boundaries and its desire "to possess forever the earth" (Sib. Or. 8.30) were contrasted with the eschatological Golden Age, when "property and wealth will be common to all" and "the earth will be equally shared with all, not divided by walls or fences" (Sib. Or. 8.208–210).

The attention of the study returned to Luke-Acts in Chapter 4. Here I treated three issues that were preliminaries to an analysis and interpretation of the summaries themselves. First, I argued that Acts 2:42–47 and 4:32–35 depict an eschatological lifestyle, since both passages narrate the effects of the Spirit whose coming marks the "last days" (Acts 2:17). Second, I showed that Luke had a strong interest in Rome and occasionally appropriated imperial titles and concepts to portray Jesus. The function of Luke's use of imperial language was identified as "supra-imperial": it implied that Christ was more properly called "Savior" and "Lord" than Caesar was, even if no open hostility toward the latter was expressed. Third, I judged claims that Luke alluded to the Golden Age myth in his infancy narrative to be inconclusive. As such, the supplementary criterion of "recurrence in the same author" was not satisfied, although Luke's use of imperial language and imagery elsewhere in Luke-Acts did provide a close analogue to the proposed Golden Age allusion in the Acts summaries.

Finally, Chapter 5 made the argument that the accounts of the early believers' lifestyle in Acts 2:42–47 and 4:32–35 allude to the Golden Age myth. After examining five specific exegetical issues in these passages, I made the case for the distinctiveness of these summaries, especially the repeated claim that the community "had all things in common" (Acts 2:44; 4:32). In addition to this common property motif, I noted several other shared themes between the Golden Age myth and Luke's descriptions, including divine blessing, human harmony, simplicity, the idea of a "new age," the ephemeral nature of these utopian conditions, and the association of later ages/outsiders with greed and privatizing of wealth. Luke's use of this community to foreshadow the final

---

[1] West, *Hesiod*, 177.

"universal restoration" also corresponded to Sib. Or. 1–2's application of the Golden Age myth. Finally, an allusion to this imperial myth paralleled other Lukan appropriations of imperial discourse, as discussed in Chapter 4. Taken together, these shared features were sufficient to fulfill the necessary criterion of "markedness."

The one remaining necessary criterion for an allusion that Chapter 1 identified was "sense," and the remainder of Chapter 5 satisfied this by suggesting two meanings that were communicated by Luke's Golden Age allusion. First, alluding to this myth of a (potentially returning) primeval utopia advanced Luke's presentation of the coming of the Spirit as marking the beginning of the "last days," the beginning of the "universal restoration" that would come to completion at the return of Christ. Second, attributing the dawning of this restoration to Christ's sending of the Spirit constituted a supra-imperial claim. Although Roman emperors had been credited with bringing about a return of the Golden Age for over a century (and would continue to be for centuries more), Luke implied that it was Christ who had truly restored the human-divine relationship and brought about a renewed human community.

Bibliography

Adams, James N. *Bilingualism and the Latin Language*. New York: Cambridge University Press, 2003.
Ahn, Yong-Sung. *The Reign of God and Rome in Luke's Passion Narrative: An East Asian Global Perspective*. BibInt 80. Leiden: Brill, 2006.
Alexander, Loveday. "The Acts of the Apostles as an Apologetic Text." Pages 15–44 in *Apologetics in the Roman Empire: Pagans, Jews and Christians*. Edited by Mark Edwards, Martin Goodman, and Simon Price. Oxford: Oxford University Press, 1999.
Alonso-Núñez, J. M. "An Augustan World History: The 'Historiae Philippicae' of Pompeius Trogus." *GR* 34 (1987): 56–72.
Alpers, Paul J. *The Singer of the Eclogues: A Study of Virgilian Pastoral*. Berkeley: University of California Press, 1979.
Andersen, T. David. "The Meaning of ΕΧΟΝΤΕΣ ΧΑΡΙΝ ΠΡΟΣ in Acts 2,47." *NTS* 34 (1988): 604–10.
Anderson, Charles A. *Philo of Alexandria's Views of the Physical World*. WUNT 2/309. Tübingen: Mohr Siebeck, 2011.
Anderson, Kevin L. "*But God Raised Him from the Dead*": *The Theology of Jesus' Resurrection in Luke-Acts*. Paternoster Biblical Monographs. Bletchley: Paternoster, 2001.
Anderson, William S., ed. *Ovid's* Metamorphoses: *Books 1–5*. Norman: University of Oklahoma Press, 1997.
Attridge, Harold W. *The Interpretation of Biblical History in the* Antiquitates Judaicae *of Flavius Josephus*. HDR 7. Missoula, MT: Scholars Press, 1976.
Aune, David, and Eric Stewart. "From the Idealized Past to the Imaginary Future: Eschatological Restoration in Jewish Apocalyptic Literature." Pages 147–77 in *Restoration: Old Testament, Jewish, and Christian Perspectives*. Edited by James M. Scott. Supplements to the Journal for the Study of Judaism 72. Leiden: Brill, 2001.
Austin, Roland G., ed. *Aeneidos: liber primus*. Oxford: Clarendon, 1971.
Baldry, H. C. "Who Invented the Golden Age?" *ClQ* 2 (1952): 83–92.
Barker, Duncan. "'The Golden Age Is Proclaimed'? The 'Carmen Saeculare' and the Renascence of the Golden Race." *ClQ* 46 (1996): 434–46.
Barnes, Timothy D. "The Date of the *Octavia*." *Museum Helveticum* 39 (1982): 215–17.
Barraclough, Ray. "Philo's Politics: Roman Rule and Hellenistic Judaism." *ANRW* 21.2: 417–553. Part 2, *Principat*, 21.2. Edited by W. Haase and H. Temporini. Berlin: de Gruyter, 1984.
Barreto, Eric D. "Crafting Colonial Identities: Hybridity and the Roman Empire in Luke-Acts." Pages 107–21 in *An Introduction to Empire in the New Testament*. Edited by Adam Winn. RBS 84. Atlanta: SBL Press, 2016.
Barrett, C. K. *A Critical and Exegetical Commentary on the Acts of the Apostles*. 2 vols. ICC. Edinburgh: T&T Clark, 1994.
Barrett, C. K. "Faith and Eschatology in Acts 3." Pages 1–17 in *Glaube und Eschatologie: Festschrift für Werner Georg Kümmel zum 80. Geburtstag*. Edited by Erich Grässer and Otto Merk. Tübingen: Mohr, 1985.

Barrett, C. K. *Luke the Historian in Recent Study*. A. S. Peake Memorial Lecture 6. London: Epworth, 1961.
Barsby, John A. *Ovid*. Greece & Rome: New Surveys in the Classics 12. Oxford: Clarendon, 1978.
Bartchy, S. Scott. "Community of Goods in Acts: Idealization or Social Reality?" Pages 309-18 in *The Dead Sea Scrolls as Background to Postbiblical Judaism and Early Christianity: Papers from an International Conference at St Andrews in 2001*. Edited by James Davila. STDJ 46. Leiden: Brill, 2003.
Basser, H. W. "Josephus as Exegete." *JAOS* 107 (1987): 21-30.
Bauckham, Richard. "The Early Jerusalem Church, Qumran, and the Essenes." Pages 63-89 in *The Dead Sea Scrolls as Background to Postbiblical Judaism and Early Christianity: Papers from an International Conference at St. Andrews in 2001*. Edited by James R. Davila. STDJ 46. Leiden: Brill, 2003.
Bauer, Walter, Frederick W. Danker, William F. Arndt, and F. Wilbur Gingrich. *A Greek-English Lexicon of the New Testament and Other Early Christian Literature*. 3rd ed. Chicago: University of Chicago Press, 2000.
Baumert, Norbert. *KOINONEIN und METECHEIN—synonym? Eine umfassende semantische Untersuchung*. SBB 51. Stuttgart: Katholisches Bibelwerk, 2003.
Beetham, Christopher A. *Echoes of Scripture in the Letter of Paul to the Colossians*. BibInt 96. Leiden: Brill, 2008.
Begg, Christopher, ed. *Judean Antiquities Books 5-7*. Flavius Josephus Translation and Commentary 4. Leiden: Brill, 2005.
Behr, Charles A., ed. *P. Aelius Aristides: The Complete Works*. Leiden: Brill, 1981.
Bellen, Heinz. "SAEculum AUReum: das Säkularbewusstsein des Kaisers Hadrian im Spiegel der Münzen." Pages 135-49 in *Politik, Recht, Gesellschaft: Studien zur alten Geschichte*. Edited by Leonhard Schumacher. Historia Einzelschriften 115. Stuttgart: Steiner, 1997.
Benardete, Seth. "Hesiod's *Works and Days*: A First Reading." *Agon* 1 (1967): 150-74.
Benoit, Pierre. "Remarques sur les 'sommaires' de Actes 2.42 à 5." Pages 1-10 in *Aux sources de la tradition chrétienne: Mélanges offerts à M. Maurice Goguel à l'occasion de son soixante-dixième anniversaire*. Edited by P. H. Menoud and Oscar Cullmann. Neuchâtel: Delachaux & Niestlé, 1950.
Berthelot, Katell. "Philo's Perception of the Roman Empire." *JSJ* 42 (2011): 166-87.
Bilde, Per. *Flavius Josephus between Jerusalem and Rome: His Life, His Works and Their Importance*. JSPSup 2. Sheffield: JSOT Press, 1988.
Bilde, Per. "Philo as a Polemist and a Political Apologist: An Investigation of His Two Historical Treatises *against Flaccus* and *The Embassy to Gaius*." Pages 97-114 in *Alexandria: A Cultural and Religious Melting Pot*. Edited by Per Bilde and Minna Skafte Jensen. Aarhus Studies in Mediterranean Antiquity. Santa Barbara: Aarhus University Press, 2010.
Billings, Bradley. "'At the Age of 12': The Boy Jesus in the Temple (Luke 2:41-52), the Emperor Augustus, and the Social Setting of the Third Gospel." *JTS* 60 (2009): 70-89.
Blickman, Daniel R. "Lucretius, Epicurus, and Prehistory." *HSCP* 92 (1989): 157-91.
Bloch, René S. *Moses und der Mythos: Die Auseinandersetzung mit der griechischen Mythologie bei jüdisch-hellenistischen Autoren*. Supplements to the Journal for the Study of Judaism 145. Leiden: Brill, 2011.
Blumenthal, Christian. "Augustus' Erlass und Gottes Macht: Überlegungen zur Charakterisierung der Augustusfigur und ihrer erzählstrategischen Funktion in der lukanischen Erzählung." *NTS* 57 (2011): 1-30.

Blumhofer, C. M. "Luke's Alteration of Joel 3.1–5 in Acts 2.17–21." *NTS* 62 (2016): 499–516.
Blundell, Sue. *The Origins of Civilization in Greek and Roman Thought*. London: Croom Helm, 1986.
Bock, Darrell L. *Acts*. BECNT. Grand Rapids: Baker Academic, 2007.
Bock, Darrell L. *Proclamation from Prophecy and Pattern: Lucan Old Testament Christology*. JSNTSup 12. Sheffield: JSOT Press, 1987.
Bock, Darrell L. *A Theology of Luke and Acts*. Biblical Theology of the New Testament. Grand Rapids: Zondervan, 2012.
Bonz, Marianne Palmer. *The Past as Legacy: Luke-Acts and Ancient Epic*. Minneapolis: Fortress, 2000.
Borgen, Peder. *Philo of Alexandria: An Exegete for His Time*. NovTSup 86. Leiden: Brill, 1997.
Bousset, Wilhelm. "Sibyllen und Sibyllinische Bücher." *RE* 18:265–80.
Bovon, François. *Luke 1: A Commentary on the Gospel of Luke 1:1–9:50*. Translated by Christine M. Thomas. Hermeneia. Minneapolis: Fortress, 2002.
Boyce, Mary. "On the Antiquity of Zoroastrian Apocalyptic." *BSOAS* 47 (1984): 57–75.
Boyd, Barbara Weiden. *Ovid's Literary Loves: Influence and Innovation in the* Amores. Ann Arbor: University of Michigan Press, 1997.
Boyle, Anthony J., ed. *Octavia: Attributed to Seneca*. Oxford: Oxford University Press, 2008.
Boys-Stones, G. R. *Post-Hellenistic Philosophy: A Study of Its Development from the Stoics to Origen*. Oxford: Oxford University Press, 2001.
Braun, Herbert. *Qumran und das Neue Testament*. 2 vols. Tübingen: Mohr, 1966.
Braund, Susanna, ed. *Seneca: De clementia*. Oxford: Oxford University Press, 2009.
Breed, Brian W. *Pastoral Inscriptions: Reading and Writing Virgil's* Eclogues. Classical Literature and Society. London: Bloomsbury Academic, 2012.
Brent, Allen. *The Imperial Cult and the Origins of Church Order: Concepts and Images of Authority in Paganism and Early Christianity before the Age of Cyprian*. Supplements to Vigiliae Christianae 45. Leiden: Brill, 1999.
Brent, Allen. "Luke-Acts and the Imperial Cult in Asia Minor." *JTS* 48 (1997): 411–38.
Brent, Allen. *A Political History of Early Christianity*. London: T&T Clark, 2009.
Brisson, Luc. "Interprétation du mythe du *Politique*." Pages 349–63 in *Reading the Statesman: Proceedings of the III Symposium Platonicum*. Edited by Christopher J. Rowe. International Plato Studies 4. Sankt Augustin, DE: Academia, 1995.
Brown, Raymond E. *The Birth of the Messiah: A Commentary on the Infancy Narratives in the Gospels of Matthew and Luke*. ABRL. New York: Doubleday, 1993.
Brown, Schuyler. *Apostasy and Perseverance in the Theology of Luke*. AnBib 36. Rome: Pontifical Biblical Institute, 1969.
Bruce, F. F. *The Acts of the Apostles: The Greek Text with Introduction and Commentary*. 3rd ed. Grand Rapids: Eerdmans, 1990.
Bryan, Christopher. *Render to Caesar: Jesus, the Early Church, and the Roman Superpower*. Oxford: Oxford University Press, 2005.
Buitenwerf, Rieuwerd. *Book III of the Sibylline Oracles and Its Social Setting*. SVTP 17. Leiden: Brill, 2003.
Burrus, Virginia. "The Gospel of Luke and the Acts of the Apostles." Pages 133–55 in *A Postcolonial Commentary on the New Testament*. Edited by Fernando F. Segovia and Rasiah S. Sugirtharajah. Bible and Postcolonialism 13. London: T&T Clark, 2009.

Campbell, Gorden Lindsay. *Lucretius on Creation and Evolution: A Commentary on* De rerum natura, *Book Five, Lines 772–1104*. Oxford Classical Monographs. Oxford: Oxford University Press, 2003.
Campbell, J. Y. "ΚΟΙΝΩΝΙΑ and Its Cognates in the New Testament." *JBL* 51 (1932): 352–80.
Canevaro, Lilah Grace. *Hesiod's "Works and Days": How to Teach Self-Sufficiency*. Oxford: Oxford University Press, 2015.
Capper, Brian. "Community of Goods in the Early Jerusalem Church." *ANRW* 26.2: 1730–74. Part 2, *Principat*, 26.2. Edited by W. Haase and H. Temporini. Berlin: de Gruyter, 1995.
Capper, Brian. "The Palestinian Cultural Context of Earliest Christian Community of Goods." Pages 324–56 in *The Book of Acts in Its Palestinian Setting*. Edited by Richard Bauckham. BAFCS 4. Grand Rapids: Eerdmans, 1995.
Capper, Brian. "Reciprocity and the Ethic of Acts." Pages 500–18 in *Witness to the Gospel: The Theology of Acts*. I. Edited by Howard Marshall and David Peterson. Grand Rapids: Eerdmans, 1998.
Carroll, John T. *Luke: A Commentary*. NTL. Louisville: Westminster John Knox, 2012.
Carroll, John T. *Response to the End of History: Eschatology and Situation in Luke-Acts*. SBLDS 92. Decatur, GA: Scholars Press, 1988.
Cassidy, Richard J. *Jesus, Politics, and Society: A Study of Luke's Gospel*. Maryknoll, NY: Orbis Books, 1983.
Cassidy, Richard J. *Society and Politics in the Acts of the Apostles*. Maryknoll, NY: Orbis Books, 1983.
Castriota, David. *The Ara Pacis Augustae and the Imagery of Abundance in Later Greek and Early Roman Imperial Art*. Princeton: Princeton University Press, 1995.
Cereti, Carlo G. *The Zand i Wahman Yasn: A Zoroastrian Apocalypse*. Serie Orientale Roma 75. Rome: Istituto per il Medio ed Estremo Oriente, 1995.
Cerfaux, Lucien. "La première communauté chrétienne a Jérusalem (Act., II, 41–V, 42)." *ETL* 16 (1939): 5–31.
Champion, Edward. "The Life and Times of Calpurnius Siculus." *JRS* 68 (1978): 95–110.
Chance, Bradley J. *Jerusalem, the Temple, and the New Age in Luke-Acts*. Macon, GA: Mercer University Press, 1988.
Cheetham, F. P. "Acts ii. 47: ἔχοντες χάριν πρὸς ὅλον τὸν λαόν." *ExpTim* 74 (1963): 214–15.
Clay, Jenny Strauss. *Hesiod's Cosmos*. Cambridge: Cambridge University Press, 2002.
Clay, Jenny Strauss. "*Works and Days*: Tracing the Path to *Arete*." Pages 71–90 in *Brill's Companion to Hesiod*. Edited by Franco Montanari, Antonios Rengakos, and Christos Tsagalis. Leiden: Brill, 2009.
Clough, Arthur Hugh, ed. *The Lives of the Noble Grecians and Romans*. 2 vols. New York: Modern Library, 1992.
Co, Maria Anicia. "The Major Summaries in Acts: Acts 2,42–47; 4,32–35; 5,12–16: Linguistics and Literary Relationship." *ETL* 68 (1992): 49–85.
Coffey, Michael, and Roland Mayer, eds. *Phaedra*. Cambridge Greek and Latin Classics. Cambridge: Cambridge University Press, 1990.
Coleman, Kathleen M., ed. *Silvae IV*. Oxford: Clarendon, 1988.
Collins, John J. *Daniel: A Commentary on the Book of Daniel*. Hermeneia. Minneapolis: Fortress, 1993.
Collins, John J. "The Development of the Sibylline Tradition." *ANRW* 20.1: 421–59. Part 2, *Principat*, 20.1. Edited by W. Haase and H. Temporini. Berlin: de Gruyter, 1987.

Collins, John J. *Seers, Sibyls and Sages in Hellenistic-Roman Judaism*. Supplements to the Journal for the Study of Judaism 54. Leiden: Brill, 1997.
Collins, John J. "Sibylline Oracles." Pages 317–472 in vol. 1 of *The Old Testament Pseudepigrapha*. Edited by James H. Charlesworth. Peabody: Hendrickson, 2009.
Collins, John J. *The Sibylline Oracles of Egyptian Judaism*. SBLDS 13. Missoula, MT: Scholars Press, 1974.
Conington, John, and Henry Nettleship, eds. *The Works of Virgil*. 3 vols. Hildesheim: Olms, 1963.
Conzelmann, Hans. *Acts of the Apostles*. Translated by James Limburg, A. Thomas Krabel, and Donald H. Juel. Hermeneia. Philadelphia: Fortress, 1987.
Conzelmann, Hans. *The Theology of St. Luke*. Translated by Geoffrey Buswell. New York: Harper, 1961.
Costa, Charles D. N., ed. *17 Letters*. Classical Texts. Warminster: Aris & Phillips, 1988.
Courtney, Edward. *A Commentary on the Satires of Juvenal*. London: Athlone, 1980.
D'Espèrey, S. Franchet. "Les Métamorphoses d'Astrée." *Revue des Études Latines* 75 (1997): 175–91.
Davis, Peter J. *Ovid and Augustus: A Political Reading of Ovid's Erotic Poems*. London: Duckworth, 2006.
Develin, Robert. Introduction to *Epitome of the Philippic History of Pompeius*. Edited by John C. Yardley. Classical Resources 3. Atlanta: Scholars Press, 1994.
Downing, Gerald. "Common Strands in Pagan, Jewish and Christian Eschatologies in the First Century." *TZ* 51 (1995): 196–211.
Downing, Gerald. Review of *Weihnachtspolitik: Lukas 1–2 und das Goldene Zeitalter*, by Stefan Schreiber. *JSNT* 33 (2011): 68–9.
Droge, Arthur J. *Homer or Moses? Early Christian Interpretations of the History of Culture*. HUT 26. Tübingen: Mohr Siebeck, 1989.
Du Quesnay, Ian M. le M. "The *Amores*." Pages 1–48 in *Ovid*. Edited by J. W. Binns. Greek and Latin Studies. London: Routledge & Kegan Paul, 1973.
Du Quesnay, Ian M. le M. "Virgil's Fourth *Eclogue*." *Papers of the Liverpool Latin Seminar* 1 (1976): 25–99.
Dunn, James D. G. *Baptism in the Holy Spirit: A Re-Examination of the New Testament Teaching on the Gift of the Spirit in Relation to Pentecostalism Today*. SBT 15. Naperville, IL: Allenson, 1970.
Dupertuis, Rubén R. "The Summaries in Acts 2, 4 and 5 and Greek Utopian Literary Traditions." PhD diss., The Claremont Graduate University, 2005.
Dupont, Jacques. "The Community of Goods in the Early Church." Pages 85–102 in *The Salvation of the Gentiles: Essays on the Acts of the Apostles*. Translated by John R. Keating. Paulist Press Exploration Books. New York: Paulist, 1979.
El Murr, Dimitri. "Hesiod, Plato, and the Golden Age: Hesiodic Motifs in the Myth of the *Politicus* 1." Pages 276–97 in *Plato and Hesiod*. Edited by G. R. Boys-Stones and Johannes Haubold. Oxford: Oxford University Press, 2010.
Ellis, E. Earle. *Eschatology in Luke*. FBBS 30. Philadelphia: Fortress, 1972.
Epp, Eldon J. *Tendency of Codex Bezae Cantabrigiensis in Acts*. SNTSMS 3. Cambridge: Cambridge University Press, 1966.
Esler, Philip Francis. *Community and Gospel in Luke-Acts: The Social and Political Motivations of Lucan Theology*. SNTSMS 57. Cambridge: Cambridge University Press, 1987.
Evans, Craig A. "The Pseudepigrapha and the Problem of Background 'Parallels' in the Study of the Acts of the Apostles." Pages 139–50 in *The Pseudepigrapha and Christian*

Origins. Edited by Gerbern S. Oegema and James H. Charlesworth. Jewish and Christian Texts in Contexts and Related Studies 4. New York: T&T Clark, 2008.
Evans, Rhiannon. *Utopia Antiqua: Readings of the Golden Age and Decline at Rome*. London: Routledge, 2008.
Fantazzi, Charles. "Golden Age in Arcadia." *Latomus* 33 (1974): 280–305.
Fantham, Elain. "Ovid's *Fasti*: Politics, History, and Religion." Pages 197–233 in *Brill's Companion to Ovid*. Edited by Barbara Weiden Boyd. Leiden: Brill, 2002.
Fantuzzi, Marco, and Richard L. Hunter. *Tradition and Innovation in Hellenistic Poetry*. Cambridge: Cambridge University Press, 2004.
Farrington, Benjamin. "*Vita Prior* in Lucretius." *Herm* 81 (1953): 59–62.
Feeney, Denis C. *Caesar's Calendar: Ancient Time and the Beginnings of History*. Berkeley: University of California Press, 2007.
Feldman, Louis H. "Hellenizations in Josephus' Portrayal of Man's Decline." Pages 336–53 in *Religions in Antiquity: Essays in Memory of Erwin Ramsdell Goodenough*. Edited by Jacob Neusner. SHR 14. Leiden: Brill, 1968.
Feldman, Louis H. *Josephus's Interpretation of the Bible*. HCS 27. Berkeley: University of California Press, 1998.
Ferguson, Everett. "'When You Come Together': *Epi To Auto* in Early Christian Literature." *ResQ* 16 (1973): 202–8.
Ferguson, John. *Utopias of the Classical World*. Aspects of Greek and Roman Life. Ithaca, NY: Cornell University Press, 1975.
Ferri, Rolando, ed. *Octavia: A Play Attributed to Seneca*. Cambridge Classical Texts and Commentaries 41. Cambridge: Cambridge University Press, 2003.
Finger, Reta. *Of Widows and Meals: Communal Meals in the Book of Acts*. Grand Rapids: Eerdmans, 2007.
Finkelpearl, Ellen D. *Metamorphosis of Language in Apuleius: A Study of Allusion in the Novel*. Ann Arbor: University of Michigan Press, 1998.
Fitzmyer, Joseph A. *The Acts of the Apostles*. AB 31. New York: Doubleday, 1998.
Fitzmyer, Joseph A. *The Gospel according to Luke I-IX: A New Translation with Introduction and Commentary*. AB 28. New Haven: Yale University Press, 2009.
Fitzmyer, Joseph A. "Jewish Christianity in Acts in Light of the Qumran Scrolls." Pages 233–57 in *Studies in Luke-Acts*. Edited by Leander E. Keck and J. Louis Martyn. Nashville: Abingdon, 1966.
Flacelière, Robert, Emile Chambry, and Marcel Juneaux, eds. *Plutarque: Vies*. 16 vols. Collection des universités de France. Paris: Belles Lettres, 1964–1983.
Fontanella, Francesca. "The Encomium on Rome as a Response to Polybius' Doubts about the Roman Empire." Pages 203–16 in *Aelius Aristides between Greece, Rome, and the Gods*. Edited by William V. Harris and Brooke Holmes. Columbia Studies in the Classical Tradition 33. Leiden: Brill, 2008.
Fowler, Don P. "Lucretius and Politics." Pages 120–50 in *Philosopha Togata: Essays on Philosophy and Roman Society*. Edited by Miriam T. Griffin and Jonathan Barnes. Oxford: Clarendon; New York: Oxford University Press, 1989.
Fowler, Don P. "On the Shoulders of Giants: Intertextuality and Classical Studies." *Materiali e discussioni per l'analisi dei testi classici* 39 (1997): 13–34.
Francis, Fred O. "Eschatology and History in Luke-Acts." *JAAR* 37 (1969): 49–63.
Franxman, Thomas W. *Genesis and the "Jewish Antiquities" of Flavius Josephus*. BibOr 35. Rome: Biblical Institute Press, 1979.
Frey, Jörg. "The Impact of the Dead Sea Scrolls on New Testament Interpretation: Proposals, Problems, and Further Perspectives." Pages 406–71 in *The Scrolls and*

Christian Origins. Edited by James H. Charlesworth. Vol. 3 of *The Bible and the Dead Sea Scrolls*. Edited by James H. Charlesworth. Waco: Baylor University Press, 2006.
Furley, David J. "Lucretius the Epicurean: On the History of Man." Pages 1–27 in *Lucrèce: Huit exposés*. Edited by David J. Furley and Olof Gigon. Entretiens sur l'Antiquité classique 24. Geneva: Fondation Hardt, 1978.
Gain, D. B., ed. *The Aratus ascribed to Germanicus Caesar*. Classical Studies 8. London: Athlone, 1976.
Gale, Monica, ed. *De rerum natura V*. Classical Texts. Oxford: Oxbow, 2009.
Gale, Monica, ed. *Myth and Poetry in Lucretius*. Cambridge Classical Studies. Cambridge: Cambridge University Press, 1994.
Gale, Monica, ed. *Virgil on the Nature of Things: The Georgics, Lucretius, and the Didactic Tradition*. Cambridge: Cambridge University Press, 2000.
Galinsky, Karl. *Augustan Culture: An Interpretive Introduction*. Princeton: Princeton University Press, 1996.
Galinsky, Karl. "Some Aspects of Ovid's Golden Age." *Grazer Beiträge* 10 (1981): 193–205.
Galinsky, Karl. "In the Shadow (or Not) of the Imperial Cult: A Cooperative Agenda." Pages 215–25 in *Rome and Religion: A Cross-Disciplinary Dialogue on the Imperial Cult*. Edited by Jeffrey Brodd and Jonathan L. Reed. WGRWSup 5. Atlanta: SBL Press, 2011.
Gamba, Giuseppe. "Significato letterale e portata dottrinale dell'inciso participiale di Atti 2,47b: ἔχοντες χάριν πρὸς ὅλον τὸν λαόν." *Salesianum* 43 (1981): 45–70.
Gambetti, Sandra. *The Alexandrian Riots of 38 C.E. and the Persecution of the Jews: A Historical Reconstruction*. Supplements to the Journal for the Study of Judaism 135. Leiden: Brill, 2009.
Garnsey, Peter. *Thinking about Property: From Antiquity to the Age of Revolution*. Ideas in Context 90. Cambridge: Cambridge University Press, 2007.
Garthwaite, John. "Martial, Book 6, on Domitian's Moral Censorship." *Prudentia* 22 (1990): 13–22.
Gatz, Bodo. *Weltalter, goldene Zeit und sinnverwandte Vorstellungen*. Hildesheim: Olms, 1967.
Gauger, Jörg-Dieter. *Sibyllinische Weissagungen: griechisch-deutsch*. Sammlung Tusculum. Düsseldorf: Artemis & Winkler, 1998.
Gaventa, Beverly Roberts. *The Acts of the Apostles*. ANTC. Nashville: Abingdon, 2003.
Gaventa, Beverly Roberts. "The Eschatology of Luke-Acts Revisited." *Enc* 43 (1982): 27–42.
Gee, Emma. *Aratus and the Astronomical Tradition*. Classical Culture and Society. New York: Oxford University Press, 2013.
Geffcken, Johannes. "Die Hirten auf dem Feld." *Hermes* 49 (1914): 321–51.
Geffcken, Johannes. *Komposition und Entstehungszeit der Oracula Sibyllina*. Leipzig: Hinrichs, 1902.
Gilbert, Gary. "The List of Nations in Acts 2: Roman Propaganda and the Lukan Response." *JBL* 121 (2002): 497–529.
Gilbert, Gary. "Luke-Acts and Negotiations of Authority and Identity in the Roman World." Pages 83–104 in *The Multivalence of Biblical Texts and Theological Meanings*. Edited by Christine Helmer. SymS 37. Atlanta: SBL Press, 2006.
Gilbert, Gary. "Roman Propaganda and Christian Identity in the Worldview of Luke-Acts." Pages 233–56 in *Contextualizing Acts: Lukan Narrative and Greco-Roman Discourse*. Edited by Todd Penner and Caroline Vander Stichele. SymS 20. Atlanta: SBL Press, 2003.
González-Reimann, Luis. *The Mahabharata and the Yugas: India's Great Epic Poem and the Hindu System of World Ages*. Asian Thought and Culture 51. New York: Lang, 2002.

Goodenough, E. R. *The Politics of Philo Judaeus: Practice and Theory*. New Haven: Yale University Press; London: Oxford University Press, 1938.
Goodman, Martin. "Jewish Writings under Gentile Pseudonyms." Pages 617–94 in vol. 3 of *The History of the Jewish People in the Age of Jesus Christ*. Edited by Emil Schürer. Revised and edited by Géza Vermès, Fergus Millar, and Martin Goodman. Edinburgh: T&T Clark, 1986.
Green, Joel B. *The Gospel of Luke*. NICNT. Grand Rapids: Eerdmans, 1997.
Green, Steven J. *Fasti 1: A Commentary*. Mnemosyne 251. Leiden: Brill, 2004.
Griffin, Miriam T. "The Elder Seneca and Spain." *JRS* 62 (1972): 1–19.
Griffin, Miriam T. *Seneca: A Philosopher in Politics*. Oxford: Clarendon, 1976.
Hadas-Lebel, Mireille. "L'évolution de l'image de Rome auprès des Juifs en deux siècles de relations judéo-romaines—164 à +70." *ANRW* 20.2: 715–856. Part 2, *Principat*, 20.2. Edited by W. Haase and H. Temporini. Berlin: de Gruyter, 1987.
Haenchen, Ernst. *The Acts of the Apostles*. Translated by Bernard Noble and Gerald Shinn. Philadelphia: Westminster, 1971.
Haley, Evan. "Hadrian as Romulus or the Self-Representation of a Roman Emperor." *Latomus* 64 (2005): 969–80.
Harris, Sarah. *The Davidic Shepherd King in the Lukan Narrative*. LNTS 558. New York: T&T Clark, 2016.
Hays, Christopher M. *Luke's Wealth Ethics: A Study in Their Coherence and Character*. WUNT 2/275. Tübingen: Mohr Siebeck, 2010.
Hays, Richard B. *Echoes of Scripture in the Letters of Paul*. New Haven: Yale University Press, 1989.
Heath, Malcolm. "Hesiod's Didactic Poetry." *ClQ* 35 (1985): 245–63.
Heen, Erik M. "The Role of Symbolic Inversion in Utopian Discourse: Apocalyptic Reversal in Paul and in the Festival of the Saturnalia/Kronia." Pages 123–44 in *Hidden Transcripts and the Arts of Resistance: Applying the Work of James C. Scott to Jesus and Paul*. Edited by Richard A. Horsley. Semeia 48. Atlanta: Society of Biblical Literature, 2004.
Heilig, Christoph. *Hidden Criticism? The Methodology and Plausibility of the Search for a Counter-Imperial Subtext in Paul*. WUNT 2/392. Tübingen: Mohr Siebeck, 2015.
Hengel, Martin. *Property and Riches in the Early Church: Aspects of a Social History of Early Christianity*. Translated by J. Bowden. Philadelphia: Fortress, 1974.
Hesiod. Translated by Glenn W. Most. 2 vols. LCL. Cambridge: Harvard University Press, 2006.
Höffken, Peter. "Überlegungen zum Leserkreis der 'Antiquitates' des Josephus." *JSJ* 38 (2007): 328–41.
Holladay, Carl R. *Acts: A Commentary*. NTL. Louisville: Westminster John Knox, 2016.
Holtz, Gudrun. *Damit Gott sei alles in allem: Studien zum paulinischen und frühjüdischen Universalismus*. BZNW 149. Berlin: de Gruyter, 2007.
Horn, Friedrich W. "Die Gütergemeinschaft der Urgemeinde." *EvT* 58 (1998): 370–83.
Horsley, Richard A. *The Liberation of Christmas: The Infancy Narratives in Social Context*. New York: Crossroad, 1989.
Hubbard, Thomas K. *The Pipes of Pan: Intertextuality and Literary Filiation in the Pastoral Tradition from Theocritus to Milton*. Ann Arbor: University of Michigan Press, 1998.
Hume, Douglas A. *The Early Christian Community: A Narrative Analysis of Acts 2:41–47 and 4:32–35*. WUNT 2/298. Tübingen: Mohr Siebeck, 2011.
Hutchison, G. O. "The Date of *De Rerum Natura*." *ClQ* 51 (2001): 150–62.
Irmscher, Johannes. "Vergil in der griechischen Antike." *Klio* 67 (1985): 281–5.
Jenkyns, Richard. "*Labor Improbus*." *ClQ* 43 (1993): 243–8.

Jervell, Jacob. *The Theology of the Acts of the Apostles*. New Testament Theology. Cambridge: Cambridge University Press, 1996.
Johnson, Luke Timothy. *The Acts of the Apostles*. SP 5. Collegeville, MN: Liturgical Press, 1992.
Johnson, Luke Timothy. *The Literary Function of Possessions in Luke-Acts*. SBLDS 39. Missoula, MT: Scholars Press, 1977.
Johnson, Luke Timothy. "Making Connections: The Material Expression of Friendship in the New Testament." *Int* 58 (2004): 158–71.
Johnston, Patricia A. *Vergil's Agricultural Golden Age: A Study of the Georgics*. Mnemosyne 60. Leiden: Brill, 1980.
Johnston, Patricia A. "Vergil's Conception of Saturn." *California Studies in Classical Antiquity* 10 (1977): 57–70.
Jones, C. P. "Towards a Chronology of Plutarch's Works." *JRS* 56 (1966): 61–74.
Kahl, Brigitte. "Acts of the Apostles: Pro(to)-Imperial Script and Hidden Transcript." Pages 137–56 in *In the Shadow of Empire: Reclaiming the Bible as a History of Faithful Resistance*. Edited by Richard A. Horsley. Louisville: Westminster John Knox, 2008.
Kahn, Charles H. "The Myth of the *Statesman*." Pages 148–66 in *Plato's Myths*. Edited by Catalin Partenie. Cambridge: Cambridge University Press, 2009.
Keener, Craig S. *Acts: An Exegetical Commentary. Introduction and 1:1–2:47*. Grand Rapids: Baker Academic, 2012.
Keener, Craig S. *Acts: An Exegetical Commentary. 3:1–14:28*. Grand Rapids: Baker Academic, 2013.
Kim, Seyoon. *Christ and Caesar: The Gospel and the Roman Empire in the Writings of Paul and Luke*. Grand Rapids: Eerdmans, 2008.
Kittel, Gerhard, and Gerhard Friedrich, eds. *Theological Dictionary of the New Testament*. Translated by Geoffrey W. Bromiley. 10 vols. Grand Rapids: Eerdmans, 1964–1976.
Klauck, Hans-Josef. "Gütergemeinschaft in der klassischen antike, in Qumran und im Neuen Testament." *RevQ* 11 (1982): 47–79.
Klauck, Hans-Josef. *Judas, ein Jünger des Herrn*. QD 111. Freiburg: Herder, 1987.
Klein, Richard. "Zur Datierung der Romrede des Aelius Aristides." *Historia* 30 (1981): 337–50.
Kloppenborg, John S. "The Power and Surveillance of the Divine Judge in the Early Synoptic Tradition." Pages 147–84 in *Christ and the Emperor: The Gospel Evidence*. Edited by Gilbert van Belle and Jozef Verheyden. BTS 20. Leuven: Peeters, 2014.
Koch, Klaus. *Daniel: Kapital 1,1–4,34*. BKAT 22.1. Neukirchen-Vluyn: Neukirchener Verlag, 2005.
Koenen, Ludwig. "Greece, the Near East, and Egypt: Cyclic Destruction in Hesiod and the Catalogue of Women." *TAPA* 124 (1994): 1–34.
Korzeniewski, Dietmar. "Die 'Panegyrische Tendenz' in den Carmina Einsidlensia." *Hermes* 94 (1966): 344–60.
Kragelund, Patrick. *Prophecy, Populism, and Propaganda in the* Octavia. Opuscula Graecolatina 25. Copenhagen: Museum Tusculanum, 1982.
Kraggerud, Egil. "Which Julius Caesar? On *Aen.* 1, 286–296." *SO* 67 (1992): 103–12.
Kubusch, Klaus. *Aurea saecula, Mythos und Geschichte: Untersuchung eines Motivs in der antiken Literatur bis Ovid*. Studien zur klassischen Philologie 28. Frankfurt am Main: Lang, 1986.
Kuecker, Aaron. *The Spirit and the "Other": Social Identity, Ethnicity and Intergroup Reconciliation in Luke-Acts*. LNTS 444. London: T&T Clark, 2011.
Kurfess, Alfons. "Ad oracula Sibyllina." *SO* 28 (1950): 95–104.

Kurfess, Alfons. "Christian Sibyllines." Pages 703–45 in vol. 1 of *New Testament Apocrypha*. Edited by Edgar Hennecke and Wilhelm Schneemelcher. Translated by Robert McLachlan Wilson. Philadelphia: Westminster, 1965.

Kurfess, Alfons. "Homer und Hesiod im 1. Buch der Oracula Sibyllina." *Philologus* 100 (1956): 147–53.

Kurfess, Alfons. "Oracula Sibyllina I/II." *ZNW* 40 (1941): 151–65.

Kurz, William. "Acts 3:19–26 as a Test of the Role of Eschatology in Lukan Christology." SBLSP 16 (1977): 309–23.

Laks, André. "Private Matters in Plato's Laws." Pages 165–88 in *Platon: Gesetze/Nomoi*. Edited by Christoph Horn. Klassiker auslegen 55. Berlin: Akademie, 2013.

Le Boeuffle, André., ed. *Les Phénomènes d'Aratos*. Collection des universités de France. Paris: Belles Lettres, 1975.

Leach, Eleanor Winsor. "Corydon Revisited: An Interpretation of the Political Eclogues of Calpurnius Siculus." *Ramus* 2 (1973): 53–97.

Leddy, Michael. "Limits of Allusion." *British Journal of Aesthetics* 32 (1992): 110–22.

Lee, DooHee. *Luke-Acts and "Tragic History": Communicating Gospel with the World*. WUNT 2/346. Tübingen: Mohr Siebeck, 2013.

Levison, John R. *Portraits of Adam in Early Judaism: From Sirach to 2 Baruch*. JSPSup 1. Sheffield: JSOT Press, 1988.

Liddell, Henry George, Robert Scott, Henry Stuart Jones, and Roderick McKenzie. 9th ed. with revised supplement. Oxford: Clarendon, 1996.

Lightfoot, Jane L. *The Sibylline Oracles: With Introduction, Translation, and Commentary on the First and Second Books*. Oxford: Oxford University Press, 2007.

Little, Douglas. "The Non-Augustanism of Ovid's 'Metamorphoses.'" *Mnemosyne* 25 (1972): 389–401.

Lovejoy, Arthur O., and George Boas. *Primitivism and Related Ideas in Antiquity*. Baltimore: Johns Hopkins University Press, 1935.

MacDonald, Dennis R. *Does the New Testament Imitate Homer? Four Cases from the Acts of the Apostles*. New Haven: Yale University Press, 2003.

MacDonald, Dennis R. *The Gospels and Homer: Imitations of Greek Epic in Mark and Luke-Acts*. The New Testament and Greek Literature 1. Lanham, MD: Rowman & Littlefield, 2015.

MacDonald, Dennis R. *The Homeric Epics and the Gospel of Mark*. New Haven: Yale University Press, 2000.

MacDonald, Dennis R. *Luke and Vergil: Imitations of Classical Greek Literature*. The New Testament and Greek Literature 2. Lanham: Rowman & Littlefield, 2015.

Maddox, Robert L. *The Purpose of Luke-Acts*. FRLANT 126. Göttingen: Vandenhoeck & Ruprecht, 1982.

Maier, Harry O. "Colossians, Ephesians, and Empire." Pages 185–202 in *An Introduction to Empire in the New Testament*. Edited by Adam Winn. RBS 84. Atlanta: SBL Press, 2016.

Maltby, Robert. *Tibullus: Elegies: Text, Introduction and Commentary*. ARCA Classical and Medieval Texts, Papers, and Monographs 41. Cambridge: Cairns, 2002.

Marguerat, Daniel. *Les Actes des apôtres (1–12)*. CNT 5A. Geneva: Labor et Fides, 2007.

Marguerat, Daniel. *The First Christian Historian: Writing the "Acts of the Apostles."* Translated by Ken McKinney, Gregory J. Laughery, and Richard Bauckham. SNTSMS 121. Cambridge: Cambridge University Press, 2002.

Marshall, I. Howard. *Luke: Historian and Theologian*. 3rd ed. Grand Rapids: Academie, 1989.

Martin, Beatrice. "Calpurnius Siculus' 'New' *Aurea Aetas*." *Acta Classica* 39 (1996): 17–38.

Martin, R. H. "The Golden Age and the ΚΥΚΛΟΣ ΓΕΝΕΣΕΩΝ (Cyclical Theory) in Greek and Latin Literature." *GR* 12 (1943): 62–71.
Martinez, Florentino García, and A. S. van der Woude. "A 'Groningen' Hypothesis of Qumran Origins and Early History." *RevQ* 14 (1990): 31–52.
Mason, Steve. Introduction to *Judean Antiquities 1–4*. Edited by Louis H. Feldman. Flavius Josephus Translation and Commentary 3. Leiden: Brill, 2004.
Mason, Steve. *Josephus, Judea, and Christian Origins: Methods and Categories*. Peabody: Hendrickson, 2009.
Mason, Steve. "'Should Any Wish to Enquire Further' (*Ant.* 1.25): The Aim and Audience of Josephus's *Judean Antiquities/Life*." Pages 64–103 in *Understanding Josephus: Seven Perspectives*. Edited by Steve Mason. JSPSup 32. Sheffield: Sheffield Academic, 1998.
Mattill Jr., Andrew Jacob. "Naherwartung, Fernerwartung, and the Purpose of Luke-Acts: Weymouth Reconsidered." *CBQ* 34 (1972): 276–93.
Maurach, Gregor. *Germanicus und sein Arat. Eine vergleichende Auslegung von V. 1–327 der Phaenomena*. Wissenschaftliche Kommentare zu griechischen und lateinischen Schriftstellern. Heidelberg: Winter, 1978.
Mayer, Roland. "Latin Pastoral after Virgil." Pages 451–66 in *Brill's Companion to Greek and Latin Pastoral*. Edited by Marco Fantuzzi and Theodore D. Papanghelis. Leiden: Brill, 2006.
Mealand, David L. "Community of Goods and Utopian Allusions in Acts II–IV." *JTS* 28 (1977): 96–9.
Meek, Russell L. "Intertextuality, Inner-Biblical Exegesis, and Inner-Biblical Allusion: The Ethics of a Methodology." *Bib* 95 (2014): 280–91.
Menzies, Robert P. *Empowered for Witness: The Spirit in Luke-Acts*. Journal of Pentecostal Theology Supplement Series 6. Sheffield: Sheffield Academic, 1994.
Metzger, Bruce M. *A Textual Commentary on the Greek New Testament*. 2nd ed. Stuttgart: Deutsche Bibelgesellschaft; United Bible Societies, 1998.
Miller, Amanda C. *Rumors of Resistance: Status Reversals and Hidden Transcripts in the Gospel of Luke*. Minneapolis: Fortress, 2014.
Miller, John F. "The *Fasti*: Style, Structure, and Time." Pages 167–96 in *Brill's Companion to Ovid*. Edited by Barbara Weiden Boyd. Leiden: Brill, 2002.
Mitchell, Alan C. "'Greet the Friends by Name': New Testament Evidence for the Greco-Roman *Topos* on Friendship." Pages 225–62 in *Greco-Roman Perspectives on Friendship*. Edited by John T. Fitzgerald. RBS 34. Atlanta: Scholars Press, 1997.
Mitchell, Alan C. "The Social Function of Friendship in Acts 2:44–47 and 4:32–37." *JBL* 111 (1992): 255–72.
Moles, John. "Accommodation, Opposition or Other? *Luke-Acts*' Stance towards Rome." Pages 79–104 in *Roman Rule in Greek and Latin Writing: Double Vision*. Edited by Jesper Majborn Madsen and Roger Rees. Impact of Empire. Leiden: Brill, 2014.
Momigliano, Arnaldo. "Literary Chronology of the Neronian Age." *ClQ* 38 (1944): 96–100.
Momigliano, Arnaldo. "From the Pagan to the Christian Sibyl: Prophecy as History of Religion." Pages 725–44 in *Nono contributo alla storia degli studi classici e del mondo antico*. Edited by Riccardo Di Donato. Storia e letteratura 180. Rome: Edizioni di storia e letteratura, 1992.
Most, Glenn W. "Hesiod's Myth of the Five (or Three or Four) Races." *Proceedings of the Cambridge Philological Society* 43 (1997): 104–27.
Mowery, Robert L. "Son of God in Roman Imperial Titles and Matthew." *Bib* 83 (2002): 100–10.
Muñoz-Larrondo, Rubén. *A Post-Colonial Reading of the Acts of the Apostles*. StBibLit 147. New York: Lang, 2012.

Muraoka, Takamitsu. *A Greek-English Lexicon of the Septuagint*. Leuven: Peeters, 2009.
Murgatroyd, Paul. *Tibullus I: A Commentary on the First Book of the Elegies of Albius Tibullus*. Pietermaritzburg: University of Natal Press, 1980.
Mussner, Franz. "'In den letzten Tag' (Apg 2,17a)." *BZ* 5 (1961): 263–5.
Mynors, Roger A. B., ed. *Georgics*. Oxford: Clarendon, 1990.
Nadeau, Yvan. *A Commentary on the Sixth Satire of Juvenal*. Collection Latomus 329. Brussels: Latomus, 2011.
Nauta, Ruurd R. *Poetry for Patrons: Literary Communication in the Age of Domitian*. Mnemosyne Supplements 206. Leiden: Brill, 2002.
Nauta, Ruurd R. "Seneca's *Apocolocyntosis* as Saturnalian Literature." *Mnemosyne* 40 (1987): 69–96.
Neagoe, Alexandru. *The Trial of the Gospel: An Apologetic Reading of Luke's Trial Narratives*. SNTSMS 116. Cambridge: Cambridge University Press, 2002.
Newlands, Carole E. *Statius' Silvae and the Poetics of Empire*. Cambridge: Cambridge University Press, 2002.
Newman, J. K. "*Saturno Rege*: Themes of the Golden Age in Tibullus and Other Augustan Poets." Pages 225–46 in *Candide iudex: Beiträge zur augusteischen Dichtung*. Edited by Anne-Ilse Radke. Stuttgart: Steiner, 1998.
Nikiprowetzky, Valentin. *La troisième Sibylle*. Etudes juives 9. Paris: Mouton, 1970.
Noble, Joshua. "The Meaning of ἔχοντες χάριν πρός in Acts 2:47: Resolving Some Recent Confusion." *NTS* 64 (2018): 573–9.
Nodet, Étienne. "Flavius Josèphe: Création et histoire." *RB* 100 (1993): 5–40.
Nolland, John. "Salvation-History and Eschatology." Pages 64–81 in *Witness to the Gospel: The Theology of Acts*. Edited by I. Howard Marshall and David Peterson. Grand Rapids: Eerdmans, 1998.
Norden, Eduard. *Beiträge zur Geschichte der griechischen Philosophie*. Leipzig: Teubner, 1893.
Ogereau, Julien M. *Paul's Koinonia with the Philippians: A Socio-Historical Investigation of a Pauline Economic Partnership*. WUNT 2/377. Tübingen: Mohr Siebeck, 2014.
Ogereau, Julien M. "A Survey of Κοινωνία and Its Cognates in Documentary Sources." *NovT* 57 (2015): 275–94.
Oliver, James. *The Ruling Power: A Study of the Roman Empire in the Second Century after Christ through the Roman Oration of Aelius Aristides*. TAPS 43. Philadelphia: American Philosophical Society, 1953.
Panikulam, Georg. *Koinōnia in the New Testament: A Dynamic Expression of Christian Life*. AnBib 85. Rome: Biblical Institute Press, 1979.
Park, Hyung Dae. *Finding Herem? A Study of Luke-Acts in the Light of Herem*. LNTS 357. London: T&T Clark, 2007.
Parke, Herbert W. *Sibyls and Sibylline Prophecy in Classical Antiquity*. Croom Helm Classical Studies. London: Routledge, 1988.
Parker, James. *The Concept of Apokatastasis in Acts: A Study in Primitive Christian Theology*. Austin: Schola, 1978.
Pelletier, André, ed. *Legatio ad Caium*. Paris: Cerf, 1972.
Perkell, Christine. *The Poet's Truth: A Study of the Poet in Vergil's Georgics*. Berkeley: University of California Press, 1989.
Pernot, Laurent. *Éloges grecs de Rome: Discours*. Roue à livres 32. Paris: Belles Lettres, 1997.
Perutelli, Alessandro. "Bucolics." Pages 27–62 in *A Companion to the Study of Virgil*. Edited by Nicholas Horsfall. Mnemosyne 151. Leiden: Brill, 1995.

Pervo, Richard I. *Acts: A Commentary*. Hermeneia. Minneapolis: Fortress, 2009.
Pervo, Richard I. *Dating Acts: Between the Evangelists and the Apologists*. Santa Rosa, CA: Polebridge, 2006.
Pesch, Rudolf. *Die Apostelgeschichte*. EKKNT 5. Zurich: Benzinger, 1986.
Petersen, Anders Klostergaard. "Imperial Politics in Paul: Scholarly Phantom or Actual Textual Phenomenon?" Pages 101–27 in *People under Power: Early Jewish and Christian Responses to the Roman Empire*. Edited by Michael Labahn and Outi Lehtipuu. Early Christianity in the Roman World 1. Amsterdam: Amsterdam University Press, 2015.
Peterson, David. *The Acts of the Apostles*. Pillar New Testament Commentary. Grand Rapids: Eerdmans; Nottingham: Apollos, 2009.
Pickett, Raymond. "Luke and Empire: An Introduction." Pages 1–22 in *Luke-Acts and Empire: Essays in Honor of Robert L. Brawley*. Edited by David Rhoads, David Esterline, and Jae-won Lee. Princeton Theological Monograph Series 151. Eugene, OR: Pickwick, 2011.
Pinter, Dean. "The Gospel of Luke and the Roman Empire." Pages 101–15 in *Jesus Is Lord, Caesar Is Not: Evaluating Empire in New Testament Studies*. Edited by Scot McKnight and Joseph Modica. Downers Grove, IL: InterVarsity Press, 2013.
Pixner, Bargil. "An Essene Quarter on Mount Zion?" Pages 245–84 in vol. 1 of *Studia Hierosolymitana: In onore del P. Bellarmino Bagatti*. Edited by Ignacio Mancini, Michele Piccirillo, and Emmanuele Testa. Collectio Maior 22. Jerusalem: Franciscan, 1976.
Plaza, Maria. *The Function of Humour in Roman Verse Satire: Laughing and Lying*. Oxford: Oxford University Press, 2006.
Plümacher, Eckhard. *Lukas als hellenistischer Schriftsteller: Studien zur Apostelgeschichte*. SUNT 9. Göttingen: Vandenhoeck & Ruprecht, 1972.
Plutarch. *Lives*. Translated by Bernadotte Perrin. 11 vols. LCL. Cambridge: Harvard University Press, 1990–2001.
Pollini, John. *From Republic to Empire: Rhetoric, Religion, and Power in the Visual Culture of Ancient Rome*. Oklahoma Series in Classical Culture 48. Norman: University of Oklahoma Press, 2012.
Porter, Stanley E. "Scripture Justifies Mission: The Use of the Old Testament in Luke-Acts." Pages 104–22 in *Hearing the Old Testament in the New Testament*. Edited by Stanley E. Porter. McMaster New Testament Studies. Grand Rapids: Eerdmans, 2006.
Possanza, Mark D. *Translating the Heavens: Aratus, Germanicus, and the Poetics of Latin Translation*. Lang Classical Studies 14. New York: Lang, 2004.
Potter, David. "Sibyls in the Greek and Roman World." *JRA* 3 (1990): 471–83.
Putnam, Michael C. J. *Tibullus: A Commentary*. American Philological Association Series of Classical Texts. Norman: University of Oklahoma Press, 1973.
Regev, Eyal. *Sectarianism in Qumran: A Cross-Cultural Perspective*. Religion and Society 45. Berlin: de Gruyter, 2007.
Reimer, Ivoni Richter. *Women in the Acts of the Apostles: A Feminist Liberation Perspective*. Translated by Linda M. Maloney. Minneapolis: Fortress, 1995.
Reitzenstein, Richard. "Altgriechische Theologie und ihre Quellen." Pages 523–44 in *Hesiod*. Edited by Ernst Heitsch. Wege der Forschung 44. Darmstadt: Wissenschaftliche Buchgesellschaft, 1966.
Riesner, Rainer. "Das Jerusalemer Essenerviertel und die Urgemeinde: Josephus, Bellum Judaicum V 145; 11QMiqdasch 46,13–16; Apostelgeschichte 1–6 und die Archäologie."

ANRW 26.2: 1775–922. Part 2, *Principat*, 26.2. Edited by W. Haase and H. Temporini. Berlin: de Gruyter, 1995.

Rimaud, Didier. "La première prière liturgique dans le livre des Actes." *La Maison-Dieu* 51 (1957): 99–115.

Robertson, Jesse E. *The Death of Judas: The Characterization of Judas Iscariot in Three Early Christian Accounts of His Death.* New Testament Monographs 33. Sheffield: Sheffield Phoenix, 2012.

Rochette, Bruno. *Le latin dans le monde grec: Recherches sur la diffusion de la langue et des lettres latines dans les provinces hellénophones de l'Empire romain.* Collection Latomus 233. Brussels: Latomus, 1997.

Rosen, Ralph M. "Homer and Hesiod." Pages 463–88 in *A New Companion to Homer.* Edited by Barry Powell and Ian Morris. Mnemosyne 163. Leiden: Brill, 1997.

Rowe, C. Kavin. "Luke-Acts and the Imperial Cult: A Way through the Conundrum?" *JSNT* 27 (2005): 279–300.

Rowe, C. Kavin. *World Upside Down: Reading Acts in the Graeco-Roman Age.* New York: Oxford University Press, 2009.

Rowe, Christopher J. "On Grey-Haired Babies: Plato, Hesiod, and Visions of the Past (and Future)." Pages 298–316 in *Plato and Hesiod.* Edited by G. R. Boys-Stones and Johannes Haubold. Oxford: Oxford University Press, 2010.

Runia, David T. "Philo of Alexandria, 'Legatio ad Gaium' 1–7." Pages 349–70 in *Neotestamentica et Philonica: Studies in Honor of Peder Borgen.* Edited by David E. Aune, Torrey Seland, and Jarl Henning Ulrichsen. NovTSup 106. Boston: Brill, 2003.

Ryberg, Inez Scott. "Vergil's Golden Age." *TAPA* 89 (1958): 112–31.

Rzach, Aloisius. "Sibyllinische Orakel." *Realencyclopädie der classischen Altertumswissenschaft* 2: 2073–183.

Sauzeau, Pierre, and André Sauzeau. "Le symbolisme des métaux et le mythe des races métalliques." *RHR* 219 (2002): 259–97.

Schiesaro, Alessandro. "Aratus' Myth of Dike." *Materiali e discussioni per l'analisi dei testi classici* 37 (1996): 9–26.

Schiesaro, Alessandro. "Lucretius and Roman Politics and History." Pages 41–58 in *The Cambridge Companion to Lucretius.* Edited by Stuart Gillespie and Philip R. Hardie. Cambridge Companions to Literature. Cambridge: Cambridge University Press, 2007.

Schnabel, Eckhard. *Acts.* Zondervan Exegetical Commentary on the New Testament 5. Grand Rapids: Zondervan, 2012.

Schneider, Gerhard. *Die Apostelgeschichte.* 2 vols. HThKNT 5. Freiburg im Breisgau: Herder, 1980.

Schoonhoven, Henk, ed. *The Pseudo-Ovidian* Ad Liviam de morte Drusi (Consolatio ad Liviam, Epicedium Drusi): *A Critical Text with Introduction and Commentary.* Groningen: Forsten, 1992.

Schottroff, Luise, and Wolfgang Stegemann. *Jesus and the Hope of the Poor.* Translated by Matthew J. O'Connell. Maryknoll, NY: Orbis Books, 1986.

Schreiber, Stefan. *Weihnachtspolitik: Lukas 1–2 und das Goldene Zeitalter.* NTOA. SUNT 82. Göttingen: Vandenhoeck & Ruprecht, 2009.

Schwazer, Oliver. "The Pseudo-Senecan *Seneca* on the Good Old Days: The Motif of the Golden Age in the *Octavia.*" *Scripta Classica Israelica* 36 (2017): 2–13.

Schweizer, Eduard. *The Holy Spirit.* Translated by Reginald H. Fuller and Ilse Fuller. Philadelphia: Fortress, 1980.

Scott, Walter. "The Last Sibylline Oracle of Alexandria." *ClQ* 9 (1915): 144–66.

Seccombe, David P. *Possessions and the Poor in Luke-Acts*. SNTSU B/6. Linz, AT: Fuchs, 1982.
Seland, Torrey. "'Colony' and 'Metropolis' in Philo: Examples of Mimicry and Hybridity in Philo's Writing Back from the Empire?" *Études Platoniciennes* 7 (2010): 11–33.
Sellar, W. Y. *The Roman Poets of the Augustan Age: Virgil*. Oxford: Clarendon, 1883.
Seo, Pyung Soo. *Luke's Jesus in the Roman Empire and the Emperor in the Gospel of Luke*. Eugene, OR: Pickwick, 2015.
Shepherd, William H. *The Narrative Function of the Holy Spirit as a Character in Luke-Acts*. SBLDS 147. Atlanta: Scholars Press, 1994.
Sihvola, Juha. *Decay, Progress, the Good Life? Hesiod and Protagoras on the Development of Culture*. Commentationes humanarum litterarum 89. Helsinki: Societas Scientarum Fennica, 1989.
Singleton, David. "Juvenal VI. 1–20 and Some Ancient Attitudes to the Golden Age." *GR* 19 (1972): 151–65.
Smallwood, Mary E., ed. *Legatio ad Gaium*. Leiden: Brill, 1961.
Solmsen, Friedrich. "Hesiodic Motifs in Plato." Pages 173–96 in *Hésiode et son influence: six exposés et discussions*. Edited by Olivier Reverdin. Entretiens sur l'Antiquité classique 7. Geneva: Fondation Hardt, 1962.
Sorabji, Richard. *Gandhi and the Stoics: Modern Experiments on Ancient Values*. Oxford: Oxford University Press, 2012.
Steele, R. B. "Pompeius Trogus and Justinus." *AJP* 38 (1917): 19–41.
Steinmetz, Peter. "Germanicus, der römische Arat." *Hermes* 94 (1966): 450–82.
Sterling, Gregory. "'Athletes of Virtue': An Analysis of the Summaries in Acts." *JBL* 113 (1994): 679–96.
Sterling, Gregory. *Historiography and Self-Definition: Josephos, Luke-Acts, and Apologetic Historiography*. NovTSup 64. Leiden: Brill, 1991.
Still, Todd D., and Bruce W. Longenecker. *Thinking through Paul: A Survey of His Life, Letters, and Theology*. Grand Rapids: Zondervan, 2014.
Stokes, George Thomas. *The Acts of the Apostles*. 2 vols. Expositor's Bible 34–35. New York: Armstrong, 1891.
Sullivan, John P. *Literature and Politics in the Age of Nero*. Ithaca, NY: Cornell University Press, 1985.
Sussman, Lewis A. *The Elder Seneca*. Mnemosyne 51. Leiden: Brill, 1978.
Syme, Ronald. "The Date of Justin and the Discovery of Trogus." *Historia* 37 (1988): 358–71.
Talbert, Charles H. *Literary Patterns, Theological Themes, and the Genre of Luke-Acts*. SBLMS 20. Cambridge: Society of Biblical Literature, 1974.
Tarrant, R. J. "Poetry and Power: Virgil's Poetry in Contemporary Context." Pages 169–87 in *The Cambridge Companion to Virgil*. Edited by Charles Martindale. Cambridge Companions to Literature. Cambridge: Cambridge University Press, 1997.
Taylor, Justin. "The Community of Goods among the First Christians and among the Essenes." Pages 147–61 in *Historical Perspectives: From the Hasmoneans to Bar Kokhba in Light of the Dead Sea Scrolls*. Edited by David M. Goodblatt, Avital Pinnick, and Daniel R. Schwartz. STDJ 37. Boston: Brill, 2001.
Theissen, Gerd. "Urchristlicher Liebeskommunismus: Zum 'Sitz im Leben' des Topos ἅπαντα κοινά in Apg 2,44 und 4,32." Pages 689–712 in *Texts and Contexts: Biblical Texts in Their Textual and Situational Contexts*. Edited by Tord Fornberg and David Hellholm. Oslo: Scandinavian University Press, 1995.

Thomas, Richard F. *Virgil and the Augustan Reception*. Cambridge: Cambridge University Press, 2001.
Thomas, Richard F. "Virgil's *Georgics* and the Art of Reference." *HSCP* 90 (1986): 171–98.
Thompson, Alan J. *One Lord, One People: The Unity of the Church in Acts in Its Literary Setting*. LNTS 359. London: T&T Clark, 2008.
Toomer, G. J. "Aratus (1)." *OCD* 132.
Turner, Max. *Power from on High: The Spirit in Israel's Restoration and Witness in Luke-Acts*. Sheffield: Sheffield Academic, 1996.
Van der Horst, Pieter. "The Jews of Ancient Phrygia." *European Journal of Jewish Studies* 2 (2008): 283–92.
Van Noorden, Helen. *Playing Hesiod: The "Myth of the Races" in Classical Antiquity*. Cambridge Classical Studies. Cambridge: Cambridge University Press, 2014.
Van Nuffelen, Peter. *Rethinking the Gods: Philosophical Readings of Religion in the Post-Hellenistic Period*. Greek Culture in the Roman World. Cambridge: Cambridge University Press, 2011.
Van Nuffelen, Peter, and Lieve van Hoof. "Posidonius and the Golden Age: A Note on Seneca, *Epistulae morales* 90." *Latomus* 72 (2013): 186–95.
Vazakas, A. A. "Is Acts I–XV.35 a Literal Translation from an Aramaic Original?" *JBL* 37 (1918): 105–10.
Verdenius, Willem J. *A Commentary on Hesiod: Works and Days, vv. 1–382*. Mnemosyne 86. Leiden: Brill, 1985.
Vernant, Jean-Pierre. "Le mythe hésiodique des races: Essai d'analyse structural." *RHR* 157 (1960): 21–54.
Versnel, Henk S. *Transition and Reversal in Myth and Ritual*. Vol. 2 of *Inconsistencies in Greek and Roman Religion*. Studies in Greek and Roman Religion 6. Leiden: Brill, 1994.
Voit, Ludwig. "Die geteilte Welt. Zu Germanicus und den augusteischen Dichtern." *Gymnasium* 94 (1987): 498–524.
Volk, Katharina. "*Aetna* oder Wie man ein Lehrgedicht schreibt." Pages 68–89 in *Die Appendix Vergiliana: Pseudepigraphen im literarischen Kontext*. Edited by Niklas Holzberg. Classica Monacensia 30. Tübingen: Narr, 2005.
Volk, Katharina. "Aratus." Pages 197–210 in *A Companion to Hellenistic Literature*. Edited by James J. Clauss and Martine Cuypers. Chichester: Wiley-Blackwell, 2010.
Walaskay, Paul W. *"And So We Came to Rome": The Political Perspective of St. Luke*. SNTSMS 49. Cambridge: Cambridge University Press, 1983.
Wallace-Hadrill, Andrew. "The Golden Age and Sin in Augustan Ideology." *Past & Present* 95 (1982): 19–36.
Walton, Steve. "Ὁμοθυμαδόν in Acts: Co-location, Common Action or 'Of One Heart and Mind'?" Pages 89–105 in *The New Testament in Its First Century Setting: Essays on Context and Background in Honour of B. W. Winter on His 65th Birthday*. Edited by P. J. Williams, Andrew D. Clarke, Peter M. Head, and David Instone-Brewer. Grand Rapids: Eerdmans, 2004.
Walton, Steve. "Primitive Communism in Acts? Does Acts Present the Community of Goods (2:44–45; 4:32–35) as Mistaken?" *EvQ* 80 (2008): 99–111.
Walton, Steve. "The State They Were In: Luke's View of the Roman Empire." Pages 1–41 in *Rome in the Bible and the Early Church*. Edited by Peter Oakes. Grand Rapids: Baker Academic, 2002.
Wassmuth, Olaf. *Sibyllinische Orakel 1–2: Studien und Kommentar*. AGJU 76. Leiden: Brill, 2011.

Watson, Lindsay, and Patricia Watson, eds. *Juvenal: Satire 6*. Cambridge Greek and Latin Classics. Cambridge: Cambridge University Press, 2014.
Weiser, Alfons. "Das Gottesurteil über Hananias und Saphira: Apg 5,1–11." *TGl* 69 (1979): 148–58.
Wengst, Klaus. *Pax Romana and the Peace of Jesus Christ*. Translated by John Bowden. Philadelphia: Fortress, 1987.
Wenk, Matthias. *Community-Forming Power: The Socio-Ethical Role of the Spirit in Luke-Acts*. Sheffield: Sheffield Academic, 2000.
West, Martin L., ed. *Hesiod: Works and Days*. Oxford: Clarendon, 1978.
Wettstein, Johann Jakob. *Novum Testamentum graecum*. 2 vols. Amsterdam: Officina Dommeriana, 1751–2.
White, Joel. "Anti-Imperial Subtexts in Paul: An Attempt at Building a Firmer Foundation." *Bib* 90 (2009): 305–33.
White, Peter. "Ovid and the Augustan Milieu." Pages 1–25 in *Brill's Companion to Ovid*. Edited by Barbara Weiden Boyd. Leiden: Brill, 2002.
Whitlark, Jason A. *Resisting Empire: Rethinking the Purpose of the Letter to "the Hebrews."* LNTS 484. London: Bloomsbury, 2014.
Wiefel, Wolfgang. *Das Evangelium nach Lukas*. THKNT 3. Berlin: Evangelische Verlagsanstalt, 1988.
Williams, Gareth. "Politics in Ovid." Pages 203–24 in *Writing Politics in Imperial Rome*. Edited by William J. Dominik, John Garthwaite, and Paul A. Roche. Leiden: Brill, 2009.
Williams, Robert D., ed. *Aeneid: Books I–VI*. London: Macmillan, 1972.
Wilson, S. G. "Lukan Eschatology." *NTS* 16 (1969–1970): 330–47.
Winkler, Martin M. *The Persona in Three Satires of Juvenal*. Altertumswissenschaftliche Texte und Studien 10. Hildesheim: Olms, 1983.
Wiseman, Timothy P. "Calpurnius Siculus and the Claudian Civil War." *JRS* 72 (1982): 57–67.
Witherington III, Ben. *The Acts of the Apostles: A Socio-Rhetorical Commentary*. Grand Rapids: Eerdmans; Carlilse: Paternoster, 1998.
Wolter, Michael. "Die Hirten in der Weihnachtsgeschichte (Lk 2,8–20)." Pages 501–17 in *Religionsgeschichte des Neuen Testaments: Festschrift für Klaus Berger zum 60. Geburtstag*. Edited by Axel von Dobbeler, Kurt Erlemann, and Roman Heiligenthal. Tübingen: Francke, 2000.
Woodward, Roger D. "Hesiod and Greek Myth." Pages 83–165 in *The Cambridge Companion to Greek Mythology*. Edited by Roger D. Woodward. Cambridge: Cambridge University Press, 2007.
Yamazaki-Ransom, Kazuhiko. *The Roman Empire in Luke's Narrative*. LNTS 404. London: T&T Clark, 2010.
Yardley, John C., and Waldemar Heckel, eds. *Epitome of the Philippic History of Pompeius Trogus*. Clarendon Ancient History Series. Oxford: Clarendon, 1997.
Yoder, Joshua P. *Representatives of Roman Rule: Roman Provincial Governors in Luke-Acts*. BZNW 209. Berlin: de Gruyter, 2014.
Zanker, Andreas T. "Late Horatian Lyric and the Virgilian Golden Age." *AJP* 131 (2010): 495–516.
Zanker, Paul. *The Power of Images in the Age of Augustus*. Translated by Alan Shapiro. Jerome Lectures Series 16. Ann Arbor: University of Michigan Press, 1988.
Zwiep, Arie W. *Judas and the Choice of Matthias: A Study on Context and Concern of Acts 1:15–26*. WUNT 2/187. Tübingen: Mohr Siebeck, 2004.

Ancient Sources Index

OLD TESTAMENT

Genesis
- 4:1 — 62 n. 30
- 4:2 — 62
- 4:17 — 63 n. 33
- 11:1–9 — 133

Leviticus
- 4:27 — 4 n. 13
- 5:21 — 110 n. 7

Numbers
- 11:25 — 140
- 15:27 — 4 n. 13
- 31:28 — 4 n. 13

Deuteronomy
- 6:5 — 3 n. 8
- 15:4 — 115 n. 29

Joshua
- 7:1 — 127 n. 72

1 Samuel
- 10 — 140
- 19 — 140

1 Chronicles
- 12:39 — 5 n. 14
- 28:17 — 112 n. 15

Psalms
- 2:4 — 130
- 2:10–11 — 130
- 146:3 — 130
- 146:6 — 130

Wisdom
- 1:1 — 112 n. 15
- 8:8 — 110 n. 7

Isaiah
- 65:17 — 132 n. 95
- 66:22 — 132 n. 95

Daniel
- 2:32–33 — 16

Joel
- 3:1–5 — 87, 139, 141
- 3:4 — 88 n. 16

APOCRYPHA

3 Maccabees
- 4:6 — 110 n. 7

NEW TESTAMENT

Matthew
- 11:5 — 78 n. 101
- 22:17 — 91 n. 34
- 22:21 — 91 n. 34

Mark
- 12:14 — 91 n. 34
- 12:16 — 91 n. 34
- 12:17 — 91 n. 34
- 13 — 86 n. 10

Luke
- 1–2 — 104–6, 129–30
- 1:35 — 97, 98, 129, 130
- 1:47 — 97 n. 60
- 1:76 — 96, 97, 99
- 1:76–2:14 — 99
- 1:79 — 95, 96, 97, 99
- 2 — 102–4, 146
- 2:1 — 91 n. 34, 91 n. 35, 95, 97, 99, 105, 129, 129 n. 83, 130
- 2:7 — 130

2:8	103	2:41–42	90
2:10	130	2:41–47	7
2:11	96, 97, 98, 99	2:41–5:42	119
2:14	95, 96, 99, 130	2:42	44 n. 135, 90 n. 25, 109, 119
2:40	113		
3:1	91 n. 34, 91 n. 35	2:42–47	1, 2, 3, 7, 12, 13, 64, 85, 89–91, 89 n. 24, 107, 118–22, 123–38, 145–6, 147–8
11:20	86 n. 10		
17:35	111		
19:11	86 n. 10		
20:22	91 n. 34	2:44	1, 4, 6, 65 n. 45, 110–111, 115–16, 117, 118, 119, 120, 124, 125, 130, 145, 148
20:24	91 n. 34		
20:25	91 n. 34		
21:5–36	86 n. 10		
21:31–32	86 n. 10	2:44–45	114–15, 118
22:3	126	2:45	116–17, 116 n. 35, 116 n. 36, 117–18, 120, 125, 127
22:5	126		
23:2	91 n. 34		
		2:46	7 n. 26, 111–12, 124, 125 n. 62
John			
4:42	97	2:46–47	124
11:48	91 n. 33	2:47	65 n. 45, 110–11, 112–14, 116, 124, 137
19:12	91 n. 34		
19:15	91 n. 34	3:19–21	131–2
		3:21	132, 135, 139, 147
Acts		4:4	116
1–2	129–30	4:12	144
1:6	132	4:21	112
1:8	129, 130	4:23	90
1:14	125 n. 62	4:23–31	130
1:15	111, 127	4:24	125 n. 62, 130
1:18	127	4:25–26	130
1:25	127, 127 n. 68	4:26	111
2:1	111	4:26–27	130
2:1–13	133	4:28	130
2:3	140	4:31	90, 90 n. 27, 91, 107, 138, 140
2:4	130		
2:5	129, 130	4:32	1, 3, 4, 5, 6, 110, 114–15, 115–16, 118, 119, 120, 124, 125, 126, 127, 127 n. 68, 145, 148
2:5–11	129 n. 83		
2:9–10	130		
2:9–11	129		
2:10	91 n. 33	4:32–35	1, 2, 3, 7, 12, 13, 64, 85, 89–91, 107, 118–22, 123–38, 145–6, 147–8
2:14–40	87		
2:17	13, 87–8, 89, 107, 131, 135, 148		
		4:33	112–14, 137
2:17–21	86, 87, 88–9	4:34	116–17, 116 n. 35, 116 n. 36, 118, 120, 121, 126, 127
2:18	88 n. 15		
2:33	138		
2:38	89 n. 24, 90, 124	4:34–35	114–15, 117, 120, 121 n. 49, 125
2:41	7 n. 26, 90, 90 n. 25, 91, 107, 130, 138		
		4:35	117–18, 120

4:36–37	120	25:25	91 n. 36
4:37	117	26:32	91 n. 34
5:1–11	119	27:1	91 n. 36
5:1	116 n. 33, 127	27:24	91 n. 34
5:1–2	120	28:14	91 n. 33
5:2	117, 127	28:16	91 n. 33
5:3	127	28:17	91 n. 33
5:4	121, 121 n. 49	28:19	91 n. 34
5:12	125 n. 62		
5:12–16	1 n. 1	Romans	
5:13	114	1:7	91 n. 33
5:13–16	112	1:15	91 n. 33
5:26	112		
5:31	98	1 Corinthians	
7:57	125 n. 62	8:6	99
8:6	125 n. 62		
9:20	98	Galatians	
10	140, 146	2:9	110 n. 7
10:14	119		
10:28	119	Ephesians	
10:36	94, 95, 96, 97, 99	6:5	112 n. 15
11:8	119		
12:12	121	Philippians	
12:20	125 n. 62	3:20	99
13:23	98	4:22	91 n. 34
15:10	140		
15:25	125 n. 62	Colossians	
16:21	91 n. 33	3:22	112 n. 15
16:37	91 n. 33		
16:38	91 n. 33	2 Timothy	
17:7	91 n. 34	1:17	91 n. 33
17:28	25 n. 45		
18:2	91 n. 33	Hebrews	
18:12	125 n. 62	13:16	110 n. 7
19	140		
19:21	91 n. 33	Revelation	
19:29	125 n. 62	20	77
22:25	91 n. 33		
22:26	91 n. 33	PSEUDEPIGRAPHA	
22:27	91 n. 33		
22:29	91 n. 33	2 Baruch	
23:11	91 n. 33	32:6	132 n. 95
23:27	91 n. 33	44:12	132 n. 95
25:8	91 n. 34	57:2	132 n. 95
25:10	91 n. 34		
25:11	91 n. 34	1 Enoch	
25:12	91 n. 34	45:4–5	132 n. 95
25:16	91 n. 33	72:1	132 n. 95
25:21	91 n. 34, 91 n. 36	91:16	132 n. 95

4 Ezra
  8:52   132 n. 95

Jubilees
  1:29   132 n. 95
  4:26   132 n. 95

Liber antiquitatum biblicarum
  3:10   132 n. 95
  5:1   71 n. 72

Testament of Abraham
  9:8   4 n. 13
  11:12   4 n. 13
  12:4   4 n. 13

Testament of Issachar
  3:8   112 n. 15, 112 n. 17
  4:1   112 n. 15
  7:7   112 n. 15

Testament of Reuben
  4:1   112 n. 15

MIDRASH

Midrash on the Psalms
  14:6   89 n. 21

Numbers Rabbah
  15:25   89 n. 21

CLASSICAL AND OTHER ANCIENT
          WRITINGS

Aelius Aristides
  Or.
  26.65   51
  26.101   51
  26.106   50

Aetna
  9   52

Aratus
  Phaen.
  5   25 n. 45
  97   102 n. 83
  108–111   28

  108–114   25
  100–101   61 n. 25
  115–128   25
  118–119   63 n. 33
  125   123
  131–146   26
  136   102 n. 83

Aristotle
  Eth. eud.
  1240b   5 n. 15

  Eth. nic.
  1159b   6 n. 23
  1159b32   115 n. 31
  1168b   3, 4, 5 n. 15

  Pol.
  1263a39–40   24 n. 44
  1263b18–23   24 n. 44
  1263b24–26   24 n. 44
  1309b25–26   113 n. 24
  1320b   5 n. 18

Arrian
  Ind.
  11.1–8   7 n. 26

Bahman Yasht
  1.3   16

Calpurnius Siculus
  Ecl.
  1   102, 104, 106
  1.37–41   103
  1.42   48, 123, 139, 143
  1.64   48
  4.6–8   48

Cicero
  Amic.
  25.92   5 n. 15

  Flac.
  67–68   69 n. 58
  68   117 n. 40

Consolatio ad Liviam
  343–344   47

Ancient Sources Index

Corippus
  Laud. Just.
  3.78 — 51

Cyranides
  1.8.27 — 113 n. 24
  3.9.15–16 — 113 n. 24

Demosthenes
  Fals. leg.
  227 — 4 n. 13

Denkard
  9.8 — 16 n. 4

Dio Cassius
  Hist. rom.
  57.8.2 — 40 n. 111

Diodorus Siculus
  Bib. hist.
  33.1.5 — 128

Diogenes Laertius
  Vit. phil.
  8.23.4 — 6 n. 23

Dionysius of Halicarnassus
  Ant. rom.
  6.10.1 — 5 n. 14

Einsiedeln Eclogues
  2.22–24 — 49, 123
  2.23 — 143
  2.23–24 — 139

Epictetus
  Diatr.
  4.1.12–13 — 96
  4.4.39 — 6 n. 23

Euripides
  Alc.
  54 — 4 n. 13

  Andr.
  376 — 6 n. 23

  Hipp.
  721 — 4 n. 13

  Med.
  247 — 4 n. 13

  Orest.
  1046 — 5 n. 15

Germanicus
  Arat.
  112–119 — 40
  113 — 123, 140
  116–117 — 62 n. 31
  117–118 — 61 n. 25
  118 — 82
  118–119 — 9 n. 43, 45

Hesiod
  Op.
  106 — 19 n. 24
  109–120 — 17–18
  109 — 26
  111 — 26
  112–113 — 61 n. 25
  113 — 26, 63 n. 34
  113–114 — 61 n. 25
  114 — 63 n. 34
  115 — 61 n. 25
  116 — 70
  117 — 68 n. 54
  117–118 — 61 n. 25
  118 — 63 n. 34
  118–119 — 20 n. 25
  119 — 123
  120 — 19, 61 n. 25, 123
  127 — 18
  134–137 — 18
  145–151 — 18
  152 — 18
  158 — 18, 19
  159–160 — 18
  173 — 68 n. 54
  174–175 — 18
  175 — 19
  176–196 — 19
  182–188 — 123

185	70 n. 68	Juvenal	
237	68 n. 54	*Sat.*	
		6.1–4	43
Homer		6.17–18	44
Il.		6.407–411	43 n. 128
2.751	20 n. 25	13.28–29	143
15.193	51 n. 166	13.38–59	43 n. 128
Od.		Lucian	
20.336–337	20 n. 25	*Dial. meretr.*	
Horace		14.3	117 n. 40
Saec.		*Merc. cond.*	
5	68 n. 52	20.6	6 n. 23
Iamblichus		*Sat.*	
Vit. pyth.		7	57, 57 n. 7
96–100	7 n. 26	31	5 n. 18
168	5 n. 18, 6 n. 23, 115 n. 31	Lucretius	
Josephus		*Rer.*	
A.J.		5.925–926	27
1.15–16	10	5.933–944	27
1.17	10, 60	5.938	29
1.45	60	5.956–957	29
1.46	63 n. 34	5.958	33
1.46–47	60–1	5.958–961	28
1.46–62	141	5.991	29
1.49	61	5.996–997	29
1.52	62	5.999–1001	28
1.53	61	5.1006	28
1.54	62	5.1011	28
1.61–62	62	5.1019–1020	28
1.62	62, 63, 81, 82	5.1024–1025	28
1.105	63	5.1110	30
1.108	63	5.1108–1111	28, 32
6.86	113 n. 23	5.1113–1123	29
14.146	112 n. 22	5.1129–1130	29, 34
14.148	112 n. 22	5.1430–1433	29
18.18–22	7 n. 26, 124 n. 59	5.1432–1433	30
18.20	5 n. 18	5.1441	30
B.J.		Lycurgus	
2.119–161	124 n. 59	*Leocr.*	
2.120–161	7 n. 26	100.61	4 n. 13
2.122	117 n. 38		
2.151	66 n. 47	Mahabharata	
2.625	117 n. 40	3.148.12–13	16
		3.148.34	16

Martial
  Ep.
  6.3.5   49 n. 157

Melito of Sardis
  Pasch.
  826   111

Musonius Rufus
  frag. 13a, 4   6 n. 23

Nicolaus of Damascus
  FGH
  90f.104   5

Octavia
  394–396   43
  397–399   61 n. 25
  400–403   43
  401–402   63 n. 33
  403   45, 82, 123, 126
  404–405   61 n. 25
  413–414   62 n. 32
  416–426   43
  425–426   62 n. 31
  430–431   143

Ovid
  Am.
  3.8.35–44   35
  3.8.41   62 n. 32
  3.8.41–42   9 n. 43, 45, 63 n. 33
  3.8.42   82
  3.8.48   35
  3.8.55   35, 37

  Ars
  2.277   38
  2.277–278   36, 37
  3.113–114   36

  Fast.
  1.193–195   37
  1.196   37, 123, 127
  1.217–218   37

  Metam.
  1.89   122
  1.89–102   36
  1.94–96   73 n. 79
  1.97   63 n. 33
  1.101   62 n. 32
  1.102   61 n. 25
  1.127   36
  1.128–150   36–7
  1.131   30, 37, 62 n. 31, 76, 123, 127
  1.135   37, 76, 82
  1.135–136   9 n. 43, 45, 63 n. 33
  1.136   76, 82
  1.142   76
  1.145–148   76

  Trist.
  2.549   37 n. 99

Philo
  Cher.
  52   62 n. 30

  Conf.
  116   113 n. 23

  Decal.
  171–172   128

  Flacc.
  74   98

  Hypoth.
  11.1–18   7 n. 26, 64, 66, 124 n. 59
  11.4   6 n. 23

  Legat.
  1   57
  1–21   58, 59
  3–7   58
  8–9   56
  13   56, 143
  21   57, 58
  21–22   143
  21–23   57
  27   4 n. 13
  33   58 n. 13
  107   56 n. 3
  141–142   58 n. 13
  143–149   58 n. 13
  206   56 n. 3
  309–310   58 n. 13, 96
  318   58 n. 13

356	96	4.713e	24
		5.739b–c	23 n. 40
Migr.		5.740a	23 n. 40
60	4 n. 13	7.802a	6 n. 21
		10.898c	4 n. 13
Mos.			
1.86	5 n. 14	*Pol.*	
		271d	61 n. 25
Opif.		271e	24, 61 n. 25, 123, 124, 140
84	59		
		271e–272a	21
Praem.		272b	21
87	82	274b	22, 26, 123
87–88	58, 66, 81	274c	22
88	82		
		Resp.	
Prob.		3.415a	20
75–91	7 n. 26, 64, 66, 124 n. 59	3.416e–417a	21
		4.424a	6 n. 21
86	117 n. 38	5.464c	24
88	135	5.464d	5 n. 18, 6
		5.464d–e	24
Sacr.		5.468e–469a	20 n. 28
3	4 n. 13	5.469a	20 n. 27
		8.547a	20 n. 28
Spec.		8.543b	5 n. 20
4.72	5 n. 18		
		Tim.	
Philostratus		18b	5 n. 20
Vit. Apoll.			
3.10–51	7 n. 26		
3.15.3	7 n. 29	Pliny the Elder	
6.6	7 n. 26	*Nat.*	
		5.73	7 n. 26
Plato			
Crat.		Plutarch	
398a	20 n. 27	*Cat. Min.*	
		73.4	4 n. 13
Crit.			
110c–d	24 n. 42	*Cim.*	
110d	5, 5 n. 20, 6	10.6	82
		10.6–7	44, 45, 53, 110, 126, 134
Gorg.			
501d	4 n. 13	10.7	82
513d	4 n. 13		
		Conj. praec.	
Leg.		140f	6 n. 23
4.713b	22	143a	6 n. 23
4.713c–e	23		

Dem.		90.40	45, 123, 125, 126
7.3	113, 113 n. 25	90.40–41	42
Frat. amor.		*Phaed.*	
96f	4 n. 13	526–533	41
		527	61 n. 25
Pyth. orac.		527–528	62 n. 31
397a–b	67	528–529	9 n. 43, 45, 63 n. 33
		529	82
Polybius		531–532	63 n. 33
Hist.		537	61 n. 25
6.48.4	4 n. 13	540	41, 123
8.3.3	4 n. 13		
8.7.7	4 n. 13	*Polyb.*	
9.22.1	4 n. 13	8.2	53 n. 177
10.16.6–9	128	11.5–6	53 n. 177
Pompeius Trogus		Servius	
Ep.		*Ecl.*	
43.1.3	7, 39–40, 45, 82, 123, 126, 148	4.4	71 n. 71
Porphyry		Sibylline Oracles	
Abst.		1.1–323	68, 68 n. 55, 72
4.6–8	7 n. 26	1.65–86	72
		1.67–78	70
Pseudo-Hippocrates		1.70–71	70
Ep.		1.74	72–3
13.5	5 n. 14	1.86	70
		1.120	71
Seneca the Elder		1.283–301	71
Contr.		1.284	134
2.7.7	47, 51 n. 171	1.294	71–2
		1.261–265	69 n. 58
Seneca the Younger		1.323	68
Apoc.		1.353–355	77–8, 78 n. 101
4.1	48, 123	1.393	69
		1.324–400	68–9
Clem.		2.6–26	72 n. 75
2.1.4	48	2.6–33	68, 68 n. 55, 72, 73 n. 81
Ep.		2.15–18	72
90.5	41	2.27–33	72, 74
90.36	45, 62 n. 31, 82	2.29–33	76
90.36–38	41–2	2.30	73, 80
90.38	45, 53, 82, 123, 126, 127	2.30–33	81
		2.30–31	73
90.38–39	42	2.31	82
90.39	82	2.33	72, 73, 80

2.313–338	74, 78, 79	14.351–354	79, 81
2.319–320	73, 78	14.351–361	79
2.319–324	73	14.354	82
2.320	82		
2.321	72, 73 n. 79, 81, 82, 123	Sophocles *Oed. col.*	
2.322–324	77	499	4 n. 13
2.324	77, 81, 82		
3.263	68 n. 54	Statius	
3.367–370	103, 103 n. 93	*Silv.*	
3.372	103, 104	1.6.39–42	49
8.1–216	75, 77, 77 n. 98, 78, 78 n. 103, 80	4.3.147	50
8.2	75	Strabo	
8.9	75, 144	*Geogr.*	
8.10	75	7.3.7	6 n. 23, 115 n. 31
8.17–26	76	7.3.9	5 n. 18, 6 n. 23
8.17–36	75–6, 77, 79	17.1.8	5 n. 18
8.18	79		
8.18–36	78 n. 104	Suetonius	
8.28	82	*Tib.*	
8:28–29	81	59.1	47, 143
8.28–35	76		
8.29	82	Tibullus	
8:30	148	*El.*	
8.34	79	1.3.36–44	39
8.37	76	1.3.37–40	73 n. 79
8.40	76	1.3.39	62 n. 31
8.50–59	75	1.3.43–44	9 n. 43, 45, 63 n. 33
8.54–55	76	1.3.44	82
8.68–72	75	1.3.45–46	61 n. 25
8.69–70	76	1.10.9–10	103 n. 89
8.73–106	77	2.3.36	39
8.93	77		
8.103–104	77	Vettius Valens *Anth.*	
8.121	81, 82, 144	3:10	111 n. 13
8.169–216	77 n. 98	6	111 n. 13
8.171	78		
8.188–189	78	Virgil	
8.196–197	77	*Aen.*	
8.199	78	1.286–291	33
8.205–207	77, 78 n. 101	1.294	33 n. 84
8.205–212	77–8, 79	6.791–795	34
8.207–210	78	6.792–793	1, 123, 139, 143, 148
8.208	77, 80, 82	6.851	34
8.208–210	81, 148	8.319–327	34
8.210	82	8.327	30, 34, 37, 62 n. 31, 123, 127
8.217–500	75		

Ecl.		*Georg.*	
4.4	68 n. 52	1.24–25	32
4.4–10	30–1	1.121–128	32
4.5	50 n. 160, 122	1.125	62 n. 32
4.6	102 n. 83, 139	1.126	82
4.8–9	147	1.126–127	9 n. 43, 45, 63 n. 33, 148
4.10	46 n. 139	1.127	82
4:15	101	1.127–128	61 n. 25
4.15–16	61 n. 25	1.145–146	33
4.15–17	31	1.155–159	33
4.18	31, 61 n. 25		
4.21	31	Xenophon	
4.29	31	*Cyr.*	
4.32–33	63 n. 33	4.2.42	128
4.38–39	73 n. 79		
4.38–41	31		
4.40	62 n. 32		

Subject Index

Acts (*see also* common property, eschatology, Golden Age allusions in Acts 2:42–47 and 4:32–35, imperial language)
  Acts 1–2 as describing birth of church 129–30
  Acts 1–2 parallels with Luke 1–2 129–30
  Acts 2:17, original text of 87–8
  Acts 2:17–21 as example of present eschatology 87–9, 139
  Acts 2:42–47 as description of Spirit's effects 89–90
  Acts 2:42–47 and 4:32–35 as eschatological 89–91, 123, 139
  Acts 3:19–21 as example of future eschatology 131–2, 139
  Acts 4:23–31, political perspective of 130–1
  Acts 4:32 parallels in Golden Age accounts 126
  Acts 4:32–35 as describing the Spirit's effects 90
  Acts 4:32–35 in tension with Acts 4:36–37 and 5:1–2 120–1
  date 55 n. 1
  distinctive vocabulary in Acts 2:42–47 and 4:32–35 119–20
  meaning of ἀφελότης in Acts 2:46 111–12
  meaning of ἀποκατάστασις in Acts 3:19 131–2
  meaning of ἐπὶ τὸ αὐτό in Acts 2:44, 47 110–11
  meaning of ἔχειν χάριν πρός in Acts 2:47 112–13
  meaning of κοινός in Acts 2:44 and 4:32 4–6, 82, 110, 115, 118–20
  meaning of κοινωνία in Acts 2:42 109–10
  meaning of νοσφίζομαι in Acts 5:2 126–7
  meaning of χάρις in Acts 4:33 113–14
  property arrangement in Acts 2:42–47 and 4:32–35 114–18
  universalizing language in Acts 2:42–47 and 4:32–35 118, 125
allusions, criteria for detecting 10–12
  availability 10, 52
  later recognition 11–12
  markedness 10–12, 118–22
  occurrence in other authors 11, 80
  recurrence in the same author 11, 101, 107
  sense 11, 135–45
Ananias and Sapphira 120–1, 125, 127–8
Andersen, T. David 112–13
Ara Pacis 46–7
Augustus 33–4, 38, 46–7, 94–7, 99, 104–6, 129

Barnabas 120
Brent, Allen 101–2

Cain 61–3
Capper, Brian 3, 8
common property 45
  absent from Greek accounts of the myth 27
  absent from rest of Bible 7–8, 121–2, 125
  appearances in Jewish and Christian uses of the myth 81
  arrangement in Acts 114–18
  common in Latin accounts of the myth 45–6
  as defining feature of Golden Age 44, 46, 81, 123
  in early imperial authors 38–44
  as ephemeral in Acts 123–4, 140
  as eschatological characteristic 58–9, 64–7, 72–4, 78–80
  expanded notion in Trogus 39–40
  in Josephus 62

language used to describe 82
Lucretius as Virgil's source 28–30
in Ovid 35, 37
in Philo of Alexandria 58–9, 66
in Plato 21, 23–4
in the Sibylline Oracles 72–4, 76–80
in Virgil 32–3
Conzelmann, Hans 85–6

eschatology (*see also* Acts, common property)
connection with Golden Age myth 58–9, 72–4, 123
in Luke-Acts 85–6, 89–91, 131–4
in Philo of Alexandria 58–9
in the Sibylline Oracles 72–4, 77–80
Essenes 7
as eschatological foreshadowing 66–7
relationship with Acts 2:42–47 and 4:32–35 64–5, 67
ethnographic tradition 6–7

Feldman, Louis 60–1, 63
friendship traditions 3–5

Gaius 55–8
Golden Age allusions in Acts 2:42–47 and 4:32–35
common property 125–8
descriptions of ephemeral utopia 123–4
divine favor 124
eschatological depictions 89–91, 123, 131–4
imperial context 128–31
objections to 9–10
previous claims 7–9
previous interpretations 136–7
as sign of the Spirit 138–41
as supra-imperial 141–5
unity 124–5
Golden Age myth, origin 15–17
Golden Age myth, political use of 46–52, 59, 74–8, 123, 143
criticism of Nero 43, 49
criticism of Tiberius 47
first in Virgil 33–4
in Philo of Alexandria 57–9
praise of Antoninus Pius 50–1

praise of Augustus 33–4
praise of Domitian 49–50
praise of Hadrian 50
praise of Nero 48–9
in the Sibylline Oracles 74, 76–80
Golden Age myth, prominence in early Empire 9, 51–2
Golden Age/Race, characteristics of
common property 32, 35, 39, 41–3, 44, 72–4, 78, 123
differences between Greek and Latin accounts 52
divine blessing 18, 21, 23, 25, 31, 41, 72, 123
general outline 52, 122–3
lack of sailing 25, 31, 35–6, 39–40
peace 18, 21, 23, 25, 31, 34, 36, 40–1, 43, 72, 123
spontaneous fertility 17–18, 21, 23, 31–2, 35–6, 40, 71, 74, 106
Golden Age/Race, return of
attributed to emperor 51–3, 143–4
first in Virgil 30–1, 33–4
in the Sibylline Oracles 72–3, 80

Hadrian's *saeculum aureum* coin 50

ideal state descriptions 5–6
imperial language
in Acts 10:36 94, 96–7, 99
detecting 99
in Luke 1:76–2:14 95–9
εἰρήνη 95–6
κύριος 95–7
σωτήρ 97–8
υἱὸς θεοῦ 97–8
Iron Age/Race, characteristics of
discord 19, 36, 43
divine abandonment 19, 36, 43
envy 19
greed 36, 41–3
private property 36, 43
sailing 36
toil 19

Judas 126–7

Ludi saeculares 46–7
Luke (*see also* eschatology, imperial language, Rome)

infancy narrative 101–7, 129–30, 142
knowledge of Latin 53
possible Golden Age allusions 101–6

Mealand, David 5–6

Pentecost 132–3, 138–41
Pilate 130–1
Priene inscription 94–5

Rome (*see also* imperial language)
    in context of Acts 2:42–47 and 4:32–35 129–31
    Luke's interest in 91, 129–31
    Luke's perspective on 92–4, 100, 129–31, 142–5

Philo of Alexandria's perspective on 58–9, 144–5
in the Sibylline Oracles 72, 74–9, 145

Saturnalia 49, 57
Schreiber, Stefan 8–9, 104–6
shepherds 102–4
Sterling, Gregory 6–7
supra-imperial 100, 142–5

Tiberius 40, 47
Tower of Babel 133

Wolter, Michael 102–4

www.ingramcontent.com/pod-product-compliance
Lightning Source LLC
Chambersburg PA
CBHW070638300426
44111CB00013B/2161